PRACTICAL REAL ESTATE MATH

Second Edition

PRACTICAL REAL ESTATE MATH

Second Edition

Betty J. Armbrust
Hugh H. Bradley
John W. Armbrust

Australia · Canada · Mexico · Singapore · Spain · United Kingdom · United States

Practical Real Estate Math, 2e
by
Betty J. Armbrust
Hugh H. Bradley
John W. Armbrust

Printed in the United States of America
6 7 8 09 08 07

For more information contact South-Western Publishing, 5101 Madison Road, Cincinnati, Ohio, 45227. Or you can visit our Internet site at http://www.swcollege.com

For permission to use material from this text or product contact us by
- **telephone: 1-800-730-2214**
- **fax: 1-800-730-2215**
- **web: http://www.thomsonrights.com**

ISBN-13: 978-0-324-14360-7
ISBN-10: 0-324-14360-5

Contents

3
MASTERING DECIMALS 39

4
PERCENT IN REAL ESTATE 53

5
RATIO, PROPORTION, AND SCALE 71

6
MEASUREMENTS IN REAL ESTATE 79

Table of Measurements

Measure of Length

1 foot (ft.)	= 12 inches (in.)		
1 yard (yd.)	= 3 feet (ft.)	= 36 inches (in.)	
1 rod (rd.)	= $16\frac{1}{2}$ feet (ft.)	= $5\frac{1}{2}$ yards (yds.)	
statute mile	= 5,280 feet (ft.)	= 1,760 yards (yds.)	= 320 rods (rds.)

Measure of Area

1 square foot (sq. ft.)	= 144 square inches (sq. in.)
1 square yard (sq. yd.)	= 9 square feet (sq. ft.)
1 square rod (sq. rd.)	= 30.25 square yards (sq. yds.)
1 acre	= 43,560 square feet (sq. ft.)
	= 4,840 square yards (sq. yds.)
	= 160 square rods (sq. rd.)
1 square mile	= 640 acres

Measure of Volume

1 cubic foot (cu. ft.)	= 1,728 cubic inches (cu. in.)
1 cubic yard (cu. yd.)	= 27 cubic feet (cu. ft.)

Measure of Time

1 minute (min.)	= 60 seconds (sec.)
1 hour (hr.)	= 60 minutes (min.)
1 day (da.)	= 24 hours (hr.)
1 week (wk.)	= 7 days (da.)
1 year (yr.)	= 12 months (mo.)
	= 52 weeks (wk.)
	= 360 days (da.)
	= 365 days (da.)

PREFACE

Practical Real Estate Math is designed for those who need to learn more about the math used in real estate. The book emphasizes those math skills needed in the real estate business and in preparation for real estate license examinations. Students will learn (or refresh!) basic computational skills and develop greater competence and accuracy in using those skills. Another of the book's guiding objectives is to enable readers to organize and interpret data when solving common real estate problems.

Many beginning and even experienced practitioners are intimidated by those aspects of a transaction involving math. In most cases, the problems are actually quite simple and can be solved with fundamental arithmetic. We will attempt to alleviate this "fear of math" by first reviewing and practicing basic arithmetic functions, applying them to those types of calculations faced by real estate practitioners in their daily tasks. Mastery of these simple techniques will provide a firm foundation for solving more advanced problems, and later chapters in the book give students the opportunity to practice real estate math using realistic problems and scenarios.

In general, each topic is developed by a learning pattern that includes:

1. Introduction of each new principle or process in a meaningful and concrete manner.
2. Background information for a clear understanding of the new principle or process.
3. An example and simple explanation of the solution.
4. An exercise for practice consisting of similar problems.
5. A review of problems, as we progress, to ensure that students retain what has been learned.

Practical Real Estate Math contains 12 chapters, each broken into several sections. We follow a step-by-step process, with new principles and problems introduced in sequence one at a time. Each section offers a clear explanation, examples that illustrate, and model solutions.

Every effort has been made to keep explanations and solutions as simple as possible. We suggest you work through this textbook with pencil and paper and do the problems with thought and care. Only through practice will you remember and learn to apply what you have studied.

Chapters 1 through 3 of the book provide a review of whole numbers, fractions, and decimals. Chapter 4 discusses percentages in real estate. Chapter 5 addresses ratio, proportion, and scale. Chapter 6 studies measurement pertinent to the real estate field, and Chapter 7 presents a study of land descriptions. Chapter 8 discusses mortgage math, including how to prepay on a mortgage. Chapter 9 is an overview of real estate appraisal; Chapter 10 sets forth real estate prorations; and Chapter 11 discusses real estate settlement. Finally, Chapter 12 provides an introduction to investment math. A basic explanation of the use of the standard calculator and the Hewlett-Packard 12C, 10B, 17BII, and 19BII models appears in the appendix.

To assess your arithmetic skill, begin with the pretest on page xiii. You may safely skip those sections of the text that address areas in which you find you are already proficient.

Acknowledgments

Many thanks to Joe Irwin, Houston Community College; Gwen Nichols, Western Schools of Real Estate; and David Wheeling, Western Piedmont Community College for their constructive reviews during various stages of this project. The book is improved as a result of their efforts. Thanks also to Arlyne Geschwender, Randall School of Real Estate, for her help with the material on depreciation.

We wish to acknowledge the efforts of Stephanie Ratzell and Robyn Heine for the many hours spent typing the manuscript; Arlea Bradley for proofreading; Robyn Heine for artwork; and Roberta Pierce, Robyn, and Stephanie for the extra hours they worked as a result of the book.

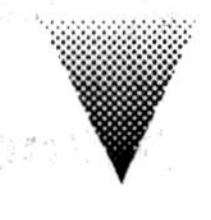

PRETEST

This pretest is intended to help you determine areas in which you need further study. Allow yourself one hour, and if you score 80% or higher, you may want to study sections where a weakness occurs. If you score below 80%, you should study all sections thoroughly. Questions 1–30 can be used to identify weaknesses in basic arithmetic manipulations. Do not use a calculator. Do not refer to answers in the back of the book.

1. Write $\frac{14}{18}$ in lowest terms.

2. Which of the following is equal to 1?

a. $\frac{2}{1}$

b. $\frac{2}{7}$

c. $\frac{173}{173}$

3. Order these fractions with the greatest first: $\frac{2}{3}, \frac{3}{4}, \frac{5}{7}$.

4. Write $7\frac{2}{3}$ as an improper fraction.

5. Simplify the following:

a. $15 + 8\frac{9}{11}$

b. $12\frac{2}{5} - 8\frac{5}{6}$

c. $5\frac{3}{4} \times 2\frac{2}{7}$

d. $\frac{5}{7} \div \frac{15}{28}$

6. Ed had $50. He spent $16 for shoes and $12 for shirts. What fraction of his money did he have left?

7. One pattern calls for $4\frac{7}{8}$ yards of material. Another calls for 4.8 yards. Which calls for more material?

8. One puppy increased from 31.78 to 34 pounds in weight one month and a second puppy increased from $29\frac{7}{8}$ to 32 pounds in a month. Which gained more?

9. Convert to a decimal:

a. $\frac{16}{30}$

b. $\frac{9}{2}$

10. Convert to a percent:

a. $\frac{5}{8}$

b. $\frac{7}{8}$

11. Convert to a decimal:

a. 92%

b. 112%

12. Convert to a fractional form:

a. 130%

b. 80%

Simplify problems 13–21.

13. $2.68 + 17.3 + .062 + .2698$

14. $17.25 - 13.89$

15. 26.582×0.341 (round to nearest hundredth)

16. $18\frac{2}{5} \times 4.75$

17. $97.785 \div 26.5$ (round to nearest hundredth)

18. $18.75 \div 3\frac{1}{4}$ (round to nearest tenth)

19. $\frac{1}{2} + \frac{3}{5} - \frac{5}{6}$

20. $2\frac{1}{2} \times \frac{1}{6} \div 1\frac{1}{4}$

21. Select the smallest of the following: $\frac{3}{4}, \frac{17}{32}, \frac{35}{64}, \frac{9}{16}, \frac{3}{8}$

22. Estimate the value of $\frac{68 \times 2{,}010}{97}$

23. Simplify: $7 \div \frac{.7}{5}$

24. How many 30–man squads can be formed from 3,240 men?

25. How many 24ths are there in $\frac{83\frac{1}{3}}{100}$?

26. Find the missing term in the following set: 10, 15, 22, 31, 42, (?)

27. Fred estimates that his car uses gasoline at an average rate of 15 miles per gallon on the road. He is to take a trip of 2,250 miles. How much money should he set aside to purchase gasoline that costs $1.00 per gallon?

28. How many 25-cent stamps are there in 2 dozen?

29. Simplify and round to nearest tenth: $\frac{1}{4} + 10(.072) - \frac{1.38}{10}$

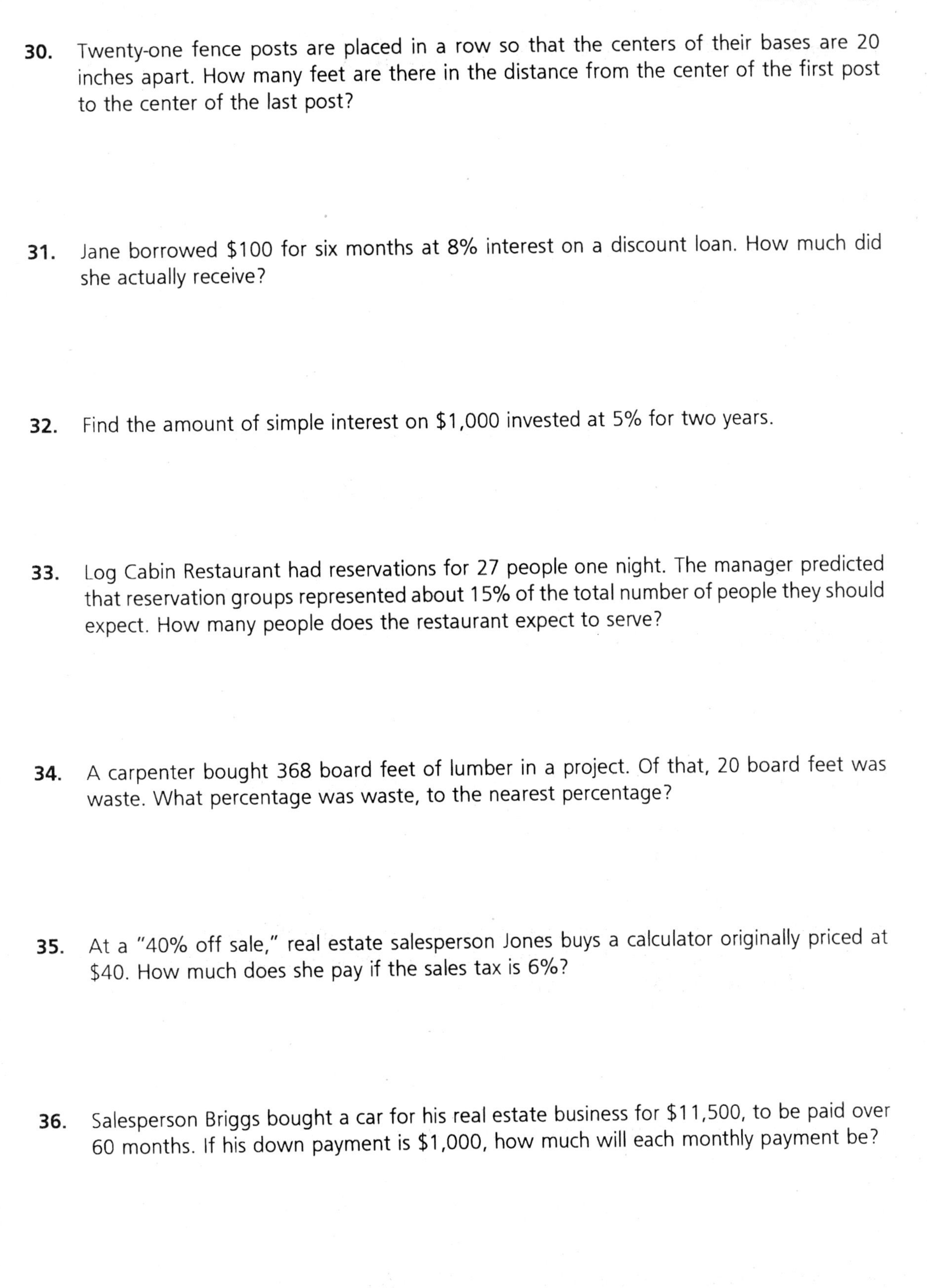

30. Twenty-one fence posts are placed in a row so that the centers of their bases are 20 inches apart. How many feet are there in the distance from the center of the first post to the center of the last post?

31. Jane borrowed $100 for six months at 8% interest on a discount loan. How much did she actually receive?

32. Find the amount of simple interest on $1,000 invested at 5% for two years.

33. Log Cabin Restaurant had reservations for 27 people one night. The manager predicted that reservation groups represented about 15% of the total number of people they should expect. How many people does the restaurant expect to serve?

34. A carpenter bought 368 board feet of lumber in a project. Of that, 20 board feet was waste. What percentage was waste, to the nearest percentage?

35. At a "40% off sale," real estate salesperson Jones buys a calculator originally priced at $40. How much does she pay if the sales tax is 6%?

36. Salesperson Briggs bought a car for his real estate business for $11,500, to be paid over 60 months. If his down payment is $1,000, how much will each monthly payment be?

37. Salesperson Jones needed to replace four automobile tires selling at $40.95 each. Find her total cost if sales tax is 6%.

38. Two 60-foot lots were purchased for $18,000 each. They were then divided into three lots and sold for $15,000 each. What was the seller's percentage of return?

39. A person in real estate sales buys an automobile for $12,250 and five years later trades it in for $7,000. What is the total depreciation? What is the annual depreciation?

40. On a certain date of this year, Eunice Larson deposited the following into her checking account: 150 pennies, 75 nickels, 30 dimes, 35 quarters, 30 $1 bills, 15 $5 bills, and a check for $50.22. How much money did she deposit?

41. "A" purchased a lot that had 150 linear feet and 17,500 square feet. "A" wanted to expand and decided to purchase two adjacent lots, one to the left and one to the right, each being 150 feet deep and 6,000 square feet. What is the front footage of the three lots combined, to the nearest foot?

42. A salesperson is paid $60 a week plus a commission of 6% on sales above a quota of $800. Last week his sales were $2,500. What were his total earnings for the week?

43. A real estate salesperson earns a commission of 3%. If she sold one house for $45,000 and another for $50,000, how much commission did she earn on the two houses?

44. A real estate secretary is paid $5.10 an hour for a 40-hour week, plus time and a half for overtime. Find her total earnings for last week, when she worked 45 hours.

45. Fred's retired father works 40 hours a week at $4.25 per hour transporting closing statements to real estate offices. How much does he earn in a year? (He is paid for 52 weeks each year.)

46. The Smiths have a 30-year mortgage on their house for $72,500 with an interest rate of 7%. If the monthly principal and interest payment is $6.65 for each $1,000 of the loan, what is the monthly principal and interest payment?

47. The Smiths bought a house for $70,250 and made a down payment of 20%. What is the amount of down payment?

48. A real estate salesperson traveled the following number of business miles: Monday, 92; Tuesday, 125; Wednesday, 116; Thursday, 135; Friday, 112. What is the average number of miles traveled per day?

49. The Wilsons own a home that has a 25-year mortgage. The monthly payments to the bank are $565. How much will they pay to the bank in 25 years?

50. Salesperson Riley owned a rental in which he had to replace carpeting in a family room that measured 40 square yards. The replacement carpeting cost $6.99 per square yard, a $\frac{9}{16}$" padding cost $2.50 per square yard, state tax was $11.38, city tax was $7.59, and an additional tax of $2.65 was charged. Installation cost was $116. What was the cost to Riley?

1

WORKING WITH WHOLE NUMBERS

Goals

1. Read and write whole numbers.
2. Add, subtract, multiply, and divide whole numbers.
3. Solve problems involving whole numbers.

It is necessary that you have a good understanding of whole numbers and arithmetic skills in order to solve problems. A calculator may help you in solving operations but you should know what to do in solving a problem. If you have good arithmetic skills, this chapter may be used as review where needed. The test at the end of the chapter may be used as a pretest in order to determine your strengths and weaknesses.

PLACE VALUE

The population of Chicago is about 7,258,582.
The number of people who attended a Rose Bowl football game was 101,289.

The numbers 0, 1, 2, 3, 4, 5, 6, 7, 8, 9, 10, etc., are called whole numbers. Whole numbers other than 0 are called the counting numbers or natural numbers. To read and write numbers, it is necessary to understand place value. In our number system, numbers are made from the digits 0, 1, 2, 3, 4, 5, 6, 7, 8, 9, and the value of a digit depends on its place in the number. In the number 845, the 8 represents 8 hundreds, the 4 represents 4 tens, and the 5 represents 5 ones or units.

$$845 = 8 \times 100 + 4 \times 10 + 5 \times 1 \text{ or } 800 + 40 + 5$$

In 962, the 6 represents 6 tens.

$$962 = 900 + 60 + 2$$

A number such as 962 is called a three-digit number. A decimal point or a dot located immediately after the ones place (often referred to as the units digit) shows that place values to the right of the decimal are less than 1. A digit's relationship to the decimal determines its value. For example, the second digit to the left of the decimal has a place value ten times greater than that of the first digit to the left of the decimal. Therefore, any digit has a place value ten times greater than the place value of a digit to its right. As an example:

5,280

Value is 5,000	Value is 200	Value is 80	Value is 0
5 × 1,000	2 × 100	8 × 10	0 × 1

5,280 = 5 (thousands) + 2 (hundreds) + 8 (tens) + 0 (ones) OR

5,280 = 5 × 1,000 + 2 × 100 + 8 × 10 + 0 × 1 = 5,000 + 200 + 80 + 0

Look at the place value chart in Figure 1–1 and note that the farther left of the decimal a digit is located, the greater the number. The number represented in the figure reads, "four trillion, three hundred twenty-one billion, nine hundred eighty-seven million, six hundred fifty-four thousand, three hundred twenty-one." Note that the digits are divided into groups of three, and each group is named by the place name at the right of the group. Thus, 987,000,000 is read, "nine hundred eighty-seven million," since the seven is in the millions place.

Example:

5,280 Think 5,000 + 200 + 80
Write five thousand, two hundred eighty

Figure 1–1 shows that the periods are ones, thousands, millions, billions, and trillions. The next seven periods are quadrillions, quintillions, sextillions, septillions, octillions, nonillions, and decillions. Very large numbers are generally expressed in scientific notation (for example, 10^3 means the same as 10 × 10 × 10, or 1,000).

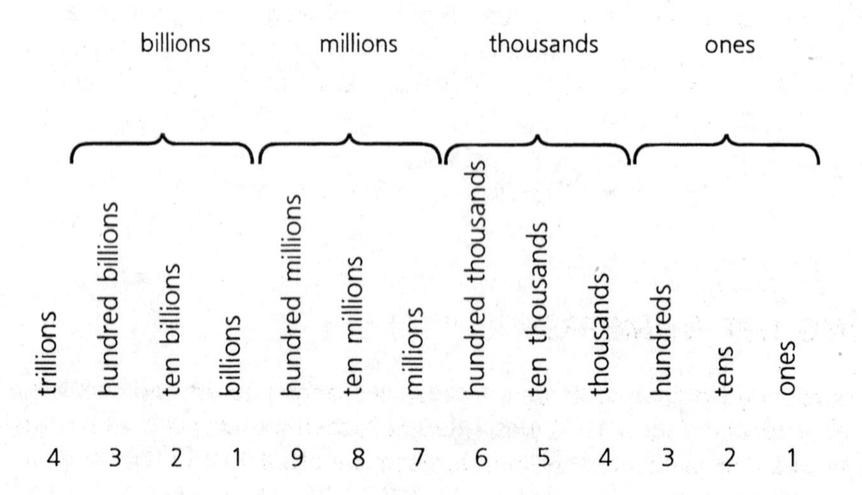

Figure 1–1

Exercises

1. Tell the value of 5 in each number:
   a. 845
   b. 5,000,000,000
   c. 7,005,241
   d. 52,143
   e. 98,245,018
   f. 231,452

Write the following as a single number:

2. 6 hundreds + 5 ones.

3. 4 ten thousands + 2 thousands + 8 hundreds.

4. 3 millions + 2 hundred thousands + 3 ten thousands + 8 thousands.

Write in words each of the following:

5. 2,408

6. 2,089,654,213

ROUNDING OFF NUMBERS

A number is rounded off when its actual value is changed to an approximate value. If the population of New York City in 1970 was 7,895,563, then we can say that the population was 8,000,000, rounded to the nearest million. Numbers are often rounded off when an exact value is not necessary.

Suppose that 75,961 people attended a football game, and in the morning newspapers the attendance is reported as 76,000. This number is attained by rounding the actual attendance to the nearest thousand. Rounding reduces the accuracy of a number value and replaces it with a more generalized or approximate value. Before rounding off any number, you must decide on the value to which you are going to round off, or the value of the digit in the rounded number that comes just before the 0s. In the number 8,000,000, for example, the digit 8 has a value of millions. In the number 600, the digit 6 has a value of hundreds. Figure 1–1 in the previous section gives such values from one to one trillion.

REMEMBER

Once you decide upon the degree of accuracy, use the following guideline for rounding numbers:

1. Underline all digits to the right of this value.
2. If the leftmost digit underlined is 5 or more, add 1 to the first value to the left of the underlined digits. If the leftmost digit underlined is less than 5, do not add 1 to the first value to the left of the underlined digits.
3. Substitute zeros for the underlined digits.

Example

Round off 5,287 to the nearest ten.

Step 1: Underline the digit to the right of the tens value.

$$5{,}28\underline{7}$$

Step 2: Because the underlined value is 5 or more, add 1 to the tens digit.

$$\begin{array}{r} 5{,}28\underline{7} \\ \underline{+1\ } \\ 5{,}29\underline{7} \end{array}$$

Step 3: Substitute zeros for the underlined digit. $5{,}29\underline{0}$.

Answer: 5,290

After some practice, steps 2 and 3 can be performed mentally.

Exercises

1. Round off to the nearest ten:
   a. 571
   b. 529

2. Round off to the nearest hundred:
   a. 2,752
   b. 3,091

3. Round off to the nearest thousand:
   a. 13,499
   b. 22,790

4. Round off to the nearest ten thousand:
  a. 541,288
  b. 668,999

5. Round off to the nearest hundred thousand:
  a. 5,720,123
  b. 7,892,225

6. Round off to the nearest million:
  a. 37,425,000
  b. 40,920,800

ADDING WHOLE NUMBERS

When the values of two or more numbers are combined to form a larger number, the process is called *addition*. The numbers that are added are called *addends,* and the number resulting from addition is called the *sum* or the *total.* Addition is indicated by writing the symbol "+" with the numbers to be added or addends.

In setting up the numbers to be added you must always be sure to line up your digits correctly—the ones digit under the ones digit, the tens digit under the tens digit, and so forth. The rightmost column containing the ones digits is called the ones column, the column of tens digits is called the tens column, and to the left are the hundreds column, the thousands column, and so forth, according to place values given in Figure 1–1.

Since all calculation is based on the use of the nine Arabic numerals, mastery of the combinations is essential. Everyone has learned "the simple number facts," and many of us grow "rusty" on these combinations; therefore, it will be useful to review simple combinations, since all other arithmetical calculation depends upon these principles.

If we add 1 + 5 + 3, we may place them in a row or in a column. The column technique is better when adding larger numbers. In column addition, we may add either up or down, and it is a good idea to form the habit of performing such additions mentally, without saying the words, but simply calling the results, as shown below.

(adding down)	(adding up)
1 one	1 nine
5 six	5 eight
3 nine	3 three
9	9

When numbers to be added have more than one digit, begin with the right-hand column and sum those digits. If the sum of the right-hand column is greater than 9, write the units digit of the sum under the ones column and "carry" the tens digit, which represents the number of tens to the tens column and add it to the numbers that appear there. If the resulting sum of the tens column is greater than 9, write the units digit of the sum under the tens column and "carry" the tens digit, which represents the number of hundreds to the hundreds column and add it to the numbers that appear there. Repeat this process until a sum is found to the proper number of columns.

In the example below, begin with the right-hand column and write the 1 under the ones column. Then "carry" the 1 (which represents the number of tens) to the tens column and add it to the numbers that appear there. Add the hundreds column the same way.

(sum of digits in right-hand column)

```
  1
 83 three
 76 nine
 62 eleven
 --
  1
```

(sum of digits in left-hand column)

```
  1
 83 nine
 76 sixteen
 62 twenty-two
---
221
```

The answer is 221. This procedure may be repeated for any number of columns.

Exercises

1. The local library has 5,322 books of fiction, 3,150 nonfiction books, 1,232 reference books, and 572 magazines. What is the total number of books and magazines?

2. After traveling 435 miles the first day and 568 miles the second day, a traveler was 357 miles from his destination. How far is the place of starting from the destination?

3. Eight states have the following areas: 265,896 square miles, 70,057 square miles, 48,506 square miles, 53,335 square miles, 48,865 square miles, 51,998 square miles, 42,022 square miles, and 20,968 square miles. What is the area of all these states?

4. A tank has two pipes. The first discharges 119 gallons per minute and the second 17 gallons more per minute than the first. How many gallons will both pipes discharge in one minute?

SUBTRACTING WHOLE NUMBERS

When the value of a smaller number is "taken away" from the value of a larger number, the process is called *subtraction*. The number that results from subtraction is called the *difference* or *remainder*. The larger number is called the *minuend,* and the smaller number, the number that is subtracted, is called the *subtrahend*. Subtraction is indicated by the symbol "–" in front of the number to be subtracted. To indicate that 13 is to be subtracted from 89, write 89 – 13 or

$$\begin{array}{rl} 89 & \leftarrow \text{minuend} \\ \underline{-13} & \leftarrow \text{subtrahend} \end{array}$$

Setting up a subtraction problem is similar to setting up an addition problem. Be certain to line up the digits correctly: ones under ones, tens under tens, hundreds under hundreds, and so on, always placing the larger number above the smaller one.

Example

Subtract 334 from 658.

Step 1: Write the minuend (658) on top and the subtrahend (334) under it and correctly align the digits. Subtract 8 – 4 = 4.

$$\begin{array}{rl} 658 & \leftarrow \text{minuend} \\ \underline{-334} & \leftarrow \text{subtrahend} \\ 324 & \leftarrow \text{difference} \end{array}$$

Step 2: Write the 4 under the ones column. Subtract 5 – 3 = 2 and write the 2 under the tens column. Subtract 6 – 3 = 3 and write the 3 under the hundreds column.

Answer: 324.

In doing subtraction problems, you may find that you have a larger digit to take from a smaller digit. In such a case, you will have to borrow from the digit to the left of the one you are working with.

Example

Subtract 88 from 122.

$$\begin{array}{r} 122 \\ \underline{-88} \end{array}$$

Step 1: To subtract the ones column, 2 – 8, you must borrow from the tens column.

$$\begin{array}{r} {}^{1}\phantom{{}^{1}2} \\ 1\not{2}{}^{1}2 \\ -88 \\ \hline 4 \end{array}$$

Step 2: The problem now becomes 12 – 8 = 4. The same thing must be done to subtract the tens column.

$$\begin{array}{r} {}^{0\,11}\phantom{{}^{1}2} \\ \not{1}\not{2}{}^{1}2 \\ -88 \\ \hline 34 \end{array}$$

Step 3: By borrowing from the hundreds column, which now becomes 0, the problem is 11 – 8 = 3.

Answer: 34

Exercises

1. A real estate salesperson sold a home for $60,950, which included a commission of $4,267. What was the cost of the home without the commission?

2. At the beginning of the year, the odometer of Mr. Wilson's car read 21,925 miles. At the end of the year, the reading was 40,700. How many miles did Mr. Wilson drive that year?

3. A real estate company has $41,524 in its commercial account. Checks for $800, $253, and $817.50 were written against the account. What is the balance?

4. A hiker camped at the 11,798-foot level of Long's Peak, which has an elevation of 14,255 feet. How much higher did he have to climb to reach the summit?

5. Sue Wilson earns $15,000 a year and pays a total of $3,650 in taxes. How much does she earn in a year after taxes?

MULTIPLYING WHOLE NUMBERS

When the number 8 is repeated 4 times, the four 8s add up to 32. We say that 8 is multiplied by 4, or 8 × 4 = 32. The symbol × indicates multiplication. In multiplication, the number being multiplied is the *multiplicand* and the number doing the multiplying is the *multiplier*. The answer to a multiplication problem is the *product*.

Multiplication is a shortcut method of doing addition. When you multiply numbers, you really add groups of numbers. Multiplying 8 × 4, which is read "8 times 4," is the same as adding four 8s: (8 × 4 = 8 + 8 + 8 + 8 = 32).

Example

Multiply 325 × 43.

Multiplication problems are set up like this:

```
  325 ← multiplicand
×  43 ← multiplier
```

Notice the digits are aligned as in addition and subtraction. Since the multiplier, 43, has two digits you must multiply the multiplicand two times: first by the ones digit, 3; then by the tens digit, 4.

Using the digit 3 as a multiplier, multiply right to left:

Step 1: 3 × 5 = 15. Write the 5 directly under the 3, the digit you are multiplying with. Carry the 1 to the next digit, the 2. 3 × 2 = 6 plus the 1 you carried equals 7. Write the 7 directly under the 4. 3 × 3 = 9. Write the 9 in the hundreds place. The number 975 is the partial answer.

```
   1
  325
×  43
  975 (partial answer)
```

Step 2: Multiply with the next digit, 4. Write the first digit of this partial answer directly under the 4, the digit you multiplied with: 4 × 5 = 20. Write the 0 directly under the 4 and carry the 2 to the next digit, the 2. 4 × 2 = 8, plus the 2 you carried, equals 10. Write 0 in the hundreds place and carry the 1 to the next digit, the 3. 4 × 3 = 12, plus the 1 you carried, equals 13. Write the 13 in the next two places to the left. (3 in the thousands place and 1 in the ten-thousands place.)

```
  1 2
  325
×  43
  975 (partial answer)
 1300  (partial answer)
```

Step 3: Draw a line under the partial answers and add the two numbers to get the final answer, the product. Be sure to keep partial answers correctly aligned.

```
   325
 ×  43
   975
 1300
 13975
```

Answer: 13,975

• ▼ • •

Exercises

1. Mr. Wilson works a 35-hour week for 36 weeks of the year. How many hours will he work in 25 years?

2. A rural Transportation Department ordered 78 buses at $30,950 each. What is the total cost?

3. The Smiths own a home that has a 30-year mortgage. The monthly payment to the bank is $548.20. What is the total amount they will pay the bank in paying off the mortgage?

4. A train travels at a steady rate of 55 miles per hour. How far does it travel in 14 hours?

5. There are 275 sheets of paper in a tablet. How many sheets are in 25 tablets?

DIVIDING WHOLE NUMBERS

When a pack of 52 playing cards is dealt to 4 players, each hand consists of 13 cards. The pack has been divided among the 4 players. When a number is broken down into smaller groups of numbers, the process is called *division*. In division, the number being divided is called the *dividend* and the number doing the division is called the *divisor*. The answer to a division problem is the *quotient*.

$$\begin{array}{r} 13 \leftarrow \text{quotient} \\ \text{divisor} \rightarrow 4\,\overline{)\,52} \leftarrow \text{dividend} \end{array}$$

Division is the opposite of multiplication. In performing division, you find out how many times a smaller number is contained in a larger number. How many 6s are there in 36? Since $6 \times 6 = 36$, there are six 6s in 36; the number 36 has been broken down into six groups of 6, and we say "36 divided by 6 equals 6." The quotient is 6. The following symbols are used to indicate division: ÷, /, $\overline{)\ }$. Each of the following expressions means "30 divided by 5": 30 ÷ 5, 30/5, $5\overline{)30}$.

Suppose we have 848 pairs of socks and we issue them to 212 men so that each will get an equal share. How many pairs will each man receive? We could subtract 212 from 848 and keep subtracting 212 from the resulting answer until we finally reach zero. Counting the number of subtractions would indicate the number of pairs to be distributed to each man, in this case, 4.

$$\begin{array}{r} 848 \\ -\underline{212} \\ 636 \\ -\underline{212} \\ 424 \\ -\underline{212} \\ 212 \\ -\underline{212} \\ 0 \end{array}$$

This is a cumbersome process, particularly if the number of pairs of socks were very large and the number of men in each group very small.

Making use of our knowledge that division is the opposite of multiplication, we may ask, "What number multiplied by 212 gives 848?" From what we know of numbers, 212 = 200 + 10 + 2 and 848 = 800 + 40 + 8. We see readily that 4 times 200 gives 800, 4 times 10 gives 40, and 4 times 2 gives 8; or that 4 times 212 gives 848. The reverse would also be true, that 848 ÷ 4 gives 212.

$$212\,\overline{)\,848}^{\;4} \qquad\qquad 4\,\overline{)\,848}^{\;212}$$

Not all division problems, however, work out so evenly. If we had 5,238 men to be divided into 6 groups, it would be more difficult if we broke the number up into the parts, 5,000 + 200 + 30 + 8, since no part is exactly divisible by 6. The following reasoning would apply:

1. There are 8 complete 6s in 50 and 800 complete 6s in 5,000.
2. Subtracting 4,800 from 5,238 leaves 438 men we still want to count out.
3. There are 7 complete 6s in 43 and 70 complete 6s in 438.
4. Subtracting 420 from 438 leaves us 18 men to be counted out.
5. There are 3 complete 6s in 18.
6. Adding our quotients, 800 + 70 + 3 = 873.

$$\begin{array}{rrl} & 873 & (800 + 70 + 3) \\ 6\,) & \overline{5,238} & \\ & \underline{-4,800} & (6 \times 800) \\ & 438 & \\ & \underline{-420} & (6 \times 70) \\ & 18 & \\ & \underline{-18} & (6 \times 3) \\ & 0 & \end{array}$$

Since numbers are "placed" (i.e., their placement value is set) when written in the proper column, the process can be shortened by omitting zeros and bringing down only numbers that are used in the next part of the example. Be sure to exercise care in placing the numbers directly under the columns in which they first appear.

```
       873
  6 ) 5,238
     -48
       43
      -42
        18
       -18
         0
```

From these steps the transition to long division is not difficult.

Exercises

1. Last year a real estate salesperson earned $20,800. How much did he earn per week?

2. There are 480 eggs in a crate. How many dozen are in the crate?

3. How many hours will it take to fill a tank that holds 1,575 gallons with a pipe that pours into it at the rate of 175 gallons an hour?

4. A jet airliner averages 650 miles per hour. How many hours will it take to travel 8,775 miles?

5. A salesperson earned the following commissions in the last five months: $925, $1,125, $875.25, $1,025.50, $750.75. What is the average monthly commission?

CHAPTER TEST

1. Tell the value of the 4 in each number:
   a. 5,340
   b. 4,000,093
   c. 837,498

2. Total sales for one day in 18 departments of a store were $19,134. What were the average sales for each department?

3. The Smith family spends $217 per month to repay their home mortgage. How much do they spend in a year on the mortgage?

4. The highest point in Colorado is Mt. Elbert, elevation 14,433 feet. The lowest point is 3,350 feet, along the Arkansas River. What is the difference in elevations?

5. A department store did $3,298,046 in business one year and $2,957,938 the next. What was the total business volume for the two years?

6. Helen Jones planned to buy a car. The basic price was $8,995. Options she wanted cost $75, $386, and $125. She had saved $3,500. How much more did she need?

7. The Smiths bought a washer and dryer for $800. If they paid $112 down and agreed to pay the remainder in 16 equal installments, how much is each remaining payment?

8. A rectangular lot has a frontage of 60 feet and a total area of 6,300 square yards. What is the depth of the lot?

9. Mr. Wilson's monthly mortgage payment for principal and interest is $372.75. If his annual property taxes are $660 and a three-year homeowner's insurance premium is $756, what will his total monthly payment be, including taxes and insurance?

10. A developer is subdividing a 15-acre tract into lots measuring 75′ × 100′. Each lot has a perimeter of 350 feet and will sell for $5,400. He has allowed 112,500 square feet for required streets, sidewalks, and recreational facilities.
    a. What is the area of each lot in square feet?

    b. How many saleable lots will he have?

11. Mr. Smith would like to completely fence a yard that measures 60′ × 50′. If he places fence posts 10 feet apart, how many posts are needed?

12. Ms. Jones can either sell 30 acres for $6,000 per acre or divide it into half-acre lots at a total cost of $40,000 and sell each lot for $4,000. How much more will she make by subdividing and selling?

13. Mr. Allen wants to buy a stereo costing $1,600. If he borrows the money from his credit union, he can repay it in 40 payments of $50. How much would he save by paying cash?

14. Salesperson Watts bought a new car for her real estate work for $11,250. She also bought the following extras: power brakes, $125; power steering, $155; air conditioning, $475; undercoating, $50; and radio and speakers, $350. Find the total cost.

15. A toll charge on a bridge is 75 cents for every car and $1.00 for every two occupants. At one time, a group of cars containing two occupants each passed over the bridge. If the tolls they paid totaled $22.75, how many persons crossed the bridge in these cars?

16. The Jones family bought a house for $72,525 and made the following improvements: fence, $472; central air conditioning, $1,575; patio, $835; and gas barbecue, $275. What was the total cost of the house, including improvements?

17. The Schroeders bought a house for $52,830. Nine years later they sold it for $65,756. How much profit did they make on the sale of the house?

18. The Blacks bought a house for $85,750. If they made a down payment of $17,150, how much more remains to be paid?

19. A real estate salesperson sold a home for $95,875, which included his commission of $2,397. What was the cost of the home without the commission?

20. Mrs. Gray has a 25-payment life insurance policy and must pay yearly premiums for 25 years. If her premiums are $317 a year, how much will she pay in premiums?

21. The Wilsons own a home that has a 30-year mortgage. The monthly payments are $554. How much will they pay in 30 years?

22. A salesperson traveled 600 miles, using 39 gallons of gasoline. Assuming that each gallon gave the same mileage, how many miles did she travel on one gallon of gasoline? Round your answer to the nearest tenth.

23. A house sold for $82,500, with a broker fee of $4,950. If additional closing costs were $500, how much did the seller receive from the sale?

24. Ten years ago a double was built for $155,000. The land was worth $45,000. The double has since lost $25,000 in value and the land has increased its value by $5,000. How much is the property worth today?

25. The Schwartzes purchased a house for $92,000. XYZ Title Insurance Company issued a title insurance policy at a premium of $4.25 per $1,000 of coverage. What was the premium payment at closing?

2

UNDERSTANDING FRACTIONS

Goals

1. Determine when fractions are equivalent, and find fractions equivalent to a given fraction.
2. Add, subtract, multiply, and divide with fractions.
3. Write improper fractions as mixed numbers and mixed numbers as improper fractions.
4. Add, subtract, multiply, and divide with fractions and mixed numbers.

So far in our discussion of operations with numbers, we have been dealing with whole numbers. It is often necessary to deal with a part of a thing. Sometimes we have special names for these parts, as when we say that an hour is divided into minutes or a foot into inches. In everyday language, a *fraction* is "part of something." We talk of "a fraction of an inch" or of a new track record that beat the old record by "a fraction of a second." In mathematics, we call the inch or the second a unit. Units may be inches, seconds, pounds, or anything that we can count or measure. We define a fraction as "part of a unit."

PARTS OF A FRACTION

Something divided equally into two parts is said to be divided into halves. We express the division arithmetically by writing 1 (the unit) as the *numerator* of the fraction and the 2 (signifying the number of division) as the *denominator*.

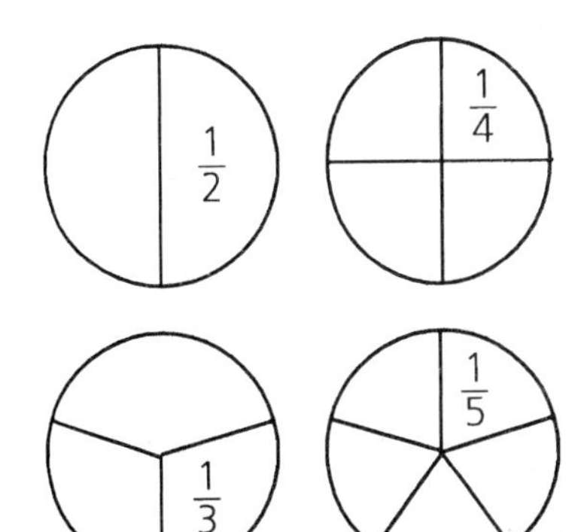

thus: 1 ←numerator
– ←fraction bar
2 ←denominator

This may be interpreted as one divided into two parts. If divided into three equal parts, the object is said to be divided into thirds, each part being expressed as $\frac{1}{3}$. Similarly, an object divided into four equal parts is said to be divided into fourths, the notation being $\frac{1}{4}$.

REMEMBER

> A fraction tells you two things:
> 1. The bottom number (denominator) tells you into how many parts the unit has been divided.
> 2. The top number (numerator) tells you how many of those parts are represented by the fraction.

If three pounds of steak are to be divided into four equal portions, each portion will weigh $\frac{3}{4}$ of a pound. In symbols, $3 \div 4 = \frac{3}{4}$. The fraction bar and the division symbol ÷ both mean "divided by."

Any fraction in which the numerator is smaller than the denominator is known as a *common,* or *proper,* fraction. Examples of common fractions are $\frac{2}{3}$, $\frac{5}{7}$, and $\frac{6}{11}$.

A foot-rule divided into inches is divided into 12 equal parts, each considered as one-twelfth ($\frac{1}{12}$). The divisions of an inch are customarily marked on a ruler as quarters, eighths, and sixteenths. If we want to express three-quarters, then

$$\frac{1}{4} + \frac{1}{4} + \frac{1}{4} \text{ or } \frac{1+1+1}{4} = \frac{3}{4} \text{ of an inch.}$$

From this it is evident that two halves or three thirds or four fourths added together would give a whole unit. Thus, $\frac{2}{2}$, $\frac{3}{3}$, $\frac{4}{4}$, etc., are each equal to a whole.

Exercises

1. Twelve students are absent from a class of 36.

a. Write as a fraction the number of students absent.

b. Write as a fraction the number of students present.

2. A jacket selling for $80 is on a "$\frac{1}{4}$ off" sale. Write the sale price of the coat as a fraction.

3. A team lost 1 out of 3 games. If the team played 105 games, how many games did the team win?

4. Salesperson Wilson earns $250 a week. He spends $100 on food, deposits $25 in his savings account, and deposits the rest of his money in his checking account. Write the above amounts as fractions by comparing each item with salesperson Wilson's weekly salary.

a. food

b. savings

c. checking

5. A basket contains 350 pieces of fruit consisting of oranges and grapefruit. If there are 70 grapefruit,

a. What fraction of the basket is grapefruit?

b. What fraction of the basket is oranges?

REDUCING FRACTIONS TO LOWEST TERMS

The numerator and denominator of a fraction are called *terms*. The fractions $3/6$ and $1/2$ have the same value, but they are written with different terms. Expressing $3/6$ of a pound as $1/2$ of a pound is reducing $3/6$ to its lowest terms. In general when you change fractions to simplest terms, you reduce them to lowest terms.

When you reduce a fraction to its lowest terms, you do not change its value.

Example

Reduce $\frac{15}{45}$ to its lowest terms.

$$\frac{15}{45} = \frac{1 \times 15}{3 \times 15} = \frac{1}{3} \times 1 = \frac{1}{3}$$

If you cannot immediately visualize that 15 is a common factor of the numerator and denominator, you can perform the operation in two steps:

$$\frac{15}{45} = \frac{3 \times 5}{9 \times 5} = \frac{3}{9} = \frac{1 \times 3}{3 \times 3} = \frac{1}{3}$$

You can also arrange the reducing procedure in the following manner, first dividing numerator and denominator by 5

$$\frac{\overset{3}{\cancel{15}}}{\underset{9}{\cancel{45}}} = \frac{3}{9}$$

and then dividing the numerator 3 and the denominator 9 by 3 to get

$$\frac{\overset{\overset{1}{\cancel{3}}}{\cancel{15}}}{\underset{\underset{3}{\cancel{9}}}{\cancel{45}}} = \frac{1}{3}$$

When reducing by the latter method, your solution should be found in one step. Divide the numerator and denominator by 15:

$$\frac{\overset{1}{\cancel{15}}}{\underset{3}{\cancel{45}}} = \frac{1}{3}$$

Exercises

Reduce each fraction to lowest terms.

1. $\frac{15}{60}$

2. $\frac{35}{45}$

3. $\frac{72}{84}$

4. $\frac{25}{150}$

5. $\frac{120}{360}$

EQUIVALENT FRACTIONS

When fractions have the same value, we call them equivalent fractions. For example, $\frac{1}{5}$ and $\frac{4}{20}$ are equivalent fractions. When fractions are added or subtracted, it is often necessary to change a given fraction to an equivalent fraction. This can be done by multiplying the numerator and the denominator by the same number without changing the value of the fraction. For example, the fraction $\frac{1}{2}$ is equivalent to $\frac{6}{12}$, since the numerator and denominator can each be multiplied by 6:

$$\frac{1 \times 6}{2 \times 6} = \frac{6}{12}.$$

Example

Change $\frac{2}{3}$ to an equivalent fraction with a denominator of 18.

To raise $\frac{2}{3}$ to 18ths, you must find how many 18ths are contained in $\frac{2}{3}$. Set up the problem like this:

$$\frac{2}{3} = \frac{?}{18}$$

To find how the 3 is changed to 18, divide 3 into 18. The quotient is 6.

$$\frac{2}{\underset{\text{into}}{3 \rightarrow}} = \frac{}{\underset{\text{is}}{18 \rightarrow 6}}$$

Multiply the numerator 2 by the quotient just found, 6. The product is 12. Write this product over 18.

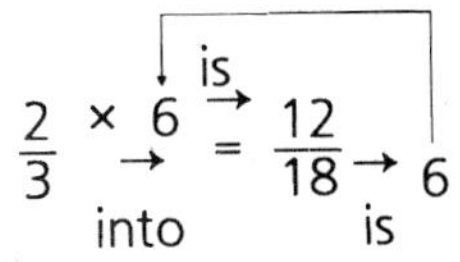

$$\frac{2}{3} \times 6 = \frac{12}{18} \rightarrow 6$$

(2 × 6 is 12; 3 into 18 is 6)

Answer: $\frac{2}{3} = \frac{12}{18}$.

Changing fractions to equivalent fractions is so often necessary in adding and subtracting fractions that it is beneficial to be able to perform this process mentally.

REMEMBER

To change a fraction to an equivalent fraction with a larger denominator:

1. Divide the denominator of the given fraction into the denominator of the equivalent fraction.
2. Multiply the numerator of the given fraction by the quotient found in step 1 and write the product over the equivalent denominator.

Exercises

1. How many pints are there in $\frac{3}{4}$ of a gallon?

2. How many 16ths of an inch are there in $\frac{3}{4}$ of an inch?

3. Change $\frac{3}{4}$ of a pound to ounces.

4. Mrs. Smith bought $\frac{5}{9}$ of a yard of material. How many inches did she buy?

5. Change $\frac{5}{9}$ to 27ths.

COMPARING FRACTIONS

To compare the values of two or more fractions means to determine the fraction that has the largest value. The process of comparing fractions is as follows:

1. Change the given fractions to equivalent fractions that have the same denominator.
2. Compare the numerators. The fraction with the largest numerator has the largest value.

Example

Which fraction is larger, $\frac{1}{2}$ or $\frac{5}{8}$?

$\frac{1}{2} = \frac{4}{8}$ and $\frac{5}{8} = \frac{5}{8}$

Since 5 is larger than 4, then $\frac{5}{8}$ is larger than $\frac{4}{8}$, and $\frac{5}{8}$ is larger than $\frac{1}{2}$.

Exercises

1. In the final week of the baseball season the catcher had 11 hits for 28 times at bat and the pitcher had 3 hits for 7 times at bat. Who had the better batting average?

2. Fred lives $\frac{5}{8}$ of a mile from school and Joe lives $\frac{11}{16}$ of a mile from school. Who lives closer to school?

3. Cindy ran a race in $5\frac{3}{10}$ minutes and Susan ran the same race in $5\frac{2}{5}$ minutes. Who won the race?

4. One savings bank offers $12\frac{3}{4}$ % interest and another bank offers $12\frac{7}{8}$% interest. Which rate of interest is higher?

5. One pipe measures $15\frac{5}{8}$ inches in diameter and another pipe measures $15\frac{17}{32}$ inches in diameter. Which pipe has the larger diameter?

IMPROPER FRACTIONS AND MIXED NUMBERS

As we mentioned before, a fraction is defined as a part of a unit. At times, however, a fraction means more than a unit. When you buy 24 oz. of ice cream, for example, you have $^{24}/_{16}$ of a pound. But $^{24}/_{16}$ of a pound is the same as $^{3}/_{2}$ of a pound or $1\frac{1}{2}$ pounds (1 pound = 16 oz.). We call $^{3}/_{2}$ an *improper fraction* and define an improper fraction as a fraction whose numerator is as large as or larger than its denominator. Examples of improper fractions are $^{7}/_{4}$, $^{5}/_{4}$, and $^{4}/_{4}$.

We refer to $1\frac{1}{2}$ as a *mixed number* and define a mixed number as a counting number followed by a fraction. Examples of mixed numbers are $2\frac{3}{8}$, $3\frac{1}{3}$, and $1\frac{7}{8}$.

When we have an improper fraction such as $^{4}/_{3}$, the following information helps us to change an improper fraction to a mixed number: $^{4}/_{3}$ may be considered as the sum of $^{3}/_{3} + ^{1}/_{3}$; the $^{3}/_{3}$ is equal to 1; therefore, $^{4}/_{3} = 1\frac{1}{3}$. We may shorten the process by this simple rule: divide the numerator by the denominator; write the quotient as a whole number followed by a fraction in which the remainder is expressed as a numerator over the same denominator as before.

Example

Change $\frac{52}{15}$ to a mixed number.

$$\begin{array}{r} 3 \\ 15 \overline{)\,52} \\ \underline{45} \\ 7 \end{array}$$

$\frac{52}{15} = 3\frac{7}{15}$, since 15 is contained in 52 three times with a remainder of 7.

REMEMBER

> To change an improper fraction to a mixed number, divide the numerator by the denominator.

Example

Change $7\frac{3}{4}$ to an improper fraction.

Set up the problem $7\frac{3}{4} = \frac{?}{4}$

Think: "4 × 7 = 28, and 28 + 3 = 31." Write 31 over the same denominator:

$$7\frac{3}{4} = \frac{31}{4}$$

REMEMBER

> To change a mixed number to an improper fraction, multiply the denominator by the whole number and add the numerator. This gives a new numerator which you write over the same denominator.

Exercises

1. How many $\frac{1}{5}$ cups of sugar can you get from a bag that holds $8\frac{3}{5}$ cups?

2. How many hours does the film *Gone with the Wind* run if it runs 210 minutes?

3. How many $\frac{1}{7}$-inch-thick slices of bread can be cut from a loaf of bread that measures $12\frac{5}{7}$ inches long?

4. Change $\frac{23}{8}$ to a mixed number.

5. Change $12\frac{2}{3}$ to an improper fraction.

MULTIPLYING FRACTIONS

With a few simple principles in mind, any of the four fundamental operations (addition, subtraction, multiplication, or division) may be performed with fractions almost as easily as with whole numbers.

Perhaps the easiest of the four operations with fractions is multiplication. Since every fraction is made up of a numerator (top number) and denominator (bottom number), we multiply numerator by numerator and denominator by denominator to get a single fraction. The total operation is easily seen in this example:

$$\frac{2}{3} \times \frac{4}{5} = \frac{2 \times 4}{3 \times 5} = \frac{8}{15}$$

REMEMBER

To multiply fractions, multiply numerator by numerator and denominator by denominator to get a single fraction.

Both multiplication and division of fractions may be simplified by performing certain divisions between numerators and denominators before proceeding with the necessary multiplications of numerators or denominators. To multiply $5/12 \times 14/15$, instead of writing

$$\frac{5 \times 14}{12 \times 15} = \frac{70}{180}$$

and then reducing by dividing both numerator and denominator by 10 (the common divisor of 70 and 180) to get

$$\frac{70 \div 10}{180 \div 10} = \frac{7}{18}$$

we may obtain the result more directly by using the process of *cancellation*. To cancel out, we see that the numerator of the first fraction (5) and the denominator of the second fraction (15) can be divided by 5. The remaining denominator (12) and numerator (14) can be divided by 2. To finish the problem, multiply the resulting fractions.

$$\frac{\overset{1}{\cancel{5}}}{\underset{6}{\cancel{12}}} \times \frac{\overset{7}{\cancel{14}}}{\underset{3}{\cancel{15}}} = \frac{7}{18}$$

When mixed numbers are to be multiplied, we change each to an improper fraction, cancel out where possible, and proceed as above.

Exercises

1. The width of a door is $\frac{1}{3}$ of its height. What is the width if the height is $8\frac{1}{3}$ ft.?

2. The number of pages in a 90-page manual was increased by $\frac{1}{5}$. How many pages were added?

3. The width of a river is $\frac{3}{8}$ of a mile. How far from either shore is a boat located exactly in midstream?

4. Multiply: $5\frac{2}{5} \times 4\frac{2}{3}$.

5. Multiply: $650 \times 78\frac{7}{10}$.

DIVIDING FRACTIONS

The process of dividing by a fraction is one of the most confusing processes in arithmetic. Let's look at a simple example. If we wish to convert a ten-dollar bill into quarters, we would obtain 40 quarters; that is, 10 divided into quarters would give 40 quarters ($10 \div \frac{1}{4} = 40$). Similarly, a five-dollar bill converted into dimes would give 50 dimes ($5 \div \frac{1}{10} = 50$). This is the same as multiplying 10 by 4 in the first case or 5 by 10 in the second case. Recall that a division problem asks how many times a divisor is contained in the dividend. The first example asks, "how many ¼ths are there in 10?" Since there are four ¼ths in 1 then there must be 40 ¼ths in 10.

From this we can arrive at a rule to divide one fraction by another. When the division symbol (÷) is used, the right-hand fraction is the divisor. Hence, in the problem $\frac{2}{3} \div \frac{3}{8}$, the divisor is $\frac{3}{8}$.

REMEMBER

> To divide one fraction by another, indicate the division with the ÷ symbol, invert the divisor (right-hand fraction), and change the problem to multiplication.

To invert a fraction, interchange the numerator and denominator. When you invert $\frac{3}{4}$, you get $\frac{4}{3}$. When you invert $\frac{5}{8}$, you get $\frac{8}{5}$. Thus,

$$\frac{3}{4} \div \frac{5}{7} = \frac{3}{4} \times \frac{7}{5} = \frac{21}{20} = 1\frac{1}{20}.$$

The equation $\frac{3}{4} \div \frac{5}{7}$ may also be written as $\frac{3/4}{5/7}$, and in this case we must think of a term to multiply the numerator and denominator by in order to make the denominator 1. This number is $\frac{7}{5}$ since $\frac{5}{7} \times \frac{7}{5} = \frac{35}{35} = 1$. Further, if we multiply the numerator and denominator of any fraction by the same value, the value of the fraction is not changed. Therefore,

$$\frac{\frac{3}{4} \times \frac{7}{5}}{\frac{5}{7} \times \frac{7}{5}} = \frac{\frac{21}{20}}{1} = \frac{21}{20} = 1\frac{1}{20}.$$

Note that this solution is the same as using the ÷ symbol and following the rule *to invert the divisor and multiply.*

REMEMBER

> To divide one mixed number by another mixed number, change the mixed numbers to improper fractions, then divide by inverting the divisor and multiplying.

Example

Divide $3\frac{2}{3} \div 6\frac{3}{5}$.

Step 1: $3\frac{2}{3} = \frac{11}{3}$ $\quad$ $6\frac{3}{5} = \frac{33}{5}$

Step 2: $\frac{11}{3} \div \frac{33}{5} = \frac{11}{3} \times \frac{5}{33} = \frac{5}{9}$

Answer: $3\frac{2}{3} \div 6\frac{3}{5} = \frac{5}{9}$.

Exercises

1. How many eighths are there in $\frac{3}{4}$?

2. How many containers of sand can be filled with $\frac{3}{8}$ of a ton of sand if each container can hold $\frac{1}{12}$ of a ton?

3. A yacht leaves port every three minutes on a sightseeing tour. How many yachts leave port in $\frac{3}{4}$ of an hour?

4. How many sheets of metal, each $\frac{1}{8}$″ thick, are there in a stack 4′6″ high?

5. Divide: $3\frac{2}{3} \div 7\frac{1}{2}$.

FRACTIONAL PART OF A NUMBER

Suppose that seven members of a work force are absent, and this represents $\frac{1}{6}$ of the total work force. How many members are there in the work force?

In order to find a number when you know a fractional part of it, divide the known fractional part, which is the given number, by the fraction, and the quotient will be the required number. Applying this rule to the above example, we see that

$$7 \div \frac{1}{6} = \frac{7}{1} \times \frac{6}{1} = 42 \text{ workers.}$$

Example

If a family spends $600 a month on a mortgage payment and this is $\frac{3}{5}$ of the monthly income, what is the monthly income?

Step 1: Divide $600 by $\frac{3}{5}$ to find monthly income.

$$600 \div \frac{3}{5} = 600 \times \frac{5}{3} = \frac{3{,}000}{3} = \$1{,}000.$$

Step 2: To check your answer, multiply the following:

$$\frac{3}{5} \times 1{,}000 = \frac{3{,}000}{5} = \$600.$$

Answer: The family's monthly income is $1,000. Always try to check your answer in terms of given facts.

In solving word problems that deal with fractional parts of an unknown number, it is often difficult to determine which given number should be divided into which. Remembering which number becomes the divisor and which number becomes the dividend is easier with the help of a mnemonic device, $\frac{IS}{OF}$. The number in the problem related to "IS" is written as the numerator of the fraction to be simplified, and the number related to "OF" is written as the denominator.

The given facts in the example above suggest the question, "$600 is ⅗ of what amount?" Using the $\frac{IS}{OF}$ method, write a fraction using 600 as the numerator and ⅗ as the denominator:

$$\frac{IS}{OF} = \frac{600}{\frac{3}{5}} = 600 \div \frac{3}{5} = 600 \times \frac{5}{3} = \$1{,}000$$

Regardless of the wording of a problem about fractional parts of unknown numbers, each problem can be reworded so that one number is related to "IS" and the other is related to "OF." Then use $\frac{IS}{OF}$ to write a numerical fraction that will solve the problem.

Example

What part of 81 is 27?

Step 1: Using the "part/total" method, we form the following fraction and then reduce.

$$\frac{27 \text{ (part)}}{81 \text{ (total)}} = \frac{1}{3}$$

Step 2: Using the $\frac{IS}{OF}$ method; we ask, "27 is what part of 81?"

$$\frac{IS}{OF} = \frac{27}{81} = \frac{1}{3}$$

Answer: 27 is one-third of 81.

REMEMBER

To find what fractional part one number is of another number, write a fraction with the *total* amount as the denominator and the *partial* amount as the numerator.

Exercises

1. If $\frac{3}{8}$ of a number is 15, find the number.

2. $\frac{3}{8}$ of what number is 27?

3. 45 is $\frac{5}{7}$ of what number?

4. 35 is $\frac{1}{4}$ of what number?

5. Tom saves $60 a week. If he is saving $\frac{3}{8}$ of his weekly income, how much does he earn in a week?

6. If you had $125 and you spent $30, what fractional part of your money did you spend?

7. Jill received 960 votes for class president. If this represents $\frac{3}{5}$ of the votes, how many votes were cast in the election?

8. Six hundred seniors entered the senior class at Jefferson High School, 525 received diplomas in June. What fraction of the seniors graduated?

9. An investor purchased a property for $65,000 and made a down payment of $16,250. What part of the purchase price is the down payment?

10. 34 is $\frac{2}{3}$ of what number?

ADDING AND SUBTRACTING FRACTIONS

When we come to adding or subtracting fractions, we find ourselves faced with greater difficulty. So long as the denominators are the same, we add and subtract fractions as we would whole numbers, but when the denominators are different, a new problem arises. This must be faced before we can perform the indicated addition or subtraction. When we add three-fifths and one-fifth, we get four-fifths ($3/5 + 1/5 = 4/5$); when we subtract one-fifth from four-fifths, we get three-fifths ($4/5 - 1/5 = 3/5$). We can think of these processes as being performed over one denominator:

$$\frac{3+1}{5} = \frac{4}{5} \qquad \frac{4-1}{5} = \frac{3}{5}.$$

REMEMBER

> To add or subtract fractions with the same denominator, add or subtract the numerators and write over the same denominator. Then simplify any improper fraction to a mixed number or a whole number.

When fractions have unlike denominators, it is impossible to perform addition or subtraction until the denominators have been converted to like terms. In this process you must find a *common denominator,* change each fraction to an equivalent fraction that has this same denominator, and then add or subtract as above. In a previous section you learned how to change a fraction to an equivalent fraction. This skill can now be applied to add and subtract fractions.

Example

Add $\frac{3}{5} + \frac{3}{10} + \frac{11}{20}$.

Step 1: Find the common denominator. In this problem the common denominator is 20, since 5, 10, and 20 all divide evenly into 20.

Step 2: Change each fraction to an equivalent fraction with the denominator 20. Apply the technique you learned in the previous section on equivalent fractions (i.e., divide each given denominator into the common denominator 20, then multiply the quotient by each numerator).

$\frac{3}{5} = \frac{12}{20}$ *Think:* "5 into 20 = 4, and 4 × 3 = 12." Write the 12 over 20.

$\frac{3}{10} = \frac{6}{20}$ *Think:* "10 into 20 = 2, and 2 × 3 = 6." Write the 6 over 20.

$\frac{11}{20} = \frac{11}{20}$ *Think:* "20 into 20 = 1, and 1 × 11 = 11." Write the 11 over 20.

Step 3: After you have changed each fraction to an equivalent fraction, add the numerators of the equivalent fractions and put the sum over the common denominator, 20.

$$\frac{12}{20} + \frac{6}{20} + \frac{11}{20} = \frac{29}{20}$$

Answer: $\frac{29}{20} = 1\frac{9}{20}$

Subtracting fractions is similar to adding fractions. Arrange the fractions one under the other, find a common denominator and change each fraction to an equivalent fraction. Then subtract numerators, and write the difference over the common denominator.

Example

Subtract $\frac{5}{6} - \frac{3}{8}$

Step 1: Find a common denominator.

$8 \times 6 = 48$

$\frac{5}{6} = \frac{40}{48}$

$- \frac{3}{8} = \frac{18}{48}$

Step 2: Subtract numerators.

$40 - 18 = 22$

Answer: $\frac{22}{48} = \frac{11}{24}$ (reduce!)

Another technique is to multiply the largest denominator by 2, 3, 4, etc., until you get a number that each of the other denominators will divide evenly. This is referred to as the *least common denominator*, and by using it you will not need to reduce the answer. Use this technique for the previous example.

Example

Subtract $\frac{5}{6} - \frac{3}{8}$

Step 1: Find the least common denominator. Since 6 will not divide 8 evenly, multiply the 8 to find a common denominator:

$8 \times 2 = 16$. Cannot be used since 6 does not divide 16 evenly.

$8 \times 3 = 24$. Use 24 as a common denominator since 6 will divide 24 evenly.

$$\frac{5}{6} = \frac{20}{24}$$
$$-\ \frac{3}{8} = \frac{9}{24}$$

Step 2: Subtract numerators:

$$20 - 9 = 11$$

Answer: $\frac{11}{24}$

Note that the answer is the same as the example that used 48 as the common denominator. This technique of finding the least common denominator may also be used in adding fractions.

Exercises

1. $\frac{1}{4} + \frac{1}{3}$

2. $\frac{1}{2} + \frac{3}{4} + \frac{5}{8}$

3. $\frac{2}{7} + \frac{1}{6} + \frac{1}{3}$

4. $\frac{5}{8} + \frac{3}{16} + \frac{7}{12}$

5. $\frac{3}{5} + \frac{7}{15} + \frac{7}{20}$

6. $\frac{3}{4} - \frac{3}{5}$

7. $\frac{9}{10} - \frac{4}{5}$

8. $\frac{4}{5} - \frac{2}{3}$

9. $\frac{7}{12} - \frac{1}{4}$

10. $\frac{7}{8} - \frac{3}{4}$

ADDING AND SUBTRACTING MIXED NUMBERS

In working with numbers that contain both whole numbers and fractions, it is necessary to combine several of the steps that have been discussed earlier. In adding mixed numbers, add the whole numbers just as in ordinary addition, and then add the fractions (after changing all the fractions involved to equivalent fractions). If the resulting fraction is an improper fraction, reduce it to a whole or mixed number and then add the fraction to the sum of the whole numbers. The following example will aid in making the process clear.

Example

Add $14\frac{1}{6} + 6\frac{2}{3} + 7\frac{1}{9}$.

Step 1: Add the whole numbers.

$$14 + 6 + 7 = 27$$

Step 2: Find the lowest common denominator using method learned earlier.

$9 \times 2 = 18$. Use 18 since all denominators will divide 18 evenly.

Step 3: Add the fractions.

$$\frac{3}{18} + \frac{12}{18} + \frac{2}{18} = \frac{17}{18}$$

Answer: Combine the two answers to a final sum.

$$27\frac{17}{18}$$

In subtraction of mixed numbers, if the fraction in the *minuend* is greater than the fraction in the *subtrahend,* we have no difficulty in performing subtraction. In such a case, set up the mixed numbers, one under the other and find the common denominator. Subtract the equivalent fractions first, then subtract the whole numbers, and combine these two answers for the final answer.

Example

Subtract: $24\frac{5}{8} - 13\frac{5}{16}$

$$\begin{array}{rcr} 24\frac{5}{8} & = & 24\frac{10}{16} \\ -\ 13\frac{5}{16} & = & 13\frac{5}{16} \\ \hline & & 11\frac{5}{16} \end{array}$$

The following example illustrates a problem in which the minuend is less than the subtrahend.

Example

Subtract: $12\frac{2}{5} - 8\frac{3}{4}$

$$\begin{array}{rcr} 12\frac{2}{5} & = & 12\frac{8}{20} \\ -\ 8\frac{3}{4} & = & 8\frac{15}{20} \\ \hline \end{array}$$

Step 1: Notice that the numerator of $\frac{15}{20}$ is larger than the numerator of $\frac{8}{20}$. Since you cannot subtract 15 from 4, borrow 1 from the 12 and change it to 11. Place the 1 in front of $\frac{8}{20}$, getting the mixed number $1\frac{8}{20}$.

$$\begin{array}{rcrcr} 12\frac{2}{5} & = & 12\frac{8}{20} & = & 11 + 1\frac{8}{20} \\ -\ 8\frac{3}{4} & = & 8\frac{15}{20} & = & 8\frac{15}{20} \\ \hline \end{array}$$

Step 2: Change $1\frac{8}{20}$ to an improper fraction.

Step 3: *Think:* "20 × 1 = 20, and 20 + 8 = 28."

$$1\frac{8}{20} = \frac{28}{20}$$

Step 4: Replace $1\frac{8}{20}$ with $\frac{28}{20}$ in the problem and subtract $\frac{15}{20}$ from $\frac{28}{20}$, then subtract the whole numbers, and combine the two answers for the final answer.

$$
\begin{array}{rcrcrcr}
12\frac{2}{5} & = & 12\frac{8}{20} & = & 11 + 1\frac{8}{20} & = & 11\frac{28}{20} \\
-\ 8\frac{3}{4} & = & 8\frac{15}{20} & = & 8\frac{15}{20} & = & 8\frac{15}{20} \\
\hline
 & & & & & & 3\frac{13}{20}
\end{array}
$$

Answer: $3\frac{13}{20}$

Exercises

1. A salesperson sold the following pieces of material: $2\frac{2}{3}$ yards, $4\frac{1}{4}$ yards, and $6\frac{1}{2}$ yards. How many yards were sold?

2. Add: $26\frac{3}{5} + 7\frac{9}{10} + 14\frac{1}{2}$.

3. Add: $4\frac{1}{3} + 6\frac{5}{6} + 3\frac{5}{9}$.

4. Mrs. Wilson had $12\frac{2}{3}$ cups of flour and used $4\frac{4}{5}$ cups to bake a cake. How many cups of flour are left?

5. Subtract: $72\frac{1}{3} - 37\frac{5}{12}$.

CHAPTER TEST

1. How many twentieths have a value of 1?

2. What fraction of a section is 40 acres?

3. How many acres are there in $\frac{3}{4}$ of a section?

4. Which has the larger number of acres, $\frac{8}{10}$ of a section or $\frac{15}{20}$ of a section?

5. Mr. Wilson gave $\frac{1}{4}$ of a section to each of his four grandchildren. How many acres did each grandchild receive?

6. Find $\frac{2}{5}$ of $\frac{5}{8}$ of a section to the nearest acre.

7. Divide: $\frac{5}{6} \div \frac{7}{12}$.

8. How many total acres are in an acreage if $\frac{5}{8}$ of the acreage is 25 acres?

9. On a certain farm, $\frac{1}{5}$ is pasture, $\frac{5}{8}$ is under cultivation, and the remainder is woodland. If the woodland is 56 acres, how many acres are there in the whole farm?

10. How many half-pints are there in $\frac{7}{8}$ of a gallon?

11. In the final week of the baseball season, Roy Wilson had 13 hits for 28 times at bat, and pitcher Jerry Jones had 3 hits for 7 times at bat. Who had the better batting average?

12. Fred ran a race in $4\frac{9}{10}$ minutes, and Jim ran the same race in $4\frac{4}{5}$ minutes. Who won the race?

13. Eva spent $\frac{3}{4}$ of an hour on her arithmetic homework, $\frac{2}{3}$ of an hour on history, and $\frac{1}{6}$ of an hour on English. How long did it take her to do all of her homework? Give the answer to the nearest minute.

14. Add: $32\frac{1}{4} + 12\frac{3}{8} + 15\frac{1}{2}$.

15. Add: $13\frac{3}{5} + 7\frac{11}{15} + 11\frac{5}{6}$.

16. Peggy had $\frac{3}{4}$ pounds of sugar and used $\frac{7}{16}$ pounds. How much sugar is left?

17. Subtract: $7\frac{3}{8} - 5\frac{3}{16}$.

18. Subtract: $14\frac{1}{5} - 6\frac{3}{4}$.

19. Multiply: $\frac{5}{16} \times \frac{4}{8} \times \frac{7}{10}$.

20. Multiply:

a. $8\frac{2}{9} \times 3\frac{1}{11}$.

b. $230 \times 27\frac{3}{5}$.

21. Salesperson Linda is taking a business trip of 800 miles. One-quarter of the entire distance was covered on the first day and $\frac{1}{6}$ of the remaining distance on the second day. What fraction of the entire trip remains to be covered?

22. On the same business trip, Linda took $800. During the first day she spent $\frac{1}{2}$ of the money; during the second day she spent $\frac{1}{4}$ of the remainder; and during the third day she spent $\frac{1}{5}$ of what was left. What fraction of the original sum did she still have after the third day?

23. Select the smallest of the following:

a. $\frac{5}{8}$

b. $\frac{7}{16}$

c. $\frac{23}{64}$

d. $\frac{17}{32}$

24. A salesperson had a monthly income of $1,200. During a certain month he spent $\frac{1}{3}$ of this income for food and $\frac{2}{5}$ of the remainder for rent. What fraction of the income was spent for rent?

25. A real estate salesperson received a commission of $\frac{1}{10}$ on her sales. How much total commission did she make on sales of $49,000 and $38,000?

3

MASTERING DECIMALS

Goals

1. Understand the place value of a decimal.
2. Add, subtract, multiply, and divide decimals.
3. Change a fraction to a decimal and change a decimal to a fraction.
4. Compare decimals and round off decimals.
5. Solve practical problems using decimals.

PLACE VALUE

Perhaps you have noticed that amounts of money on personal checks are often written as common fractions. Five dollars and thirty-five cents is written as $\$5^{35}/_{100}$. When you write the amount $\$5^{35}/_{100}$ as \$5.35, you express the fraction $^{35}/_{100}$ as a decimal fraction or a decimal, .35. Also, you express the mixed fraction $5^{35}/_{100}$ as a mixed decimal, 5.35. In both cases the fraction bar is replaced by a decimal.

A common fraction can have any number as its denominator, but a decimal fraction must have a denominator that is 10 or a power of 10. Recall that powers of 10 are 100, 1,000, 10,000 and so on. The denominator of a decimal fraction is never written down since it is determined by the number of digits to the right of the decimal point. Here are some examples of common fractions written as decimal fractions:

$\frac{4}{10} = .4$ Read .4 as "four tenths." Note that the 4 is one place to the right of the decimal.

$\frac{12}{100} = .12$ Read .12 as "twelve hundredths." Note that the right-hand digit is two places to the right of the decimal.

In order, then, to read and write decimals an understanding of place value is necessary. Study the place value chart in Figure 3–1.

To read a decimal, we use the name of the last place to the right as the denominator, although the denominator is not actually written down. Thus .6281 is read "six thousand, two hundred, eighty-one ten-thousandths." The decimal part of the number in the place chart of Figure 3–1 is read, "twelve thousand, three hundred, forty-five millionths." Note that we say the word "and" for the decimal point in numbers that include a whole number and a decimal.

millions	hundred thousands	ten thousands	thousands	hundreds	tens	ones		tenths	hundredths	thousandths	ten thousandths	hundred thousandths	millionths
1,	2	3	4,	5	6	7	.	0	1	2	3	4	5

Figure 3–1

Exercises

Write each of the following as a fraction.

1. 428.01

2. 73.801

3. 11.81275

Write each of the following as a decimal.

4. Two thousand, one hundred, sixteen ten-thousandths

5. Three and thirty-six hundred-thousandths

COMPARING DECIMALS AND ROUNDING OFF DECIMALS

When you compared the values of common fractions in Chapter 2, you found a common denominator. Similarly, in order to compare decimals you must make certain that each has the same number of decimal places. Changing decimal expressions so as to give each one the same number of decimal places is the same as changing their fractional equivalents to expressions having a common denominator. Hence, .06 and .56 have a common denominator of 100 and the decimals .007 and .123 have a common denominator of 1,000.

One way to compare decimals is to use a number line. Figure 3–2 illustrates that 0.6 > 0.2 (read "0.6 is greater than 0.2"), because 0.6 is to the right of 0.2 on the number line.

It is not always easy to use a number line to compare decimals; therefore, we need another way to decide which is greater.

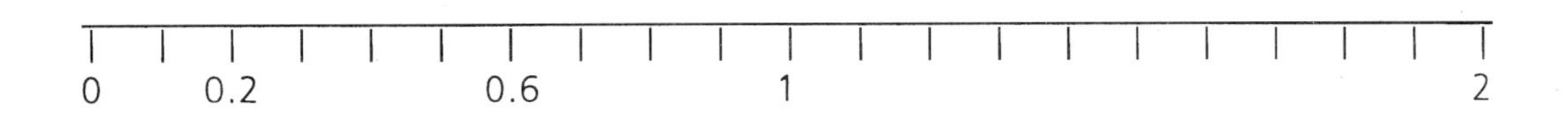

Figure 3–2

REMEMBER

To compare decimals, do the following:

1. Where necessary, add zeros to the right of the last digit until each decimal has the same number of places.
2. Compare digits in each decimal place. The largest number is the decimal with the largest value.

Example

Compare 0.942 and 0.927.

Step 1: To compare these decimals, which have the same number of places, compare the digits in each place until you find a place where the digits are different.

```
0. 9 4 2
↕  ↕ ↕ ↕
0. 9 2 7
```

Step 2: In this example we begin with the units place, not the tenths place. Each digit is the same: 0 in the units place, and 9 in the tenths place. In the hundredths place they differ, and 4 is greater than 2.

Answer: Therefore, 0.942 > 0.927.

In Chapter 1 we learned how to round off a whole number, changing it to an approximate number. To round off decimals, follow the same steps used in rounding whole numbers, except in the final step omit all digits to the right of the place to which you are rounding off.

After deciding on the value to which you will round off:

Step 1: Underline all digits to the right of this value.

Step 2: If the leftmost digit underlined is 5 or more, add 1 to the first value to the left of the underlined digits. If the leftmost digit underlined is less than 5, do not add 1 to the first value to the left of the underlined digits.

Step 3: Omit all digits underlined.

REMEMBER

To round any number to a given place, look at the digit to the right of that place. If it is 5 or more, increase the digit in the given place by 1. In a whole number, the digits to the right are replaced by zeros and in a decimal the digits are dropped.

Example

Round off .1354 to the nearest tenth.

Step 1: .1 3 5 4

Step 2: Since 3 < 5 we do not add 1 to the 1 in the tenths place.

Answer: Omitting all digits underlined, .1354 to the nearest tenth is .1.

Example

Round off .1354 to the nearest hundredth.

Step 1: .1 3 5 4

Step 2: The leftmost digit underlined is 5 so we add 1 to the hundredths place.

Answer: Omitting all digits underlined, .1354 to the nearest hundredth is .14.

Exercises

Compare the decimals in each pair. Write > (greater than) and < (less than) in the blank space.

1. .452 ________ 1.056.

2. .03 ________ .003.

3. Order the following decimals from least to greatest: 11.4, 10.43, 11.04, 11.44.

4. Round 4.18 to the nearest tenth.

5. Round .00518 to the nearest hundredth.

CHANGING FRACTIONS TO DECIMALS AND DECIMALS TO FRACTIONS

To convert a fraction to a decimal, simply divide the numerator by the denominator, adding to the numerator as many zeros as may be necessary to permit an even division, and then expressing the quotient as a decimal. Think of the line that separates the two numbers of a fraction as meaning "divided by." Thus $\frac{1}{5}$ equals 1.0 divided by 5, or 0.2; $\frac{1}{2}$ equals 1.0 divided by 2, or 0.5; $\frac{1}{8}$ equals 1.000 divided by 8, or 0.125. Note that in order to divide 8 into 1 by an even division it was necessary to annex three zeros.

To convert a decimal expression to a fraction, simply reverse the procedure. Express the decimal (with the decimal point removed) as the numerator over a denominator which is the place value of the last digit to the right of the decimal, then reduce the fraction to lowest terms. A knowledge of place value is necessary to make this conversion.

Figure 3–3 is a table of basic conversions of fractions to decimals and decimals to fractions.

Table of Common Fractions and Equivalent Decimals

Common Fraction	*Equivalent Decimal*	*Common Fraction*	*Equivalent Decimal*	*Common Fraction*	*Equivalent Decimal*
$\frac{1}{2}$	.5	$\frac{5}{6}$	.833	$\frac{3}{5}$	.6
$\frac{1}{3}$	.333	$\frac{1}{8}$	.125	$\frac{4}{5}$	.8
$\frac{2}{3}$	.667	$\frac{3}{8}$	.375	$\frac{1}{7}$	.143
$\frac{1}{10}$	.1	$\frac{5}{8}$	.625	$\frac{1}{9}$	.111
$\frac{1}{4}$	.25	$\frac{7}{8}$	.875	$\frac{1}{12}$	.083
$\frac{3}{4}$	.75	$\frac{1}{5}$	.2	$\frac{1}{16}$	.063
$\frac{1}{6}$	.167	$\frac{2}{5}$	.4		

Figure 3–3

Example

$.5 = \frac{5}{10} = \frac{1}{2}$

Example

$.125 = \frac{125}{1000} = \frac{25}{200} = \frac{5}{40} = \frac{1}{8}$

Exercises

Change the following to decimals:

1. $\frac{7}{8}$

2. $\frac{3}{8}$

3. $\frac{3}{16}$

Change the following to fractions:

4. 0.625

5. 0.3125

ADDING, SUBTRACTING, AND MULTIPLYING DECIMALS

Addition of decimals is simple to one who has mastered the general principles of addition. There is only one new rule to keep in mind and that is to line up the decimal points one under another and proceed as in ordinary addition of whole numbers. To add 41.985, 241.541, 728.4, and

9.46, we simply arrange the figures in a column with the decimal points aligned, with the sums of the digits in the same place values, carrying in cases of numbers greater than 9, and indicating the total with the decimal point directly under the points in the column.

$$\begin{array}{r} 41.985 \\ 241.541 \\ 728.4 \\ 9.46 \\ \hline 1{,}021.386 \end{array}$$

REMEMBER

> In subtracting decimals, the same rule applies. Line up the decimal points in the minuend and subtrahend and proceed as in subtraction of whole numbers. If there are fewer places to the right of the decimal in the minuend than in the subtrahend, add zeros to occupy the empty spaces.

To subtract 506.4127 from 2,408.21, note that there are four places to the right of the decimal point in the subtrahend and only two places to the right in the minuend. Hence it is necessary to add two zeros, making the minuend 2,408.2100. If there are fewer places to the right of the decimal point in the subtrahend than in the minuend, those place values can be considered as zeros. Since there is nothing to subtract, the numbers above the blank spaces are merely brought down.

$$\begin{array}{r} 2{,}408.2100 \\ -\ 506.4127 \\ \hline 1{,}901.7973 \end{array} \qquad \begin{array}{r} 30.7624 \\ -\ \ 7.06 \\ \hline 23.7024 \end{array}$$

Our experience in changing a decimal to a fraction can aid in locating the decimal point in the answer as we multiply decimals.

$$0.3 \times 0.6 = \frac{3}{10} \times \frac{6}{10} = \frac{18}{100} = .18$$

$$4.6 \times 3.16 = \frac{46}{10} \times \frac{316}{100} = \frac{14{,}536}{1{,}000} = 14.536$$

In our examples, we change each decimal to a fraction, multiply fractions, and then convert back to decimals. Let's look at the examples again and come up with a rule to find the decimal place in the product without having to change decimals to fractions and back again.

$$\begin{array}{rl} 0.3 & \leftarrow \text{1 decimal place} \\ \times\ 0.6 & \leftarrow \text{1 decimal place} \\ \hline .18 & \leftarrow \text{2 decimal places} \end{array} \qquad \begin{array}{rl} 4.6 & \leftarrow \text{1 decimal place} \\ \times\ 3.16 & \leftarrow \text{2 decimal places} \\ \hline 14.536 & \leftarrow \text{3 decimal places} \end{array}$$

REMEMBER

> In multiplying decimals, we add the number of decimal places in the top number (the multiplicand) to the number of decimal places in the bottom number (the multiplier), and moving from right to left, count as many places in the answer (product) as there are total places in the problem.

Exercises

1. A sales agent for Sunrise Realty Company earns the following commissions: $1,506.28, $5,215.75, $2,325.42, and $4,220.00. What is his total commission?

2. From what number must 63.102 be subtracted to leave 14.676?

3. Nancy earned real estate commissions of $28,517.76 last year. This year her commissions totaled $32,634.54. How much more did she earn this year?

4. A lot has measurements of 122.2 ft. by 165.79 ft. Find its area.

5. Multiply: 2.1 × .037.

DIVIDING BY DECIMALS

Dividing a whole number into a decimal is similar to dividing a whole number by another except that it is necessary to locate the decimal properly in the answer, or quotient. When the dividend is a decimal and the divisor a whole number, place the decimal point in the quotient directly above the decimal point in the dividend and then simply divide as whole numbers.

Example

Divide 1.25 ÷ 250.

Step 1: Place the decimal point in the quotient properly.

$$250 \overline{)\,1.25}$$

Step 2: Place zeros directly above 1, 2, and 5, since 250 does not go into 1 or 12 or 125. Since there is still a remainder of 125, add a zero in the dividend. We can continue to add zeros until there is a remainder of zero, or until we round off to a desired decimal place.

$$\begin{array}{r} 0.00 \\ 250 \overline{)\,1.250} \end{array}$$

Answer:

$$\begin{array}{r} 0.005 \\ 250 \overline{)\,1.250} \\ \underline{1\ 250} \\ 0 \end{array}$$

$$1.25 \div 250 = 0.005$$

When we divide a decimal by another decimal, it is necessary to find a way to write the divisor as a whole number. When we discussed division of fractions in Chapter 2, we discovered that $5 \div \frac{1}{2} = 10$. In changing the divisor $\frac{1}{2}$ to a decimal we find that $\frac{1}{2} = .5$. It follows that $5 \div .5$ also equals 10.

$$\begin{array}{r} 10 \\ .5 \overline{)\,5.0} \end{array}$$

This illustration can help us develop a rule in order to write a decimal divisor as a whole number. $5 \div .5$ can be written as $^{5}/_{.5}$.

We can further multiply the numerator and the denominator by the same number since we are essentially multiplying the fraction by 1 and hence not changing its value. When we multiply .5 by 10 its value becomes 5, and a whole number, as desired. Therefore,

$$\frac{5}{.5} = \frac{5 \times 10}{.5 \times 10} = \frac{50}{5} \text{ or } 5 \overline{)\,50.}$$

Notice that multiplying both numerator and denominator by 10 moves the decimal one place to the right and does not change the value of the original fraction. Multiplying the numerator and denominator by 100 would move the decimal two places to the right; by 1,000, three places, etc. By multiplying the divisor and the dividend by the same number we can change the division problem to a problem we can solve. From our example:

$$\frac{5}{.5} = \frac{50}{5} = 10.$$

REMEMBER

> Move the decimal point in the divisor the proper number of places in order to make the divisor a whole number. Move the decimal in the dividend the same number of places, adding zeros if necessary.

Example

Divide 1.05 ÷ 3.5.

Step 1: Move the decimal one place to the right in both the divisor and dividend and place the decimal in the quotient directly above its new location in the dividend. Observe that moving the decimal one place to the right is the same as multiplying the divisor and dividend by 10.

```
3.5 ) 1.05
```

Step 2: Complete the division as with whole numbers.

```
          0.3
3.5 ) 1.0 5
      1 0 5
          0
```

Answer: 1.05 ÷ 3.5 = 0.3

Example

Divide 2.1375 ÷ 2.85

Step 1: Move the decimal two places to the right in both dividend and divisor and proceed as when dividing whole numbers.

```
            0.7 5
2.85 ) 2.1 3 7 5
       1 9 9 5
         1 4 2 5
         1 4 2 5
               0
```

Answer: 2.1375 ÷ 2.85 = 0.75

Often, the division does not come out exactly, and in those cases we must round off the answer to a desired place. Always find the quotient to one more place than the desired place and then round off by techniques discussed in this chapter.

Exercises

1. Divide: .2 ÷ .25.

2. Divide: $9.75 \div .13$.

3. Add zeros and divide until there is a remainder of zero: $7 \div 0.2$.

4. Divide: $306.64 \div 19$. Round off to the nearest hundredth.

5. Divide: $224 \div .32$.

CHAPTER TEST

1. Mr. Owen owned 26.25 acres of land. He sold 2.5 acres to Mr. Jones and 11.75 acres to an investment corporation. How much land did he have left?

2. A real estate agent earns $12.50 for every $100 of sales. Write his earnings as a decimal.

3. What number must be subtracted from 1 to give a difference of .4124877?

4. Arrange the following decimals in descending order of size: 0.014, 0.104, 0.140, 0.0014.

5. Round off 71.85 billion to the nearest tenth of a billion.

6. The local rate for sending a parcel is 25 cents for the first pound and 40 cents for each additional 2 pounds. How many pounds does a parcel weigh if the cost for local delivery from XYZ Realty to ABC Realty is $3.45?

7. Mrs. Riggs purchased her home for $35,950 and sells it for a .13 profit. What is the selling price?

8. Change 0.325 to a fraction in lowest terms.

9. A real estate office clerk earns \$4.50 an hour for each hour before 5 P.M. and \$5.50 an hour for each hour after 5 P.M. The lunch hour is a paid hour. What amount is earned by working from 9 A.M. to 8:30 P.M.?

10. Mr. Jones paid \$20,410 for 4.5 acres of land. What was the cost per acre, to the nearest dollar?

11. Simplify the following:

a. $.06 \div \frac{.6}{.05}$

b. $.7 \div \frac{7}{5}$

c. $8 \div \frac{16}{.05}$

d. $4 \div \frac{.4}{5}$

12. Perform the indicated operation and round off the answer to the nearest hundredth:

a. $\frac{1}{4} + 10(.073) - \frac{1.32}{10}$

b. $\frac{5.72}{10} - \frac{3}{8}$

c. $\frac{2}{9} \times .63$

d. $.83\frac{1}{3} \times 10\ (.0415)$

13. Of the following numbers, select the greatest in value: $\frac{2}{.5}, \frac{.5}{2}, \frac{5}{.2}, \frac{.5}{.2}$

14. A charge for a taxi is \$.20 for the first .25 mile, then \$.10 for each additional .25 mile. How many .25 miles are there in a trip that costs \$2.20?

15. Receipts from a school athletic contest are \$150. If 100 tickets were sold to students at \$.75 each, how many tickets were sold to adults at \$1.50 each?

4

PERCENT IN REAL ESTATE

Goals

1. Change a percent to a fraction or decimal.
2. Change a fraction or a decimal to a percent.
3. Find a percent of a given amount.
4. Find what percent one number is of another number.
5. Find a number when a percent of it is known.
6. Apply percentages to real estate problems.

This chapter will help you build skills in solving percent and percentage problems, which are very important in the real estate business. The word *percent* means computing by "hundredths." 5% means 5 hundredths, 40% means 40 hundredths, and 80% means 80 hundredths. The symbol used for percent is %. You read such numbers as "5 percent," "40 percent," and "80 percent." A real estate salesperson who earns a commission of 3% earns $3 for every $100 worth of property sold, or $3 out of $100. One hundred percent means 100 hundredths, or all of something. If "100 percent of the Skyview Realty Co., staff" attended a closing seminar, then the whole staff attended.

CHANGING A PERCENT TO A FRACTION OR DECIMAL

To change a percent to a fraction, drop the percent symbol and divide by 100.

$12\% = \frac{12}{100} = \frac{3}{25}$ $\qquad$ $25\% = \frac{25}{100} = \frac{1}{4}$

$37\frac{1}{2}\% = \frac{37.5}{100} = \frac{37.5 \times 10}{100 \times 10} = \frac{375}{1,000} = \frac{3}{8}$

$150\% = \frac{150}{100} = \frac{3}{2}$

REMEMBER

To change a percent to a decimal, drop the percent symbol and move the decimal in the original percent two places to the left.

Examples

12% = .12 (move two places to the left)
25% = .25
37.5% = .375
150% = 1.50

• ▼ • •

Exercises

1. Change the following percents to fractions:
   a. 20%
   b. 30%
   c. 130%
   d. 90%

2. Change the following percents to decimals:
   a. 6.21%
   b. .71%
   c. 162%
   d. 36%

CHANGING A FRACTION OR A DECIMAL TO A PERCENT

REMEMBER

To change a fraction to a percent, check to determine if you can change the given fraction to an equivalent fraction that has a denominator of 100.

Example

Change $\frac{1}{4}$ to a percent.

Step 1: Since 4 will divide evenly into 100, $\frac{1}{4}$ can be changed to an equivalent fraction that has a denominator of 100.

$$\frac{1}{4} = \frac{\quad}{100} \qquad \frac{1}{4} \rightarrow \frac{25}{100}$$

Think: "4 into 100 is 25 and 25 × 1 = 25." Now write 25 over 100.

Answer: $\frac{1}{4} = \frac{25}{100} = 25\%$.

You may want to review equivalent fraction techniques in Chapter 2.

REMEMBER

> If the denominator of a fraction will not divide into 100 evenly, divide the numerator by the denominator, carry the answer to three decimal places, and change the decimal to a percent.

Example

Change $\frac{5}{8}$ to a percent.

Step 1: Since 8 will not divide evenly into 100, divide 8 into 5 and carry the answer to three places.

$$
\begin{array}{r}
.625 \\
8\,\overline{)\,5.000} \\
\underline{4\,8} \\
20 \\
\underline{16} \\
40
\end{array}
$$

Step 2: Change .625 to a percent by moving the decimal two places to the right and adding a % sign.

$$.625 = .625 = 62.5\%$$

Answer: $\frac{5}{8} = 62.5\%$

Figure 4–1 is a table of basic conversions of fractions to percent and percent to fractions.

Table of Common Fractions and Equivalent Percents

Common Fraction	*Equivalent Percent*	*Common Fraction*	*Equivalent Percent*	*Common Fraction*	*Equivalent Percent*
$\frac{1}{2}$	50%	$\frac{5}{6}$	83.33%	$\frac{3}{5}$	60%
$\frac{1}{3}$	33.33%	$\frac{1}{8}$	12.5%	$\frac{4}{5}$	80%
$\frac{2}{3}$	66.67%	$\frac{3}{8}$	37.5%	$\frac{1}{7}$	14.29%
$\frac{1}{10}$	10%	$\frac{5}{8}$	62.5%	$\frac{1}{9}$	11.11%
$\frac{1}{4}$	25%	$\frac{7}{8}$	87.5%	$\frac{1}{12}$	8.33%
$\frac{3}{4}$	75%	$\frac{1}{5}$	20%	$\frac{1}{16}$	6.25%
$\frac{1}{6}$	16.67%	$\frac{2}{5}$	40%		

Figure 4–1

Exercises

1. Change the following fractions to percents:
   a. $\frac{39}{100}$
   b. $\frac{2}{5}$
   c. $\frac{1}{50}$
   d. $\frac{7}{8}$

2. Change the following decimals to percents:
   a. .60
   b. .40
   c. .833
   d. .411

PROPORTION AND PERCENT

Proportions (discussed in Chapter 5) can be used in solving percent problems. One of the ratios in a proportion is always the comparison of two numbers called the *percentage* and the *base*. If 25 is being compared to 37, then 25 is the percentage and 37 is the base. The other ratio is a percent expressed as a fraction called the *rate*. Since these terms and their relationships are difficult for many people to understand, we could substitute the words "part" for "percentage" and "total" for "base," and then solve for r as a percent:

REMEMBER

"Percentage" refers to a quantity—a part of a whole; "base" refers to the total or whole amount in the problem; and "rate" means a percent.

$$\frac{\text{part}}{\text{total}} = \frac{r}{100}$$

We have previously discussed the concepts of "part" and "total" in Chapter 2, in the section "Fractional Part of a Number."

Example

30 is what percent of 80?

Rate =

Step 1: $\frac{\text{percentage}}{\text{base}} = \frac{r}{100}$ or $\frac{\text{part}}{\text{total}} = \frac{r}{100}$

Step 2: $\frac{30}{80} = \frac{r}{100}$, $r = \frac{30}{80} \times 100 = \frac{3{,}000}{80} = \frac{150}{4} = 37\frac{1}{2}$

Answer: 30 is $37\frac{1}{2}$% of 80.

Sometimes it is easier to solve a percent problem by changing it into a mathematical equation. The word "of" will suggest multiplication, while "is" will represent equality and division. The percentage is obtained when a percent of a number is taken. The rate is the percent taken of the number, and the base is the number from which a percent is taken. Use one of the following three transformation forms of the percentage rule to solve percentage problems:

1. Percentage = base × rate or part = total × rate
2. Base = $\frac{\text{percentage}}{\text{rate}}$ or total = part/rate
3. Rate = $\frac{\text{percentage}}{\text{base}}$ or rate = part/total

To find the percentage or part use form 1 of the rule.

Example

Find 10% of 130.

Rate × total = part Part = .10 × 130 = 13

Answer: 10% of 130 = 13

To find the base or total, use form 2.

Example

If 15% of a number is 30, what is the number?

Total = $\frac{30}{.15}$ = 200.

Answer: 15% of 200 = 30

To find the rate, use form 3.

Example

What percent is 50 of 80?

Rate = $\frac{50}{80}$ = .625 = 62.5%.

Answer: 50 is 62.5% of 80.

The formula $\frac{P}{B}$ = R, where P is percentage, B is base, and R is rate or percent (hundredths), can also be written as P = B × R or P = BR. Transformation forms from a formula are difficult to remember for many people, so we can use a memory aid to simplify this process. If P = BR, we draw a circle (see Figure 4–2) with a diameter representing division and place the left member of the equality sign on top and the right member, which means B × R, on the bottom.

We then cover the term we want to find and "do" as the diagram indicates to get the correct transformations.

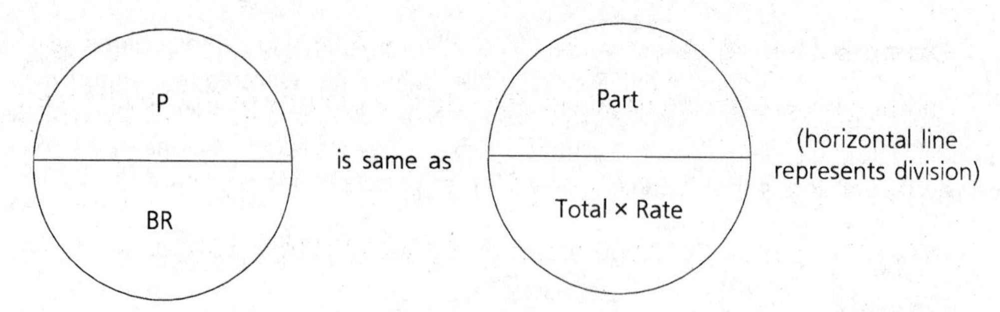

Figure 4–2

Covering P, we get $P = BR$

Covering R, we get $R = \frac{P}{B}$

Covering B, we get $B = \frac{P}{R}$

So if we know two parts of the equation we can find the third part. Let's do the previous example using our memory aid (see Figure 4–3).

Example

What percent is 50 of 80?

P = 50 percentage (part)

B = 80 base (total), so

$R = \frac{50}{80} = .625 = 62.5\%$

We can use the memory aid in all problems in real estate that use formulas.

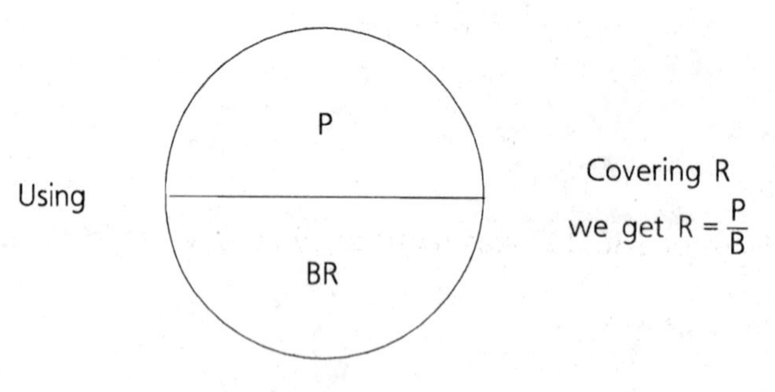

Figure 4–3

FINDING A PERCENT OF A GIVEN AMOUNT

A common problem in real estate, as well as everyday life, is finding the percent of a given amount. According to our previous discussion, percentage = base × rate, or part = total × rate.

A sales tax of 5% (5% means 5 cents per 100 cents) tells you that you pay \$.05 for every \$1.00 of purchase. A purchase of \$2.00 would be taxed \$.10. In general, if you know the given amount (base), you can find the percent of that amount by multiplying by the rate. (Remember that "of" means to multiply.)

Example

Find the amount of commission on the sale of a property of $120,000 if the commission is 7%.

Using P = B × R

Think: 7% (rate) of $120,000 (base) or .07 × $120,000 = $8,400.

Example

Find $\frac{1}{5}$% of 2,000.

Step 1: Using P = B × R R = $\frac{1}{5}$% B = 2,000

Step 2: Since $\frac{1}{5} = \frac{20}{100} = .20$ and .20% = .002

Then .002 × 2,000 = 4.000

Answer: $\frac{1}{5}$% of 2,000 = 4

Exercises

1. The Jones family bought a house for $90,500 and made a down payment of 20%. What is the amount of down payment?

2. How much do they owe on the house?

3. A home selling for $80,000 was reduced by 25%. What is the amount of the reduction?

4. Fred bought a VCR that sells for $440. He received a 20% discount. What was the discount price?

5. What is 250% of 70?

FINDING WHAT PERCENT ONE NUMBER IS OF ANOTHER NUMBER

To express a given number as a percentage of another number, divide the given number by the number with which it is being compared. As we previously discussed, rate = $\frac{\text{percentage}}{\text{base}}$ or rate = $\frac{\text{part}}{\text{total}}$. Therefore, to find what percent one number is of another number, we write a fraction and change to a decimal, comparing the first to the second number, then convert the decimal to a percent. Use the ratio $\frac{\text{part}}{\text{total}}$, which is identical to the rate formula given above.

Example

5 is what percent of 20?

Step 1: Use rate = $\frac{\text{part}}{\text{total}}$. The percentage or part is 5 and the base or total is 20.

Step 2: Rate = $\frac{5}{20}$ = .25 = 25%

Answer: 5 is 25% of 20. We can easily check this since 25% of 20 is .25 × 20, which is 5.

Example

3 is what percent of 8?

Step 1: Use rate = $\frac{\text{part}}{\text{total}}$.

Answer: Rate = $\frac{3}{8}$ = .375 = 37.5%

Note: In this example we must carry the division to three places in order to have no remainder.

Example

3 is what percent of 16?

Step 1: Use rate = $\frac{\text{part}}{\text{total}}$.

Answer: Rate = $\frac{3}{16}$ = .1875 = 18.75%

Note: In this example we must carry the division to four places in order to have no remainder.

Some fractions never come out to an even division in decimals. For example, ⅓, regardless of the number of decimal places, always leaves a remainder: ⅓ = .3333.... Therefore, we say that ⅓ = 33.3% or 33⅓%.

Exercises

1. Fred had $180 and spent $60. What percent of his money did he spend?

In questions 2–5, write the indicated ratio as a fraction. Then change the fraction to the nearest whole percent.

2. 28 is what percent of 36?

3. A foot is 12 inches and a meter is 39.37 inches. A foot is what percent of a meter?

4. 14 is what percent of 28?

5. There are 20 women and 30 men working for XYZ Realty. What percent of the workers are men?

FINDING A NUMBER WHEN A PERCENT OF IT IS KNOWN

Suppose we know that 32 is 50% of some number. By our intuition we know that the desired number is 64 because 50% of 64 is .50 × 64, which is 32. We could think ½ × 64 since 50% = .50 = ½. So in order to determine the unknown number, we simply write 50% as a decimal (.50) or fraction (½) and then divide into the given number.

$$32 \div \frac{1}{2} = 32 \times 2 = 64 \qquad \text{or} \qquad 32 \div .5 = 64$$

REMEMBER

To find a number when a percent of a given number is known, divide the known number by the decimal or fractional equivalent of the percent.

Example

18 is 60% of what number?

Step 1: Use total = $\frac{\text{part}}{\text{rate}}$.

part = 18, rate = 60%

Total = $\frac{18}{60\%}$

Think: 18 divided by the decimal or fractional equivalent of 60%.

$\frac{18}{.6} = 30$ or $18 \div \frac{3}{5} = 18 \times \frac{5}{3} = 30$

Step 2: We can check by taking 60% of 30, which gives .60 × 30, and we get 18.

Answer: 18 is 60% of 30.

Example

If a 20% reduction in price is $2,000, find the original price.

Step 1: Use total = $\frac{\text{part}}{\text{rate}}$.

part = 2,000 rate = 20%

Step 2: total = $\frac{2,000}{.20}$ = $10,000

$\frac{\$2,000}{.20} = \$10,000$, or $\$2,000 \div \frac{1}{5} = \$2,000 \times 5 = \$10,000$

If a 20% reduction is $2,000 (remember that "is" means to divide), the original price is $10,000, or $2,000 ÷ 20%.

Answer: $2,000 is 20% of $10,000.

Exercises

1. 50% of what number is 90?

2. 16 is 25% of what number?

3. 200 is 400% of what number?

4. In one year Fred earned $10 on a savings account invested at 5%. How much was the investment?

5. The price of a television set was reduced by $50. If this represents a reduction of 25%, find the original price.

APPLICATIONS OF PERCENTAGE

Many companies pay their salespeople by giving them a *commission* for each article they sell. The commission is usually a certain percent of the price of the article. The primary application in the real estate business is the calculation of commission and selling price of a property sold. Since the rate of commission is a percent, change the given percent to a decimal before multiplying.

REMEMBER

> To find the amount of commission a salesperson earns, multiply the rate of commission by the total sales (selling price).

Formula: Sales commission = rate × sale price (C = R × SP)

We can express this formula in a memory aid as discussed in the first section of this chapter (see Figure 4–4). We can cover what we are looking for and do as the memory aid indicates.

Example

Broker A receives a commission of 7% on a property he sells for $80,000. How much sales commission does he receive?

Step 1: Covering sales commission in our memory aid we find:

Commission = rate × sale price

Step 2: Commission = .07 × $80,000

Answer: Commission = $5,600

Example

Broker B received $5,000 in sales commission on a property she sold. What was the selling price if the rate of commission was 5%?

Step 1: Covering sale price in our memory aid we find:

$$\text{Sale price} = \frac{\text{commission}}{\text{rate}}$$

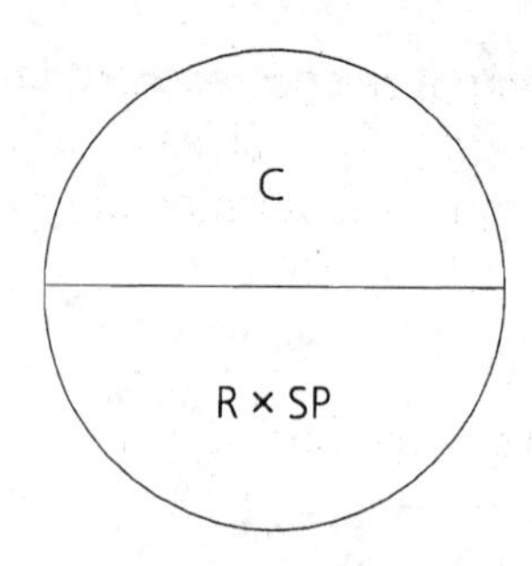

Figure 4–4

Step 2: Sale price $= \frac{\$5{,}000}{.05}$

Answer: Sale price = $100,000

All commission and selling price problems are not this easy, although all involve the same formula.

Example

A broker lists a house for $80,000 with a commission rate of 7%. Salesperson A, employed by the listing broker, receives 50% of the total commission on every house sold. If Salesperson A sells the listed house for 5% less than its listed price, what is Salesperson A's commission?

Step 1: List data given in problem:

List price: $80,000
House sale price: 95% of list price
Commission arrangement: 50% of total
Commission rate: 7%

Step 2: First find total commission:

Commission = price × rate
Commission = $80,000 × .95 × .07
Commission = $5,320

Step 3: Finally, find Salesperson A's commission:

Salesperson A's commission = .5 × $5,320

Answer: Salesperson A's commission = $2,660

Profit and Loss

Calculations involving *profit* and *loss* use the same percentage formula we used in calculating commissions. The formula for calculating sales commission had three variables:

Formula: Sales commission = rate of commission × sale price

The following is an extended discussion in that we will use sale price to calculate profit or loss. If the sale price is more than the cost, there is a profit. Conversely, if the sale price is less than the cost, there is a loss. So selling price and cost are important in profit and loss problems. Cost in real estate problems is referred to as "value" or what one paid for the property. Let's look at a couple of examples and then form our memory aid.

Example

Mr. Wilson paid $82,000 for his home and sold it five years later at a 30% profit. What was the selling price of the house?

Since a profit is realized in this transaction, the house sold for more than $82,000, or 30% more than $82,000.

Step 1: To determine the selling price, take 30% of $82,000 and add it to $82,000, or multiply $82,000 by (1 + percent of profit), which would be 1.30. The 1 here represents 100% of the $82,000 and the .30, or 30%, represents the profit added.

Answer: Selling price is $82,000 × 1.30 = $106,600.

Note: This is a one-step problem. We could have calculated the profit and added it to the $82,000:

Profit = .30 × $82,000
Profit = $24,600 and sale price =
$82,000 + $24,600 = $106,600 = sale price

We have verified that using (1 + percent of profit) is a correct technique.

Example

Mr. Wilson paid $82,000 for his home and sold it five years later at a 30% loss. What was the selling price of the house?

Since there is a loss, he sold his home for less than he paid for it (cost), i.e., 30% less than $82,000.

Step 1: As in our previous example, take (1 – percent of loss) times $82,000.

Selling price = (1 – .30) × $82,000
Selling price = .70 × $82,000
Selling price = $57,400

In order to verify this calculation, cost: $82,000
loss: $24,600

Answer: Selling price is $82,000 – $24,600 = $57,400.

Based on the examples above, Figure 4–5 illustrates our memory aid.

Example

An owner sells her house for $33,000 and realizes a gain of 10%. What was her cost?

Step 1: Using our memory aid in Figure 4–5 and covering the cost we get:

$$\text{Cost} = \frac{\$33{,}000}{1 + 10\%} = \frac{\$33{,}000}{1.10} = 30{,}000$$

Answer: Cost = $30,000

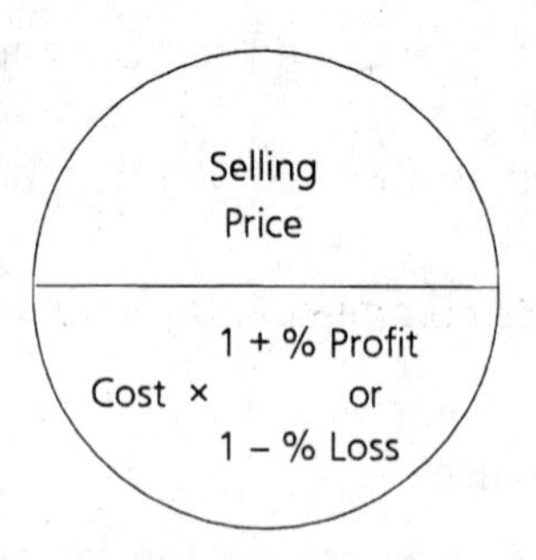

Figure 4–5

Note: Cost is less than selling price if there is a profit (gain). Another approach to this problem can use the idea that we have discussed previously, that "is" means to divide.

$33,000 "is" 110%
+10% gain

cost less if gain → cost is 100%

If 110% "is" $33,000 then $\frac{33,000}{1.10} = \$30,000.$

Answer: Cost = $30,000

Example

An owner sells her house for $33,000 and realizes a loss of 10%. What was her cost?

Step 1: Covering cost we get cost $= \frac{\$33,000}{1 - 10\%}$

Step 2: Cost $= \frac{\$33,000}{.90} = \$36,666.67$

Answer: Cost = $36,666.67

Note: Cost is greater than selling price if there is a loss!

cost greater if loss → cost is 100%
10% loss
$33,000 "is" 90%

If 90% "is" $33,000 then $\frac{\$33,000}{.90} = \$36,666.67$

Many other applications of percentage problems will be found in the following sections of this book.

Exercises

1. Broker Wilson receives a 7½% commission on a house that he sells for $120,000. What is his sales commission?

2. Salesperson A has a 50/50 split agreement on commission with her broker and she sells 40 acres for $500 per acre. The office receives a commission that is 6% of the first $15,000 and 4% of the balance of the sale. Salesperson A must pay 5% of her share of the commission to Salesperson B, who listed the property. What is the net amount received by Salesperson A?

3. Broker A has a property listed at $20,000. Jim Brown purchases it for $16,000 and sells it for $20,000. What percent of profit did he make, to the nearest percent?

4. A house sold for $99,000 at a profit of 20%. What did the house cost?

5. Adams bought a property for $25,000 and sold it one year later at a 3% loss. What was the selling price?

CHAPTER TEST

1. Change $12\frac{1}{2}\%$ to a decimal.

2. Change $12\frac{1}{2}\%$ to a fraction.

3. Express $\frac{5}{8}$ as a percent.

4. Change $.25\frac{1}{2}$ to a percent.

5. The Jones family plans to buy an $82,000 house and needs a 20% down payment. Are their savings of $20,000 enough for the down payment?

6. A salesperson received a commission of $2,200 on a property selling for $72,500. What is his commission, to the nearest percent?

7. A 20% down payment on a property amounts to $20,900. What is the selling price of the property?

8. A broker's office received a commission of $4,150 on the sale of a house. If the broker received a commission of 6%, what was the selling price of the house?

9. A house sold for $95,000 at a profit of 15%. What did the house cost?

10. Mr. Wilson purchases a property for $100,000 and sells the property for $80,000. What is his percent of loss?

11. 60 is $62\frac{1}{2}\%$ of what number?

12. Of the following, select the number having the greatest value: $\frac{1}{4}$, .2462, $24\frac{1}{2}\%$, $\frac{3}{8}$.

13. Suppose you make a 20% down payment on a tract of undeveloped land. The down payment amounts to $15,580. What is the purchase price?

14. Mrs. James received a notice from her lender that during the past year her total interest paid on a $58,000 mortgage was $4,930. What interest rate is she paying?

15. Calculate the missing element in each of the following four sales:

	Selling Price	*Commission Rate*	*Commission Earned*
a.	$55,000		$3,850
b.		6%	$3,000
c.	$82,500	7%	
d.		8%	$6,215

16. A woman provided in her will that her 130-acre farm was to be sold and the proceeds distributed as follows: 37% to her husband; 18% to each of her two sons and one daughter; the balance to be given to her college. The college received $37,000. How much is the total estate? How much did the daughter receive?

17. The Moore family sold their house for $36,850, which was 17% more than they paid for it. What was their purchase price?

5

RATIO, PROPORTION, AND SCALE

Goals

1. Compare two quantities using a ratio.
2. Find missing terms in a proportion.
3. Use proportions to solve real estate problems and scale drawings.

RATIO AND PROPORTION

When we are confronted with the problem of comparing two or more fractional quantities, it is helpful to make use of ratio and proportion. *Ratio* expresses the relative sizes of two numbers and is found by dividing one number by the number to which it is being compared. A ratio may be stated as a fraction, such as $\frac{1}{2}$, or as two numerals separated by a colon, such as 1:2 (read "one to two"). It is best to write a ratio as a fraction, so that it may be treated as a fraction.

A *proportion* is a statement that two ratios are equal. Proportions occur most often when we reduce fractions to lowest terms or when we find a common denominator and raise various fractions to equivalent fractions having that common denominator. These two procedures were discussed in Chapter 2. Consider the following proportions:

$$\frac{2}{3} = \frac{12}{18}$$

$$\frac{1}{2} = \frac{2}{4}$$

If we multiply the numerator of each fraction (ratio) by the denominator of the other, the products are equal. Thus, for the first proportion, $\frac{2}{3} = \frac{12}{18}$,

$$2 \times 18 = 3 \times 12 \text{ or } 36 = 36.$$

In the second proportion, $\frac{1}{2} = \frac{2}{4}$,

$$1 \times 4 = 2 \times 2 \text{ or } 4 = 4.$$

In a proportion, then, the cross products of the terms *must be* equal, and if three of the terms are known, we can solve for the fourth. The product of the means equals the product of the extremes.

means

$$2 : 3 = 12 : 18$$

extremes

In solving a problem in which one of the members of a proportion is not known, we may place the three known terms in our proportion, indicating the unknown by a question mark (?) or a symbol and solve by the technique discussed in the previous paragraph. For example, if we wish to determine the cost of 28 bags of concrete when we already know that 16 bags cost \$20, we can set up this problem as a proportion and solve it. Our problem would appear in either of these forms:

$$\frac{16}{28} = \frac{\$20}{?} \qquad \frac{28}{16} = \frac{?}{\$20}$$

The cross product of each proportion will be the same. Since it is always easier to solve if we set up our proportion to have the unknown part in the numerator, we would use the latter proportion:

$$\frac{28}{16} = \frac{?}{\$20} \quad \frac{7}{4}\text{(reduce!)} = \frac{?}{\$20}$$

Since the cross products must be the same, our equation becomes

$$\frac{7}{4} \times \$20 = ?$$

and the unknown part is \$35. So the proportion would read

$$\frac{7}{4} = \frac{\$35}{\$20}$$

This checks since the cross product in each case is \$140. Therefore, going back to the original proportion, 28 bags cost \$35.

Example

A piece of land containing 30 acres sells for \$5,000. At the same rate, what would 22 acres sell for?

$$\frac{\$5{,}000}{30} = \frac{?}{22} \qquad \frac{\$5{,}000}{30} \times 22 = \$3{,}666.67$$

Answer: 22 acres sell for \$3,666.67.

Example

For a 30-unit apartment complex two men are required for maintenance. A 105-unit complex would require how many men?

$$\frac{2}{30} = \frac{?}{105} \qquad \frac{2}{30} \times 105 = ? = 7$$

Answer: The 105-unit complex would need 7 men.

Example

If $2\frac{1}{2}$ gallons of gasoline will power a chainsaw for 3 hours, how many gallons are needed to saw wood for $4\frac{1}{2}$ hours?

Step 1: To help solve the problem, we can use a chart:

GALLONS OF GAS	2½	?
HOURS OF SAWING	3	4½

Step 2: So we have a proportion:

$$\frac{2\frac{1}{2}}{3} = \frac{?}{4\frac{1}{2}}$$

$$\frac{\frac{5}{2}}{3} = \frac{?}{\frac{9}{2}}$$

$$\frac{5}{2} \times \frac{1}{3} \times \frac{9}{2} = ? = \frac{15}{4} = 3\frac{3}{4} \text{ (cross multiply)}$$

Answer: Three and three-fourths gallons of gasoline are needed to saw wood for $4\frac{1}{2}$ hours.

The following is a more difficult example that necessitates setting up two proportions:

Example

If four air cargo transports use 5,000 gallons of fuel in three hours, how many air transports use 12,500 gallons in six hours?

Step 1: Organize the information into a chart:

AIR TRANSPORTS	4	?
GALLONS OF FUEL	5,000	12,500
HOURS	3	6

Step 2: Set up another proportion to eliminate one of the measurements. The easiest measure to solve is hours.

GALLONS OF FUEL	5,000	?
HOURS	3	6

$$\frac{5{,}000}{3} = \frac{?}{6} \quad \frac{5{,}000}{3} \times 6 = 10{,}000 \text{ (cross multiply)}$$

Four air transports need 10,000 gallons of fuel in six hours.

Step 3: Based on Step 2, the problem can now be organized in the following chart:

AIR TRANSPORTS	4	?
GALLONS OF FUEL	10,000	12,500

$$\frac{4}{10{,}000} = \frac{?}{12{,}500}$$

$$\frac{4}{10{,}000} \times 12{,}500 = ? \text{ (cross multiply)}$$

$$\frac{50{,}000}{10{,}000} = ? = 5$$

Answer: Five air transports

Exercises

1. Lot A is 100 feet wide and lot B is 350 feet wide. Both lots have the same depth. Lot A contains five acres. How many acres does lot B contain?

2. Sales agents A and B work in the same office and receive identical commission rates on the sale of single-family dwellings. Agent A sells a single-family home for $65,000 and receives a commission of $1,500. If agent B sells a single family dwelling for $85,000, what commission will B receive?

3. Jones and Smith pay taxes at the same tax rate. Jones pays $900 on a home worth $90,000. What tax should Smith pay on his home, which is worth $120,000?

4. A mortgage company requires a down payment of $15,000 on a $75,000 house. At the same rate, how much down payment would be required on a house costing $125,000?

5. In a recent year, $3 out of every $10 spent by XYZ Realty Company was spent on newspaper advertising. If $10,000 was spent on advertising that year, how much went to newspapers?

SCALE DRAWING

An interesting application of ratio and proportion is in scale drawing. Often a drawing of an object is needed, but it is not practical to make the drawing full size, since it may be either too small or too large. Then it is useful to make an accurate picture of the object that is of a different size. This is known as a *scale drawing*. The scale is the ratio of the length of the drawing to the length of the actual object. All parts of the drawing are then illustrated to that particular scale.

A floor plan of a house can be drawn to the scale ½ inch = 1 foot, so that for every foot of actual measurement the scale drawing would measure ½ inch. Ratio and proportion can be used to find actual dimensions of the house from the scale drawing, provided the scale is known.

Example

Using the scale $\frac{1}{2}$ inch = 1 foot, what are the actual dimensions of a house represented as 20 inches by 36 inches?

Step 1: Let W represent the width and L represent the length of the house.

Step 2: Write a proportion to find each measurement.

$$\frac{\frac{1}{2}}{1} = \frac{20}{W} \quad \text{or} \quad \frac{1}{\frac{1}{2}} = \frac{W}{20}$$

$$\frac{\frac{1}{2}}{1} = \frac{36}{L} \quad \text{or} \quad \frac{1}{\frac{1}{2}} = \frac{L}{36}$$

Step 3: It is easier to use

$$\frac{1}{\frac{1}{2}} = \frac{W}{20} \quad \text{and} \quad \frac{1}{\frac{1}{2}} = \frac{L}{36}$$

Since the cross products are equal,

$$\frac{1 \times 20}{\frac{1}{2}} = W \quad \text{and} \quad \frac{1 \times 36}{\frac{1}{2}} = L$$

$$W = 40 \text{ feet} \quad \text{and} \quad L = 72 \text{ feet}$$

Answer: The house has actual dimensions of 40 feet by 72 feet.

Example

In the scale drawing of a subdivision, $\frac{1}{2}$ inch = 100 feet. The front of a given lot is $\frac{1}{8}$ inch wide in the drawing. How wide is the actual lot?

Step 1: The ratio of the length on the map to the corresponding actual length is

$$\frac{\frac{1}{2}}{100}.$$

Step 2: Write the proportion $\frac{\frac{1}{2}}{100} = \frac{\frac{1}{8}}{W}$ or $\frac{100}{\frac{1}{2}} = \frac{W}{\frac{1}{8}}$.

Step 3: It is easier to use $\frac{100}{\frac{1}{2}} = \frac{W}{\frac{1}{8}}$.

$$\frac{100}{\frac{1}{2}} = 200$$

$$\frac{200}{1} = \frac{W}{\frac{1}{8}}$$

$$W = \frac{200}{1} \times \frac{1}{8}$$

$$W = \frac{200}{8} = 25 \text{ feet}$$

Answer: The lot is 25 feet wide.

Many real estate problems can be solved using the simple rules of proportion.

Exercises

1. If 1 inch = 20 yards, what distance is represented by (a) 4 inches? (b) 3.5 inches?

2. If $\frac{1}{8}$ inch = 2 feet, what measurement represents (a) 4 feet? (b) 30 feet?

3. A drawing has a scale of 1 inch = 10 feet. How many inches represent 150 feet?

4. A blueprint is drawn to a scale of 1:110. If the length of a boat on the blueprint is 4.5 inches, what is the actual length of the boat in feet?

5. The distance on an outline map of the United States from Boston to New York is $\frac{1}{4}$ inch. The scale is 1 inch to 750 miles. What is the distance from New York to Boston to the nearest mile?

CHAPTER TEST

1. A home valued at $90,000 has depreciated $500 in 10 years. At the same rate, what is the depreciation on a home valued at $60,000 over 10 years, to the nearest dollar?

2. The Jensons pay $850 in taxes on a house valued at $82,500. At this rate, how much tax will there be on a house valued at $92,000?

3. Find the number of inches used to represent 1,600 miles if $\frac{1}{8}$ inch represents 200 miles.

4. The Jones family spends an average of $105 on utilities every two months. How much do they spend on utilities in a year?

5. The mortgage company requires a down payment of $11,500 on a $70,000 house. How much down payment would be required on a house costing $87,500?

6. The tax rate on a house is $83 per $1,000 assessed value. What is the tax on a house assessed at $71,250?

7. The scale on a map is $\frac{1}{2}$ inch = 80 miles. Jonesville and Sunville are $\frac{3}{4}$ inch apart on the map, while Sunville and Hamlet are 2 inches apart. What is the actual distance from Jonesville to Hamlet, traveling through Sunville?

8. An architectural drawing uses a scale of 1:15. How many inches should a line in the drawing be to represent an actual length of 8.5 feet?

9. Solve for W: 6:W = 9:12.

10. A room that measures 4" × 6" on a blueprint is actually 20′ × 30′. If another room on the blueprint measures 32 square inches, how many square feet does it actually contain?

11. Salesperson Wilson has an agreement with his broker that he earns $10 for every $110 he makes in sales. How much does he earn on $2,200 worth of sales?

12. Using the scale ⅜ inch = 15 miles, how many inches in length is a blueprint land line representing a distance of 40 miles?

13. A lot measuring 60′ × 125′ costs $9,000. At the same rate, what would an 85′ × 105′ lot cost?

14. Sunshine Realty Company paid $54 for 4½ dozen advertising brochures. The company now wishes to buy 13¾ dozen of the same brochures. How many dollars must Sunshine Realty Company pay if the price per brochure is the same?

15. The scale on a map of the north side of a farm plot is ¾ inch = 6 miles. What is the length of the north side of the farm if the side measures 1¼ inches on the map?

6
Measurements in Real Estate

Goals

1. Convert a smaller measure to a larger measure.
2. Convert a larger measure to a smaller measure.
3. Calculate the perimeter of a geometric figure.
4. Calculate the area of a geometric figure.
5. Calculate the volume of a rectangular solid.
6. Calculate the volume of a cylinder.

In the United States, the basic standards for measuring length are the inch, the foot, the yard, and the mile. This chapter discusses how to solve real estate problems that involve perimeter, area, and volume. This background will help in solving problems that deal with property descriptions and appraisals.

The measure of length is the distance between the ends of the object measured. In other words, when you measure the length of an object, you find the distance between the two ends by measuring in a straight line in one direction. The width and length of a property are each really measures of length. As a result, it is easier to think of a "measure of length" as a "linear measure." A plot of ground whose length is 165 feet and width is 125 feet gives each measure as a linear measure. Let's review our table for measuring length.

REMEMBER

Measure of length and linear measure are both straight line distance.

Measures of Length

1 foot (ft.)	=	12 inches (in.)		
1 yard (yd.)	=	3 feet (ft.)	=	36 inches (in.)
1 mile	=	5,280 feet (ft.)	=	1,760 yards (yds.)

CHANGING A SMALLER MEASURE TO A LARGER MEASURE

In order to convert a smaller measure to a larger measure, find out how many units of the smaller measure are contained in one unit of the larger measure.

Example

Change 78 inches to feet.

Step 1: Since 12 inches equals 1 foot, we want to see how many times 12 is contained in 78 inches.

$\frac{78}{12} = 6.5$ ft.

(We are changing to a larger unit, so we divide.)

Answer: 78 in. = 6.5 ft.

Example

How many miles in 5,280 yards?

Step 1: Since 1,760 yds. = 1 mile, we want to see how many times 1,760 is contained in 5,280 yards.

$\frac{5{,}280}{1{,}760} = 3$ miles

(We are changing to a larger unit, so we divide.)

Answer: 5,280 yds. = 3 miles

Exercises

1. Change 102 inches to feet.

2. Change 87 inches to feet.

3. One measure of a plot of ground is 165 feet. How many yards does the side contain?

4. How many yards is 198 inches?

5. If the distance between two points is 6,160 yards, how many miles apart are they?

CHANGING A LARGER MEASURE TO A SMALLER MEASURE

To convert a larger measure to a smaller measure, find how many units of the smaller measure are contained in one unit of the larger measure, then multiply the given number of larger units by this number.

Example

Change 10 yards to feet.

1 yard = 3 feet. Therefore, 10 yards contain 10 × 3 feet = 30 feet. (We are changing to a smaller unit, so we multiply.)

Answer: 10 yards = 30 feet

Example

Change 10 yards to inches.

1 yard = 36 inches. Therefore, 10 yards contain 10 × 36 inches = 360 inches. (We are changing to a smaller unit, so we multiply.)

Answer: 10 yards = 360 inches

Example

Change 3 miles to feet.

1 mile = 5,280 feet. Therefore, 3 miles contain 3 × 5,280 feet = 15,840 feet. (We are changing to a smaller unit, so we multiply.)

Answer: 3 miles = 15,840 feet

REMEMBER

To convert a smaller measure to a larger measure or a larger measure to a smaller measure, first find how many units of the smaller measure are contained in one unit of the larger measure.

1. To change a smaller measure to a larger measure, divide by the number found.
2. To change a larger measure to a smaller measure, multiply by the number found.

1 ft. = 12 in.
1 yd. = 3 ft. = 36 in.
1 mi. = 1,760 yds. = 5,280 ft.

Exercises

1. Change 5.75 feet to inches.

2. If one measure of a plot of ground is 45 yards, how many feet is that measure?

3. Convert 2.5 miles to feet.

4. If the altitude of an airplane is 6 miles, what is its altitude in feet?

5. Change 20 yards to feet.

FINDING THE PERIMETER OF GEOMETRIC FIGURES

The study of geometry includes finding facts about points, lines, and planes. It also includes finding lengths, areas, and volumes of geometric figures or figures of various shapes. The outline of something forms a figure. Man's first measurements consisted of finding lengths of figures. Common plane figures used in real estate include the triangle, quadrilateral, rectangle, and square (see Figure 6–1).

A *triangle* is a closed figure that has three straight sides and three angles.

A *quadrilateral* is a closed figure that has four straight sides and four angles.

A *rectangle* is a closed, four-sided figure with four right angles (90-degree angles) and having opposite sides equal in length.

A *square* is a special kind of rectangle in that it has four equal sides and four right angles.

Another special quadrilateral is a *trapezoid.* A trapezoid is a closed, four-sided figure in which two opposite sides are parallel, i.e., always the same distance apart (see Figure 6–2).

Many problems in real estate and other fields deal with finding the perimeter of figures. The *perimeter* is the whole outer boundary of a figure or the measure around the sides of a figure.

REMEMBER

> To find a perimeter, find the length of each side of the figure, and add all the lengths together.

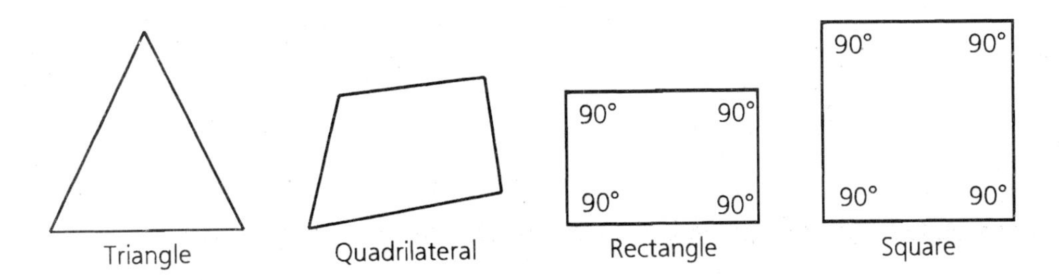

Figure 6–1

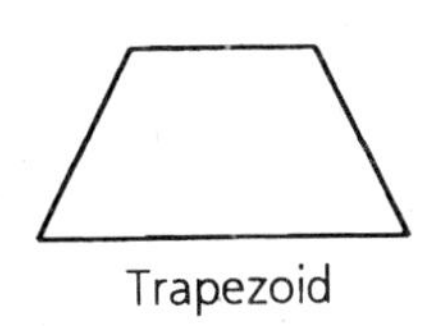

Figure 6–2

Example

Find the perimeter of each figure:

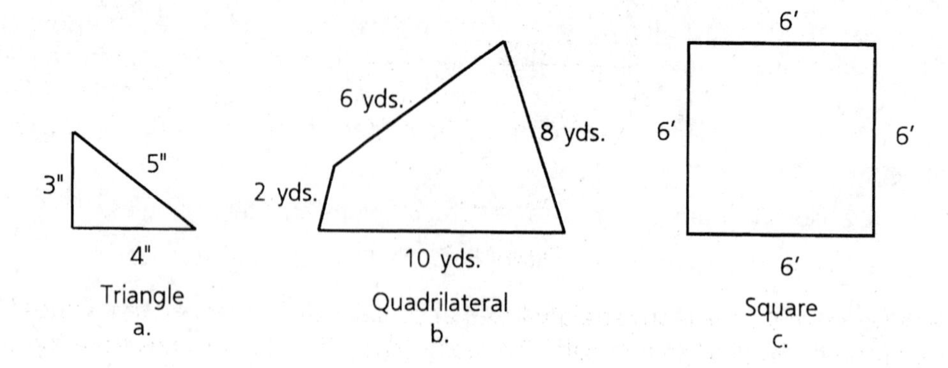

a. 4 in. + 5 in. + 3 in. = 12 in. The perimeter of the triangle is 12 in.

b. 2 yds. + 6 yds. + 8 yds. + 10 yds. = 26 yds. The perimeter of the quadrilateral is 26 yds.

c. 6 ft. + 6 ft. + 6 ft. + 6 ft. = 24 ft. Since every square has four equal sides, you can find its perimeter by multiplying the length of the side by 4: 6 ft. × 4 = 24 ft. The perimeter of the square is 24 ft.

Example

Find the perimeter of a rectangle whose length is 20 feet and whose width is 15 feet.

Step 1: Draw the four-sided closed figure with four right angles and opposite sides equal.

20′

90° 90°

15′ 15′

90° 90°

20′

From the figure, the perimeter is
20 ft. + 15 ft. + 20 ft. + 15 ft. = 70 ft.

Step 2: Note that there are two 20-foot measures and two measures of 15 feet. We could also find the perimeter:

2 × 20 ft. + 2 × 15 ft.
40 ft. + 30 ft. = 70 ft.

Answer: The perimeter of the rectangle is 70 feet.

A circle is defined as the set of all points in a plane equally distant from a given point in the plane (see Figure 6–3).

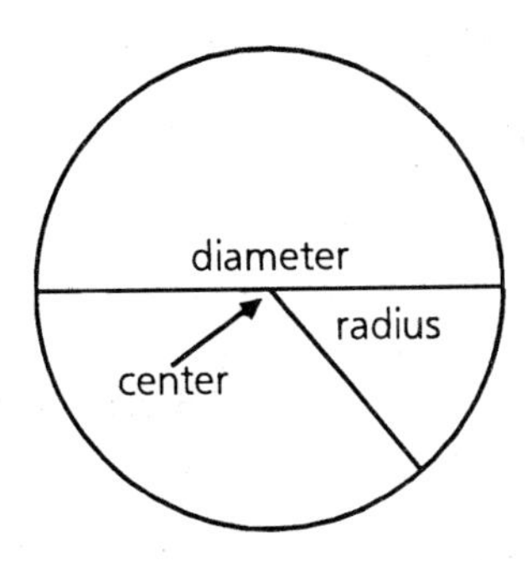

Figure 6–3

The *diameter* (d) of a circle is any straight line that contains the center and terminates (ends) on the edge of the circle, dividing it in half. The *radius* (r) is a line that extends from the center to the edge of the circle.

REMEMBER

> The *circumference* is the distance around the circle, or its perimeter. The circumference (C) of a circle equals twice the product of π (pi) and the radius.

So $C = 2\pi r$. The symbol π (pi) represents the ratio of the circumference of a circle to its diameter. Some approximate values of π are $22/7$, 3.14, 3.142, and 3.1416. Note that if $C = 2\pi r$, then $C = \pi d$, since $2r = d$.

Using our memory aid (see Figure 6–4), we can find the circumference by covering C, and we get $C = 2\pi r$. We could also find the radius, given the circumference, by covering r to get $r = \frac{C}{2\pi}$. Our main application in real estate probably is finding the circumference. Note again that $d = 2r$ or the diameter is twice the radius.

Example

Find the circumference of a circular plot of ground that has a diameter of 259 feet.

We can use our memory aid to find $C = 2\pi r$. Since $d = 2r$, then $C = \pi d$. If $d = 259$ ft. and $\pi = \frac{22}{7}$, we get

$$C = \frac{22}{7} \times 259 \text{ ft.}$$

$$C = \frac{22}{7} \times 259 \text{ ft.} = 22 \times 37 = 814 \text{ ft.}$$

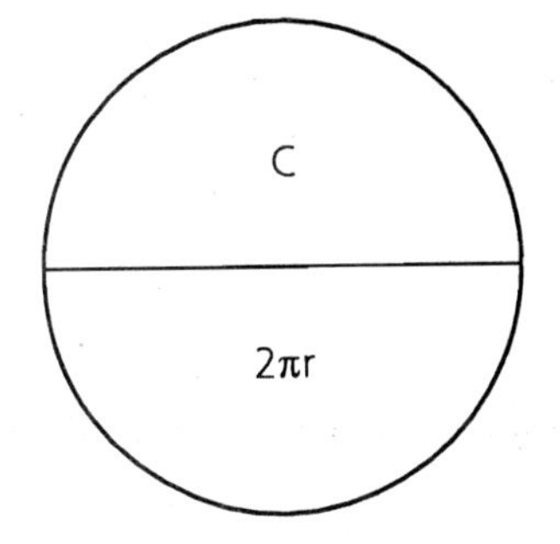

or

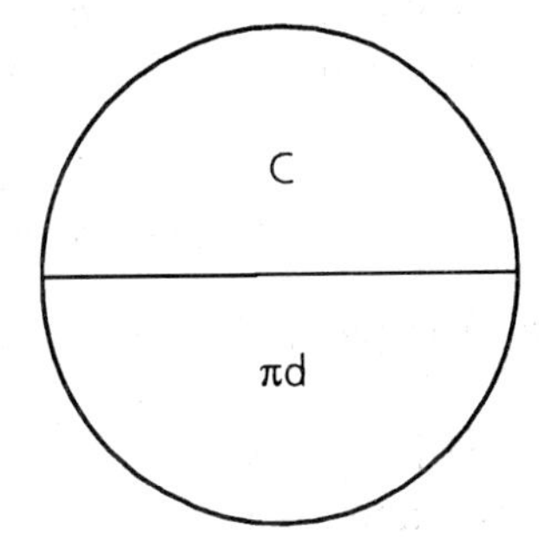

Figure 6–4

Answer: The circumference is 814 feet.

Example

The circumference of a circle is 14π feet. Find the radius.

If $C = 14\pi$ ft., then from our memory aid, $r = \frac{C}{2\pi}$.

$$r = \frac{14\pi}{2\pi} = 7$$

Answer: The radius is 7 feet.

Exercises

1. Find the perimeter of a triangle if the sides measure 5 feet, 9 feet, and 7 feet.

2. Find the perimeter of a quadrilateral if the sides measure 15 feet, 27 feet, 15 yards, 18 feet. (Hint: change 15 yards to feet).

3. Find the perimeter of a rectangle with a length of 8 feet and a width of 4 feet.

4. A baseball diamond is a square, and the distance between each of the bases is 90 feet. If a hitter hits two home runs, how far will he run around the bases?

5. Find the perimeter of the trapezoid.

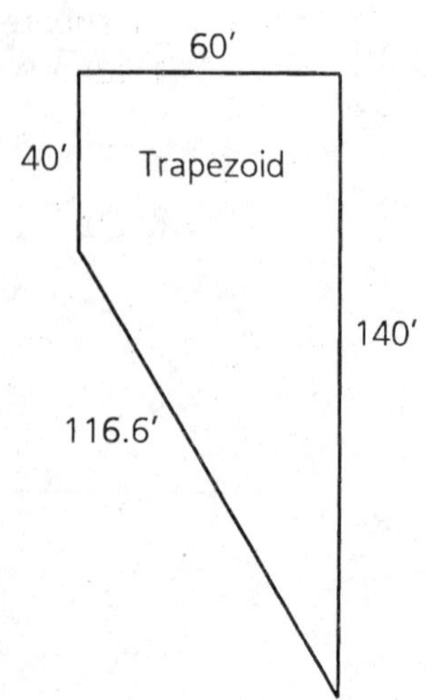

6. Let $\pi = \frac{22}{7}$. Find the circumference of a circle whose diameter is 49 yards.

7. The circumference of a circle is 28π. Find the radius.

MEASURING AREA

As pointed out at the beginning of the chapter, the basic units of linear measure are the inch, foot, yard, and mile. These are obtained by measuring in one direction; hence, measures of length such as distance and perimeter are one-dimensional.

Units of square measure such as square inch, square foot, square yard, square mile, and acre give the area of a figure. The area is found by measuring in two directions; hence, measures of area are two-dimensional.

Measures of area are common in everyday life. A farmer interested in selling his or her farm will certainly want to know the size of the farm in acres, particularly if he or she is going to sell for a certain price per acre.

The area of a figure is measured by how many times a particular unit of square measure is contained in the figure. A square unit, then, is the surface of a square whose side is one unit. A square inch is a square whose side is one inch (see Figure 6–5). Likewise, a square foot is a square whose side is one foot.

Area of a Rectangle or a Square

The area of a closed plane figure formed by line segments is the number of square units contained in its surface. For example, the area of a rectangle four inches long and two inches wide is eight square inches, since it contains eight squares, each of which is a square inch (Figure 6–6).

Let's review the basic measure of area formulas that are commonly used in real estate.

Units of Square Measure

1 square foot (sq. ft.)	=	144 square inches (sq. in.)
1 square yard (sq. yd.)	=	9 square feet (sq. ft.)
1 acre	=	43,560 square feet (sq. ft.)
1 square mile	=	640 acres

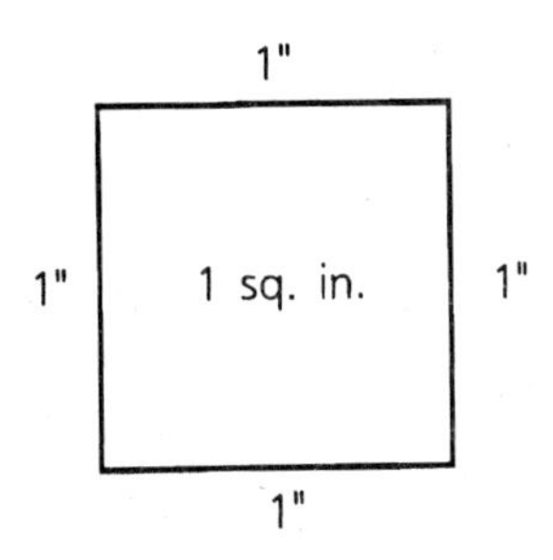

Figure 6–5

4"

1	2	3	4
5	6	7	8

8 square inches

2"

Figure 6–6

Note that an acre is already a square measure. There is no such measure as a "square acre."

Figure 6–7 shows that one square yard equals nine square feet. The figure is a square with a side of one yard or three feet.

We can use our memory aid in Figure 6–8 to find area or length or width.

Covering the part we want to find, we get

$$A = LW \qquad L = \frac{A}{W} \qquad W = \frac{A}{L}$$

Example

A rectangular kitchen measures 15 feet by 12 feet. What is its area in square yards?

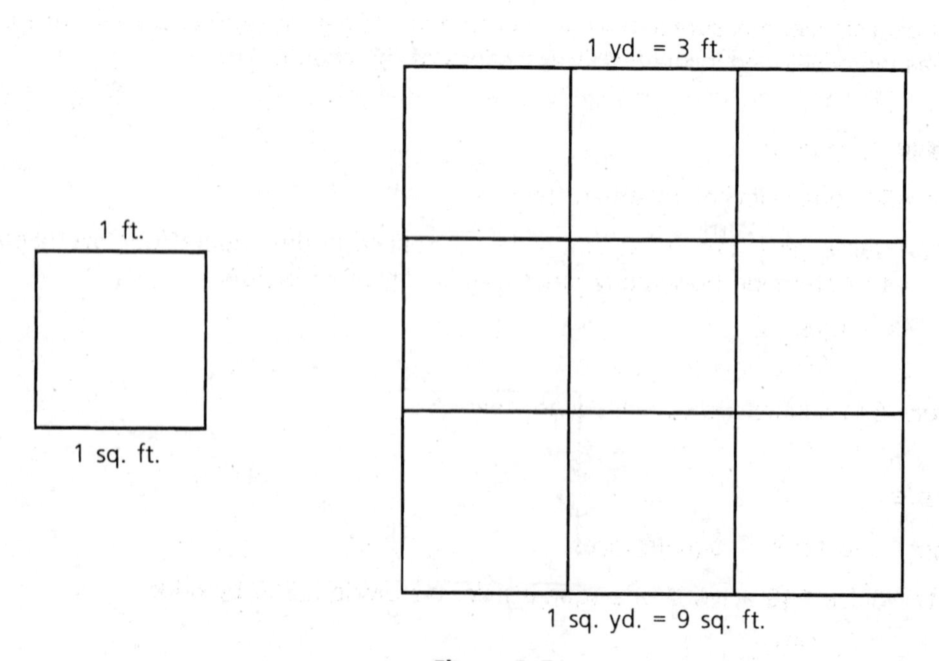

Figure 6–7

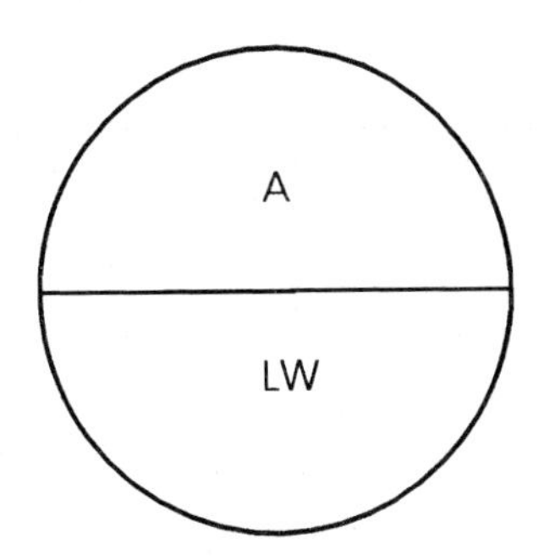

Figure 6–8

Step 1: Since 15 ft. = $\frac{15}{3}$ = 5 yds. and 12 ft. = $\frac{12}{3}$ = 4 yds., the dimensions of the kitchen are 5 yds. by 4 yds. Remember that 1 yd. = 3 ft.

Step 2: A = LW
A = 5 × 4 = 20 sq. yds.

Answer: The area of the kitchen is 20 square yards.

Example

If the area of a rectangular lot is 12,500 square feet and the width is 100 feet, what is the length of the lot?

Step 1: $L = \frac{A}{W}$, $L = \frac{12{,}500}{100} = 125$ ft.
If we know the area and the measure of a side, we divide the area by the known side.

Answer: The length of the lot is 125 feet.

To change a smaller measure to a larger measure or a larger measure to a smaller measure, use the ideas we developed in the first two sections of this chapter.

Example

Change 864 square inches to square feet.

Step 1: Since there are 144 square inches contained in one square foot, we need to determine how many times 144 is contained in 864.

$$\frac{864}{144} = 6$$

Answer: 864 square inches = 6 square feet

Example

Change 2,560 acres to square miles.

Step 1: Since 640 acres is one square mile, we divide 2,560 by 640.

$$\frac{2{,}560}{640} = 4$$

Answer: 2,560 acres = 4 square miles

Example

200 square feet equals how many square inches?

Step 1: Since 1 sq. ft. = 144 sq. in., multiply 200 by 144.

$$200 \times 144 = 28{,}800$$

Answer: 200 square feet = 28,800 square inches

The area of a rectangle is found by multiplying its length by its width (in the same linear measure). This product is the area in units of square measure. (Since a square is a rectangle whose length and width are the same, its area is the same as that of a rectangle.) If we let A mean area of the rectangle, L mean length of the rectangle, and W mean width of the rectangle, then area is

$$A = L \times W \text{ or } A = LW$$

Example

How many acres are contained in a rectangular field that is 650 feet by 300 feet? (Find to the nearest tenth of an acre.)

Step 1: Find the area in square feet and change to acres (1 acre = 43,560 square feet).

$$A = LW$$
$$A = 650 \times 300 = 195{,}000 \text{ sq. ft.}$$

Step 2: Since 1 acre = 43,560 square feet, divide 195,000 by 43,560.

$$195{,}000 \div 43{,}560 = 4.476584 \text{ acres}$$

Answer: The field contains 4.5 acres, to the nearest tenth of an acre.

A square is a special rectangle, where both the length and width are the same. Therefore, $A = L \times W = s \times s$, and $s \times s = s^2$; so $A = s^2$ for the area of a square, where s represents the side of the square.

Example

Find the area of a square with side 10.5 feet.

$$\text{Using } A = s^2$$
$$A = (10.5)^2$$
$$A = 10.5 \times 10.5$$
$$A = 110.25 \text{ sq. ft.}$$

Answer: The area is 110.25 square feet.

REMEMBER

> To find the area of a rectangle or square, you must obtain two linear dimensions, the length and the width, in the same unit of measure. Remember that a square has the length and width as equal measures. These two linear measures are then multiplied in order to obtain the area measure.

Area of a Parallelogram

A parallelogram is a special quadrilateral, a four-sided figure with opposite sides parallel and equal. Parallel lines are in the same direction but always the same distance apart. Observe the parallelogram in Figure 6–9.

Note that sides a and c are parallel and equal, and sides b and d are parallel and equal. If we cut off the triangle at the right and fit it in on the left, we would have a rectangle (see Figure 6–10).

The area of a parallelogram is the same as the area of a rectangle. Note that in finding the area of a parallelogram we do not multiply the lengths of the sides, but we multiply the length of a side and the height (altitude) of a parallelogram. The height or altitude of a parallelogram is a segment drawn from a vertex to the line containing the opposite side and perpendicular to (forming a 90° angle with) that side (see Figure 6–11).

We now find that the area of a parallelogram is the product of the length of a side and the length of the altitude (height) to that side: $A = BH$. The area of a parallelogram is introduced here to make it easier to understand the area of a triangle. In all probability you will not need to find the area of a parallelogram on your real estate licensing examination.

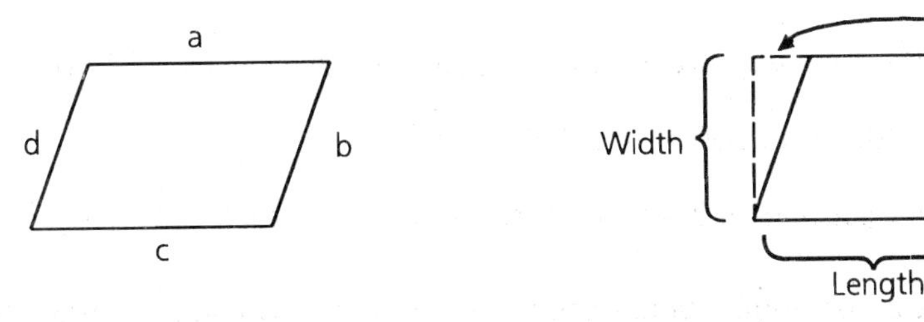

Figure 6–9

Figure 6–10

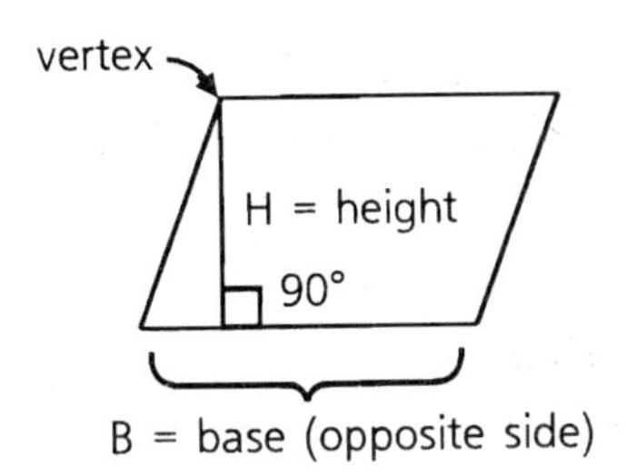

Figure 6–11

Example

Find the area of the parallelogram below:

6"

10"

$H = 6,\ B = 10$
$A = BH$
$A = 10 \times 6 = 60$

Answer: The area of the parallelogram is 60 square inches.

Area of a Triangle

A diagonal divides a parallelogram into two triangles, each of the same area. The area of a triangle, then, is simply one-half the area of the parallelogram with the same height and base (Figure 6–12).

In Figure 6–13, we see that the area of the triangle is the product of the height and the base divided by 2, since there are two triangles of equal area in a parallelogram. The base (B) can be represented by any of the three sides of the triangle but the height (H) is the length of the altitude to the line representing the base. The height is the length of the line from any vertex perpendicular (making a 90° angle) to the opposite side.

In Figure 6–14, note the illustration on the left, in which one angle of the triangle is 90°. This is called a right triangle; since the right triangle has one side perpendicular to another, either side may be the base and the other side, the height.

The formula for the area of a triangle is as follows:

$$A = \frac{1}{2}BH = \frac{BH}{2}$$

This formula can be illustrated by our memory aid in Figure 6–15 and by transformation forms:

$$A = \frac{BH}{2} \qquad B = \frac{A}{\frac{H}{2}} = \frac{2A}{H} \qquad H = \frac{A}{\frac{B}{2}} = \frac{2A}{B}$$

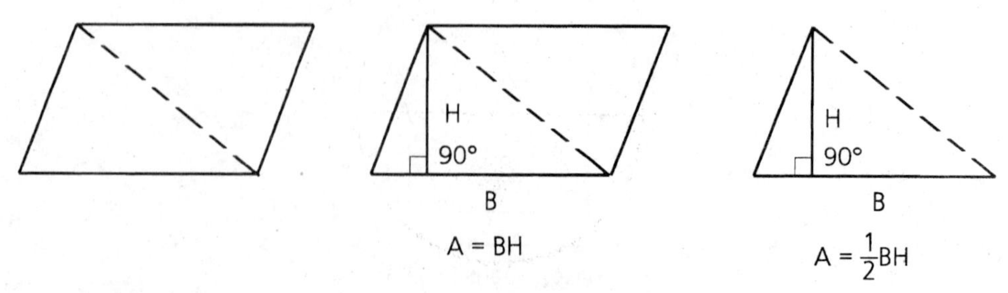

Figure 6–12 **Figure 6–13**

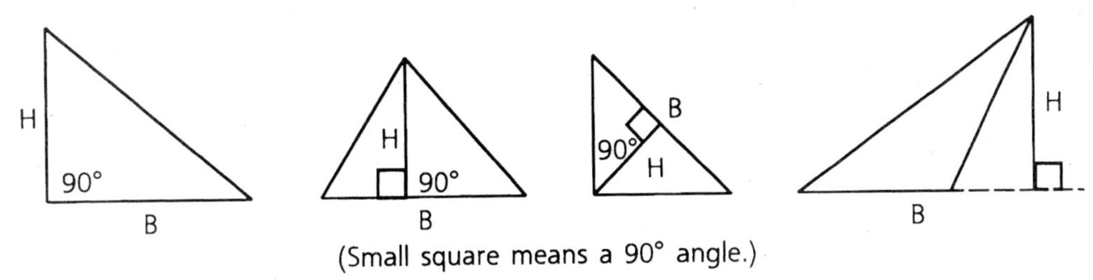

(Small square means a 90° angle.)

Figure 6–14

Example

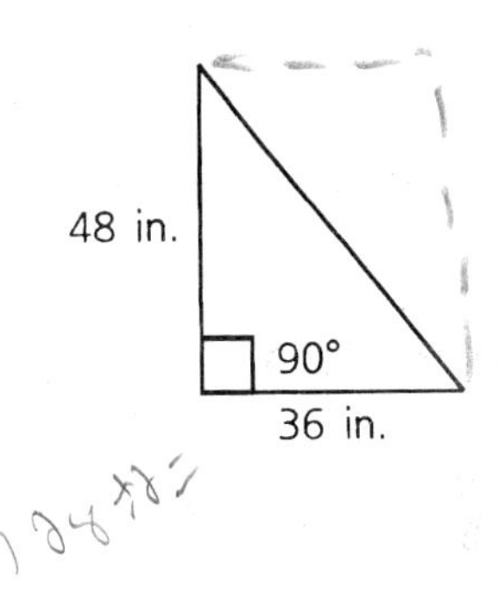

Find the area of a countertop that is in the shape of a right triangle with sides 36 inches and 48 inches.

Since the sides are perpendicular, let one side (B) be 48 and the height (H) be 36:

$$B = 48 \qquad H = 36$$

$$A = \frac{1}{2}\ BH$$

$$A = \frac{1}{2} \times 48 \times 36 = 864 \text{ sq. in.}$$

Answer: The countertop has an area of 864 square inches.

Example

What is the area of the following triangle?

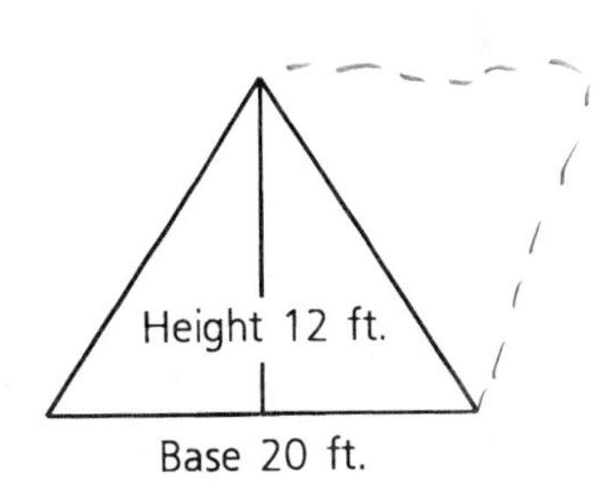

$$H = 12,\ B = 20$$

$$A = \frac{1}{2}\ BH = \frac{1}{2} \times 20 \times 12 = 120 \text{ sq. ft.}$$

Answer: The area of the triangle is 120 square feet.

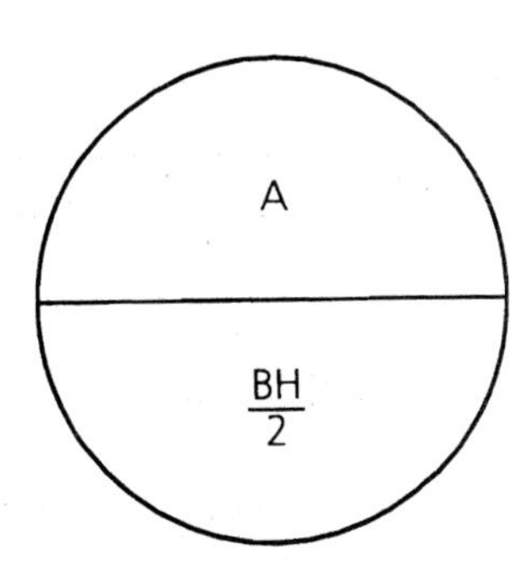

Figure 6–15

REMEMBER

> The area of a triangle is the product of the height and the base divided by 2.

A plot of ground or a building may not be in the form of a triangle but the shape may be in a combination of triangles, squares, and rectangles (see Figure 6–16). To find the area of a plot or floor space of a building, divide the shape into triangles, squares, and rectangles, and then find the area of each separate figure and add all the areas together.

Example

Find the number of square feet in the floor plan of a home with the measurements given:

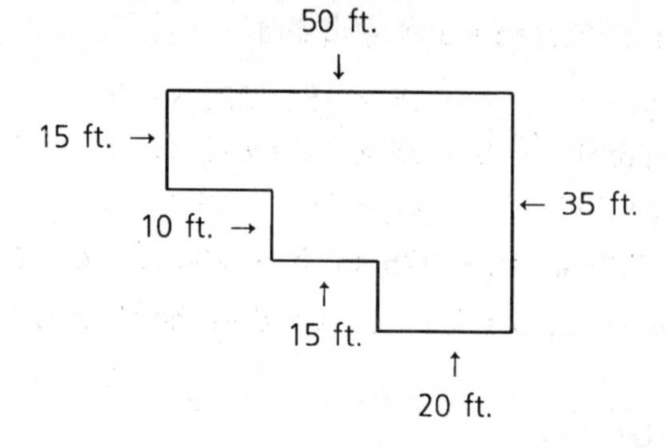

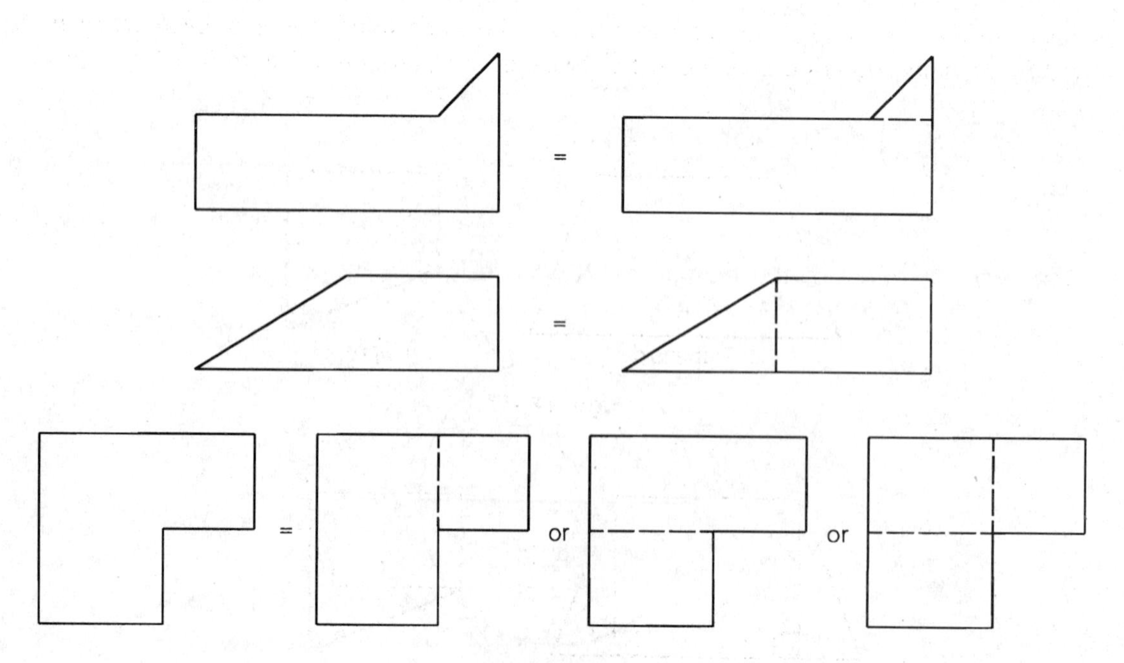

Figure 6–16

Step 1: Divide into rectangular regions I, II, and III.

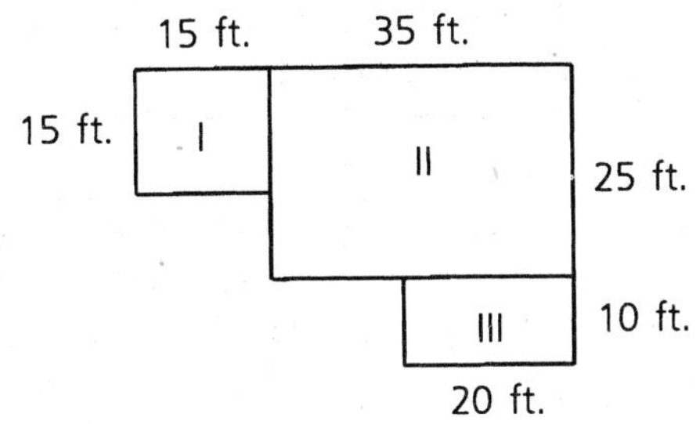

Region I is a square 15 ft. by 15 ft.
Region II is a rectangle 35 ft. by 25 ft.
Region III is a rectangle 20 ft. by 10 ft.

Step 2: A = LW for a rectangle and a square.

Area region I:	A = 15 × 15 = 225 sq. ft.
Area region II:	A = 35 × 25 = 875 sq. ft.
Area region III:	A = 20 × 10 = 200 sq. ft.

Step 3: Total area: 225 sq. ft. + 875 sq. ft. + 200 sq. ft. = 1,300 sq. ft.

Answer: The number of square feet contained in the floor is 1,300 sq. ft.

Area of a Trapezoid

We defined a trapezoid previously in this chapter as a special quadrilateral or four-sided figure with two parallel sides. Since problems involving the area of a trapezoid often appear on the licensing examination, the technique of calculating the area of a trapezoid is presented here. Figure 6–17 provides examples of trapezoids.

Note that each figure in Figure 6–17 is four-sided, with two sides parallel, so that side a is parallel to side b. A simpler notation that means the same thing is a || b. Each area can be found by dividing into areas of a rectangle, triangle, or square, as in Figure 6–18.

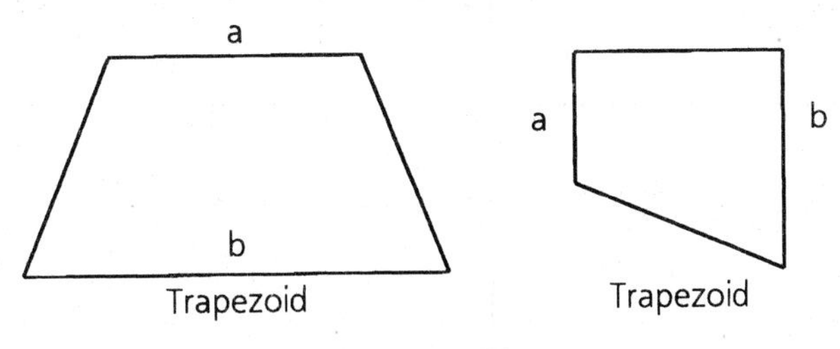

Figure 6–17

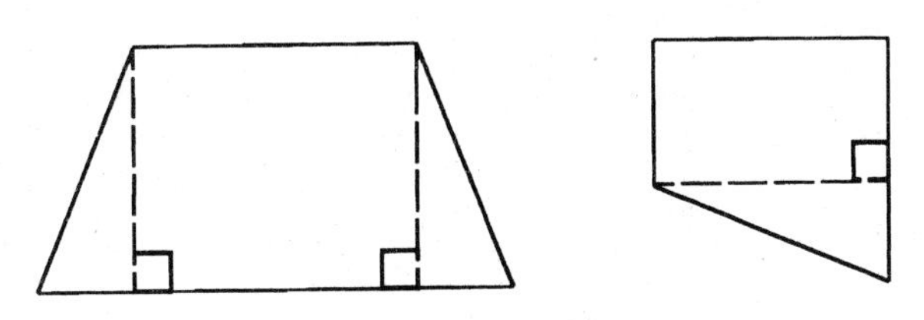

Figure 6–18

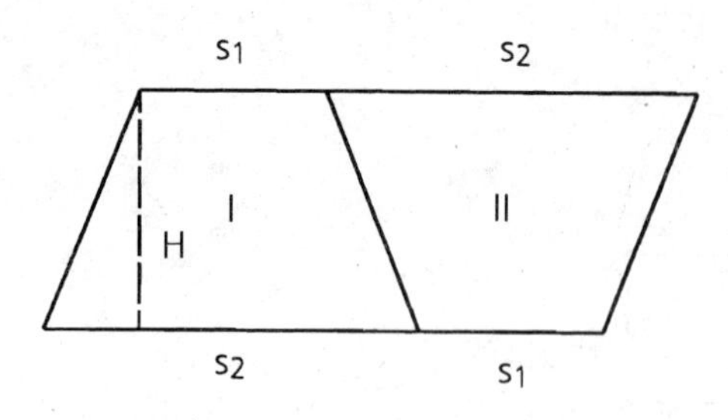

Figure 6–19

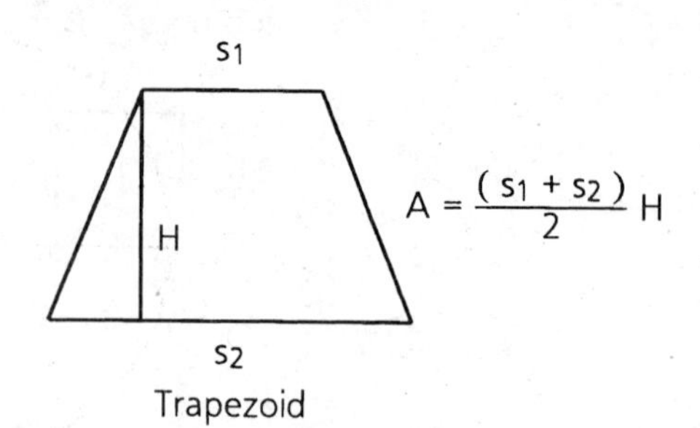

Figure 6–20

We can also use a formula to find the area of a trapezoid. If we arrange two trapezoids of the same area and same shape as shown in Figure 6–19, we have a parallelogram. The variables s_1 and s_2 represent the two parallel sides of trapezoid I and trapezoid II.

If s_1 is the length of the top parallel side, s_2 the length of the bottom parallel side, and H the height, then we have a parallelogram with base $s_1 + s_2$ and height H. Since the area of a parallelogram is equal to the product of its base multiplied by its height ($A = BH$), the area (A) of the two trapezoids is $(s_1 + s_2) \times H$, or $A = (s_1 + s_2)H$. Since there are two trapezoids in the parallelogram and each area is the same, the area of one trapezoid is one-half the area of the parallelogram:

$$\text{Area of trapezoid} = \frac{1}{2} \times (s_1 + s_2) \times H, \text{ or}$$
$$= \frac{1}{2}(s_1 + s_2)H$$

In the formula shown above, $(s_1 + s_2)$ means the sum of the lengths of the parallel sides. The area of a trapezoid is shown in Figure 6–20.

REMEMBER

To find the area of a trapezoid, add the length of the two parallel sides and divide that sum by 2 (or average the sum of the sides), and then multiply that result by the height.

In a trapezoid the parallel sides are often called the bases of a trapezoid. Using our memory aid in Figure 6–21:

Example

Find the area of the following trapezoid:

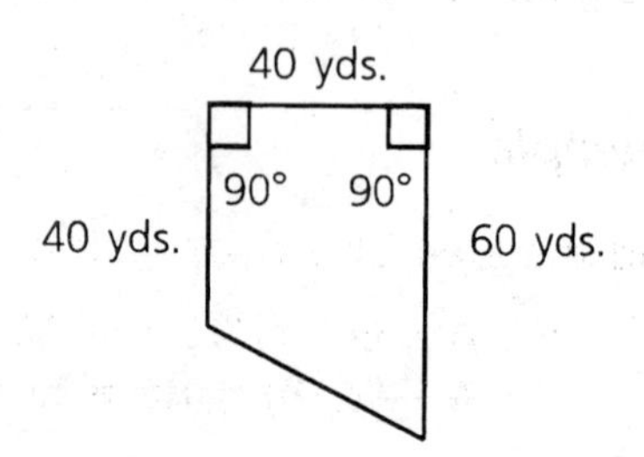

From the figure, $H = 40$, $s_1 = 40$, $s_2 = 60$.

Using our memory aid we get

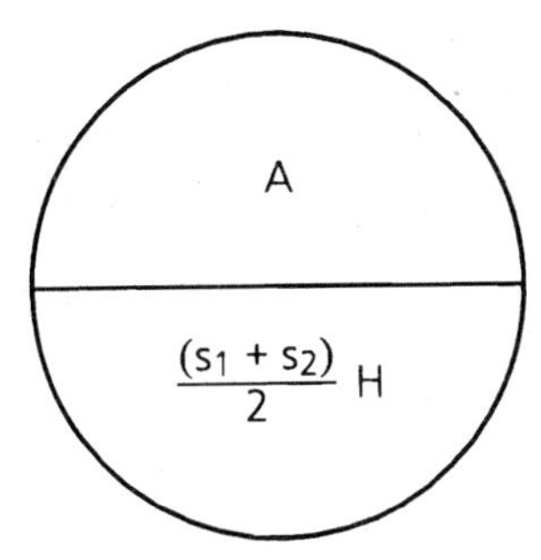

Figure 6–21

$$A = \frac{(s_1 + s_2)}{2} H$$

$$A = \frac{(40 + 60)}{2} \times 40 = \frac{100}{2} \times 40 = 50 \times 40$$

$$A = 2{,}000 \text{ sq. yds.}$$

Answer: The area of the trapezoid is 2,000 square yards.

Area of a Circle

To review, a circle consists of all points in a plane which are equally distant from a point in the plane called the center. The distance from this center point to any point on the circle is called the radius and all radii of the same circle are equal. The diameter is a line segment through the center of the circle with end points on the circle. The length of the diameter is twice the length of the radius.

REMEMBER

> The area of a circle equals the product of pi (π) and the square of the radius.

As previously stated, some approximate values of π are $^{22}/_{7}$, 3.14 to two decimal places, 3.142 to three decimal places, and 3.1416 to four decimal places. The formula for the area of a circle is as follows:

$$A = \pi r^2$$

This gives us the memory aid shown as Figure 6–22.

Example

Find the area of a circle with a radius of 10 feet.

$A = \pi r^2$ $\quad$ $r = 10$ $\quad$ $\pi = 3.14$

$A = (3.14) \times 10^2 = 3.14 \times 100 = 314$

Answer: The area is 314 square feet.

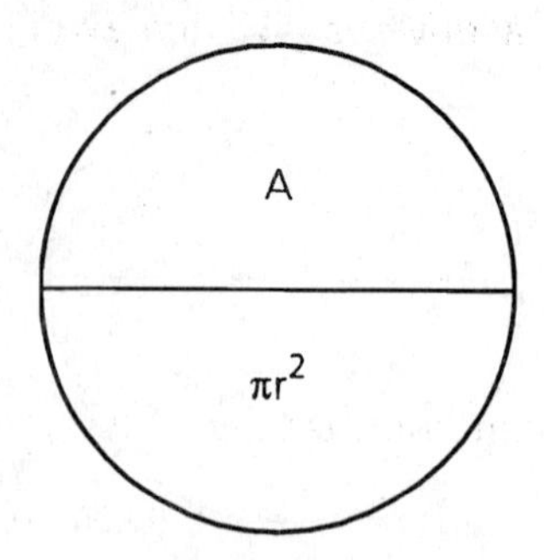

Figure 6–22

Example

What is the area of the given circular house?

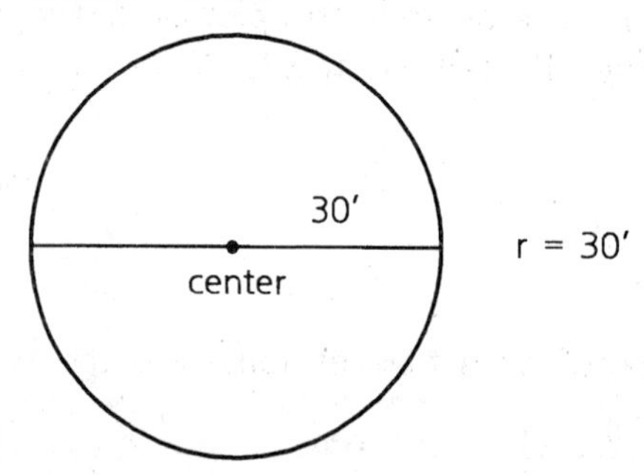

Since $A = \pi r^2$ and $r = 30$ use $\pi = 3.142$

$A = 3.142 \times 30^2 = 3.142 \times 900 = 2{,}827.8$

Answer: The area of the circular house is 2,827.8 square feet.

Exercises

1. Change 3,200 acres to square miles.

2. How many square feet are in 20 square yards?

3. How many square yards are in 20 square feet?

4. Two rectangular lots each have an area of 16,800 square feet. One has a height of 120 feet, and the other has a height of 200 feet. Find the base of each.

5. Find the cost of cementing a driveway 15 feet wide and 50 feet long at a cost of $1.50 per square foot.

6. Find the area of a parallelogram with a base of 12 yards and a height of 18 feet. Give the area in square yards.

7. A triangular piece of property has a base of 1 mile and an altitude of $\frac{1}{2}$ mile. How many square feet are contained in this plot of ground? How many acres (to the nearest acre)? What will the plot sell for at $2,000 per acre?

8. One part of a hip-roof on a tri-level home has the following dimensions:

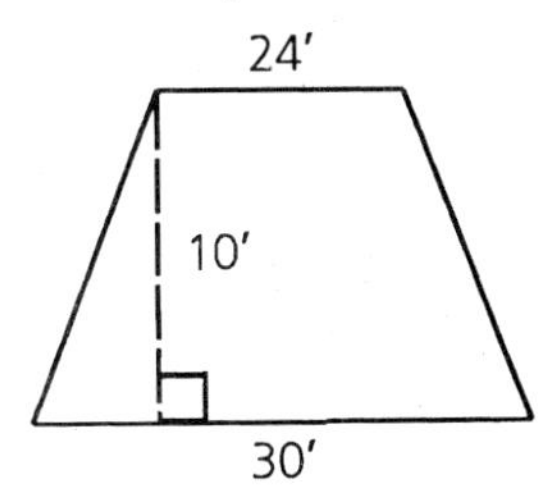

Find the area of this part of the hip-roof.

9. What is the running room (in square yards) for a dog on a 24-foot leash fastened to a stake in the ground? Let $\pi = 3.14$.

10. Find the area of the following:

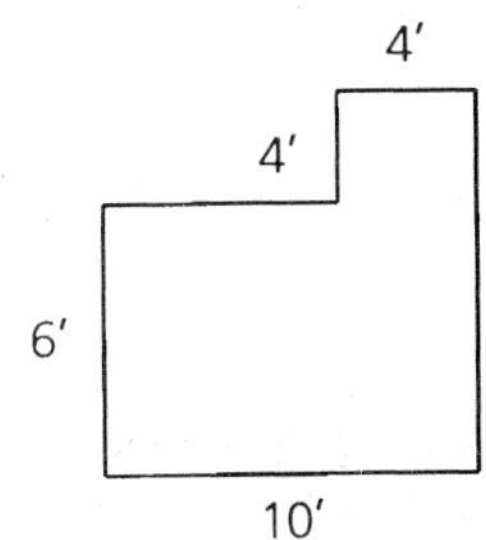

MEASURING VOLUME

The basic units of volume measure are the cubic inch, the cubic foot, and the cubic yard. Measures in volume also include three linear measures: length, width, and height. Volume measures are three-dimensional. To measure the volume of a three-dimensional figure is to measure its capacity or contents. Examples of such three-dimensional figures (called *solids* or *rectangular solids*) include such everyday items as boxes and cartons. Each solid has measures of length, width, and height. Breadth, depth, and altitude also may be used.

A *cube* is a solid made up of six squares, each meeting the others at right angles (90°). A cube is a rectangular solid in which each measure of length, width, and height is equal. A *cubic inch* is a cube that has a length of 1 inch, a width of 1 inch, and a height of 1 inch. These measures can be written as 1 inch × 1 inch × 1 inch or 1" × 1" × 1". The cube shown in Figure 6–23 contains a volume of one cubic inch. Let's review the cubic measurements used in real estate.

Units of Cubic Measure

1 cubic foot (cu. ft.)	=	1,728 cubic inches (cu. in.)
Since 1 ft.	=	12 in.,
1 cu. ft.	=	12 in. × 12 in. ×12 in. = 1,728 cu. in.
1 cubic yard (cu. yd.)	=	27 cubic feet (cu. ft.)
Since 1 yd.	=	3 ft.,
1 cu. yd.	=	3 ft. × 3 ft. × 3 ft. = 27 cu. ft.

To change larger measures of volume to smaller measures and smaller measures of volume to larger measures, use the ideas developed earlier in this chapter.

Example

Change 20 cubic feet to cubic inches.

We are changing to a smaller unit, so we multiply.
1 cu. ft. = 1,728 cu. in.
20 × 1,728 cu. in. = 34,560 cu. in.

Answer: 20 cubic feet = 34,560 cubic inches

Example

Change 8,640 cubic inches to cubic feet.

We are changing to a larger unit, so we divide.
1 cu. ft. = 1,728 cu. in.

$$\frac{8{,}640}{1{,}728} = 5 \text{ cu. ft.}$$

Answer: 8,640 cubic inches = 5 cubic feet

Example

Change 5 cubic yards to cubic feet.

We are changing to a smaller unit, so we multiply.
1 cu. yd. = 27 cu. ft.
5 cu. yds. = 5 × 27 = 135 cu. ft.

Answer: 5 cubic yards = 135 cubic feet

Volume of a Rectangular Solid

A rectangular solid (see Figure 6–24) is made up of rectangles or squares. As we discussed previously, the cube is made up of squares. In any rectangular solid, all surfaces meet at right angles (90°).

REMEMBER

> To find the volume of a rectangular solid, multiply the length by the width, and that product by the height.

All three measures must be in the same unit of linear measure. The volume is the cubic unit of measure. This rule can be written as a formula in which V is the volume, L the length, W the width, and H the height.

$$V = L \times W \times H \text{ or}$$
$$V = LWH$$

This produces the memory aid in Figure 6–25.
Covering the part we want to find, we get the following transformation forms:

$V = LWH$ $\quad L = \frac{V}{WH}$ $\quad W = \frac{V}{LH}$ $\quad H = \frac{V}{LW}$

Example

What is the volume of a rectangular solid 6 inches by 5 inches by 3 inches?

$V = LWH \quad V = 6 \times 5 \times 3 = 90$ cu. in.

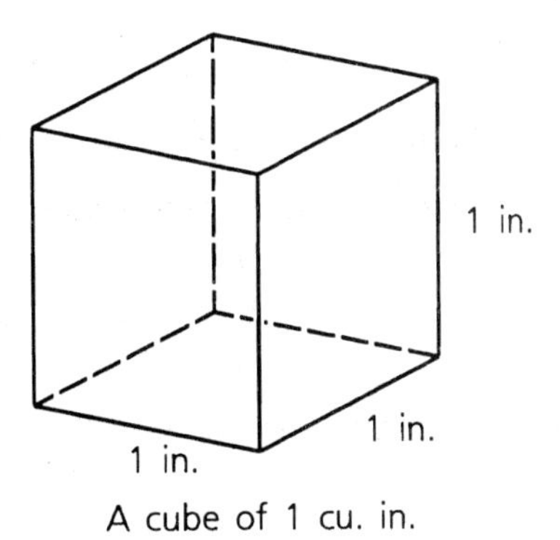

A cube of 1 cu. in.

Figure 6–23

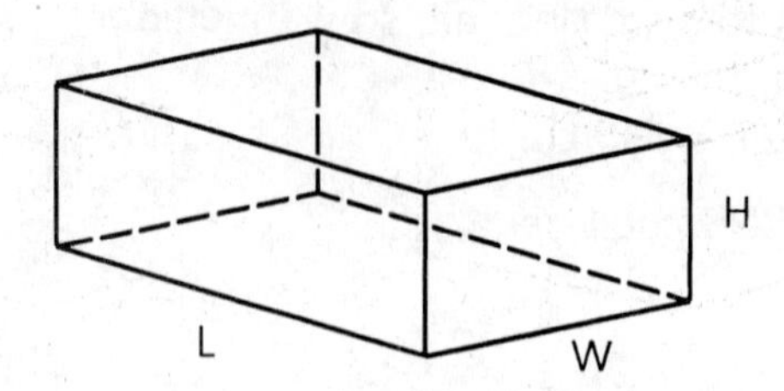

Figure 6–24

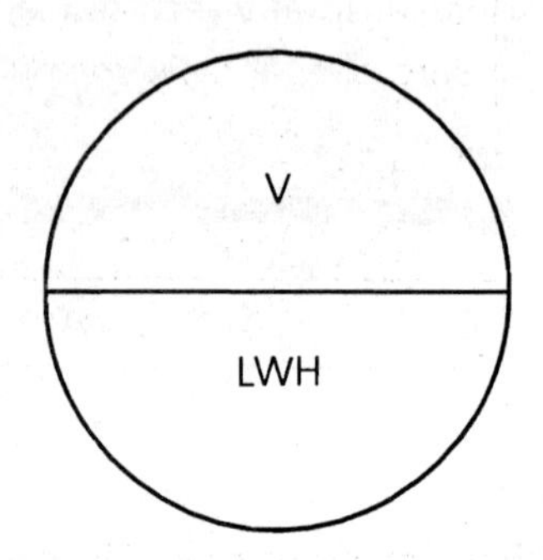

Figure 6–25

Answer: The volume is 90 cubic inches.

To visualize the example above, think of how many 1" × 1" × 1" cubes are in the given rectangular solid. It contains five rows of six cubes in each of its three layers. The volume, then, is 6 × 5 × 3, or 90 cubic inches.

To verify the volume formula, let's find the number of 1" × 1" × 1" cubes in a rectangular solid that is 3 inches by 2 inches by 1 inch. Figure 6–26 contains two rows of three cubes in one layer, or six cubes. This verifies our volume formula, V = LWH or V = 3 × 2 × 1 = 6 cubic inches.

Example

To prepare for the foundation of a building, a volume of 125 feet by 50 feet by 100 feet must be excavated. How many cubic yards of dirt must be removed?

Step 1: V = LWH

V = 125 × 50 × 100 = 625,000 cu. ft.

Step 2: Change 625,000 cu. ft. to cu. yds.

We are changing to a larger unit, so we divide.

1 cu. yd. = 27 cu. ft.

$\frac{625{,}000}{27} = 23{,}148.15$ cu. yds.

Answer: 23,148.15 cubic yards of dirt must be removed.

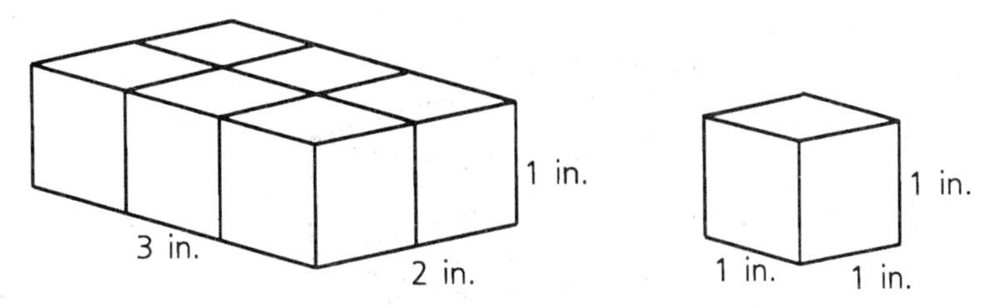

Figure 6–26

REMEMBER

A linear measure times a linear measure times a linear measure gives a cubic measure.

in. × in. × in. = cu. in.
ft. × ft. × ft. = cu. ft.
yd. × yd. × yd. = cu. yd.

Volume of a Cylinder

A cylinder is a long round figure either hollow or solid, like the form of a piston chamber in an engine. It is a solid bounded by a curved side and two flat surfaces or bases. The bases are circles and have the same area. In a right circular cylinder, such as a tin can, all lines representing the curved side of the cylinder are parallel to each other and each line is perpendicular (makes a 90° angle) with the base.

In a right circular cylinder, the radius is the radius of each base (circle). The diameter of the bases is the diameter of the cylinder. The perpendicular between the bases is the altitude or height of the cylinder (see Figure 6–27).

REMEMBER

To find the volume (V) of the cylinder, multiply the area of the base by the height.

The base is a circle with area πr^2 (r = radius). Multiplying this by the height (H), we get

$$V = \pi r^2 H$$

This translates to the memory aid in Figure 6–28.

Covering the part we want to find, we get the following transformation forms:

$$V = \pi r^2 H \qquad H = \frac{V}{\pi r^2} \qquad r^2 = \frac{V}{\pi H}$$

Example

A silo has an inside diameter of 30 feet and a height of 50 feet. How many cubic feet of grain can be stored in the silo?

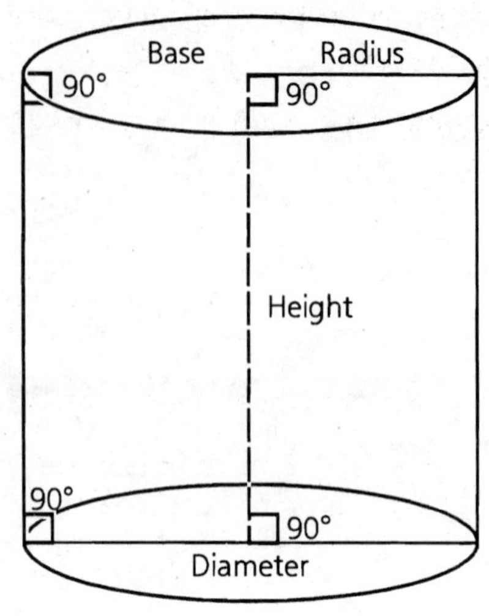

Right circular cylinder

Figure 6–27

Since the silo is a right circular cylinder we can find its volume.

$$V = \pi r^2 H,\ \pi = 3.14,\ r = \frac{30}{2} = 15,\ H = 50$$
$$V = 3.14 \times 15^2 \times 50$$
$$V = 3.14 \times 225 \times 50$$
$$V = 3.14 \times 11{,}250$$
$$V = 35{,}325 \text{ cu. ft.}$$

Answer: 35,325 cubic feet of grain can be stored in the silo.

Example

Let's assume that a farmer has 35,325 cubic feet of grain stored in a silo and sells the grain for $5.00 per cubic yard. How much will the farmer receive for the grain?

Step 1: First we need to change 35,325 cubic feet to cubic yards.
We are changing to a larger unit, so we divide.
1 cu. yd. = 27 cu. ft.
$\frac{35{,}325}{27} = 1{,}308.3$ cu. yds. (to nearest tenth)

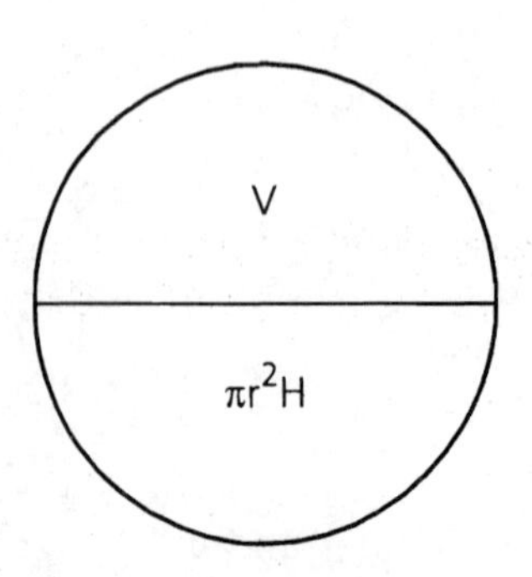

Figure 6–28

Step 2: If the farmer receives $5.00 per cubic yard, then
1,308.3 × 5 = $6,541.50.

Answer: The farmer will receive $6,541.50 for the sale of the grain.

Exercises

1. The cost to replace a home that has been destroyed by fire is $10 per cubic foot. If the ground dimensions of the home were 50 feet by 30 feet and the height was 10 feet, what will it cost to replace the home?

2. A barn is built in the form of a cube, and each side measures 30 feet. How many cubic feet of alfalfa can be stored in the barn?

3. How many boxes 4 feet by 3 feet by 6 inches can be stored in a space measuring 20 feet by 15 feet by 20 feet?

4. A container in the form of a rectangular solid 8 inches by 20 inches by 2 feet is filled with water. If all the water is to be poured into cubes 2 inches on a side, how many cubes are needed?

5. How many cubic feet of water does a cylindrical pool contain if its radius is 14 feet and the height of the water in the pool is 18 inches? (Use $\pi = \frac{22}{7}$.)

CHAPTER TEST

1. What is the depth of a rectangular lot containing 2,520 square yards with a frontage of 90 feet?

2. A tract of land contains 348,480 square feet. It sold for $950 per acre. What was the total selling price?

3. The excavation for a basement must be 27 feet by 50 feet by 10 feet deep. What will be the total cost to the owner if the rate is $5.00 per cubic yard of earth removed?

4. Mr. Wilson decided to build a fence around a lot with frontage of 125 feet and a depth of 160 feet. The cost of the fence is $1.00 per linear foot, excluding the gates at front and rear of the lot. Each gate is four feet wide and costs $30.50. What is the total cost of the fence, including the gates?

5. How many cubic yards of gravel would be needed to fill a trench 54 feet long, 10 feet wide, and 30 inches deep?

6. Find the area of the shaded lot.

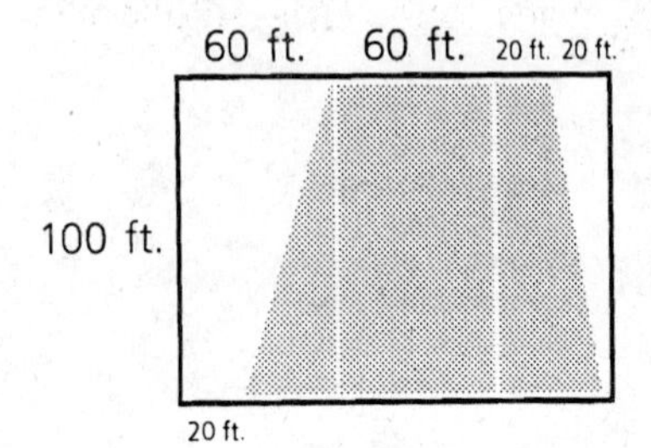

7. In the diagram below find the length of the property boundary on North Street.

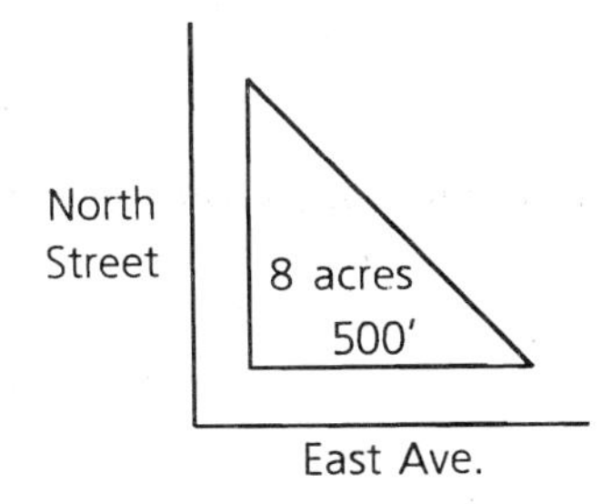

8. What is the square footage of the following diagram?

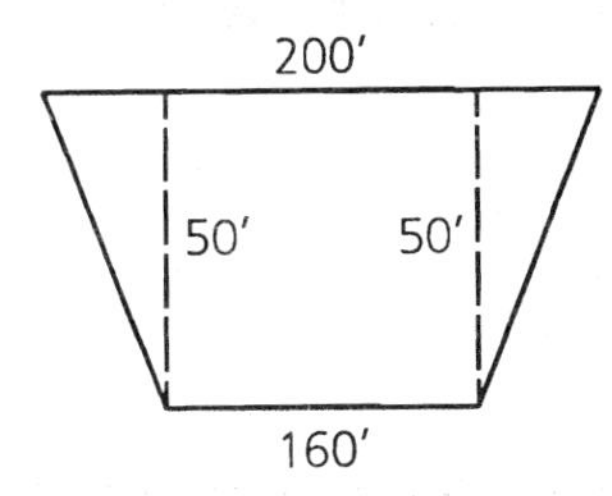

9. How many cubic feet of concrete would be needed to build a public sidewalk 48 inches wide on the street sides of a 75-foot by 114-foot corner lot? If the sidewalk is 6 inches in depth, what would it cost at $60.00 per cubic yard?

10. A silo in the shape of a cylinder has a diameter of 28 feet and a height of 50 feet. How many cubic feet of corn can be stored in the silo? (Let $\pi = \frac{22}{7}$.)

11. Find the area of a square whose sides measure 9.5 feet. Round off to the nearest whole unit.

12. Find the area of a rectangular field $\frac{1}{2}$ mile wide and $2\frac{1}{2}$ miles long. Give solution in acres.

13. Find the perimeter of a square whose side measures $1\frac{3}{4}$ inches. (Hint: In a square the length and width have the same measure.)

14. Find the volume of a cube whose side measures $4\frac{1}{2}$ inches. Round your answer to the nearest whole unit. (Hint: In a cube, the length, width, and height all have the same measure.)

15. The following lot was bought for $3.00 per square foot. What was the total cost?

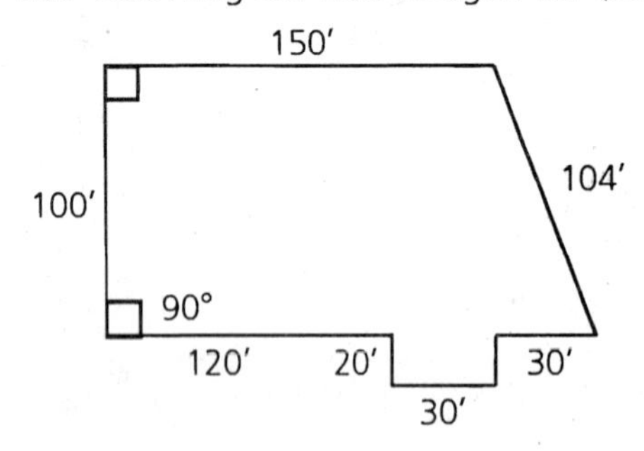

16. A real estate office building is 42 feet wide and 60 feet long. The entire building has a sidewalk around it 6 feet wide and 4 inches deep. What is the total area of the sidewalk?

17. The carpet chosen by the Kelleys for their living room was $15.50 a square yard. How much did the carpet cost if the living room was 12 feet 6 inches by 18 feet?

18. Realtor Jones must paint a bedroom in a home she has listed to make it more attractive for selling. If Jones must allow 72 square feet for openings, how many gallons of paint must she purchase in order to cover the walls and ceiling of a room 12 feet long, 9 feet 6 inches wide, and 8 feet high with two coats of paint? (One gallon will cover 450 square feet with one coat.)

19. A silo in the form of a right circular cylinder has an inside diameter of 28 feet and a height of 40 feet. If a bushel is about $1\frac{1}{4}$ cubic feet, how many bushels of corn will the silo hold?

20. The area of a trapezoid is 60 square feet and the bases are 8 feet and 12 feet. Find the height of the trapezoid in feet.

21. Which parcel has the larger area?

a. 41,371 sq. ft.
b. an acre
c. 4,017 sq. yds.
d. 196 feet square

22. A broker has the problem of subdividing a 10-acre tract into 50 × 100 foot lots. After allowing 85,600 square feet for the necessary streets, how many lots will the broker realize from this subdivision?

7

LAND DESCRIPTIONS

Goals

1. Learn the descriptions used for land.
2. Solve problems to determine approximately how much land is involved in a description.
3. Understand the importance of a complete, accurate legal description when property is encumbered or conveyed.

Three types of land descriptions are in general use in the United States today:

1. Metes and bounds
2. United States governmental survey
3. Descriptions by lot and block (recorded plat)

Other types of descriptions unique to particular states will not be discussed here.

METES AND BOUNDS

Metes and bounds is the oldest method of land description in the United States and is used worldwide when it is necessary to describe an irregular tract of land.

Elements that are necessary to make up a proper metes and bounds description are as follows:

1. An accurate and unique beginning point, referred to as the *point of beginning* (P.O.B.)
2. An accurate description of each boundary, completely enclosing the tract, with the final boundary line returning to the P.O.B.
3. The *area* of the tract in square feet, acreage, and so on

To understand the metes and bounds system, it is necessary to understand the *bearing* and *azimuth* systems, since many times a metes and bounds description will have an angular course, that is, a course not due north, south, east, or west.

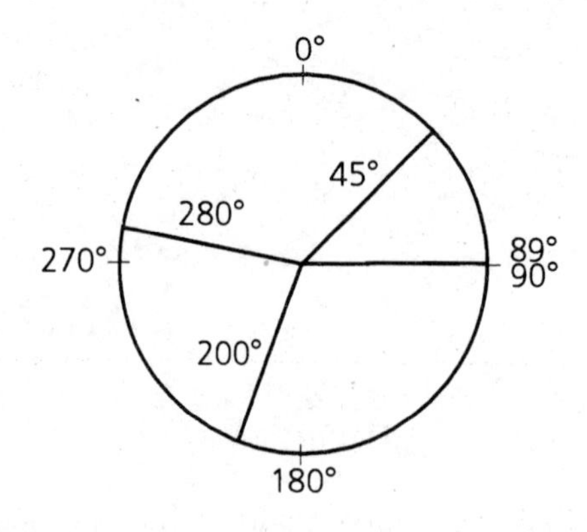

Figure 7–1

Azimuth System

In the azimuth system the compass or circle is undivided. Azimuth readings always commence from the *north* and move in a clockwise direction. Thus, a property line running due south would be described as 180°. Consider the following readings: 45°, 280°, 89°, 200°. There is only one point on the azimuth circle at which each of these readings can be located (see Figure 7–1).

Bearing System

The direction of a line is given by its *bearing*. Think of a bearing as a direction in which you are looking or traveling. A full circle, containing all directions (see Figure 7–2), is made up of four quadrants of exactly 90° each (4 × 90° = 360°).

In the bearing system, a compass is divided into four quadrants: the northeast (NE), southeast (SE), southwest (SW), and northwest (NW). A north–south line bisects the compass, as does an east–west line. A bearing is always described as *north* or *south*.

The conventional way of writing a bearing is:

1. The first letter (N or S) of the quadrant
2. The degree, minutes, and seconds
3. The second letter (E or W) of the quadrant

A bearing description reading N 45° E would be drawn as shown in Figure 7–3. (Stand in the center of the circle, face *north*, turn (bear) 45° toward the *east*).

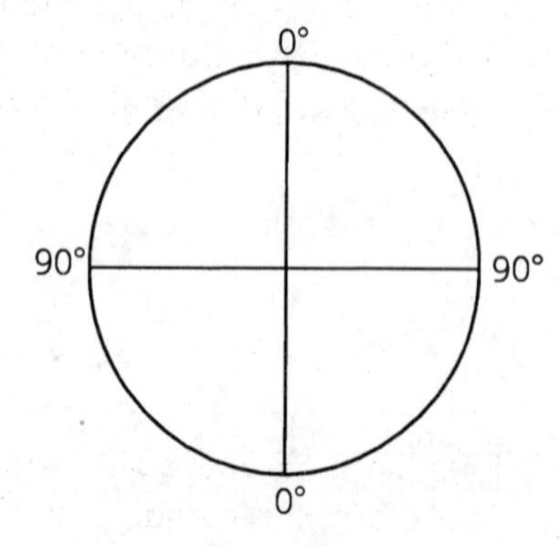

Figure 7–2

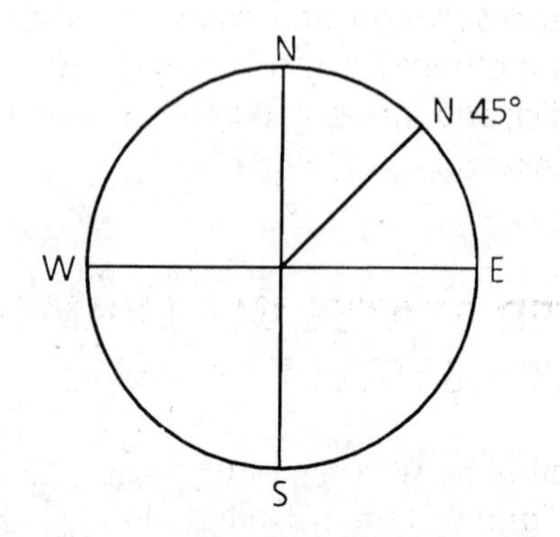

Figure 7–3

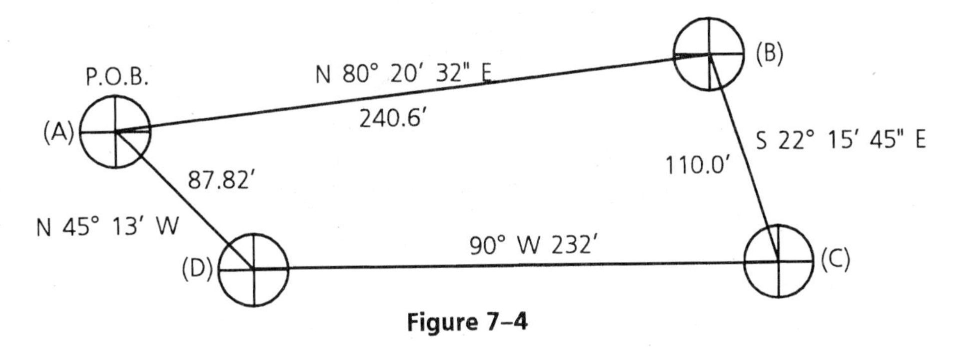

Figure 7–4

The tract shown in Figure 7–4 might, beginning with corner (A), be described as follows if you were "walking" in a clockwise direction.

Beginning at an iron pipe on the east side of J. C. Jones's property, and at a fence corner, which pipe is S 40° 22′ 36" E of the center of the intersection of Powell Avenue and Cobblestone Way; thence running with a wire fence N 80° 20′ 32" E 240.6′ to a pipe at the base of an oak tree; (B) thence S 22° 15′ 45" E 110.0′ to a pipe at the base of a stone wall; (C) thence 90° W 232′ to a stone; (D) thence N 45° 13′ W 87.82′ to the point of beginning.

Exercises

1. Locate the following bearing readings:

a. N 45° E
b. 90° E
c. S 88° W
d. S 70° E
e. N 70° W

0°
90° 90°
0°

2. Now convert each bearing reading to an azimuth.

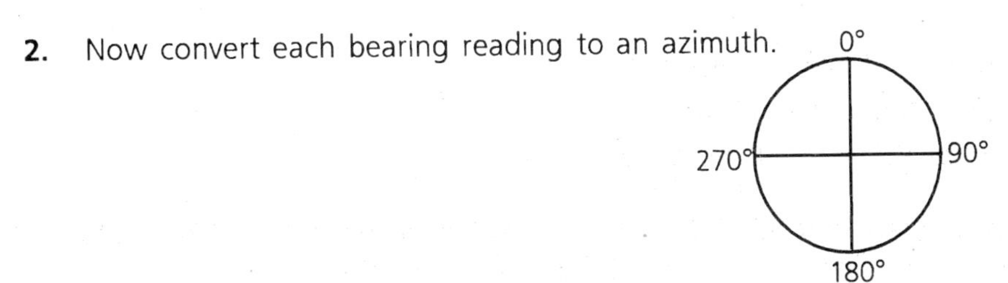

The description and survey on pages 114–115 show the application of the metes and bounds method. Figures 7–5 and 7–6 were furnished by and used with permission of Eugene A. Burdick and James E. Burdick of Burdick Engineering Company, Inc., 2103 South Wadsworth Blvd., Lakewood, CO 80227.

UNITED STATES GOVERNMENTAL SURVEY SYSTEM

The United States governmental survey system was established in 1785 and is also referred to as the "grid system," "United States public land surveys," "government rectangular survey," or just "rectangular survey."

I, Eugene A. Burdick, a Registered Professional Engineer and Land Surveyor registered in the State of Colorado, hereby certify to MEGA-BUCKS CORPORATION, a Colorado Corporation and to

that a field survey of the premises described hereon was conducted under my direction and supervision and completed on June 20, 1983; that, to the best of my information, knowledge and belief, the attached improvement survey plat correctly shows all boundaries, the location of all pins and monuments, the location of all structures situated on the described parcel, easements, visible encroachments, and any fences, hedges or walls on or within two feet of both sides of all boundaries of said parcel, the location of all visible utilities located on said parcel and all underground utilities for which there is visible surface evidence, and the location of all easements, underground utilities, tunnels for which record evidence is available from the County Clerk and Recorder or for which information was made available based on information contained in Land Title Guarantee Company title insurance commitment No. dated June 10, 1983.

LEGAL DESCRIPTION:

A parcel of land in the Northwest one-quarter of the Southwest one-quarter of Section Thirty-Six (36) Township Four (4) South, Range Seventy-Four (74) North of the 6th Principal Meridian, County of Arapahoe, State of Colorado, described as follows:

Beginning at a point 674.5 feet south of the north line and 30 feet east of the west line of said Northwest ¼ of the Southwest ¼ of Section 36, Township 4 South, Range 74 North; thence East parallel to the north line of said Northwest ¼ Southwest ¼ 300 feet; thence South parallel to the west line of said Northwest ¼ Southwest ¼ 387 feet; thence West parallel to aforesaid North line 300 feet; thence North parallel to aforesaid west line 387 feet to the point of beginning.

Eugene A. Burdick
Eugene A. Burdick, PE-LS
Colorado Reg. No. 9010

NOTICE: According to Colorado law you must commence any legal action based upon any defect in this survey within six years after you first discover such defect. In no event, may any action based upon any defect in this survey be commenced more than ten years from the date of the certification shown hereon.

No	Description	Date	By
1	[illegible]	6-27-83	CAB

REVISIONS

CERTIFICATE of SURVEY
Boundary and Improvement Survey
Part of NW¼ SW¼ Sec. 36, T4S, R74N
County of Arapahoe, Colorado

Date 6-21-83
Bk Pg
BURDICK ENGINEERING COMPANY, INC.
Engineering & Land Surveying
6001 West 16th Ave
Lakewood Colorado 80214
Job No -10003
Sheet No 1 of 1
DESIGNED BY ______ DRAWN BY ______ CHECKED BY ______

Figure 7–5

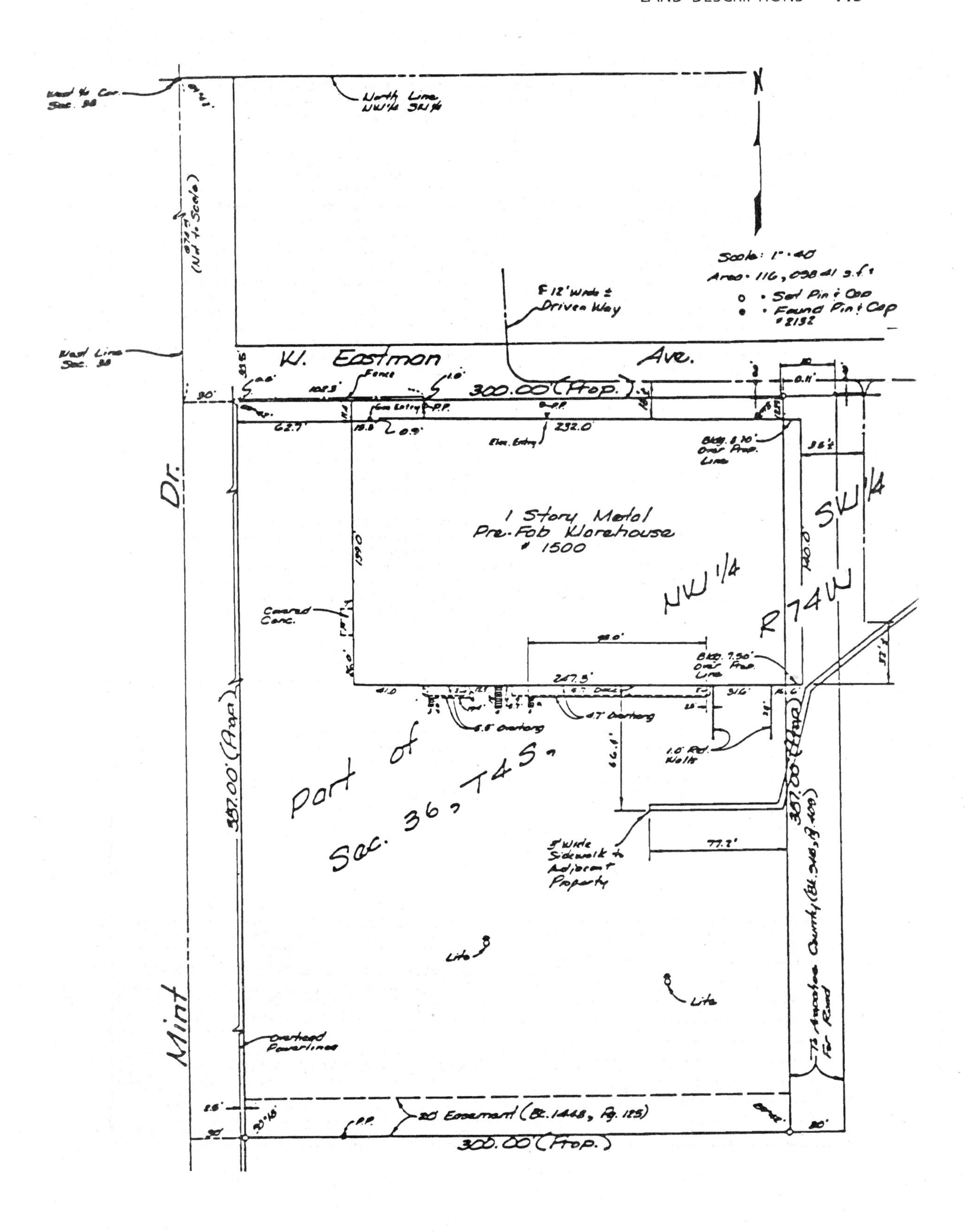
North Line NW1/4 SW1/4
Scale: 1" = 40
Area = 116,098.41 s.f.
• Set Pin & Cap
• Found Pin & Cap #2132
12' Wide ± Driven Way
W. Eastman Ave.
300.00 (Prop.)
1 Story Metal Pre-Fab Warehouse # 1500
NW 1/4
SW 1/4
R74W
Part of Sec. 36, T4S,
Mint Dr.
357.00 (Prop.)
5' Wide Sidewalk to Adjacent Property
Lite
Overhead Powerlines
20' Easement (Bk. 1448, Pg. 125)
300.00 (Prop.)

Figure 7–6

These surveys are used in the entire continental United States, except for the areas occupied by the original 13 states, parts of Ohio, and all of Hawaii and Texas. If your state is not concerned with this, you may wish to move on to the next chapter.

Principal Meridians and Baselines

To understand the rectangular survey system, one must have an understanding of *meridians* and *baselines.* A meridian is a line that runs straight north and south. A baseline runs east and west (see Figure 7–7).

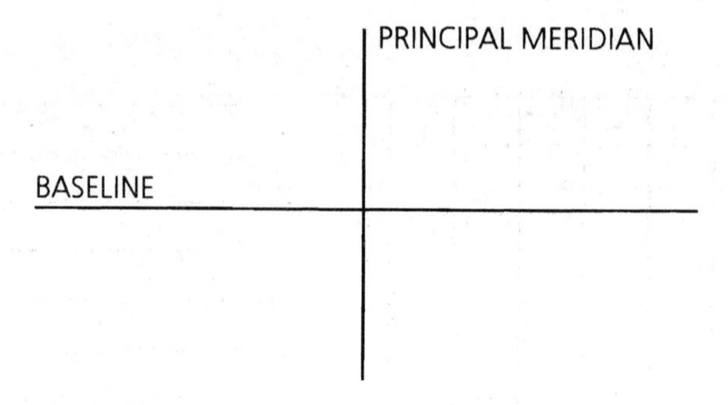

Figure 7–7

There are 36 principal meridians located in different parts of the United States.

Correction Lines and Guide Meridians

After the principal meridian and baseline were established, other lines were established running east and west, parallel to the baseline at intervals of 24 miles to the north and to the south of the baseline. These lines were referred to as *correction lines* (see Figure 7–8).

The next step consisted of establishing lines running due north and south at 24-mile intervals on each side of the principal meridian, commencing at the baseline and extending to the first correction line. These lines were called *guide meridians* and, with the correction lines, divided the territory into squares approximately 24 miles on each side. This 24-mile square is known as a *check* or a *quadrangle* (Figure 7–9).

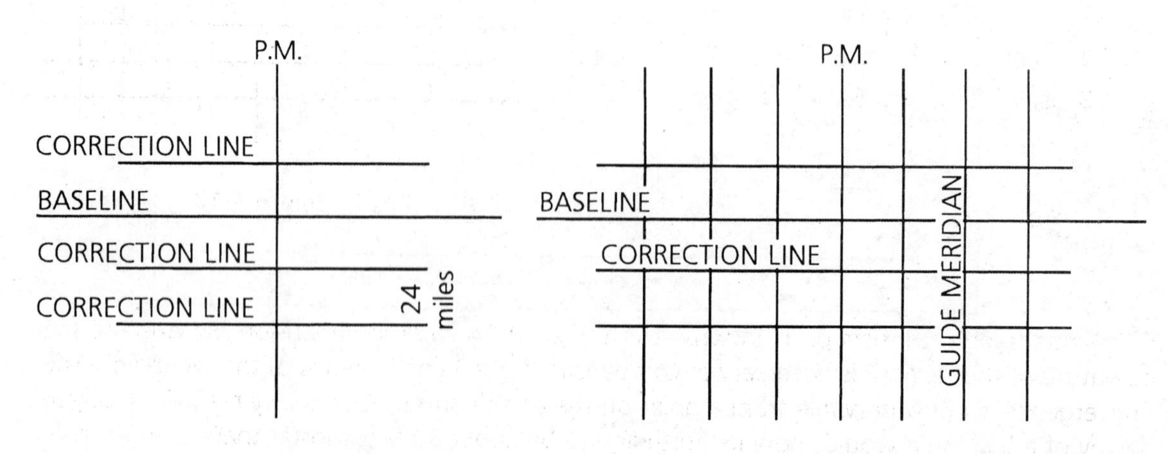

Figure 7–8 **Figure 7–9**

Township and Range Lines

The 24-mile squares (checks or quadrangles) were then divided into smaller tracts of land by lines running north and south and parallel to the principal meridian at regular six-mile intervals. These lines are known as *range lines.* At the same time, east–west lines were established at six-mile intervals and parallel to the baseline. These imaginary lines are known as *township lines.*

The six-mile strip running north and south is referred to as a "range" and numbered east and west of the principal meridian (Figure 7–10).

The six-mile strip running east and west is referred to as a *tier* (Figure 7–11).

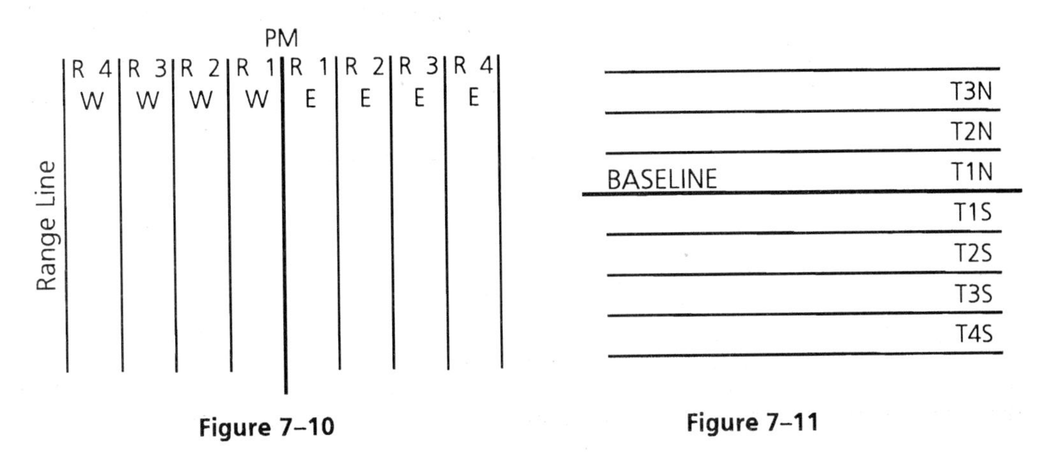

Figure 7–10

Figure 7–11

If you put Figures 7–10 and 7–11 together, the resulting blocks are known as "townships." There are 16 townships in each *check* or *quadrangle* (see Figure 7–12).

The townships labeled in Figure 7–12 would be described as follows:

1. Township 1 North, Range 2 West.
2. Township 2 South, Range 1 East.
3. Township 2 North, Range 2 East.

or

1. Twp. 1 N, R 2 W.
2. Twp. 2 S, R 1 E.
3. Twp. 2 N, R 2 E.

PM
R 4 W R 3 W R 2 W R 1 W R 1 E R 2 E R 3 E R 4 E
T4N
T3N
T2N
T1N
BASELINE
1
2
3

Figure 7–12

A quadrangle consists of 16 townships. It is 24 × 24 miles in dimension. Because of the curvature of the earth, it is necessary to compensate for the convergence of the meridians. The convergence is not observable from a point on the earth's surface but is very real. An accurate survey of a township would show its north line to be about 50 feet shorter than its south line. Thus, in the fourth township north of the baseline, the difference is 200.64 feet shorter than the south line of Township 1. To compensate for this convergence of the meridians, the south line of Township 5 is measured the full distance of six miles on the correction line (Figure 7–13).

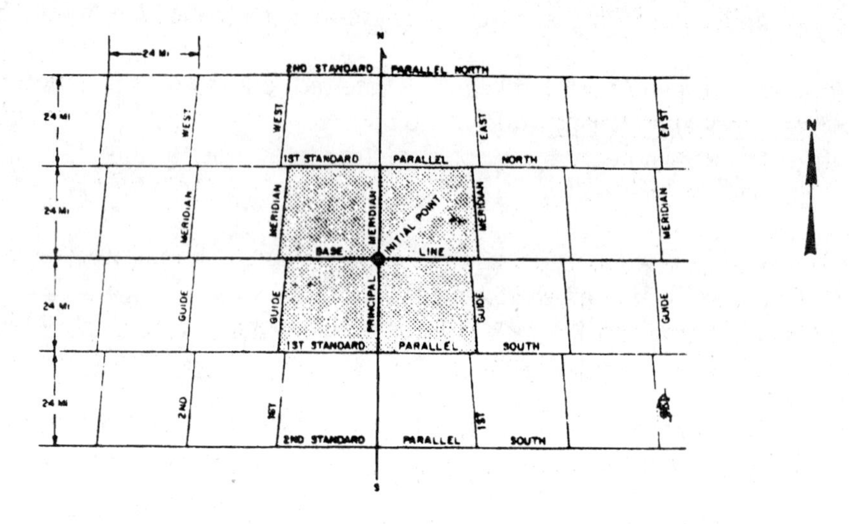

Figure 7–13

Sections

The Act of 1785 creating the Rectangular Survey System provided only for townships of six miles square, and only the outside boundaries were surveyed, although monuments were placed at every mile on the township lines.

It soon became apparent that a six-mile square was too large an area in which to describe a given tract of land, so in 1796 Congress passed an act directing that the townships be surveyed into 36 sections, each to be one mile square and "as nearly as may be" 640 acres (Figure 7–14). One acre contains 43,560 square feet. Each section corner was to be monumented, and the sections were to be numbered consecutively from 1 to 36. Number 1 was to be in the northeast

Division of Townships into Sections
1 Mile Square

6	5	4	3	2	1
7	8	9	10	11	12
18	17	16	15	14	13
19	20	21	22	23	24
30	29	28	27	26	25
31	32	33	34	35	36

Figure 7–14

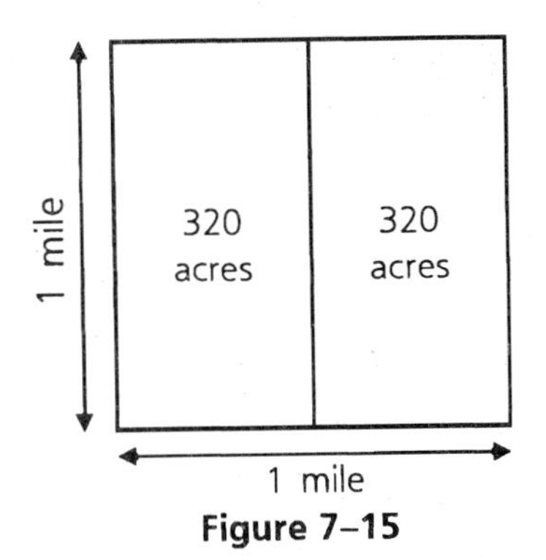

Figure 7–15

NW¼ 160 acres	NE¼ 160 acres
SW¼ 160 acres	SE¼ 160 acres

Figure 7–16

corner of the township and proceed west and east alternately through the township, ending in the southeast corner with number 36.

In 1800 Congress provided for the subdivision of *sections* (1 mile × 1 mile) into east and west halves of 320 acres each by running north and south lines through the center of the sections (Figure 7–15).

In 1805 Congress provided for the further division of sections into quarter sections by running east and west lines through the center and monumenting all quarter section corners (Figure 7–16).

80	80	80	80
80	80	80	80

Figure 7–17

40	40	40	40
40	40	40	40
40	40	40	40
40	40	40	40

Figure 7–18

In 1820 Congress directed the further division of sections into half-quarter sections by running north and south lines through all quarter sections (Figure 7–17).

Finally, in 1832 Congress directed the subdivision into quarter-quarter sections by running east and west lines through the quarter sections (Figure 7–18).

Forty acres is the smallest statutory division of legal sections. Sections can be broken up into smaller parcels of 2½ -, 5 -, 10 -, and 20-acre tracts (Figure 7–19).

REMEMBER

> One can easily locate a property described by governmental survey by *reading the description in reverse,* i.e., reading the principal meridian, then the range, township, section, part of the section, part of part of the section, and part of part of part of the section.

Assume the diagram in Figure 7–20 is Section 6 of Township 2 S of Range 70 W of the 6th P.M.

a. The SE¼ SE¼ Section 6, Twp. 2 S, R. 70 W, 6th P.M.

b. The NE¼ NW¼ SE¼ Section 6, Twp. 2 S, R. 70 W, 6th P.M.

c. The SE¼ SW¼ SW¼ Section 6, Twp. 2 S, R. 70 W, 6th P.M.

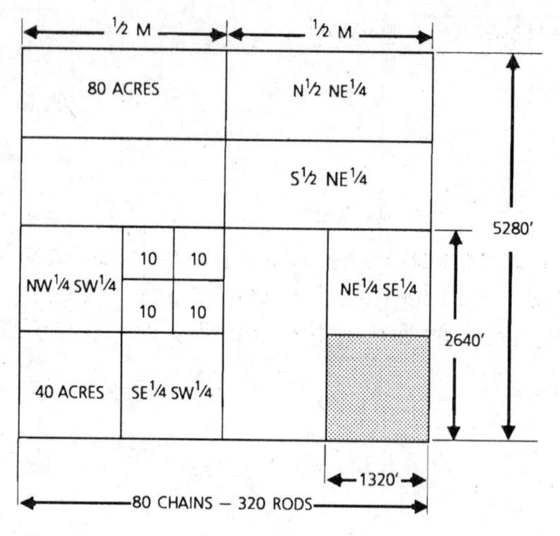

Figure 7–19

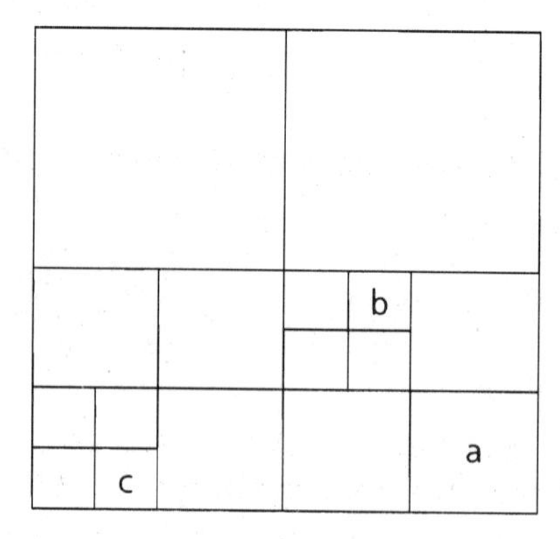

Figure 7–20

Exercises

1. An area of land 24 miles by 24 miles is how many square miles?

2. A parcel of land six miles square is referred to as a township and is how many square miles?

3. What is the perimeter of a township?

4. A property is bounded on one side by a frontage road that runs 2,640 feet, a perpendicular boundary that runs 1,320 feet, and a straight line to close. The property will sell for $2,050 per acre. How many acres are in this tract? What is the sale price?

5. How many acres are in the NW¼ NW¼ NE¼ of any section?

6. If a three-acre tract of land has a depth of 200 feet, what is the frontage of the tract?

7. A developer bought the SE¼ of the SW¼ of a section of land. He developed the NW¼ of this land and sold the remainder for $3,000 per acre. How much did he develop? What was the sale price of the remaining sold parcel?

8. Determine the number of acres in the shaded area of this sketch.

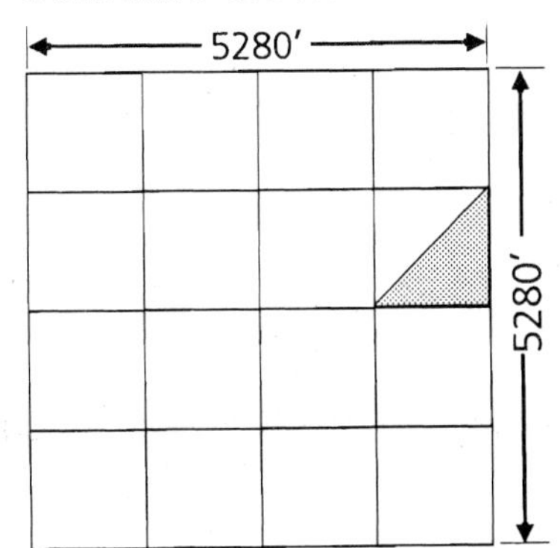

9. A developer purchased a part of a section described as the N½ of the S½ of the NE¼ for $78,400. How many acres are in the tract? What was paid per acre?

10. How many acres are included in the NE¼ of the SE¼ *and* the SE¼ of the SE¼ of the NE¼?

11. The owner of the property in question 10 sold the S½ of the NE¼ of the SE¼ for $2,500 per acre. How many acres were sold? What was the total sale price?

12. Describe the shaded areas of the section in the illustration shown below.

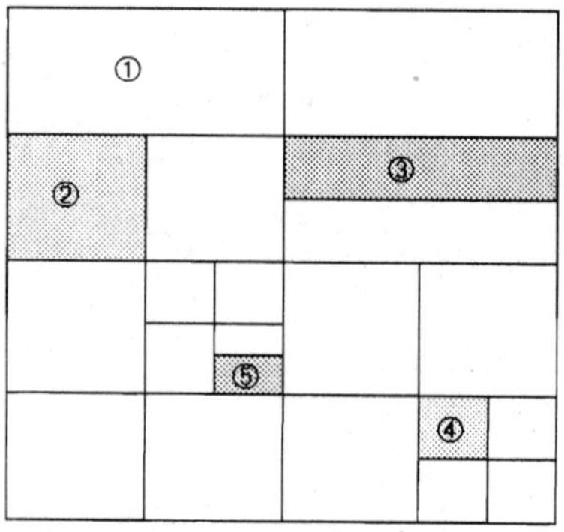

13. In the diagram in question 12, how many acres are in each of the shaded areas?

1.
2.
3.
4.
5.

LOT AND BLOCK

When an owner of a plot of land wishes to subdivide the tract into smaller parcels or lots, he or she employs a surveyor to survey the tract and draw a plat, dividing the tract into blocks separated by streets and alleys and then dividing the blocks into smaller areas called lots.

The lots and blocks are numbered, giving identification to each, and the subdivision is given a name. The jurisdiction in which the subdivision is located must grant approval, at which time the subdivision map may be placed on record and identified by lot and block number, subdivision name, and county. The subdivider may also establish easements and restrictive covenants upon the land.

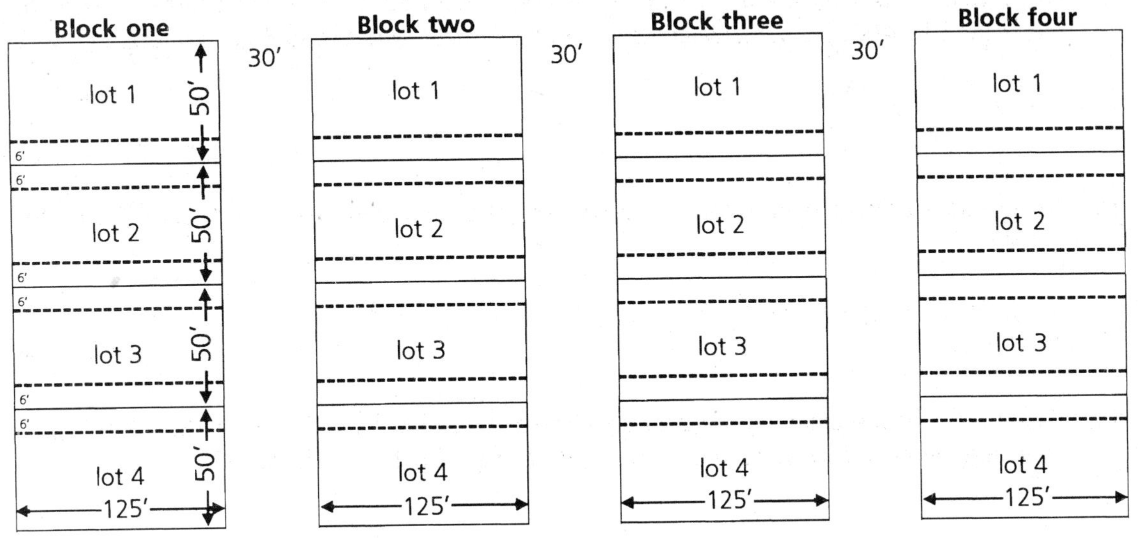

Golden Subdivision, County of Aspen, State of Colorado

Figure 7–21

Exercises

Answer questions 1–6 using subdivision shown in Figure 7–21.

1. What is the square footage of each lot in the subdivision?

2. What is the square footage of the entire subdivision?

3. How many acres are contained in the land?

4. What is the square footage allotted for easements and roadways?

5. The building department requires that each house be set back from the easement 5 feet, from the front line 30 feet, and from the rear of the property 50 feet. What is the maximum square footage allowed for a house to be built on lot 2 block 2?

6. Each lot was listed at $500 per front foot. Lot 1 sold at full price, and lot 2 sold for 15% less. What was the combined sale price?

7. A subdivider owns 40 acres of land. To subdivide the land, the county requires that two acres be dedicated to school land and three acres to open space. Streets and alleys will require four acres. If the lots are to be 100′ × 200′, how many lots can be obtained?

8. If you own a parcel of land 600 feet wide by 400 feet deep, how many $\frac{1}{4}$-acre sites can be obtained by subdividing the land?

9. How many acres are in the land described in question 8?

10. If you own seven acres of land and wish to subdivide into lots 100′ × 200′, how many lots can be obtained?

CHAPTER TEST

1. How many acres are in the following described parcel of land? Begin at a point at the NW corner of a section, thence east 2,640 feet, thence south 1,320 feet, thence west 1,320 feet, thence north 660 feet, thence west 1,320 feet, thence north to the point of beginning.

2. Draw lines in the circle approximating the following:

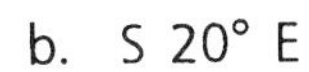

   a. N 45° W
   b. S 20° E
   c. N 10° E
   d. S 40° W

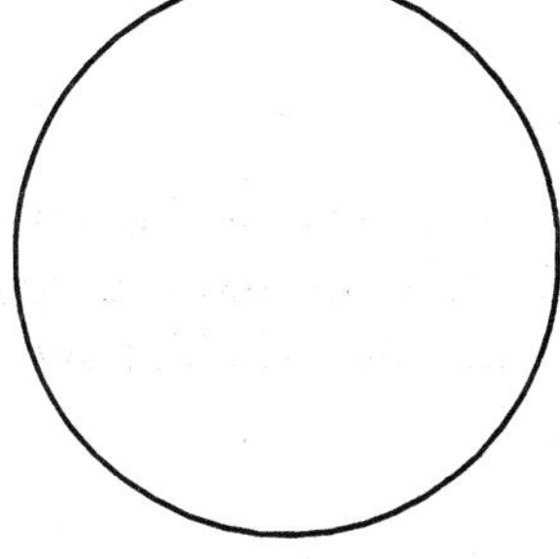

3. A commercial site contains 283,140 square feet and sold for $1,698,840. What is the cost per square foot? How many acres are in the site?

4. A 20-acre tract of land has 800 feet of frontage on a country road. What is the depth of the tract?

5. Sullivan owned the NE¼ of the SE¼ of a section. He sold the SE¼ of the NE¼ of the SE¼ to Jamison for $6,800 per acre.

   a. How many acres did Sullivan originally own?
   b. How many acres did he sell to Jamison?
   c. How much did Jamison pay?

6. Locate, shade, and describe 160 acres of the land exactly in the center of a section.

7. Ten percent of a township is how many acres?

8. An appraiser determines that market value in an area is $540 per acre. Swenson owns the N½ of the NE¼ of the SW¼ of a section. How many acres does Swenson own? How much is Swenson's land worth?

9. How many acres are in the following parcel of land? Begin at a point at the northwest corner of a section, thence due east 2,640 feet, thence due south 2,640 feet, thence in a straight line back to the point of beginning.

10. Which of the following is not an acre?

a. 43,560 square feet

b. 363′ × 120′

c. 180′ × 242′

d. 203′ × 203′

Use the following information for questions 11–14: A subdivider owns 60 acres of land and wishes to subdivide it into 25,000 square-foot lots. The law requires that 300,000 square feet be allowed for streets.

11. What is the maximum number of lots to be obtained from this site?

12. If each site is 200 feet deep, what is their width?

13. If each lot sells for $480 per front foot, what will each lot sell for?

14. What percent of the whole is allocated to streets?

15. If a subdivider is selling lots that are 75 feet wide and 200 feet deep for $45,000, what is the price per front foot?

8
MORTGAGE MATH

Goals

1. Compute simple, compound, and add-on interest problems.
2. Use a chart to determine monthly payments on an amortized loan.
3. Understand discount points charged by a lender.
4. Determine any prepayment of principal on an amortized loan.

SIMPLE INTEREST

Most interest on mortgages is calculated based upon simple interest. *Interest* is rent paid for the use of other people's money. To determine interest, use the memory aid in Figure 8–1.

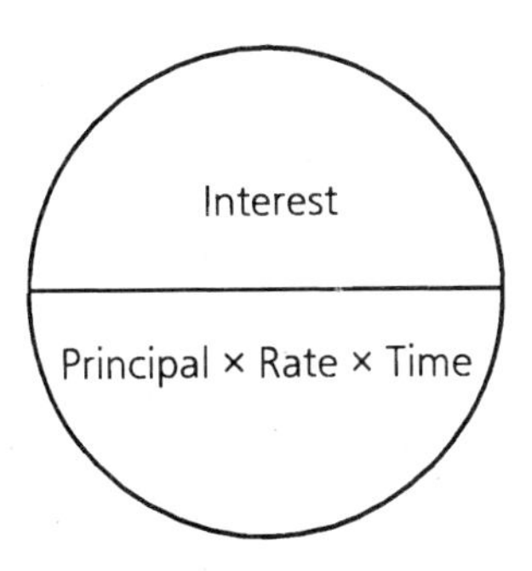

Figure 8–1

REMEMBER

> Unpaid principal balance × interest rate = interest for one year × time = interest due for this period.

For the following examples, assume that the original loan balance is $75,000, with an interest rate of 12% per annum, and amortized over 30 years.

Example

If interest is unknown, then

$75,000 × .12 = $9,000
$9,000 × 1 year = $9,000 per year

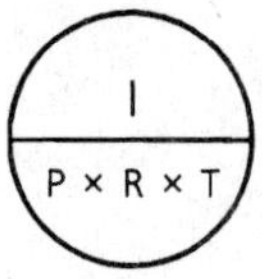

or $I = P \times R \times T$

Example

If rate is unknown, then

$9,000 ÷ 75,000 = .12 × 1 = .12 per year (or per annum)

or $R = \frac{I}{P \times T}$

Example

If principal is unknown, then

.12 × 1 = .12 per year
$9,000 ÷ .12 = $75,000

or $P = \frac{I}{R \times T}$

Example

If time is unknown (simple interest is always computed for one year), then

$75,000 × .12 = $9,000 ÷ $9,000 = 1

or $T = \frac{I}{P \times R}$

Interest may be paid in the following manner:

Monthly	=	$\frac{1}{12}$ of year
Bimonthly	=	$\frac{1}{6}$ of year
Semiannually	=	$\frac{1}{2}$ of year
Annually	=	once a year or any other period that lender and borrower agree upon

Most lenders charge interest monthly. So, based on the figures we've used in the previous examples

$9,000 ÷ 12 months = $750 per month based upon an unpaid balance of $75,000.

Monthly Payments Required to Repay a $1,000 Loan

NO. YEARS

%	5	10	15	20	25	30	35	40
6	19.33	11.10	8.44	7.16	6.44	6.00	5.70	5.50
6¼	19.45	11.23	8.57	7.31	6.60	6.16	5.87	5.68
6½	19.57	11.35	8.71	7.46	6.75	6.32	6.04	5.85
6¾	19.68	11.48	8.85	7.60	6.91	6.49	6.21	6.03
7	19.80	11.61	8.99	7.75	7.07	6.65	6.39	6.21
7¼	19.92	11.74	9.13	7.90	7.23	6.82	6.56	6.40
7½	20.04	11.87	9.27	8.06	7.39	6.99	6.74	6.58
7¾	20.16	12.00	9.41	8.21	7.55	7.16	6.92	6.77
8	20.28	12.13	9.56	8.36	7.72	7.34	7.10	6.95
8¼	20.40	12.27	9.70	8.52	7.88	7.51	7.28	7.14
8½	20.52	12.40	9.85	8.68	8.06	7.69	7.47	7.34
8¾	20.64	12.54	10.00	8.84	8.23	7.87	7.66	7.53
9	20.76	12.67	10.15	9.00	8.40	8.05	7.84	7.72
9¼	20.88	12.81	10.30	9.16	8.57	8.23	8.03	7.91
9½	21.01	12.94	10.45	9.33	8.74	8.41	8.22	8.11
9¾	21.13	13.08	10.60	9.49	8.92	8.60	8.41	8.30
10	21.25	13.22	10.75	9.66	9.09	8.78	8.60	8.50
10¼	21.38	13.36	10.90	9.82	9.27	8.97	8.79	8.69
10½	21.50	13.50	11.06	9.99	9.45	9.15	8.99	8.89
10¾	21.62	13.64	11.21	10.16	9.63	9.34	9.18	9.09
11	21.75	13.78	11.37	10.33	9.81	9.53	9.37	9.29
11¼	21.87	13.92	11.53	10.50	9.99	9.72	9.57	9.49
11½	22.00	14.06	11.69	10.67	10.17	9.91	9.77	9.69
11¾	22.12	14.21	11.85	10.84	10.35	10.10	9.96	9.89
12	22.25	14.35	12.01	11.02	10.54	10.29	10.16	10.09
12¼	22.38	14.50	12.17	11.19	10.72	10.48	10.36	10.29
12½	22.50	14.64	12.33	11.37	10.91	10.66	10.56	10.49
12¾	22.63	14.79	12.49	11.54	11.10	10.87	10.76	10.70
13	22.76	14.94	12.66	11.72	11.28	11.07	10.96	10.90

Figure 8–2

If a loan is amortized, then the monthly payments are calculated to include an additional amount to reduce the principal balance over a period of time.

To use an amortization chart, two of three facts must be known: interest rate and time of loan. In the example we've been using, we know the interest is 12% per annum. We know the loan is to be paid over a 30-year period. Match 12% to 30 years and at the intersection of the chart (see Figure 8–2) you will find $10.29 (per $1,000). If the loan to be obtained is $75,000, then $10.29 × 75 = $771.75, which is the principal and interest payment for 30 years. Suppose a borrower wishes to know how much he or she will pay the lender if no prepayment has been made on the loan. The payment as computed above is $771.75 × 360 months of payments, or $277,830. To compute the amount that would be interest to the lender, subtract the principal amount from the total principal and interest paid.

$277,830
– 75,000
$202,830 interest to be paid to lender

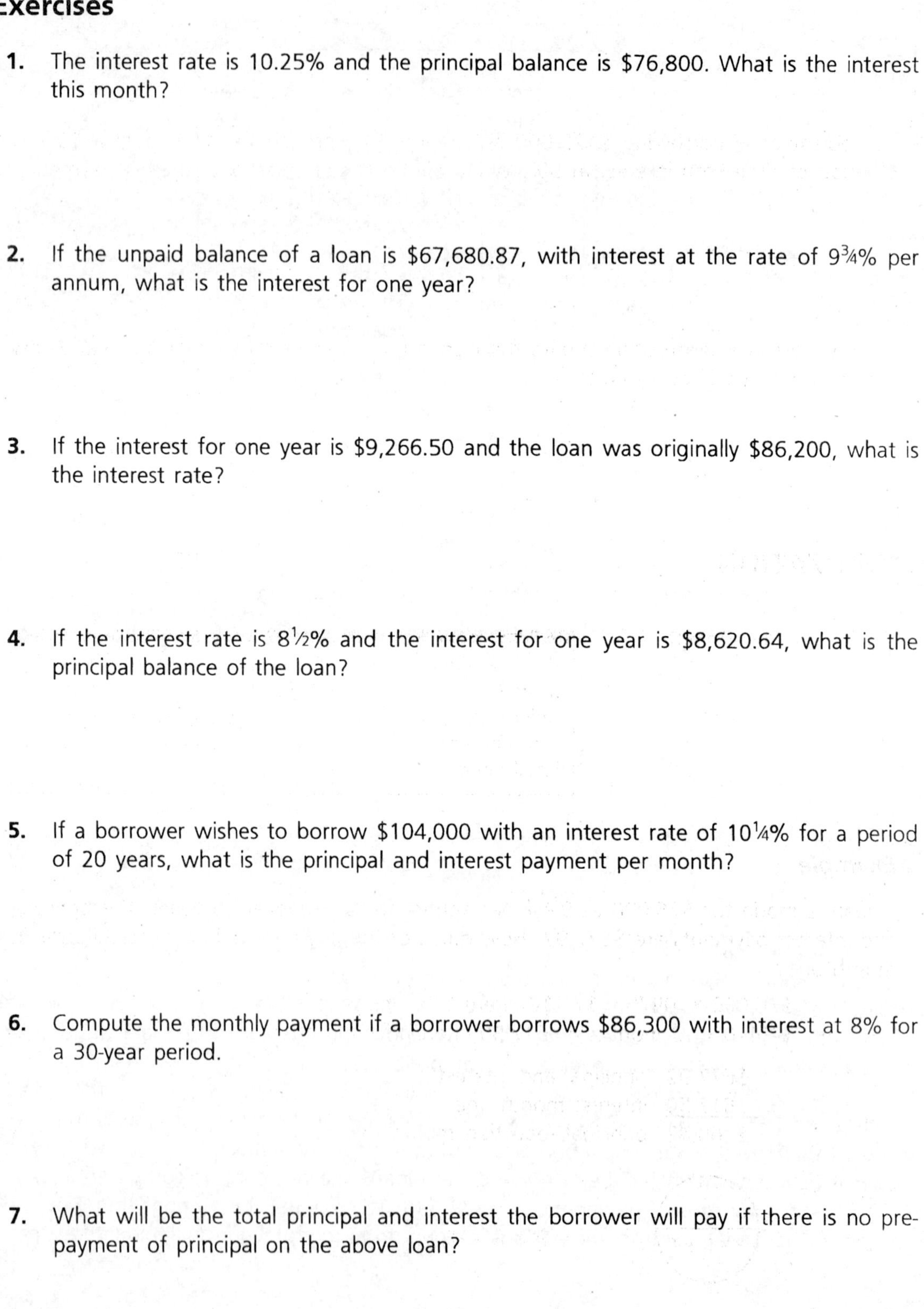

Exercises

1. The interest rate is 10.25% and the principal balance is $76,800. What is the interest this month?

2. If the unpaid balance of a loan is $67,680.87, with interest at the rate of $9\frac{3}{4}\%$ per annum, what is the interest for one year?

3. If the interest for one year is $9,266.50 and the loan was originally $86,200, what is the interest rate?

4. If the interest rate is $8\frac{1}{2}\%$ and the interest for one year is $8,620.64, what is the principal balance of the loan?

5. If a borrower wishes to borrow $104,000 with an interest rate of $10\frac{1}{4}\%$ for a period of 20 years, what is the principal and interest payment per month?

6. Compute the monthly payment if a borrower borrows $86,300 with interest at 8% for a 30-year period.

7. What will be the total principal and interest the borrower will pay if there is no prepayment of principal on the above loan?

8. How much of the above amount will be interest?

9. A borrower is borrowing $125,000 and wants to amortize this loan over a 20-year period of time with interest at 9%. What will be the principal and interest payment?

10. If the borrower in question 9 pays the loan off in 15 years rather than 20 years, how much interest will be saved?

AMORTIZATION

REMEMBER

> When a loan is amortized, interest is included with each payment, along with an additional amount necessary to reduce the principal over a given period of time. So, to *amortize* means to reduce debt based upon a series of equal installments.

Example

A loan is made for $76,000 at 9¾% per annum for a period of 25 years. The principal and interest payments are $677.92. How much of the payment will apply to principal in month one?

$76,000 × .0975 = $7,410 interest for one year
$7,410 ÷ 12 months = $617.50 interest for month one

$677.92	principal and interest
– 617.50	interest month one
$ 60.42	principal reduction month one

I / P × R × T

$I = P \times R \times T$

Example

What is the unpaid balance of the loan after payment one?

$76,000.00 unpaid balance month one
– 60.42 principal reduction
$75.939.58 unpaid balance after month one payment

Example

What is the interest for month two?

$75,939.58 × .0975 = $7404.11
Interest for one year ÷ 12 months = $617.01
The interest for month two is $617.01.

Example

What is the unpaid balance of the loan after payment two?

$677.92 principal and interest
– 617.01 interest month two
$ 60.91 principal reduction month two

$75,939.58 balance
– 60.91 principal reduction
$75,878.67 unpaid balance after month two payment

Example

Based upon an original 30-year loan for $100,000, with interest at 8% per annum and a principal and interest payment of $734.00, what will the loan balance be after three payments?

Month 1: $100,000 × .08 = $8,000/12 = $666.67 month one interest
$734.00 – $666.67 = $67.33 principal month one
$100,000 – $67.33 = $99,932.67 principal balance after month one payment

Month 2: $99,932.67 × .08 = $7,994.61/12 = $666.22 month two interest
$734.00 – $666.22 = $67.78 principal month two
$99,932.67 – $67.78 = $99,864.89 principal balance after month two payment

Month 3: $99,864.89 × .08 = $7,989.19/12 = $665.77 month three interest
$734.00 – $665.77 = $68.23 principal month three
$99,864.89 – $68.23 = $99,796.66 principal balance after month three payment

Many loans allow a buyer to prepay on principal. A borrower thus saves the *offsetting* interest and reduces the loan by the number of months prepaid on the principal.

LOAN AMOUNT	= $	75,000.00
MO. P&I PAYMENT	= $	771.75
TERM IN YEARS	=	29.891
INTEREST RATE	=	12.000%

STARTING MONTH = 9 DAY PAYMENT DUE = 1

IMPOUNDS: TAX 0.00 F/INS. 0.00 MISC 0.00 PYMT 771.75

Date	Interest	Principal	Balance
Sep. 1	750.00	21.75	74,978.25
Oct. 1	749.78	21.97	74,956.28
Nov. 1	749.56	22.19	74,934.09
Dec. 1	749.34	22.41	74,911.68
Jan. 1	749.12	22.63	74,889.05
Feb. 1	748.89	22.86	74,866.19
Mar. 1	748.66	23.09	74,843.10
Apr. 1	748.43	23.32	74,819.78
May 1	748.20	23.55	74,796.23
Jun. 1	747.96	23.79	74,772.44
Jul. 1	747.72	24.03	74,748.41
Aug. 1	747.48	24.27	74,724.14
Sep. 1	747.24	24.51	74,699.63
Oct. 1	747.00	24.75	74,674.88
Nov. 1	746.75	25.00	74,649.88
Dec. 1	746.50	25.25	74,624.63
Jan. 1	746.25	25.50	74,599.13
Feb. 1	745.99	25.76	74,573.37
Mar. 1	745.73	26.02	74,547.35
Apr. 1	745.47	26.28	74,521.07
May 1	745.21	26.54	74,494.53
Jun. 1	744.95	26.80	74,467.73
Jul. 1	744.68	27.07	74,440.66
Aug. 1	744.41	27.34	74,413.32
Sep. 1	744.13	27.62	74,385.70
Oct. 1	743.86	27.89	74,357.81
Nov. 1	743.58	28.17	74,329.64
Dec. 1	743.30	28.45	74,301.19

Figure 8–3

Example

Assume an original loan of $75,000 with interest at 12% per annum and amortized over a 30-year period (actually amortized over 29.891 years). The principal and interest payment is due September 1, 1996. See Figure 8–3 for the amortization schedule through 1998.

Notice that at the end of 1998, the loan balance would be $74,301.19, reflecting $698.81 of principal reduction after two years and four months of payments. Interest paid over that period would total $20,910.19.

Based upon the above information, what will the interest for 30 years be?

$771.75 per month × 360 months = $277,830
$277,830 – $75,000 loan = $202,830

Answer: $202,830 is the interest paid to the lender over a 30-year period if there is no prepayment of principal.

Very little of the payment in the early years of the loan is applied to principal. Assume that the borrower is not too happy with this situation and wishes to reduce not only the number of months paid on the loan but also the interest paid to the lender.

LOAN AMOUNT = $75,000.00
MO. P&I PAYMENT = $ 771.75
TERM IN YEARS = 29.891
INTEREST RATE = 12.000%
STARTING MONTH = 9 DAY PAYMENT DUE = 1
IMPOUNDS: TAX 0.00 F/INS. 0.00 MISC 0.00 PYMT 771.75

	Date		Interest		Principal	Balance
payment 1	Sep. 1		– ~~750.00~~		– –~~21.75~~	74,978.25
	Oct. 1	*save– –>*	– ~~749.78~~	*prepay– –>*	21.97	74,956.28
	Nov. 1	*save– –>*	– –~~749.56~~	*prepay– –>*	22.19	74,934.09
	Dec. 1	*save– –>*	– ~~749.34~~	*prepay– –>*	22.41	74,911.68
payment 2	Jan. 1		– ~~749.12~~		– –~~22.63~~	74,889.05
(pay Oct. 1)	Feb. 1	*save– –>*	– –~~748.89~~	*prepay– –>*	22.86	74,866.19
	Mar. 1	*save– –>*	– ~~748.66~~	*prepay– –>*	23.09	74,843.10
	Apr. 1	*save– –>*	– ~~748.43~~	*prepay– –>*	23.32	74,819.78
payment 3– –	May 1		748.20		23.55	74,796.23
(pay Nov. 1)	Jun. 1		747.96		23.79	74,772.44
	Jul. 1		747.72		24.03	74,748.41
	Aug. 1		747.48		24.27	74,724.14
	Sep. 1		747.24		24.51	74,699.63
etc.– –	Oct. 1		747.00		24.75	74,674.88
	Nov. 1		746.75		25.00	74,649.88
	Dec. 1		746.50		25.25	74,624.63
	Jan. 1		746.25		25.50	74,599.13
	Feb. 1		745.99		25.76	74,573.37
	Mar. 1		745.73		26.02	74,547.35
	Apr. 1		745.47		26.28	74,521.07
	May 1		745.21		26.54	74,494.53
	Jun. 1		744.95		26.80	74,467.73
	Jul. 1		744.68		27.07	74,440.66
	Aug. 1		744.41		27.34	74,413.32
	Sep. 1		744.13		27.62	74,385.70
	Oct. 1		743.86		27.89	74,357.81
	Nov. 1		743.58		28.17	74,329.64
	Dec. 1		743.30		28.45	74,301.19

Figure 8–4

As stated before, the borrower may *prepay* principal payments *only* and save the offsetting interest.

Say that the borrower sends the regular payment of $771.75 for payment number one. Assume he or she can afford about $75 additional each month and sends the principal payment for month two of $21.97, month three of $22.19, and month four of $22.41, or *$66.57* extra, to be applied to principal reduction only. The borrower will now scratch through all *four* payments and has saved the *offsetting* interest for month two of $749.78, month three of $749.56, and month four of $749.34, or *$2,248.68* by prepaying principal of $66.57.

It is very important to remember that *a payment must still be made every month.* Therefore, month number two, which is October 1, 1996, the borrower will be paying the January 1, 1997 payment, and the unpaid balance will be $74,889.05. Payment two is $771.75, which pays interest of $749.12 due to the lender because the borrower has used the lender's money for the *second* month. The borrower now prepays the principal for payments six, seven, and eight, or $22.86 plus $23.09 plus $23.32, or $69.27, and has saved the offsetting interest of $2,245.98, never to be recuperated by the lender. The borrower now scratches through those payments and payment number three, which is due November 1, 1996; the borrower has moved to the May 1, 1997, payment (see Figure 8–4).

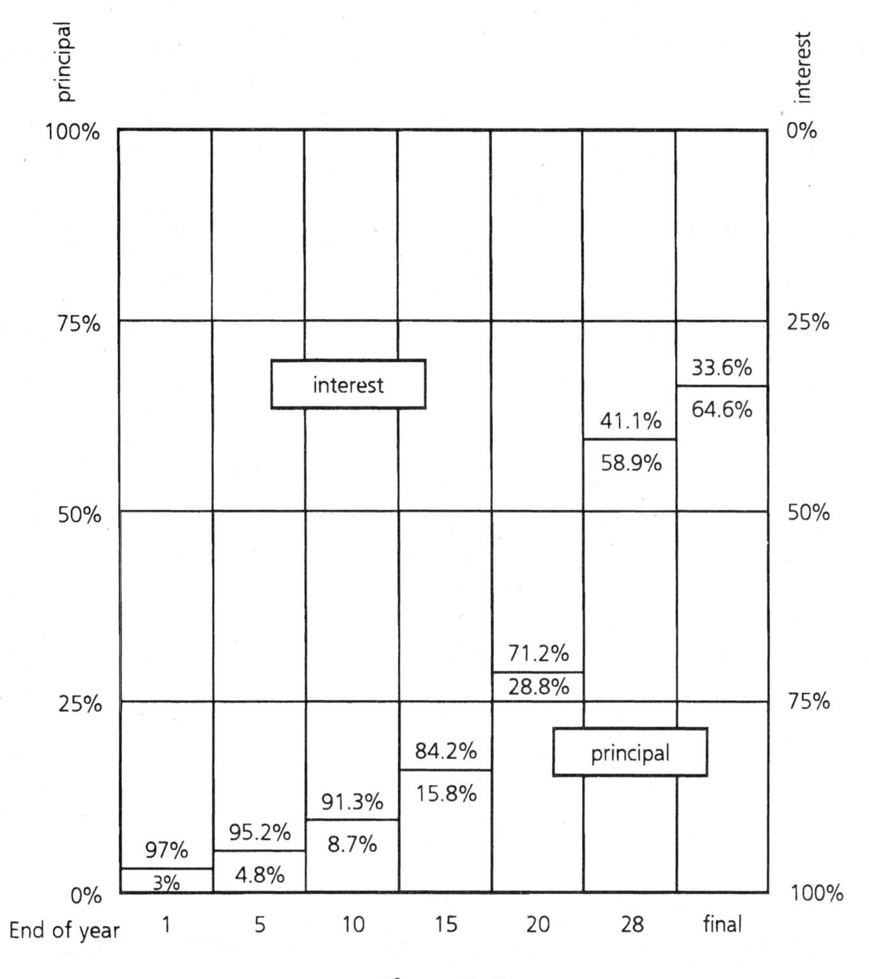

Figure 8–5

A borrower may set up any plan for prepayment as long as it is not prohibited by the mortgage/trust deed agreement. FHA and VA loans can be prepaid without penalty. Many conventional loans will limit prepayment to not more than 20% of principal in any one year. Therefore, 20% principal repayment × 5 years = entire loan payoff. So, even with limitations, the possibilities are astounding.

Many people are concerned about the interest write-off benefits for federal taxation purposes. Remember, a payment can never be skipped. Therefore, a borrower will pay 12 payments every year, which equals 12 months of interest write-off. Figure 8–5 shows the principal and interest paid as a percentage, if there are no prepayments of principal.

The principal and interest payments are equal to each other after about 24 years, at which time the principal portion increases rapidly and interest decreases in the same amount.

Exercises

For questions 1–7 use the following information: A property sells and appraises for $105,000. The lender is willing to make a loan of 80% of the appraisal.

1. What is the loan amount?

2. The interest on the loan is 12%. What is the annual interest?

3. What is the interest payment for payment number one?

4. Based upon the information in Figure 8–2, what is the principal and interest payment if the loan is amortized over 25 years?

5. How much of payment number one is applied to principal?

6. How much of payment number two is applied to principal?

7. If the borrower never prepays on the loan, how much interest will be paid?

8. Mr. Samuels had a loan for $50,000 at 14% interest. At the end of five years he had reduced the principal by 3.7%. The payments are $667.85 per month. How much of the payment went to principal in the first month of the sixth year?

9. Mr. and Mrs. Colby purchased a home for $109,000. They borrowed 80% of the purchase price from a savings and loan at 9½% interest, amortized over 30 years, payable in installments of $733.35 per month. They borrowed 10% of the purchase price from the seller at 8½% interest, amortized over 10 years, payable in installments of $135.16 per month. What will be the total principal and interest payments if there is no prepayment of the loan?

10. How much would Mr. and Mrs. Colby save in interest if they paid off the 30-year loan in 20 years?

ADD-ON INTEREST

Add-on interest is usually not used for real estate, but is commonly used for financing the purchase of chattel, such as automobiles or furniture. Interest is computed on the total principal amount *borrowed* and added on to that amount *before* the payments are applied.

Example

An automobile is purchased for $12,000. The payments will be made over a 36-month period. The interest is 9.9%. The amount due the lender in the beginning of the loan is $15,564.

$12,000 × .099 = $1,188
$1,188 × 3 years = $3,564
$12,000 + $3,564 = $15,564

Early prepayment *does not* save interest.

Exercises

1. A dining room set is financed for three years at a cost of $1,485. The interest is 14% add-on. What is the beginning balance of the loan?

2. An automobile is purchased and financed for $21,000 at 8% interest. How much must be paid back if the loan is amortized over five years?

3. What will the monthly payments be?

POINTS

One point is equal to 1% of a loan amount. The purpose of points is to equalize the yield received by the lender when the lender feels he or she is making a loan at an interest rate that is less than the market rate. Interest rates are determined by supply and demand and in some cases limited by government regulations.

REMEMBER

> A rule of thumb used to determine points is that for every ⅛% loss of interest by a lender, the "discount" should be 1% of the loan or one percentage point. This rule is based upon the theory that most loans are paid off in an average of eight years.

Example

An investor could place a loan of $60,000 at market rates of 10%. A borrower wishes a 9% loan. How many points will the lender charge?

$$\begin{array}{r} 10\% \\ -\ 9\% \\ \hline 1 \end{array} = \frac{1}{1} = \frac{8}{8}$$

In order to offset 1% loss of interest, the lender needs ⁸⁄₈% or 8 points.

$60,000 × .08 = $4,800

Discount points are paid on the original loan amount. They may be paid by either buyer or seller, split between the two, or by any other agreement unless the law prohibits one or the other from paying. When buyers or sellers pay discount points, they are paying prepaid interest to the lender.

Exercises

1. The borrower will accept a loan of $70,000 with 9½% interest. The market rate is 10%. Using the rule of thumb, how much will the lender charge in discount points?

2. If market interest is 10% and a borrower wishes to borrow $95,000 at 9¼%, what will the lender charge in discount points?

3. The loan is $60,000 and current interest rates are 11%. The borrower wishes to borrow at 10¼%. What will be the discount charged?

LOAN SERVICE FEES

Lenders charge a loan service fee to process a loan. Such a fee is usually 1% to 2% of the loan and is normally paid by the buyer at closing. This is also referred to as a loan processing or a loan origination fee. It pays the lender for the costs involved in processing the loan.

CHAPTER TEST

1. A loan has an unpaid balance after the July 1 payment of $162,680.52. The interest rate is 9%. The borrower's payments are $1,542 including principal and interest. What will the principal balance be after the September 1 payment?

2. A loan is made in the amount of $92,500. The interest for the first month is $674.48. What is the interest rate?

3. Interest paid for one year is $10,280. The interest rate is 12%. What is the principal balance of the loan?

4. Smith borrows $60,250 with interest at the rate of 11% per annum and amortized over a 20-year period. Using Figure 8–2, what are Smith's principal and interest payments?

5. Based upon the information in question 4, if Smith never prepays on his principal, what will he pay the lender in interest over the 20-year period?

6. Based upon the rule of thumb given in the text material, if the market interest rate is 10½% but the buyer requires a 10% interest rate in order to qualify for the loan, how much will be paid to the lender in discount points?

7. If the loan is $108,200, the discount points are 6% to be split between buyer and seller, the loan service fee is 2% and the buyer's other closing costs are $1,100, how much does the buyer need to close the transaction?

8. A sale was made for $90,000. The borrower was able to borrow 80% of the sale price. The discount paid by the buyer was 3¾% and the loan service fee was 2%. What were the total charges to the buyer?

9. A home was sold for $105,000 with the buyer securing a 90% loan. The seller paid $2,835 in discount points. How many points were paid?

10. The interest paid for the first month is $682.60. The loan is for 80% of the appraised value of the property and the interest rate is 11%. What is the appraised value?

11. A property is purchased for $125,000. The purchaser pays $25,000 down and requires an 80% loan to value. However, the appraisal is only $119,000. How much is the loan service fee if the lender requires 1½%?

Use the information in question 11 to answer questions 12–13.

12. How much is the buyer short of the required down payment?

13. The seller agrees to finance the difference that the purchaser is lacking in down payment, but only if the buyer agrees to pay add-on interest of 10%. How much will the buyer pay if the loan is paid off in four years?

9

Appraisal Math

Goals

1. Understand the three approaches to value.
2. Know the amount and types of data needed to complete an assignment.
3. Compute problems related to the approaches to value.
4. Know that an appraisal is an estimate or opinion of value.

The purpose of this chapter is to demonstrate some of the mathematics applicable to each of the three traditional approaches to value, i.e., the cost approach, the market or sales comparison approach, and the income approach.

The methods and techniques illustrated are introductory in nature. The serious student of appraisal is advised to pursue the courses offered by the various appraisal organizations and to use the additional study materials available.

Whenever possible and appropriate, the practitioner will utilize all three approaches to arrive at an estimate of value. The value indications disclosed by each will provide a range of value. The appraiser will then analyze and review the data in each approach, giving the greatest weight to the approach that contains the best data and is most applicable to the valuation problem at hand, rather than using an average calculated from the three approaches.

THE COST APPROACH

The cost approach is based on the estimated cost to build the improvements as of the date of the appraisal, with an allowance for accrued depreciation and the contributory value of the site. The construction cost figures may be obtained from local contractors or from various construction cost services, such as Marshall and Swift, Means, or Boeckh.

The Cost Approach Formula

cost new of improvements – depreciation + site value = indicated value

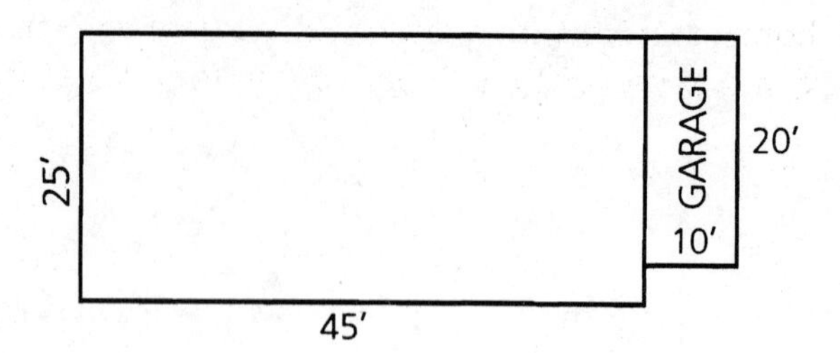

Measurements

The first step in applying the cost approach formula is to measure the exterior of the improvements to find the size or area of the building, patios, porches, basement, etc., as in the following diagram.

The second step is to multiply the area or volume by the appropriate cost figures.

House: 25 × 45 = 1,125 sq. ft. × $35.00	=	$39,375
Garage: 10 × 20 = 200 sq. ft. × $12.00		2,400
		$41,775 total value

Exercise 1

1. Find the area of this one-story house in square feet.

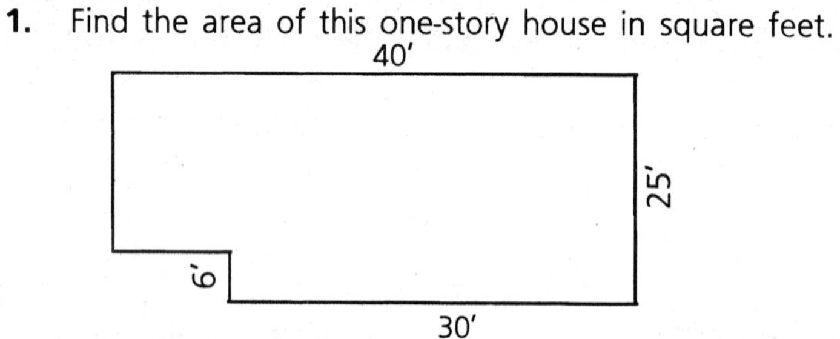

2. Find the area of this two-story house in square feet.

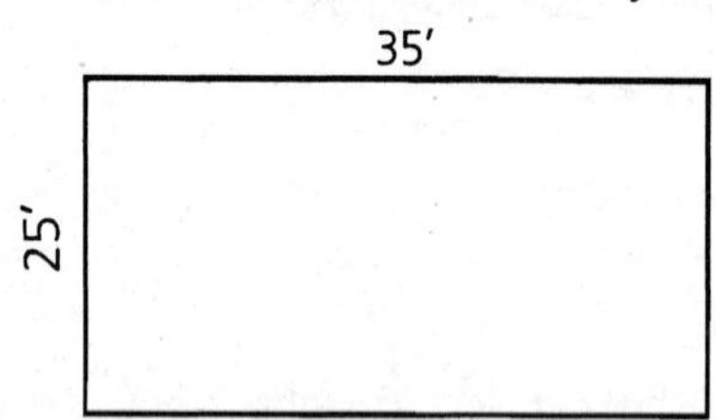

3. If the above two-story house costs $35 per square foot to build and has a two-car attached garage 20 ft. × 20 ft. with a cost of $12 per square foot, what is the indicated cost new of the improvements?

4. Using the two-story home featured in question 2, assume the property has a full, finished basement with a cost factor of $10 per square foot. What is the total cost of the improvement?

Accrued Depreciation

The third step in the cost approach is the estimate of accrued depreciation. This requires an estimate of economic or useful life and an estimate of effective age. *Economic life* is the period of time over which the improvements contribute to the value of a property. *Effective age* is the age the improvements appear to be. This is based on observed condition and comparison of the subject property to other properties. The effective age may be the same as, more than, or less than actual age.

In the age/life method of estimating depreciation, the annual rate of depreciation is found by dividing 1 or 100 by the economic life and then multiplying the result by the effective age.

100 ÷ 50 years economic life = 2% depreciation per year
100 ÷ 40 years economic life = 2.5% depreciation per year
100 ÷ 20 years economic life = 5% depreciation per year

For the first example, using an effective age of 10 years and an annual rate of depreciation of 2%, the total accrued depreciation expressed as a percent is 2% × 10 years = 20% total accrued depreciation.

To convert the accrued depreciation into dollars, the cost new is multiplied by the percent of accrued depreciation.

```
cost new $60,000
         ×   .20
         $12,000  accrued depreciation
         $60,000
         -12,000
         $48,000  current value of improvements
```

Exercise 2

1. The cost to reproduce a building is $125,000. The economic life is 45 years. What is the annual rate of depreciation in dollars?

2. In the previous problem, if the effective age is five years, find the loss from depreciation attributable to the building.

3. Given an economic life of 45 years, find the annual rate of depreciation.

4. Using an economic life of 40 years, find the annual rate of depreciation and the total accrued depreciation at the end of seven years.

5. If the cost new of the building in the previous problem is $55,000, find the total accrued depreciation in dollars at the end of seven years.

Site Value

The fourth step in the cost approach is the estimate of site value. Site value is estimated by analyzing similar site sales in the area as they compare to the subject site, with plus or minus adjustments as shown in the following example:

	Sale Price	Size	Location	Value
Sale #1	$15,000	+10%	–0–	$16,500
Sale #2	$18,000	–0–	–5%	$17,100
Sale #3	$16,000	+5%	–0–	$16,800
Sale #4	$20,000	–0–	–10%	$18,000

Each sale is compared to the subject property, and plus or minus adjustments are made for any inferior or superior item or characteristic. In this example, sale #1 is inferior to the subject in size, sale #2 is superior to the subject in location, sale #3 is inferior to the subject in size, and sale #4 is superior to the subject in location.

The final value estimate is not a result of calculating an average of the market value figures. The appraiser will review each sale, consider first those sales that required the *least net adjustment* and the *least number of adjustments*. On this basis, the above example would provide a value indication of $17,000, with the greatest weight given to sales 2 and 3.

Exercise 3

1. The cost new of a home is $75,000, and the site value is 25% of total property value. What is the site value in dollars?

2. Using the cost new of $75,000, an economic life of 60 years, and an effective age of five years, what is the value of the property with the site value from exercise 1?

MARKET OR SALES COMPARISON APPROACH

This approach is a process of comparing actual sales of similar properties to the property being appraised. The comparisons are made by a series of plus or minus adjustments *applied to the comparable sales.*

Adjustments are made for the variations in location, date of sale, physical characteristics, financing, size, or any other variable which is present.

REMEMBER

> The adjustments are always made to the comparable sale, not the subject property. The subject property always represents 100% or the norm. The comparable sales will be less than 100% or inferior to the subject, requiring a plus adjustment, or more than 100% or superior to the subject, requiring a minus adjustment.

Example

Assume that you are appraising an average quality, 10-year-old home and have obtained three comparable sales.

Data	**Comp. 1**	**Comp. 2**	**Comp. 3**
Sale Price	$120,000	$114,000	$102,000
Location	Superior	Similar	Similar
Size	Similar	Superior	Inferior
Condition	Superior	Similar	Inferior

Adjustments obtained from the market: location $8,000; size $6,000; condition $2,000.

Answer:

Data	**Comp. 1**	**Comp. 2**	**Comp. 3**
Sale Price	$120,000	$114,000	$102,000
Location	– 8,000	–0–	–0–
Size	–0–	– 6,000	+ 6,000
Condition	– 2,000	–0–	+ 2,000
Net Adjustment	– 10,000	– 6,000	+ 8,000
Value Range	$110,000	$108,000	$110,000

The subject property's indicated value = $108,000.
Comparable Sale 2 required the least net adjustment and the least number of individual adjustments. (Adjustments may be made as percentages or in dollar amounts. Dollar amounts are usually preferred.)

Sequence of Adjustments

When percentage adjustments are used alone or in combination with dollar adjustments, the recommended sequence of adjustments is as follows:

1. Property rights appraised
2. Financing terms
3. Conditions of sale
4. Market conditions
5. Location
6. Physical characteristics

Whatever method is used, the adjustments must be consistently applied to each comparable sale.

The following adjustment grid is part of the sales comparison analysis section of the Uniform Residential Appraisal Report. The grid shows those variables that are typically adjusted for when completing a residential appraisal.

Partial Reproduction of the URAR Form.

SALES COMPARISON ANALYSIS

ITEM	SUBJECT	COMPARABLE NO. 1		COMPARABLE NO. 2		COMPARABLE NO. 3	
Address							
Proximity to Subject							
Sales Price	$		$		$		$
Price/Gross Liv. Area	$ ¢	$ ¢		$ ¢		$ ¢	
Data and/or Verification Source							
VALUE ADJUSTMENTS	DESCRIPTION	DESCRIPTION	+ (-) $ Adjustment	DESCRIPTION	+ (-) $ Adjustment	DESCRIPTION	+ (-) $ Adjustment
Sales or Financing Concessions							
Date of Sale/Time							
Location							
Leasehold/Fee Simple							
Site							
View							
Design and Appeal							
Quality of Construction							
Age							
Condition							
Above Grade Room Count	Total : Bdrms : Baths	Total : Bdrms : Baths		Total : Bdrms : Baths		Total : Bdrms : Baths	
Gross Living Area	Sq. Ft.	Sq. Ft.		Sq. Ft.		Sq. Ft.	
Basement & Finished Rooms Below Grade							
Functional Utility							
Heating/Cooling							
Energy Efficient Items							
Garage/Carport							
Porch, Patio, Deck, Fireplace(s), etc.							
Fence, Pool, etc.							
Net Adj. (total)		+ -	$	+ -	$	+ -	$
Adjusted Sales Price of Comparable			$		$		$

Figure 9–1

Exercise 1

1. The subject property has a one-car garage, and the comparable sale has a two-car garage. What is the correct adjustment?

2. Which of the following is true?

   a. The subject is 100%.
   b. The subject is inferior or superior to the comparable sale.
   c. The subject is the norm that is being sought.
   d. All of the above.

3. Indicate the appropriate adjustments in the third column.

Subject Property	Comparable Property	Adjustment + – ?
1. Patio	No patio	
2. No fireplace	Fireplace	
3. Garage	No garage	
4. Full basement	Full basement	

INCOME APPROACH

The first part of this section deals with the income approach as applied to single-family residential properties up to and including four rental units.

Single-Family Properties

This type of property utilizes a gross rent multiplier and the estimated economic rent for the subject property. The multiplier and income can be developed on a monthly or annual basis. This is accomplished by obtaining the rental rates from competing properties in the area. The rental rates can be analyzed on a basis of rent per square foot, per room, or per unit.

1. *Per square foot.* A 1,000 sq. ft. house rents for $450 per month. The rental rate per square foot is $450 ÷ 1,000 = $.45 per sq. ft. per month.
2. *Per room.* A six-room house rents for $450 per month. The rate per room each month is $450 ÷ 6 = $75 per room.
3. *Per unit.* This is the total rental rate per unit, $450 for this example.

Gross Rent Multiplier

The next step is the determination of the appropriate multiplier. To abstract this data from the market, the appraiser analyzes recent sales of similar properties that were rented at the time of sale. The relationship between the rental rate and the sales price is then determined by the following formula:

sale price ÷ gross income = gross rent multiplier

	Sale Price		Monthly Income		GRM
Sale #1	$50,000	÷	$450.00	=	111.11
Sale #2	$45,000	÷	$450.00	=	100.00
Sale #3	$55,000	÷	$500.00	=	110.00
Sale #4	$47,500	÷	$425.00	=	111.76
Sale #5	$50,000	÷	$475.00	=	105.26

The multiplier may be obtained on either a monthly or annual basis and must be consistently applied to monthly or annual income.

The above example provides a range of multipliers from the neighborhood. From this data the applicable factor is arrived at by giving the most weight to sales that are most similar to the subject property, followed by those factors which appear most often in the data.

Sales 1, 3, and 4 disclose a tight range of 110 to 111.76. Assuming that these sales are most comparable to the appraised property, a monthly gross rent multiplier of 110 could be selected. With the economic rent of $450 per month, the value indicated by this method is

$450 × 110 = $49,500

To find an annual multiplier:

	Sale Price		Annual Income		GRM
Sale #1	$250,000	÷	$24,850	=	10.06
Sale #2	$280,000	÷	$26,420	=	10.59
Sale #3	$190,000	÷	$21,240	=	8.94
Sale #4	$210,000	÷	$22,650	=	9.27
Sale #5	$240,000	÷	$23,250	=	10.32

The gross rent multiplier of 10 would be applicable. With the economic rent of $25,350 per year, the value indicated by this method is

$25,350 × 10 = $253,500

Examples

1. A property is poorly located on a busy street. Due to the location, the property suffers a rental loss of $25 per month. The annual gross rent multiplier is 9.0. What is the loss in value?

$25 per month × 12 months = $300 annual income loss

$300 × 9.0 = $2,700 = loss in value

2. You are appraising a small income property for an owner, who is considering a remodeling program. The owner requests that you consider the potential increase in income and value compared to the cost of the improvements. The monthly gross rent multiplier is 100. With the following rent increases and cost figures, should the owner make the proposed changes?

	Increase in Rent	Cost
1. Add appliances	$30 per month	$2,500
2. Add a bath	$10 per month	$1,500
3. Add a garage	$40 per month	$3,000

a. $30 × 100 = $3,000 increase in value

b. $10 × 100 = $1,000 increase in value

c. $40 × 100 = $4,000 increase in value

Choices a and c are economically feasible; the increase in value exceeds the cost. Choice b should be abandoned; cost exceeds the increase in value.

Exercise 1 GRM

1. A property suffers a loss in income of $200 per month due to poor condition. Using a gross monthly rent multiplier of 110.00, find the amount of depreciation due to condition.

2. Market rent on a property is $850 per month. The gross annual multiplier based upon comparables is 9.0. What is the indicated value of the property?

3. Select a gross rent multiplier from the following comparable sales. The annual income from the subject property is $22,800. What is the indicated value?

	Sale Price	Annual Gross Income
Sale #1	$190,000	$23,750
Sale #2	$178,000	$22,250
Sale #3	$210,000	$26,250
Sale #4	$178,600	$22,325

Larger Income-Producing Properties

The analysis of larger income-producing properties is accomplished by a process of converting an income stream into a lump sum capital value, referred to as *capitalization*, utilizing the net annual operating income and an appropriate capitalization rate. The basic capitalization formula

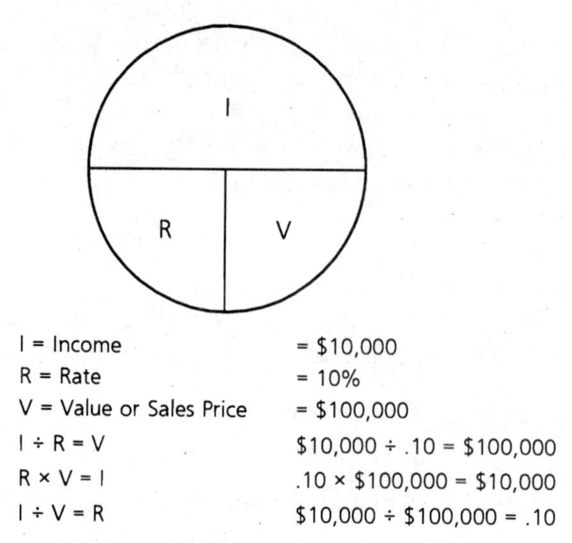

Figure 9–2

is known as "IRV," and this formula can provide any of the components needed to solve a particular problem, as shown in Figure 9–2.

REMEMBER

> The overall capitalization rate includes a return *on* investment and a return *of* investment. Improved real estate is a wasting asset. The investor must be compensated for the wearing out of the improvements. This is accomplished by adding a *return of investment,* or recapture rate, to the investor's risk interest rate or *return on investment*. The total of the two components is *the overall capitalization rate*.

Example

A review of money market conditions and the returns available on alternative investments discloses that a reasonable return on an investment is 8%. The property being considered has a remaining economic life of 25 years. The *recapture rate* or *return of investment* is 1 or 100 ÷ by 25 years = 4% return of investment.

Answer: The total capitalization rate is 8% + 4% = 12%.

Steps in the Income Approach

The first step in the income approach is the determination of the net annual operating income for the property being appraised. An operating statement is developed as follows:

market rent
×
number of units
=
scheduled gross income
−
vacancy and collection losses

=

effective gross income

−

operating expenses

=

net operating income

÷

capitalization rate

=

value indication via income approach

Example

Assume an appraisal of a 15-unit apartment building with economic rent per unit of $350 per month, or $63,000 per year, and an annual vacancy and collection loss of 5%. The operating expenses are

Taxes	$10,000
Insurance	800
Management	3,000
Repairs	1,500
Utilities	2,000
	$17,300

Answer:		
	Gross annual income	$63,000
	Less: vacancy and collection loss	3,150
	Equals effective gross income	$59,850
	Less annual operating expenses	17,300
	Equals net operating income	$42,550

The next step is obtaining the capitalization rate to be applied to the net operating income to arrive at the indicated value.

One source of capitalization rates is actual sales of similar income properties obtained by market research. This is a process of analyzing sold properties and their net operating income at the time of sale. When these data are compiled, the IRV formula is applied to disclose the capitalization rate at which the property sold:

income ÷ by sale price = rate (I ÷ SP = R)

Example

	Net Operating Income		Sale Price		Rate
Sale #1	$40,670	÷	$415,000	=	.098
Sale #2	$48,200	÷	$482,000	=	.10
Sale #3	$45,700	÷	$430,000	=	.106
Sale #4	$52,800	÷	$512,600	=	.103

Assuming the subject property is most similar to sales 1 and 2 and using a cap rate of .10, what is the indicated value of the property?

$42,550 ÷ .10 = $425,500 or rounded to $426,000

Answer: $426,000 is the indicated value of the property.

Figure 9–3, a property operating statement, was developed for a 50-unit apartment building. After deducting the vacancy and collection loss and all expenses from the gross income, the net operating income to be capitalized is $76,950.

If the appraiser concludes that the appropriate rate is 10%, the value provided by this

PROPERTY OPERATING STATEMENT

Gross Annual Income			
Market or economic income			
50 2 bedroom units @ $300 per month			
50 × $300 × 12 months			$180,000
Less: Vacancy & Collection Loss 5%			– 9,000
			171,000
Plus: Other Income (parking, laundry, etc.)			+ 5,000
Effective Annual Income			$176,000
Expenses			
Fixed expenses			
Real estate taxes	$20,000		
Insurance	2,000		
		$22,000	
Operating expenses			
Management 7%	$12,320		
Water and sewer	9,000		
Gas	12,000		
Electric	14,000		
Trash collection	1,200		
Maintenance	15,000		
Advertising	500		
Audit – legal	2,500		
		$66,520	
Reserves for replacement			
Roof	$ 3,000		
Heat/AC	3,000		
Hot water	530		
Floor cover	2,000		
Appliances	2,000		
		$10,530	
Annual expenses and reserves			$ 99,050
net annual income to be capitalized			$ 76,950

Figure 9–3

approach is

$76,950 ÷ .10 = $769,500

This is known as the property residual, or direct capitalization, method and takes into consideration the whole of the income stream, which is capitalized into value. The technique is effective and can be supported by market evidence.

There are many methods and techniques within the income approach that are available to the appraiser. The result of the income capitalization approach is the present value of the future benefit, consisting of the income stream and the reversion. The reversion might be the return of the property to the owner at the expiration of a lease, proceeds of resale at the end of a holding period, or any whole or partial interest or site value, to be returned in the future.

The technique used will vary depending upon the appraisal problem, which might require discounted cash flows, mortgage equity analyses, property residual, or leased fee valuation. These advanced topics are beyond the scope of this chapter.

Exercise 2 IRV

1. A property has a value of $150,000 with a capitalization rate of 7%. What is the value with a cap rate of 9%?

2. A property suffers a loss in income of $35 per month due to an adverse location. Using a cap rate of 12%, what is the loss in value?

3. A property is sold for $200,000 with a net annual income of $15,000. What is the cap rate?

4. A property generates a scheduled gross income of $45,000. Vacancy and collection loss is 5% of gross income, and expenses are 35% of effective gross income. Using a cap rate of 11.5, what is the property value?

5. A property sold at a 12% cap rate. The property had a remaining economic life of 20 years. What is the *return on* investment?

6. A property sold at a 12% cap rate. The return on investment is 8%. What is the remaining economic life?

RATES AND RATIOS

The *debt coverage ratio* is used to determine whether the net operating income anticipated from a property will be adequate to cover the debt service. The formula is

net operating income (NOI) ÷ debt service (DS) = debt coverage ratio

NOI $50,000 ÷ DS $40,000 = 1.25 debt coverage ratio

The debt coverage ratio indicates a net cash flow to the investor after all expenses and principal and interest payments are paid.

Expense ratio analysis provides a means of comparing the efficiency of various properties and determining typical operating costs. The formula is

operating expenses ÷ effective gross income

	Building A	**Building B**	**Building C**	**Building D**
Effective gross income	$60,000	$72,000	$55,000	$65,000
Operating expenses	$25,800	$29,500	$24,500	$28,600

Building A $25,800 ÷ $60,000 = .43 = operating ratio
Building B $29,500 ÷ $72,000 = .41 = operating ratio
Building C $24,500 ÷ $55,000 = .45 = operating ratio
Building D $28,600 ÷ $65,000 = .44 = operating ratio

The *loan-to-value ratio* expresses the relationship between the amount borrowed and the value of the property. The formula is

mortgage amount ÷ value = loan to value

$124,000 ÷ $175,000 = .71 or 71% = loan-to-value ratio

ECONOMIC RENT

An analysis of the rents generated by competing properties will provide an indication of the potential income for a property being evaluated.

Property No.	**1**	**2**	**3**	**4**
annual gross rent	$50,000	$55,000	$40,000	$48,000
number of units	15	18	12	14
number of rooms	45	54	36	42
bldg. area sq. ft.	9,000	10,800	7,200	8,400
annual rent per unit	$3,333	$3,056	$3,333	$3,429
per room	$1,111	$1,018	$1,111	$1,143
per square foot	$5.56	$5.09	$5.56	$5.71

annual rent per unit	= gross income divided by the number of units
per room	= gross income divided by the number of rooms
per square foot	= gross income divided by the square footage of building area

The *profit margin* provides a rate or relationship between the cash flow to be received and the effective gross income. The formula is

cash flow ÷ effective gross income = profit margin

cash flow $6,000 ÷ EGI $19,000 = .32 or 32% = profit margin

Return on equity investment relates to the net cash flow, either before or after income taxes, to the equity investment or down payment.

cash flow $6,000 ÷ equity $45,000 = .13 or 13% =
return on equity or cash return on cash investment

The *break-even ratio* indicates the ability of an investment to cover all operating expenses and debt services (mortgage payments). The formula is

operating expenses + debt service ÷ effective gross income

	Building 1	**Building 2**	**Building 3**	**Building 4**
Effective gross income	$75,000	$80,000	$90,000	$50,000
Operating expenses	$26,000	$28,000	$36,000	$21,000
Debt service	$40,000	$48,000	$54,000	$30,000

Bldg. 1 $26,000 + $40,000 = $66,000 ÷ $75,000 = .88
Bldg. 2 $28,000 + $48,000 = $76,000 ÷ $80,000 = .95
Bldg. 3 $36,000 + $54,000 = $90,000 ÷ $90,000 = 1.00
Bldg. 4 $21,000 + $30,000 = $51,000 ÷ $50,000 = 1.02

Buildings 1 and 2 produce a net cash flow to the investor after all expenses and debt service.
Building 3 is breaking even.
Building 4 is operating at deficit.

The *payback period* indicates the time period over which the property will return the equity investment. The formula is

investment cost or down payment ÷ net annual cash flow after all expenses and debt service have been paid.

equity invested $60,000 ÷ annual net cash flow $5,000 = 12 years payback period

This simplified method does not consider the tax aspects of the investment but is useful as a quick analysis of a property.

Exercises

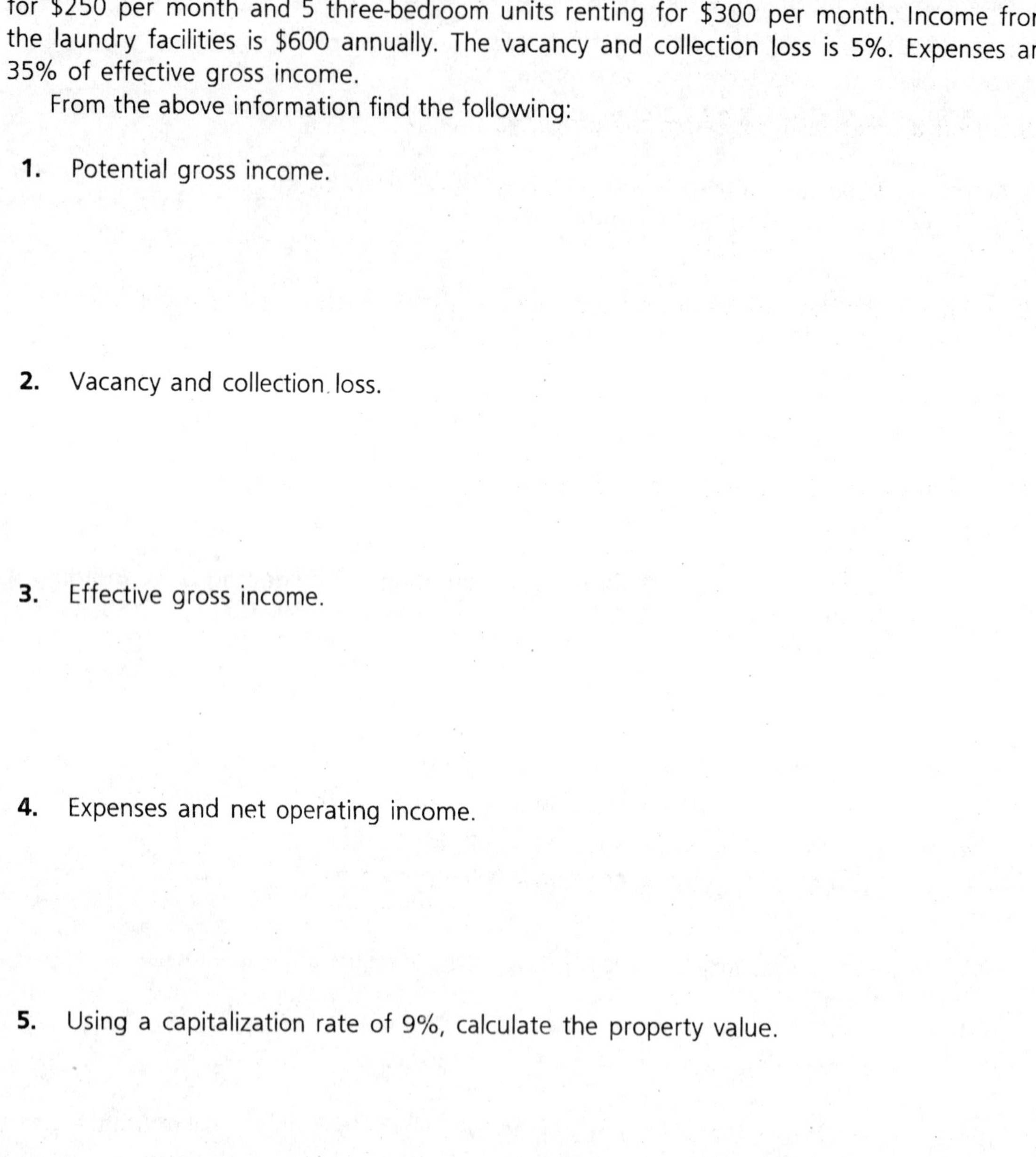

You are appraising a 20-unit apartment building consisting of 15 two-bedroom units renting for $250 per month and 5 three-bedroom units renting for $300 per month. Income from the laundry facilities is $600 annually. The vacancy and collection loss is 5%. Expenses are 35% of effective gross income.

From the above information find the following:

1. Potential gross income.

2. Vacancy and collection loss.

3. Effective gross income.

4. Expenses and net operating income.

5. Using a capitalization rate of 9%, calculate the property value.

6. Using an annual gross rent multiplier of 6.9, calculate the property value.

7. Assuming a loan for 65% of property value, amortized over 25 years with a mortgage interest rate of 9%, find the annual debt service and the down payment or equity investment. Use the average of the value indications arrived at in exercises 5 and 6 as a basis for the loan.

8. Find the net cash flow from the property.

9. What is the net cash return on the equity investment, expressed as a percentage?

10. Calculate the profit margin and debt coverage ratio.

CHAPTER TEST

1. The formula for the cost approach is a.________________ b.________________

   c.________________.

2. If a property suffers a loss of $10 per month in rental income due to condition, what is the loss in value with an annual gross rent multiplier of 12.0?

3. If the annual net loss in income is $1,200, what is the loss in value with a capitalization rate of 9.5?

4. Effective gross income is the income received after ________________ and ________________ have been deducted from scheduled gross income.

5. If a property produces a scheduled gross income of $50,000, with vacancy and collection loss of 5% and operating expenses of 35%, what is the net operating income?

6. In the above example, if the property value is $310,000, what is the capitalization rate?

7. An investor paid $450,000 for an office building. The land value is $90,000. The economic life of the building is 30 years. What is the value at the end of 10 years?

8. The cost to build a two-story home is $45 per square foot. The exterior dimensions of the home are 40 × 28. The site value is $25,000. Accrued depreciation is 10% of cost new. What is the value using the cost approach?

9. A property has a value of $60,000. The land value is $18,000, and the cost new of the improvements is $47,000. What is the total accrued depreciation?

10. An investor purchased a property for $400,000 and obtained a mortgage for 60% of the purchase price. The property generates a net operating income of $30,000. What is the return to the equity investment as a percent?

11. In question 10, if the annual debt service is $25,000, what is the debt coverage ratio?

12. In question 10, if effective gross income is $60,000, what is the expense ratio?

13. The basic capitalization formula is referred to as "IRV." Which of the following variations is *incorrect*?

    a. V × I = R

    b. I ÷ V = R

    c. I ÷ R = V

    d. R × V = I

14. The income from a property is $15,000 per year. Expenses are $6,000. The sale price was $85,000. What is the capitalization rate?

15. A property value is $125,000. The investor obtained a 70% loan, payable at $750 per month. The property produces a net income of $15,000. What is the before-tax net return to the equity investment, expressed as a percent?

10
REAL ESTATE PRORATIONS

Goals

1. Understand the proration process.
2. Compute prorations.
3. Apply the computation to a buyer and seller settlement sheet.
4. Understand debit and credit procedure.

To *prorate* means to make a proportionate distribution and to allocate an expense, whether paid in advance or in arrears, to the proper party.

Items to be prorated can be paid in advance or in arrears. When paid in arrears the current period cannot be paid until the end of the period. When items are paid in arrears the seller is debited with his or her portion of the item and the buyer is credited. At the end of the period, the buyer is responsible for payment. If payment is made in advance, the seller is credited with the unused portion of the item and the buyer debited.

States vary in custom and by contract as to how prorations are handled. In the examples that follow, unless otherwise specified, we will use actual days in each month and, 365 days in each year, and the buyer will pay the date of closing.

Examples of items to be prorated are

1. Real estate taxes
2. Property insurance
3. Rents
4. Water and sewer charges
5. Mortgage interest

REAL ESTATE TAXES

General ad valorem taxes are the regular, recurring real property taxes imposed on all privately owned properties each year. The amount of the tax is based on the value of the property. Indeed, *ad valorem* is a Latin phrase meaning "according to value." The amount of the tax depends upon the following formula:

taxes = assessed valuation × mill levy or tax rate.

Assessed valuation is the value assigned to the property by the county assessor.

assessed valuation = fair market value × a given percentage (say 21%)

The county assessor appraises the property to determine its fair market value. Suppose he or she determines the fair market value to be $100,000.

$100,000 × .21 = $21,000
The assessed valuation is $21,000.

The *mill levy* is the tax rate. One mill is equal to 1⁄10th of a cent. The following shows how it is expressed in dollars and cents:

$1.00	=	one dollar
$ .10	=	ten cents
$ .01	=	one cent
$.001	=	one mill

Some areas use a mill levy, others a given tax rate to compute the taxes. If the tax rate for a certain entity, say a recreation district, were only one mill, it would be applied as follows to the $21,000 assessed valuation used in the illustration above:

$21,000.00	assessed valuation
× .001	mill levy
$ 21.00	tax

A mill is a tax rate equivalent to $1.00 per $1,000 of assessed valuation.

Suppose the total mill levy against the property with an assessed valuation of $21,000 was 85 mills. The tax on such property would be determined as follows:

$21,000.00	assessed valuation
× .085	mill levy
$ 1785.00	tax

The assessed valuation is determined by the assessor as of a date established by the state legislature in most states. That is usually the date on which the lien of taxes attaches to the property. The following memory aid might be helpful. If taxes are known, always divide into taxes. Otherwise, multiply assessed value × mill levy or tax rate.

Formula:

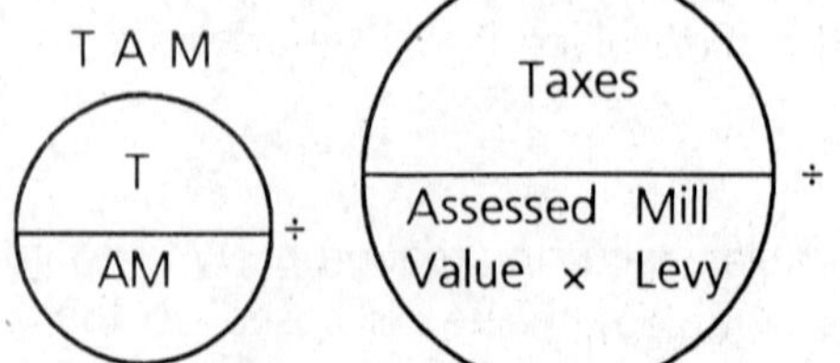

TAM

T
÷
AM

Taxes
÷
Assessed Value × Mill Levy

$$AV \overline{)\text{taxes}} = ML$$

$$ML \overline{)\text{Taxes}} = AV$$

AV × ML = taxes

Assume the taxes are paid in arrears. Closing is to take place on August 21.

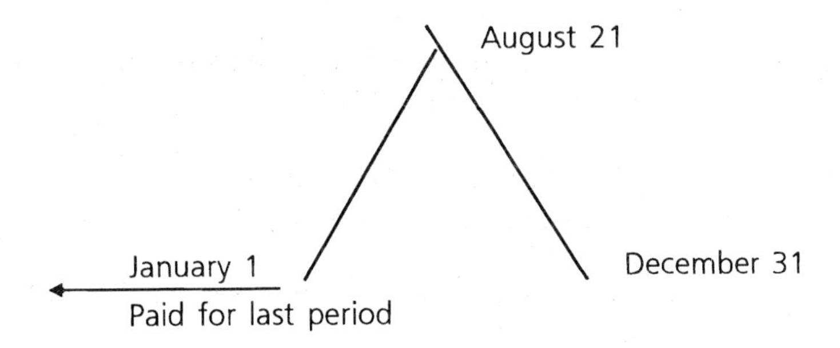

The "pyramid" represents the period of time (January 1 through December 31). The right side of the pyramid represents the buyer's period of ownership and the left side the seller's period of ownership. Periods of ownership and tax liability are as follows:

Seller: January 1 through August 20
Buyer: August 21 through December 31

Since the taxes are paid in arrears, the seller owes the buyer. On the settlement statement, the seller would be debited January 1 through August 20 (therefore paying to the date of closing) and the buyer would be credited January 1 through August 20. At the end of the period, the buyer will pay the taxes. The number of days in the period must now be counted.

January	31 days
February	28
March	31
April	30
May	31
June	30
July	31
August	20
Total	232 days owned by seller

August 21–date of closing
Seller's period of ownership 232 days
Buyer's period of ownership 133 days
January 1
December 31

taxes = $1,785 ÷ 365 days = 4.890411 per day.
(If a figure is carried out to the *sixth* place it will be accurate.)

$4.890411	per day
× 232	days owned by seller
$1,134.575	debit seller and credit buyer, since the buyer will pay the tax at the end of the period
or	
$1,134.58	

Now assume, as for most uniform examinations, that there are 30 days in every month and 360 days in every year and the *seller* pays through the date of closing.

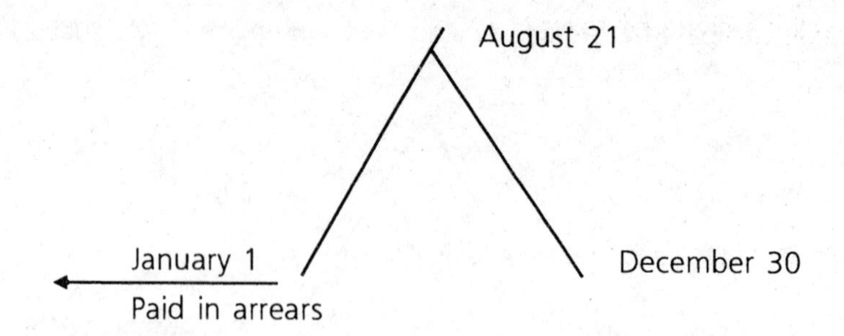

January through July = 7 months × 30 days = 210 days
August = 21 days
231 days

taxes = \$1,785 ÷ 360 =	\$ 4.958333	per day
×	231	days
	\$ 1,145.38	debit seller and credit buyer

Now assume that the taxes are paid in *advance* annually. Use 30 days in each month and 360 days in each year for your computations. The seller pays the date of closing.

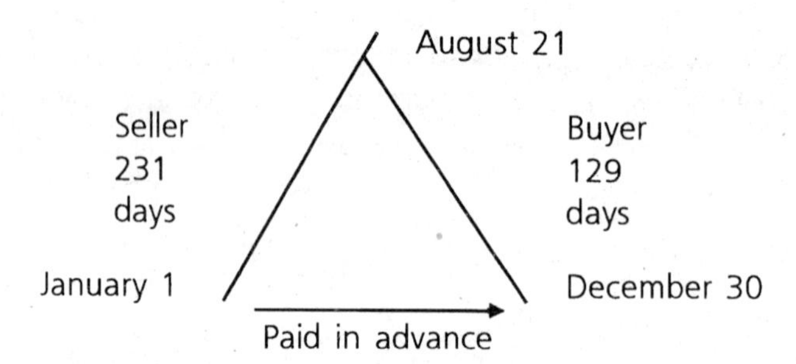

taxes = \$1,785 ÷ 360 =	\$4.958333	per day
×	129	days
	\$ 639.62	debit buyer and credit seller

Some jurisdictions charge a real property transfer tax upon the transfer of any real estate within the tax district. This is usually a percentage of the sales price and is paid by the buyer or seller by agreement or statute. Transfer tax is typically collected by the broker or closing party and forwarded to the local jurisdiction that is making the charge. It is not a proration item.

Exercises

Use 360 days in the year. The seller is to pay the day of closing. The tax year is January to January, and taxes are paid in arrears. The closing date is June 15. The assessed value is \$15,000 and the mill levy is 80.

1. What are the taxes for the year?

2. What is the seller's share of taxes?

3. What is the buyer's share of taxes?

4. When will the taxes be paid and who will pay them?

A closing is held on October 30. Taxes are $927 and paid in advance. The seller has paid the first half of the taxes. The second half is now due and must be collected by the closer. Use 360 days in the year for your computations.

5. How much does the seller owe?

6. How much does the buyer owe?

Use 360 days in the year in the following exercises. The seller is to pay the date of closing.

7. Taxes are $1,120 per year, paid in advance by the seller. How much is the debit and credit if the closing takes place August 17?

8. Taxes are $1,540 per year, paid in arrears. How much is the debit and credit if the closing takes place May 20?

9. Taxes are $2,050 per year, and the seller has paid the first half of the year. The second half is due now. The closing will be held October 18. Compute the proration and decide who pays the taxes.

10. Taxes are $745.60 per year, payable in arrears. The closing is July 21. How much is the debit and credit?

PROPERTY INSURANCE

Insurance must be paid in advance and usually is written for a one-year period. Assume that a one-year insurance policy was paid by the seller. The policy was $640 per year and will expire at 12:01 A.M. next March 24. The closing is to take place September 23, and the buyer will pay the date of closing.

$640 ÷ 365 days = $1.753425 per day
Unused = 182 days

September	8			
October	31		$1.753425	per day
November	30	×	182	days
December	31	$	319.12	debit buyer
January	31			and
February	28			credit seller
March	23			
	182 days unused			

Exercises

An insurance policy is $360 per year and is to be prorated at closing. The policy will expire next year at 12:01 A.M. March 28. The closing is this year on August 31. The seller is to pay the date of closing. Use 365 days in the year.

1. How many days are remaining unused of the policy?

2. What is the seller's credit?

An insurance policy is $282.50 per year and is to be prorated at closing. The closing is July 15, and the policy expires at 12:01 A.M. next May 11. As in the example above, the seller is to pay the date of closing. Use 365 days in the year.

3. How many days of the policy has the seller used?

4. The seller's used portion of the policy is how many dollars?

5. The buyer will be debited and the seller credited with how many dollars?

6. The insurance policy is $280 per year paid in advance on October 1. The closing will take place March 28, and the seller will pay date of closing. Use 30 days in each month.

   a. The seller will be credited $________?

   b. The buyer will be debited $________?

Compute the unused portion of insurance and the debit and credit on the following problems. Use 30 days in each month. The buyer is to pay the date of closing.

7. A closing is to take place May 17, 1996. The insurance policy of $560 was paid November 20, 1994 for a three-year period.

8. Insurance was paid on February 18 for the year in the amount of $340. The closing is December 17.

9. The seller paid the insurance policy on July 18 in the amount of $680. The closing is January 14.

10. Insurance is $420, paid on October 21 for one year. The closing will take place July 27th.

RENTS

Rents are usually paid in advance, on a period-to-period basis. Therefore, the seller will owe the buyer for the period of time collected and *unearned.*

Assume a closing is to take place June 24. The property has two units. Both units are rented. The rent for unit number one is $680 per month, due the first of each month. The rent for unit number two is $740 per month, due the 15th of each month.

Unit one

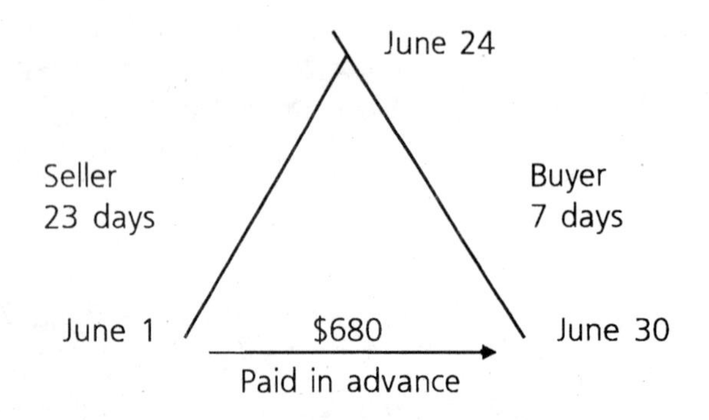

$680 ÷ 30 days =
$ 22.666666 per day
× 7 days
$158.666666 seller

Rounded to $158.67
seller owes buyer

Unit two

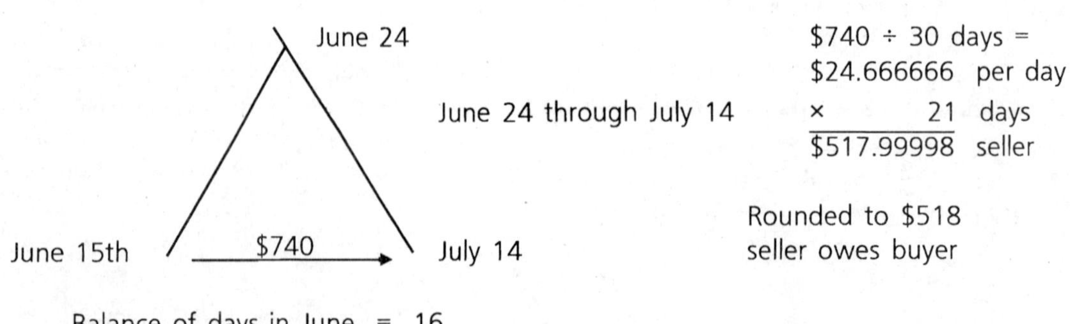

Balance of days in June = 16
July = 14
30 days in period.

So: $158.67
+518.00
$676.67 debit seller and credit buyer

Exercises

An income property closed on the 23rd of June. The rent is $600 for unit number one, due the first of each month, and $725 for unit number two, due the 10th of each month, both collected in advance by the seller. The seller owns to the date of closing.

1. What is the daily rent for unit number one?

2. What is the daily rent for unit number two?

3. How much of the total rent does the seller get to keep?

4. How much of the total rent will be credited to the buyer?

5. Rent is $860 per month, paid in advance. The closing is to take place June 28. How much is the debit and credit if the seller pays all costs through the date of closing?

6. Rent is $1,490 per month, and the seller is charged to the date of closing, which takes place on September 9. How much is the debit and credit?

7. Mr. Adams owns a six-unit apartment complex. The rent on each unit is $450 per month. The rent is paid in advance on the first of each month. Adams sold the complex to Mr. and Mrs. Baker, and the closing is to take place November 22. The Bakers will pay all costs beginning the date of closing. How much does the seller owe the buyer for rent?

8. The closing for an eight-unit apartment building is August 27. Six of the units are two-bedroom and rent for $480 per month. Two of the units are three-bedroom and rent for $560 per month. Use actual days in the month. The seller is to pay through the date of closing.

9. Use 30 days in the month. The buyer is to receive credit for the date of closing, which is July 16. The rent on a two-unit property is $290 per unit, and both are paid in advance. Unit one rent was due and paid on the fifth, and unit two rent was due and paid on the first. Prorate the rentals.

10. Rent is paid in advance on the first in the amount of $780. The closing is on April 20. The buyer will own the property the date of closing. Use 30 days.

WATER AND SEWER CHARGES

Water and sewer charges might be combined into one bill or billed separately. They could be payable in advance (flat rate) or in arrears (usually metered) for a period of time, usually from one to three months.

Assume water and sewer charges are $30 flat rate per month, paid in advance for two months on November 1 by the seller. The closing is December 4.

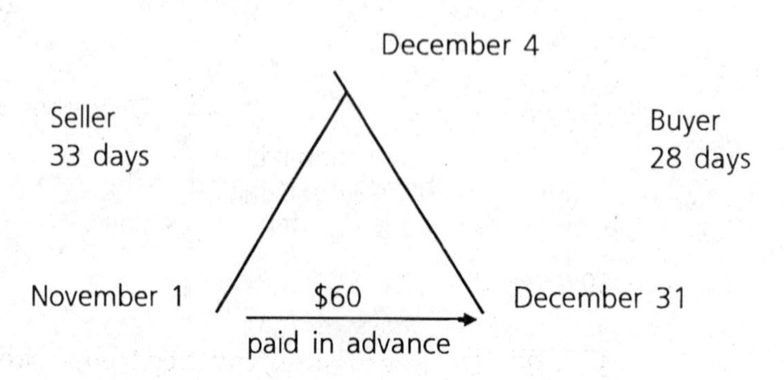

$30 per month × 2 months =	$60	
November	30	days
December	31	days
	61	days

$60 ÷ 61 days = $0.983607 per day
Water is paid by the seller to be used by the buyer.

So:

	$.983607	
×	28	days
$	27.54	debit buyer and credit seller

Assume the bill was due but unpaid on the date of closing.

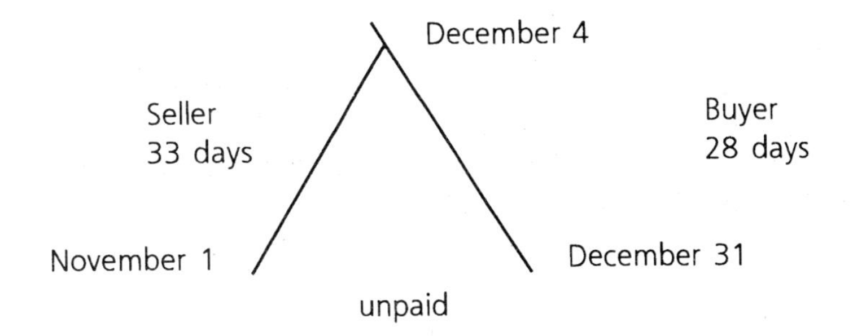

	$0.983607	
×	33	days seller
$	32.46	debit seller

	$0.983607	
×	28	days buyer
$	27.54	debit buyer

So:

$32.46	debit seller
27.54	debit buyer
$60.00	credit closing agent who will pay the bill

Assume the bill was to be paid in arrears.

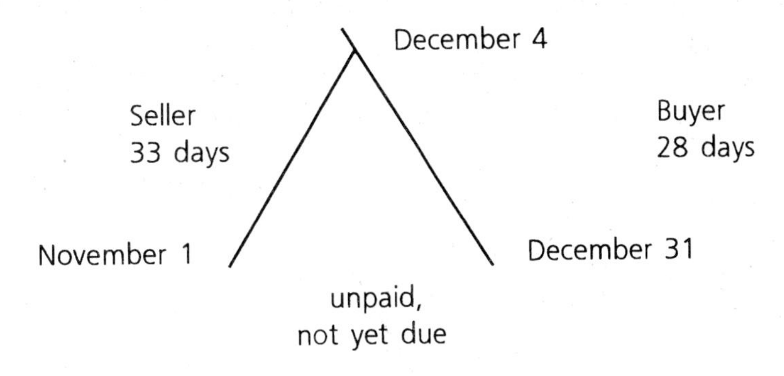

	$0.983607	
×	33	days seller
$	32.46	debit seller and credit buyer who will pay the bill when due

Exercises

The water bill is $16 each month, payable in advance for three months. The last bill was paid on March 1. The closing is April 20. Use actual days in the month. The buyer is to pay the date of closing.

1. How many days are in the period?

2. How manys days are unused?

3. What is the dollar amount of the proration?

4. What is the debit and credit?

5. The water and sewer bill are $26.82, payable in arrears for a two-month period beginning August 1 and closing September 20. What is the proration and the debit and credit?

6. The water bill is paid in advance by the seller for May, June, and July. The bill is $78.62. The date of closing is June 28, and the seller is to pay through the date of closing. Use actual days in each month in your proration. How much is the debit and credit?

7. The water bill was due and unpaid on March 1 for March and April in the amount of \$24.87. The closing is to be held April 14. Use actual days in the period. The seller is to pay for the day of closing. What is the proration and the debit and credit?

Use 30 days in each month and the buyer to pay the date of closing in the following:

8. The water bill is flat rate and paid in advance quarterly. The bill is \$86.40 for this quarter. The closing is March 18. Compute the proration.

9. The sewer bill for one year is due September 20. The bill is now due and *not paid* in the amount of \$124. The closing is October 28. Compute the proration.

10. The water bill is \$19.80 for the month, payable in arrears. The closing is on the 16th. Compute the proration.

MORTGAGE INTEREST

A borrower usually pays interest in arrears unless otherwise agreed upon, based upon a payment period. When a loan is assumed the interest for the payment period that is within the closing time must be settled between the parties. (See also Chapter 8 "Mortgage Math.")

The closing is September 13. The buyer is assuming a loan in the unpaid balance of \$76,286. The interest rate is 11% per annum.

$$\$76{,}286 \times .11 = 8{,}391.46 \text{ per year}$$

Formula:

$$\frac{I}{PRT} \qquad \begin{array}{c} I \\ \hline PRT \end{array} \qquad \div \qquad \frac{\text{interest}}{\text{principal} \times \text{rate} \times \text{time}}$$

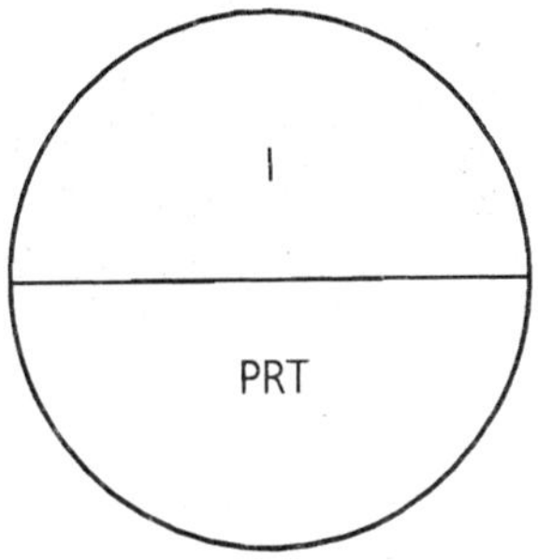

principal × rate	= interest for one year
interest ÷ principal	= rate per annum
interest ÷ rate	= principal balance
interest ÷ time	= interest for period

Now because each interest period incorporates a different number of days, *you do not* divide by 365 days but by 12 months, since the lender is charging *this* month, 1/12th of the annual interest.

$8,391.46 ÷ 12 mo. = 699.288333 rounded to
699.29 *this* month

Now divide *this* month's interest by the number of days in this month.

$699.29 ÷ 30 = $23.309667 per day
or $23.31

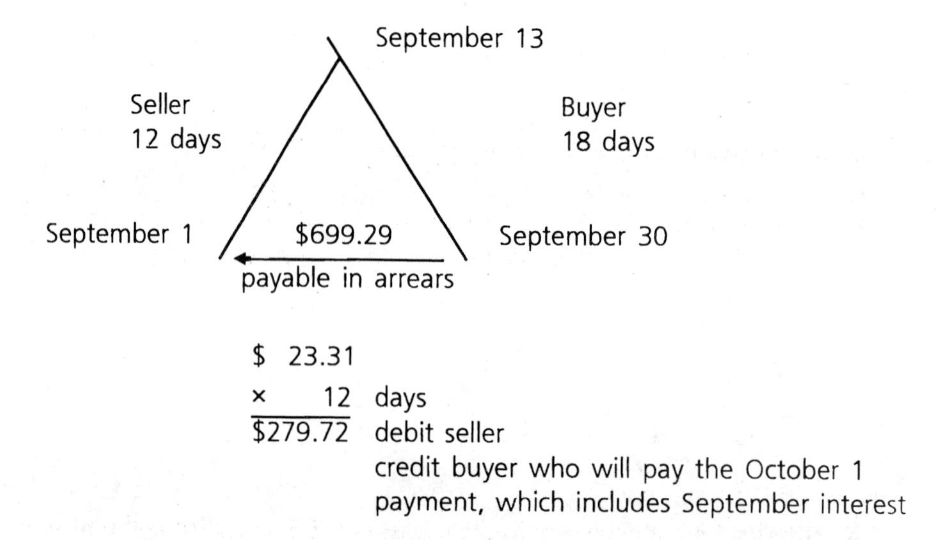

Using the same example, assume interest is payable in advance and the seller pays through the date of closing.

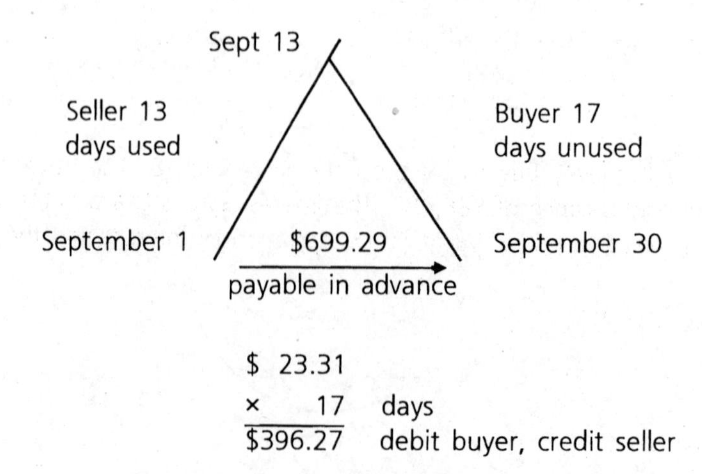

Exercises

Using the same example, assume interest is payable in advance and the seller pays through the date of closing.

1. A closing takes place August 18. The August 1 payment paid August interest. How many days does the buyer owe for interest?

2. If the interest is $23.40 per day, what is the seller's credit?

For the following problems, use actual days in the year. The seller is to pay the date of closing.

3. The unpaid balance of the loan is $42,600 and the interest rate is 10%. The closing is April 23. Interest is paid in arrears. What is the proration of interest and the debit and credit?

4. The interest for the month of August is $780 and paid by the seller in advance. The closing will take place August 14. What is the proration of interest and the debit and credit?

5. The seller will convey title to his property on March 18. The buyer will assume the loan with an unpaid balance of $86,480. The interest rate is 8% payable in arrears. The March 1 payment has been paid. What is the proration of interest and the debit and credit?

For the following problems, use 30 days in each month. The buyer is to pay the date of closing.

6. The interest is payable in arrears. The unpaid balance of the loan is $60,280 with interest at 12% per annum. The closing is July 14. What is the proration?

7. Interest is payable in advance on a $36,000 loan with interest at 7¾%. The payment was due and paid on the 10th of the month and included interest for that day. The closing is on the 28th. What is the proration of interest and the debit and credit?

8. On March 16, the buyer assumed a home loan with an unpaid balance of $52,800 as of March 1. The interest is 8.5% payable in advance. What is the proration of interest and the debit and credit?

9. After the August 1 payment of $686 principal and interest, the unpaid balance of the loan is $42,800. The payment included interest in advance. The interest rate is 6.5% and closing is August 21. Compute the proration and determine the debit and credit.

10. The unpaid balance of a loan is $98,200. Interest is 12.5% and payable in advance. The monthly payment is due on the first and includes interest for the entire month. The closing will take place on May 17. Compute the proration and determine the debit and credit.

CHAPTER TEST

1. A buyer assumes a $43,500 loan at 9½% interest. Interest payments are in arrears. The last payment paid was September 1, and the closing is September 20. The buyer is responsible for the date of closing. How much interest is the buyer given credit for?

2. The real value of a property as determined by the county assessor is $82,600. The percentage of real-to-assessed value is 18%. The mill levy as established is 81.6 mills. What are the taxes?

3. An income property closed on April 23. The buyer was credited with the day of closing. The rents are $325 for one unit and $350 for one unit, both collected on the first of the month by the seller. What is the debit and credit?

4. Mr. Wilson is purchasing a home from Ms. Collins. The closing will be held August 12 of the current year. Since Mr. Wilson is short on funds to close, it is decided that it will be less expensive for him to assume Ms. Collins's hazard insurance policy than to purchase a new one, since her policy will expire October 24 at 12:01 A.M. The premium amount is $276. Using a 30-day month and charging Ms. Collins with the day of closing, how much will Mr. Wilson owe Ms. Collins at the closing?

5. A buyer wishes to assume a loan with an unpaid balance after the September 1 payment of $86,222.60. The interest rate is 8% paid in arrears. The closing date is September 9, and the seller will pay for the date of closing. What is the debit and the credit for interest?

6. Use 360 days in the year. The seller is to pay for the day of closing. The closing date is January 21. The assessed value is $12,000 and the mill levy is 80.5. The tax year begins January 1 and taxes are paid in arrears. What would be the seller's charge for taxes?

7. Closing is June 12 of the current year. The water bill is flat rate and paid in arrears. The bill is $41.69 for the period June 1 through June 30. The buyer is to pay the date of closing. What is the debit and credit?

8. The taxes are $858.92 for January 1 through December 31. The taxes are paid in arrears. The closing is July 16 and the buyer owns the date of closing. What is the debit and credit?

9. The insurance premium is $198.76, paid annually. The closing is August 13 and the policy expires April 15 at 12:01 A.M. next year. Use 365 days. The seller pays the date of closing. What is the debit and credit?

10. The taxes are $964.50 paid in advance. The closing is November 3. Use actual days in the year. The seller is to pay for the date of closing. What is the debit and credit?

11. The taxes on a property were $616. The tax rate is $38.50 per $1,000 of assessed value. The taxing authority has assessed property at 50% of appraised value. What is the assessed value of the property?

12. The taxes from January 1 to January 1 on a property were $846 and have been paid in full by the owner. What refund will she receive as credit from the buyer if the sale of the property closes September 15 and the seller is charged the day of closing?

13. A house is insured for $70,000 at a cost of $.75 per $100 for one year. If a three-year insurance policy costs $2\frac{1}{2}$ times as much as a one-year policy, what will it cost to insure the house for three years?

11

SETTLEMENT STATEMENTS

Goals

1. Understand the debit-credit procedure.
2. Determine the amount of money a seller and a buyer receive or bring to a real estate settlement.
3. Properly prepare and explain the seller and buyer settlement statement.
4. Compute the broker's reconciliation of funds to determine if there is enough money being received to pay the bills that must be paid.

Prior to most real estate transfers, there will be a settlement, or closing. A closing statement might be a standardized form peculiar to an area, or one prepared or computer-generated using only the line items required. Many brokers use a four-column worksheet with a separate form for the broker reconciliation of funds. Figure 11–1 is a six-column worksheet similar to that used in some areas.* It includes the seller statement, the buyer statement, and the broker reconciliation statement. This form is the broker's organization worksheet. Once it is completed, the broker will prepare separate statements for the buyer and seller, who will see only their individual settlement statements.

In most areas, brokers close using the settlement statement referred to as the HUD-1 form (see Figure 11–2). Since the HUD-1 form contains no broker debit or credit (money-in, money-out) columns, if the form is used you may want to do your own broker reconciliation of funds. (You will see an example later, in Figure 11–5.) If the closing is finalized using the HUD-1 in your state, please study the solution to each practice problem and complete sample problems 1–4, including the broker reconciliations. The solutions to these problems are included in the answer key at the back of the text.

*Figure 11–1 and the other printed portions of the closing statements used in this chapter other than the HUD-1 forms are approved by the Colorado Real Estate Commission Form #SS-61-7-71 and used here with permission.

Figure 11–1 Sample six-column settlement statement

	SELLER		BUYER		BROKER	
	Debit	Credit	Debit	Credit	Debit	Credit
1. Selling Price						
2. Deposit, paid to						
3. Trust Deed, payable to						
4. Trust Deed, payable to						
5. Trust Deed, payoff to						
6. Interest on Loan Assumed						
7. Title Ins. Premium						
8. Abstracting: Before Sale						
9. After Sale						
10. Title Exam by						
11. Recording: Warranty Deed						
12. Trust Deed						
13. Release						
14. Other						
15. Documentary Fee						
16. Certificate of Taxes Due						
17. Taxes for Preceding Year(s)						
18. Taxes for Current Year						
19. Tax Reserve						
20. Special Taxes						
21. Personal Property Taxes						
22. Hazard Ins. Prem. Assumed						
23. Premium for New Insurance						
24. Hazard Ins. Reserve						
25. FHA Mortgage Ins. Assumed						
26. FHA Mortgage Ins. Reserve						
27. Loan Service Fee (Buyer)						
28. Loan Discount Fee (Seller)						
29. Interest on New Loan						
30. Survey and/or Credit Report						
31. Appraisal Fee						
32. Water and/or Sewer						
33. Rents						
34. Security Deposits						
35. Loan Transfer Fee						
36. Loan Payment Due						
37. Broker's Fee						
Sub-Totals						
Balance due to/from Seller						
Balance due to/from Buyer						
TOTALS						

The printed portions of this form aproved by the Colorado Real Estate Commission (88-41-7-71)

Figure 11–2 Sample HUD-1 settlement statement

HUD-1 (3-86) | OMB NO. 2502-0265

A. U.S. DEPARTMENT OF HOUSING AND URBAN DEVELOPMENT

SETTLEMENT STATEMENT

B. TYPE OF LOAN		
1. ☐ FHA	2. ☐ FMHA	3. ☐ CONV. UNINS.
4. ☐ VA	5. ☐ CONV. INS.	
6. FILE NUMBER:	7. LOAN NUMBER:	
8. MORTGAGE INSURANCE CASE NUMBER:		

C. NOTE: This form is furnished to give you a statement of actual settlement costs. Amounts paid to and by the settlement agent are shown. Items marked *"(p.o.c.)"* were paid outside the closing; they are shown here for informational purposes and are not included in totals.

D. NAME OF BORROWER:	E. NAME OF SELLER:	F. NAME OF LENDER:
G. PROPERTY LOCATION:	H. SETTLEMENT AGENT:	PLACE OF SETTLEMENT
	I. SETTLEMENT DATE:	

J. SUMMARY OF BORROWER'S TRANSACTION		K. SUMMARY OF SELLER'S TRANSACTION	
100. GROSS AMOUNT DUE FROM BORROWER:		**400. GROSS AMOUNT DUE TO SELLER:**	
101. Contract sales price		401. Contract sales price	
102. Personal property		402. Personal property	
103. Settlement charges to borrower *(line 1400)*		403.	
104.		404.	
105.		405.	
Adjustments for items paid by seller in advance		*Adjustments for items paid by seller in advance*	
106. City/town taxes to		406. City/town taxes to	
107. County taxes to		407. County taxes to	
108. Assessments to		408. Assessments to	
109.		409.	
110.		410.	
111.		411.	
112.		412.	
120. GROSS AMOUNT DUE FROM BORROWER		**420. GROSS AMOUNT DUE TO SELLER**	
200. AMOUNTS PAID BY OR IN BEHALF OF BORROWER:		**500. REDUCTIONS IN AMOUNT DUE TO SELLER:**	
201. Deposit or earnest money		501. Excess deposit (see instructions)	
202. Principal amount of new loan(s)		502. Settlement charges to seller *(line 1400)*	
203. Existing loan(s) taken subject to		503. Existing loan(s) taken subject to	
204.		504. Payoff of first mortgage loan	
205.		505. Payoff of second mortgage loan	
206.		506.	
207.		507.	
208.		508.	
209.		509.	
Adjustments for items unpaid by seller:		*Adjustments for items unpaid by seller:*	
210. City/town taxes to		510. City/town taxes to	
211. County taxes to		511. County taxes to	
212. Assessments to		512. Assessments to	
213.		513.	
214.		514.	
215.		515.	
216.		516.	
217.		517.	
218.		518.	
219.		519.	
220. TOTAL PAID BY/FOR BORROWER		**520. TOTAL REDUCTION AMOUNT DUE SELLER**	
300. CASH AT SETTLEMENT FROM/TO BORROWER		**600. CASH AT SETTLEMENT TO/FROM SELLER**	
301. Gross amount due from borrower *(line 120)*		601. Gross amount due to seller *(line 420)*	
302. Less amounts paid by/for borrower *(line 220)*	( )	602. Less reductions in amt. due to seller *(line 520)*	( )
303. CASH (☐ FROM) (☐ TO) BORROWER		**603. CASH (☐ TO) (☐ FROM) SELLER**	

RESPA, [illegible] 4305

(continued)

Figure 11–2 continued

HUD-1 (3-86)

L. SETTLEMENT CHARGES	PAID FROM BORROWER'S FUNDS AT SETTLEMENT	PAID FROM SELLER'S FUNDS AT SETTLEMENT
700. **TOTAL SALES/BROKER'S COMMISSION** based on price $ @ % =		
Division of Commission (line 700) as follows:		
701. $ to		
702. $ to		
703. Commission paid at Settlement		
704.		
800. ITEMS PAYABLE IN CONNECTION WITH LOAN		
801. Loan Origination Fee %		
802. Loan Discount %		
803. Appraisal Fee to		
804. Credit Report to		
805. Lender's Inspection Fee		
806. Mortgage Insurance Application Fee to		
807. Assumption Fee		
808.		
809.		
810.		
811.		
900. ITEMS REQUIRED BY LENDER TO BE PAID IN ADVANCE		
901. Interest from to @ $ /day		
902. Mortgage Insurance Premium for months to		
903. Hazard Insurance Premium for years to		
904. years to		
905.		
1000. **1000. RESERVES DEPOSITED WITH LENDER**		
1001. Hazard insurance months @ $ per month		
1002. Mortgage insurance months @ $ per month		
1003. City property taxes months @ $ per month		
1004. County property taxes months @ $ per month		
1005. Annual assessments months @ $ per month		
1006. months @ $ per month		
1007. months @ $ per month		
1008. months @ $ per month		
1100. TITLE CHARGES		
1101. Settlement or closing fee to		
1102. Abstract or title search to		
1103. Title examination to		
1104. Title insurance binder to		
1105. Document preparation to		
1106. Notary fees to		
1107. Attorney's fees to		
(includes above items numbers;)		
1108. Title insurance to		
(includes above items numbers;)		
1109. Lender's coverage $		
1110. Owner's coverage $		
1111. Tax Certificate		
1112.		
1113.		
1200. GOVERNMENT RECORDING AND TRANSFER CHARGES		
1201. Recording fees: Deed $; Mortgage $; Releases $		
1202. City/county tax/stamps: Deed $; Mortgage $		
1203. State tax/stamps: Deed $; Mortgage $		
1204.		
1205.		
1300. ADDITIONAL SETTLEMENT CHARGES		
1301. Survey to		
1302. Pest inspection to		
1303.		
1304.		
1305.		
1400. **TOTAL SETTLEMENT CHARGES** *(enter on lines 103, Section J and 502, Section K)*		

I have carefully reviewed the HUD-1 Settlement Statement and to the best of my knowledge and belief, it is a true and accurate statement of all receipts and disbursements made on my account or by me in this transaction. I further certify that I have received a copy of the HUD-1 Settlement Statement.

Borrowers

Sellers

To the best of my knowledge, the HUD-1 Settlement Statement which I have prepared is a true and accurate account of this transaction. I have caused or will cause the funds to be disbursed in accordance with this statement.

Settlement Agent

Date

WARNING: It is a crime to knowingly make a false statement to the United States on this or any other similar form. Penalties upon conviction can include a fine and imprisonment. For details see: Title 18 U.S. Code Section 1001 and Section 1010.

ASSUMPTIONS

Example

In the following problem all prorations are completed for you. Please follow along as we explain the problem line by line. In the table below and on pages 188–191, the corresponding six-column line numbers are shown in *italic* while the HUD–1 line numbers are shown in **boldface.** The closing date is May 1. Please assume for this problem that all months contain 30 days. For the completed settlement statement, see Figures 11–3 and 11–4.

		6-column	**HUD-1**
Sale price	$89,000.00	*Line 1*	**101–401**
Deposit given to broker by the buyer as contract was signed	$ 2,500.00	*Line 2*	**201**
Trust deed to assume after May 1 payment	$68,500.00	*Line 3*	**203, 503**
The April interest has been paid with the May 1 payment. Collect loan payment	$ 983.00	*Line 36*	**506**
Second trust deed to seller	$ 3,500.00	*Line 4*	**204, 507**
Owner's title insurance policy	$ 560.00	*Line 7*	**1108**
Mortgagee's title insurance policy	$ 50.00	*Line 7*	**1108**
Examination of title by buyer's attorney	$ 350.00	*Line 10*	**1103**
Recording of warranty deed	$ 3.00	*Line 11*	**1201**
Recording second trust deed to seller	$ 9.00	*Line 12*	**1201**
Documentary fee (some states), 1¢ per $100	$ 8.90	*Line 15*	**1203**
Tax certificate	$ 15.00	*Line 16*	**1111**
Tax adjustment: $1,260, last year's taxes paid. Charge four months to seller	$ 420.00	*Line 18*	**211, 511**
*Tax reserve in seller's account	$ 420.00	*Line 19*	**109, 409**
Insurance premium paid $432 Used four months: Eight months remaining	$ 288.00	*Line 22*	**111, 411**
*Insurance reserve in seller's account	$ 360.00	*Line 24*	**110, 410**
Credit report, $56; Survey, $140	$ 196.00	*Line 30*	**1301, 1303**
Three months water paid by seller, two months used, $45 total	$ 15.00	*Line 32*	**112, 412**
Transfer fee to loan company, 1%	$ 685.00	*Line 35*	**807**
Commission, 6% on sale	$ 5,340.00	*Line 37*	**703**

*Reserves are monies paid monthly by the owner, held by the lender, and out of which taxes and insurance are paid as they are due.

Line 1; **101, 401;** Sale Price:

A credit to the seller and debit to the buyer. This is considered to be the "check" or the amount that the seller would receive and the buyer would pay if there were no other considerations. Therefore, any additional credit to the seller will *increase* the "check" to the seller, and any debit to the seller will *decrease* the "check" to the seller. Any additional debit to the buyer will *increase* the "check" the buyer must bring to the closing, and any additional credit will *decrease* the "check" the buyer must bring to the closing. The costs vary from area to area and from closing to closing. It may also be customary in one area for a seller to pay for certain items, while in other areas the buyer would pay for title insurance, tax certificates, etc. All items are negotiable between the parties. The final result will be the amount of money the seller receives or must bring to the closing and the amount that the buyer receives or must bring to the closing.

Line 2; **201;** Deposit, Paid to:

The buyer *has given $2,500 in earnest money to the broker. Credit the buyer, decreasing* the funds needed to close, and *debit* the *broker*. Broker debit consists of funds actually received by the broker and deposited in the broker's trust account (money in). Broker credit is checks actually written *out* by broker or disbursing agent (money out).

Line 3; **203–503;** Trust Deed Payable to:

Since this is a loan assumption, the unpaid balance of the loan is a debit to the seller and a credit to the buyer, thereby *decreasing* each party's check by that amount since the seller owes the debt and the buyer is assuming the debt.

Line 4; **204–507;** Trust Deed Payable to Seller:

In this problem the seller has agreed to carry back a second deed of trust/mortgage. A debit to the seller *decreases* the check he or she will receive today as he or she will be receiving the funds later, usually payable in monthly installments. The buyer is credited, thereby *decreasing* the funds to be brought to the closing.

Line 5; **504–505;** Trust Deed/Mortgage Payoff:

Debit the seller any payoff and credit the broker who will write the check for the payoff. Any reserve accounts held by the old lender reduce the payoff.

Line 6; **213–513;** Interest on Loan Assumed:

Not used in this instance because the closing date is May 1. When making the May 1 payment, the seller is paying April interest (in arrears in this case); therefore, there is no debit of interest to the seller. If the closing had been on May 5, the seller would have been debited four days if the seller pays expenses *to* the date of closing, or five days if the seller pays *through* date of closing. The buyer would be credited the interest since the buyer will be paying the June 1 payment. If interest is paid in advance, the buyer will be debited the entire month of May and the seller credited, since the seller pays the interest with the loan payment.

Line 7; **1108;** Title Ins. Premium:

In some parts of the country the seller pays the Owner's Policy of Insurance, and in other areas the buyer customarily pays. The buyer usually pays to insure a *new lender* (mortgagee's policy) against defect in title. In this case the *seller* is the new lender. Debit the proper party and credit the broker. The broker will write the check to the title company.

Lines 8–9; **1102;** Abstract/After Sale:

The seller usually pays to bring an abstract to date and certify. The buyer usually pays after-sale abstracting and certification.

Line 10; **1103;** Title Exam By:

The title is always examined by the buyer's or lender's attorney. Debit the buyer and credit the *broker*. The broker will write the check to the attorney.

Lines 11–14; **1201;** Recording Fees:

The buyer usually pays to record the deed as well as the deed of trust/mortgage. The seller usually pays to record releases or documents necessary to perfect title.

Line 15; **1203;** Documentary Fee:

In some states this might be called deed stamps or tax stamps. Depending on the area, the documentary fee may or may not apply. Either the buyer or the seller may pay.

Line 16; **1111;** Certificate of Taxes Due:

This is usually obtained from the county treasurer to determine whether there are back taxes unpaid and taxes due now. It may be paid by the buyer or seller. The cost varies by area.

Line 17; **511;** Taxes for Preceding Year(s):

The seller pays (i.e., is debited with) any back property taxes or property taxes now due to or through the date of closing. The broker is credited. If the money to pay the taxes is in escrow with the lender and the *lender* will pay the taxes, then because the buyer is buying the escrow (reserve) account (see line 19) and taxes will be paid from *buyer* funds after closing, the seller is debited with the taxes now due and the buyer is credited.

Line 18; **211;** Taxes for Current Year:

If due in advance and paid, debit the buyer with the balance of the year and credit the seller, who has paid the taxes. If due in advance and not paid, debit the seller's share to the seller, debit the buyer's share to the buyer, and credit the broker with the total amount to be paid. If due in arrears (as on most state exams), then debit the seller's share to the seller and credit buyer, who will pay the taxes when they become due.

Line 19; **109;** Tax Reserve:

When the loan is assumed, the buyer purchases all reserve accounts held by the lender. Debit the buyer and credit the seller. With a new loan, reserves are *established* and the seller is not involved; debit the buyer only.

Line 20; **108, 408;** Special Taxes:

These include taxes for street, sidewalk, and sewer assessments. In most instances the seller is debited and the broker is credited.

Line 21; **513;** Personal Property Taxes:

See Line 18 explanation.

Line 22; **111, 411;** Hazard Ins. Premium Assumed:

In this problem, the buyer agrees to assume the seller's insurance, which is paid in advance. Debit the buyer and credit the seller with the unused portion.

Line 23; **111;** Premium for New Ins.:

If a new policy, debit the buyer and credit the broker.

Line 24; **110, 410;** Hazard Ins. Reserve:
See Line 19 explanation.

Line 25; **110, 410;** FHA Mortgage Ins. Assumed:
If paid in arrears (prior to 9–1–83), debit the seller and credit the buyer. When paid in advance (9–1–83 and later), credit the seller with the unused portion and debit the buyer. Use this line also for private mortgage insurance, which is usually paid annually in advance.

Line 26; **110, 410;** FHA Mortgage Ins. Reserves:
See Line 19 explanation. Use this line also for private mortgage insurance reserves.

Line 27; **801;** Loan Service Fee:
Usually the buyer pays this when securing a new loan.

Line 28; **802;** Loan Discount Fee:
This is by contractual agreement.

Line 29; **901;** Interest on New Loan:
Usually the lender will charge the buyer interest from the date of closing to the end of the month when the buyer is securing a new loan. (See Exercise 3.)

Line 30; **1301;** Suvey and/or Credit Report:
Usually the buyer is debited.

Line 31; **1303;** Appraisal Fee:
By agreement, either buyer or seller may pay if applicable.

Line 32; **112, 412;** Water and/or Sewer:
If paid in advance, the seller receives credit and the buyer is debited. If paid in arrears, debit the seller to or through the date of closing and credit the buyer. If due now, debit the seller and credit the broker. Water is a lien on property in many areas, and the broker will collect and pay any unpaid bills.

Line 33; **214, 514;** Rents:
Rent is usually paid in advance. The seller is debited and the buyer credited.

Line 34; **208, 508;** Security Deposits:
Debit the seller and credit the buyer.

Line 35; **807;** Loan Transfer Fee:
In this problem the fee is 1% of unpaid balance of loan. Debit the buyer and credit the broker. This is usually a buyer expense.

Line 36; **206, 506;** Loan Payment Due:
This is dependent upon the assumption statement. If the loan balance at closing is *after* the principal part of a payment due is credited against the loan, then debit the seller. If the unpaid balance of the loan at closing is *before* the principal part of a payment due is credited against the loan, then debit the buyer. Credit the broker, who will send the payment to the lender, along with the assumption package.

Line 37; **703;** Broker Fee:
By agreement, this is a seller debit and/or buyer debit and broker credit. The broker and others involved in the commission are paid by the broker.

Subtotals; **1400, 220, 520:**

Total all columns:

Balance Due to/from Seller; **603:**

Subtract the smaller from the larger dollar figure in the subtotal column, then *add* the difference to the *smaller* figure on subtotal line. If the difference is in the *debit* column, the seller *receives* this amount at closing; therefore, *credit* the broker this amount. The broker will pay the seller. If the difference is in the *credit* column, the seller must bring funds to the closing. In this instance *debit* the broker (money in), and the broker will use the funds to pay the bills.

Seller Final Total; **N/A:**

Debit and credit must be equal.

Balance Due to/from Buyer; **303:**

Subtract the smaller from the larger dollar figure in the subtotal column, then *add* the difference to the *smaller* figure on subtotal line. If the difference is in the *credit* column, the buyer must bring funds to the closing, so *debit* the broker (money in). If the difference is in the debit column, the buyer *receives* money back at the closing. Credit the broker, and the broker will draw the check for overpayment to the buyer.

Buyer Final Total; **N/A:**

Debit and credit must be equal.

Broker Final Total; **N/A:**

This is the broker's final reconciliation. Does the broker have enough money in (i.e., debit) to pay all funds to be paid out (i.e., credit)? If these columns do not balance, then there is an error in debits, credits, or subtotals in the statement that must be found and corrected.

Figure 11–3 Six-column settlement statement, example 1

May 1 This Year	SELLER Decrease Check Debit	SELLER Increase Check Credit	BUYER Increase Check Debit	BUYER Decrease Check Credit	BROKER Money to Closer Debit	BROKER Paid out by Closer Credit
1. Selling Price The Check		$ 89,000 00	$ 89,000 00			
2. Deposit, paid to				$ 2,500 00	$ 2,500 00	
3. Trust Deed, payable to	$ 68,500 00			68,500 00		
4. Trust Deed, payable to	3,500 00			3,500 00		
5. Trust Deed, payoff to						
6. Interest on Loan Assumed						
7. Title Ins. Premium Owners/Mortgage	560 00		50 00			610 00
8. Abstracting: Before Sale						
9. After Sale						
10. Title Exam by Buyer Attorney			350 00			350 00
11. Recording: Warranty Deed			3 00			3 00
12. Trust Deed			9 00			9 00
13. Release						
14. Other						
15. Documentary Fee 1c each $100 of price			8 90			8 90
16. Certificate of Taxes Due			15 00			15 00
17. Taxes for Preceding Year(s) paid $1,260.00						
18. Taxes for Current Year 4 months	420 00			420 00		
19. Tax Reserve		420 00	420 00			
20. Special Taxes						
21. Personal Property Taxes						
22. Hazard Ins. Prem. Assumed 8 months left		288 00	288 00			
23. Premium for New Insurance						
24. Hazard Ins. Reserve		360 00	360 00			
25. FHA Mortgage Ins. Assumed						
26. FHA Mortgage Ins. Reserve						
27. Loan Service Fee (Buyer)						
28. Loan Discount Fee (Seller)						
29. Interest on New Loan						
30. Survey and/or Credit Report $140.00/$56.00			196 00			196 00
31. Appraisal Fee						
32. Water and/or Sewer 2 months used		15 00	15 00			
33. Rents						
34. Security Deposits						
35. Loan Transfer Fee 1% loan amount			685 00			685 00
36. Loan Payment Due Pay April interest	983 00					983 00
37. Broker's Fee 6%	5,340 00					5,340 00
Sub-Totals	$ 79,303 00	$ 90,083 00	$ 91,399 90	$ 74,920 00	$ 2,500 00	$ 8,199 00
Balance due to/~~from~~ Seller	10,780 00					10,780. 00
Balance due ~~to~~/from Buyer				16,479 00	16,479 00	
TOTALS	90,083 00	90,083 00	91,399 90	91,399 00	18,979 00	18,979 00

The printed portions of this form aproved by the Colorado Real Estate Commission (88-41-7-71)

Figure 11–4 HUD-1 settlement statement, example 1

HUD-1 (3-86) OMB NO. 2502-0265

A. U.S. DEPARTMENT OF HOUSING AND URBAN DEVELOPMENT

SETTLEMENT STATEMENT

B. TYPE OF LOAN

1. ☐ FHA 2. ☐ FMHA 3. ☐ CONV. UNINS.
4. ☐ VA 5. ☐ CONV. INS.

6. FILE NUMBER: 7. LOAN NUMBER:

8. MORTGAGE INSURANCE CASE NUMBER:

C. NOTE: This form is furnished to give you a statement of actual settlement costs. Amounts paid to and by the settlement agent are shown. Items marked "(p.o.c.)" were paid outside the closing; they are shown here for informational purposes and are not included in totals.

D. NAME OF BORROWER: Solution to Closing Problem Practice Problem

E. NAME OF SELLER:

F. NAME OF LENDER:

G. PROPERTY LOCATION:

H. SETTLEMENT AGENT:

PLACE OF SETTLEMENT:

I. SETTLEMENT DATE: May 1, 19–

J. SUMMARY OF BORROWER'S TRANSACTION		K. SUMMARY OF SELLER'S TRANSACTION	
100. GROSS AMOUNT DUE FROM BORROWER: (Buyer debits)		**400. GROSS AMOUNT DUE TO SELLER:** (Seller credits)	
101. Contract sales price	$ 89,000.00	401. Contract sales price	$89,000.00
102. Personal property		402. Personal property	
103. Settlement charges to borrower *(line 1400)*	1,316.90	403.	
104.		404.	
105.		405.	
Adjustments for items paid by seller in advance		*Adjustments for items paid by seller in advance*	
106. City/town taxes to		406. City/town taxes to	
107. County taxes to		407. County taxes to	
108. Assessments to		408. Assessments to	
109. Reserve Taxes	420.00	409. Reserve Taxes	420.00
110. Reserve Insurance	360.00	410. Reserve Insurance	360.00
111. Hazard Insurance 8 months	288.00	411. Hazard Insurance	288.00
112. Water 1 month	15.00	412. Water 1 month	15.00
120. GROSS AMOUNT DUE FROM BORROWER	$ 91,399.90	**420. GROSS AMOUNT DUE TO SELLER**	$90,083.00
200. AMOUNTS PAID BY OR IN BEHALF OF BORROWER: credit		**500. REDUCTIONS IN AMOUNT DUE TO SELLER:** debits	
201. Deposit or earnest money	2,500.00	501. Excess deposit (see instructions)	
202. Principal amount of new loan(s)		502. Settlement charges to seller *(line 1400)*	5,900.00
203. Existing loan(s) ~~taken subject to~~ assume	68,500.00	503. Existing loan(s) ~~taken subject to~~ assume	68,500.00
204. 2nd Mortgage/trust deed	3,500.00	504. Payoff of first mortgage loan	
205.		505. Payoff of second mortgage loan	
206.		506. Loan payment due	983.00
207.		507. 2nd Mortgage/trust deed	3,500.00
208.		508.	
209.		509.	
Adjustments for items unpaid by seller:		*Adjustments for items unpaid by seller:*	
210. City/town taxes to		510. City/town taxes to	
211. County taxes 4 months to	420.00	511. County taxes 4 months to	420.00
212. Assessments to		512. Assessments to	
213.		513.	
214.		514.	
215.		515.	
216.		516.	
217.		517.	
218.		518.	
219.		519.	
220. TOTAL PAID BY/FOR BORROWER	$ 74,920.00	**520. TOTAL REDUCTION AMOUNT DUE SELLER**	$79,303.00
300. CASH AT SETTLEMENT FROM/TO BORROWER		**600. CASH AT SETTLEMENT TO/FROM SELLER**	
301. Gross amount due from borrower *(line 120)*	91,399.90	601. Gross amount due to seller *(line 420)*	$90,083.00
302. Less amounts paid by/for borrower *(line 220)*	(74,920.00)	602. Less reductions in amt. due to seller *(line 520)*	(79,303.00)
303. CASH (☒ FROM) (☐ TO) BORROWER	$ 16,479.90	**603. CASH (☒ TO) (☐ FROM) SELLER**	$10,780.00

RESPA, HB 4305.2

(continued)

Figure 11–4 continued

HUD-1 (3-86)

L. SETTLEMENT CHARGES	(debits) PAID FROM BORROWER'S FUNDS AT SETTLEMENT	(debits) PAID FROM SELLER'S FUNDS AT SETTLEMENT
700. TOTAL SALES/BROKER'S COMMISSION based on price $89,00.00 @ 6% = 5340. *Division of Commission (line 700) as follows:*		
701. $ to		
702. $ to		
703. Commission paid at Settlement		$ 5,340.00
704.		
800. ITEMS PAYABLE IN CONNECTION WITH LOAN		
801. Loan Origination Fee %		
802. Loan Discount %		
803. Appraisal Fee to		
804. Credit Report to		
805. Lender's Inspection Fee		
806. Mortgage Insurance Application Fee to		
807. Assumption Fee	685.00	
808.		
809.		
810.		
811.		
900. ITEMS REQUIRED BY LENDER TO BE PAID IN ADVANCE		
901. Interest from to @ $ /day		
902. Mortgage Insurance Premium for months to		
903. Hazard Insurance Premium for years to		
904. years to		
905.		
1000. **1000. RESERVES DEPOSITED WITH LENDER**		
1001. Hazard insurance months @ $ per month		
1002. Mortgage insurance months @ $ per month		
1003. City property taxes months @ $ per month		
1004. County property taxes months @ $ per month		
1005. Annual assessments months @ $ per month		
1006. months @ $ per month		
1007. months @ $ per month		
1008. months @ $ per month		
1100. TITLE CHARGES		
1101. Settlement or closing fee to		
1102. Abstract or title search to		
1103. Title examination to Buyers attorney	350.00	
1104. Title insurance binder to		
1105. Document preparation to		
1106. Notary fees to		
1107. Attorney's fees to		
(includes above items numbers;)		
1108. Title insurance to	50.00	560.00
(includes above items numbers;)		
1109. Lender's coverage $ 50.00		
1110. Owner's coverage $ 560.00		
1111. Tax Certificate	15.00	
1112.		
1113.		
1200. GOVERNMENT RECORDING AND TRANSFER CHARGES		
1201. Recording fees: Deed $ 3.00 ; Mortgage $ 9.00 ; Releases $	12.00	
1202. City/county tax/stamps: Deed $; Mortgage $		
1203. State tax/stamps: Deed $ 8.90 ; Mortgage $	8.90	
1204.		
1205.		
1300. ADDITIONAL SETTLEMENT CHARGES		
1301. Survey to Survey Company	140.00	
1302. Pest inspection to		
1303.		
1304. Credit report	56.00	
1305.		
1400. TOTAL SETTLEMENT CHARGES *(enter on lines 103, Section J and 502, Section K)*	$1316.90	$5,900.00

I have carefully reviewed the HUD-1 Settlement Statement and to the best of my knowledge and belief, it is a true and accurate statement of all receipts and disbursements made on my account or by me in this transaction. I further certify that I have received a copy of the HUD-1 Settlement Statement.

Borrowers

Sellers

To the best of my knowledge, the HUD-1 Settlement Statement which I have prepared is a true and accurate account of this transaction. I have caused or will cause the funds to be disbursed in accordance with this statement.

Settlement Agent

Date

WARNING: It is a crime to knowingly make a false statement to the United States on this or any other similar form. Penalties upon conviction can include a fine and imprisonment. For details see: Title 18 U.S. Code Section 1001 and Section 1010.

Broker's reconciliation, example 1

HUD-1 Practice Problem	
Funds received:	
Earnest deposit	$ 2,500.00
Buyer funds to close	16,479.00
Total funds received	$18,979.00
Funds to disburse:	
Seller funds	$10,780.00
Title insurance	610.00
Buyer attorney	350.00
Record warranty deed	3.00
Record trust deed	9.00
State tax	8.90
Tax certificate	15.00
Survey	140.00
Credit report	56.00
Loan transfer fee	685.00
Loan payment due	983.00
Broker's fee	5340.00
Total funds to be disbursed:	$18,979.00

Figure 11–5

Solve the following exercises using 30 days in each month and the seller paying through the date of closing. Refer to Chapter 10, on prorations. Use the blank statement forms provided. See Answer Key for solutions.

Practice Problem 1

1. The closing is to take place October 20 of the current year.
2. The sale price is $105,000.
3. The earnest deposit is $2,000.
4. The purchaser will assume the existing loan with an unpaid balance of $84,600.
5. The seller has paid the October payment of $918, which paid interest for September.
6. The interest rate is 10%.
7. The title insurance, which the seller will pay, is $627.
8. Cost to record the deed is $5 (buyer pays).
9. Cost of tax stamps are $10.50 (buyer pays).
10. The tax certificate is $13 (buyer pays).
11. The taxes are paid in arrears. This year's taxes are estimated at $1,082.
12. The reserve for taxes is $880, and the insurance reserve is $192.
13. The hazard insurance is to be assumed by the purchaser and is $380 per year. This was paid May 10.
14. The water bill of $32 is to be paid in advance. The bill is unpaid for October.
15. The broker commission is 6%.

Figure 11–6 Six-column settlement statement for practice problem 1

	SELLER		BUYER		BROKER	
	Debit	Credit	Debit	Credit	Debit	Credit
1. Selling Price						
2. Deposit, paid to						
3. Trust Deed, payable to						
4. Trust Deed, payable to						
5. Trust Deed, payoff to						
6. Interest on Loan Assumed						
7. Title Ins. Premium						
8. Abstracting: Before Sale						
9. After Sale						
10. Title Exam by						
11. Recording: Warranty Deed						
12. Trust Deed						
13. Release						
14. Other						
15. Documentary Fee						
16. Certificate of Taxes Due						
17. Taxes for Preceding Year(s)						
18. Taxes for Current Year						
19. Tax Reserve						
20. Special Taxes						
21. Personal Property Taxes						
22. Hazard Ins. Prem. Assumed						
23. Premium for New Insurance						
24. Hazard Ins. Reserve						
25. FHA Mortgage Ins. Assumed						
26. FHA Mortgage Ins. Reserve						
27. Loan Service Fee (Buyer)						
28. Loan Discount Fee (Seller)						
29. Interest on New Loan						
30. Survey and/or Credit Report						
31. Appraisal Fee						
32. Water and/or Sewer						
33. Rents						
34. Security Deposits						
35. Loan Transfer Fee						
36. Loan Payment Due						
37. Broker's Fee						
Sub-Totals						
Balance due to/from Seller						
Balance due to/from Buyer						
TOTALS						

The printed portions of this form aproved by the Colorado Real Estate Commission (88-41-7-71)

Figure 11–7 HUD-1 settlement statement for practice problem 1

HUD-1 (3-86) OMB NO. 2502-0265

A.

U.S. DEPARTMENT OF HOUSING AND URBAN DEVELOPMENT

SETTLEMENT STATEMENT

B. TYPE OF LOAN

1. ☐ FHA 2. ☐ FMHA 3. ☐ CONV. UNINS.
4. ☐ VA 5. ☐ CONV. INS.

6. FILE NUMBER: 7. LOAN NUMBER:

8. MORTGAGE INSURANCE CASE NUMBER:

C. NOTE: This form is furnished to give you a statement of actual settlement costs. Amounts paid to and by the settlement agent are shown. Items marked *"(p.o.c.)"* were paid outside the closing; they are shown here for informational purposes and are not included in totals.

D. NAME OF BORROWER:	E. NAME OF SELLER:	F. NAME OF LENDER:

G. PROPERTY LOCATION:	H. SETTLEMENT AGENT:	PLACE OF SETTLEMENT
	I. SETTLEMENT DATE:	

J. SUMMARY OF BORROWER'S TRANSACTION		K. SUMMARY OF SELLER'S TRANSACTION	
100. GROSS AMOUNT DUE FROM BORROWER:		**400. GROSS AMOUNT DUE TO SELLER:**	
101. Contract sales price		401. Contract sales price	
102. Personal property		402. Personal property	
103. Settlement charges to borrower *(line 1400)*		403.	
104.		404.	
105.		405.	
Adjustments for items paid by seller in advance		*Adjustments for items paid by seller in advance*	
106. City/town taxes to		406. City/town taxes to	
107. County taxes to		407. County taxes to	
108. Assessments to		408. Assessments to	
109.		409.	
110.		410.	
111.		411.	
112.		412.	
120. GROSS AMOUNT DUE FROM BORROWER		**420. GROSS AMOUNT DUE TO SELLER**	
200. AMOUNTS PAID BY OR IN BEHALF OF BORROWER:		**500. REDUCTIONS IN AMOUNT DUE TO SELLER:**	
201. Deposit or earnest money		501. Excess deposit (see instructions)	
202. Principal amount of new loan(s)		502. Settlement charges to seller *(line 1400)*	
203. Existing loan(s) taken subject to		503. Existing loan(s) taken subject to	
204.		504. Payoff of first mortgage loan	
205.		505. Payoff of second mortgage loan	
206.		506.	
207.		507.	
208.		508.	
209.		509.	
Adjustments for items unpaid by seller:		*Adjustments for items unpaid by seller:*	
210. City/town taxes to		510. City/town taxes to	
211. County taxes to		511. County taxes to	
212. Assessments to		512. Assessments to	
213.		513.	
214.		514.	
215.		515.	
216.		516.	
217.		517.	
218.		518.	
219.		519.	
220. TOTAL PAID BY/FOR BORROWER		**520. TOTAL REDUCTION AMOUNT DUE SELLER**	
300. CASH AT SETTLEMENT FROM/TO BORROWER		**600. CASH AT SETTLEMENT TO/FROM SELLER**	
301. Gross amount due from borrower *(line 120)*		601. Gross amount due to seller *(line 420)*	
302. Less amounts paid by/for borrower *(line 220)*	( )	602. Less reductions in amt. due to seller *(line 520)*	( )
303. CASH (☐ FROM) (☐ TO) BORROWER		**603. CASH (☐ TO) (☐ FROM) SELLER**	

(continued)

Figure 11–7 continued

HUD-1 (3-86)

L. SETTLEMENT CHARGES	PAID FROM BORROWER'S FUNDS AT SETTLEMENT	PAID FROM SELLER'S FUNDS AT SETTLEMENT
700. TOTAL SALES/BROKER'S COMMISSION based on price $ @ % = *Division of Commission (line 700) as follows:*		
701. $ to		
702. $ to		
703. Commission paid at Settlement		
704.		
800. ITEMS PAYABLE IN CONNECTION WITH LOAN		
801. Loan Origination Fee %		
802. Loan Discount %		
803. Appraisal Fee to		
804. Credit Report to		
805. Lender's Inspection Fee		
806. Mortgage Insurance Application Fee to		
807. Assumption Fee		
808.		
809.		
810.		
811.		
900. ITEMS REQUIRED BY LENDER TO BE PAID IN ADVANCE		
901. Interest from to @ $ /day		
902. Mortgage Insurance Premium for months to		
903. Hazard Insurance Premium for years to		
904. years to		
905.		
1000. **1000. RESERVES DEPOSITED WITH LENDER**		
1001. Hazard insurance months @ $ per month		
1002. Mortgage insurance months @ $ per month		
1003. City property taxes months @ $ per month		
1004. County property taxes months @ $ per month		
1005. Annual assessments months @ $ per month		
1006. months @ $ per month		
1007. months @ $ per month		
1008. months @ $ per month		
1100. TITLE CHARGES		
1101. Settlement or closing fee to		
1102. Abstract or title search to		
1103. Title examination to		
1104. Title insurance binder to		
1105. Document preparation to		
1106. Notary fees to		
1107. Attorney's fees to		
(includes above items numbers;)		
1108. Title insurance to		
(includes above items numbers;)		
1109. Lender's coverage $		
1110. Owner's coverage $		
1111. Tax Certificate		
1112.		
1113.		
1200. GOVERNMENT RECORDING AND TRANSFER CHARGES		
1201. Recording fees: Deed $; Mortgage $; Releases $		
1202. City/county tax/stamps: Deed $; Mortgage $		
1203. State tax/stamps: Deed $; Mortgage $		
1204.		
1205.		
1300. ADDITIONAL SETTLEMENT CHARGES		
1301. Survey to		
1302. Pest inspection to		
1303.		
1304.		
1305.		
1400. TOTAL SETTLEMENT CHARGES *(enter on lines 103, Section J and 502, Section K)*		

I have carefully reviewed the HUD-1 Settlement Statement and to the best of my knowledge and belief, it is a true and accurate statement of all receipts and disbursements made on my account or by me in this transaction. I further certify that I have received a copy of the HUD-1 Settlement Statement.

Borrowers

Sellers

To the best of my knowledge, the HUD-1 Settlement Statement which I have prepared is a true and accurate account of this transaction. I have caused or will cause the funds to be disbursed in accordance with this statement.

Settlement Agent

Date

WARNING: It is a crime to knowingly make a false statement to the United States on this or any other similar form. Penalties upon conviction can include a fine and imprisonment. For details see: Title 18 U.S. Code Section 1001 and Section 1010.

Practice Problem 2

1. The closing is to take place May 4 of the current year.
2. The sale price is $86,800.
3. The earnest deposit is $5,000.
4. The purchaser will assume the existing loan with an unpaid balance after the May 1 payment of $72,600.
5. The May 1 payment is not paid. You are to collect $773.25.
6. Interest is 10.5% per annum and paid in advance.
7. Title insurance is $584, which the buyer has agreed to pay.
8. Recording fees are $10.
9. Tax stamps are $8.68.
10. Tax certificate which the seller has agreed to pay is $15.
11. Taxes are paid in advance for the current year and are $720.
12. Tax reserves are $315 and insurance reserves are $187.
13. The hazard insurance policy was paid by the seller last November 15, in the amount of $320.
14. The water bill is $45, payable in arrears for April and May.
15. It is a two-unit property. Unit one rents for $500 per month, and unit two rents for $620 per month. The seller collected for both units on May 1.
16. Each tenant has given the seller a $200 security deposit.
17. There is a loan transfer fee of $125.
18. The broker commission is 8%.

Figure 11–8 Six-column settlement statement for practice problem 2

	SELLER		BUYER		BROKER	
	Debit	Credit	Debit	Credit	Debit	Credit
1. Selling Price						
2. Deposit, paid to						
3. Trust Deed, payable to						
4. Trust Deed, payable to						
5. Trust Deed, payoff to						
6. Interest on Loan Assumed						
7. Title Ins. Premium						
8. Abstracting: Before Sale						
9. After Sale						
10. Title Exam by						
11. Recording: Warranty Deed						
12. Trust Deed						
13. Release						
14. Other						
15. Documentary Fee						
16. Certificate of Taxes Due						
17. Taxes for Preceding Year(s)						
18. Taxes for Current Year						
19. Tax Reserve						
20. Special Taxes						
21. Personal Property Taxes						
22. Hazard Ins. Prem. Assumed						
23. Premium for New Insurance						
24. Hazard Ins. Reserve						
25. FHA Mortgage Ins. Assumed						
26. FHA Mortgage Ins. Reserve						
27. Loan Service Fee (Buyer)						
28. Loan Discount Fee (Seller)						
29. Interest on New Loan						
30. Survey and/or Credit Report						
31. Appraisal Fee						
32. Water and/or Sewer						
33. Rents						
34. Security Deposits						
35. Loan Transfer Fee						
36. Loan Payment Due						
37. Broker's Fee						
Sub-Totals						
Balance due to/from Seller						
Balance due to/from Buyer						
TOTALS						

The printed portions of this form aproved by the Colorado Real Estate Commission (88-41-7-71)

Figure 11–9 HUD-1 settlement statement for practice problem 2

HUD-1 (3-86) OMB NO. 2502-0265

A. U.S. DEPARTMENT OF HOUSING AND URBAN DEVELOPMENT SETTLEMENT STATEMENT	B. TYPE OF LOAN 1. ☐FHA 2. ☐FMHA 3. ☐CONV. UNINS. 4. ☐VA 5. ☐CONV. INS.	
	6. FILE NUMBER:	7. LOAN NUMBER:
	8. MORTGAGE INSURANCE CASE NUMBER:	

C. NOTE: This form is furnished to give you a statement of actual settlement costs. Amounts paid to and by the settlement agent are shown. Items marked "(p.o.c.)" were paid outside the closing; they are shown here for informational purposes and are not included in totals.

D. NAME OF BORROWER:	E. NAME OF SELLER:	F. NAME OF LENDER:
G. PROPERTY LOCATION:	H. SETTLEMENT AGENT: I. SETTLEMENT DATE:	PLACE OF SETTLEMENT

J. SUMMARY OF BORROWER'S TRANSACTION		K. SUMMARY OF SELLER'S TRANSACTION	
100. GROSS AMOUNT DUE FROM BORROWER:		**400. GROSS AMOUNT DUE TO SELLER:**	
101. Contract sales price		401. Contract sales price	
102. Personal property		402. Personal property	
103. Settlement charges to borrower *(line 1400)*		403.	
104.		404.	
105.		405.	
Adjustments for items paid by seller in advance		*Adjustments for items paid by seller in advance*	
106. City/town taxes to		406. City/town taxes to	
107. County taxes to		407. County taxes to	
108. Assessments to		408. Assessments to	
109.		409.	
110.		410.	
111.		411.	
112.		412.	
120. GROSS AMOUNT DUE FROM BORROWER		420. GROSS AMOUNT DUE TO SELLER	
200. AMOUNTS PAID BY OR IN BEHALF OF BORROWER:		**500. REDUCTIONS IN AMOUNT DUE TO SELLER:**	
201. Deposit or earnest money		501. Excess deposit (see instructions)	
202. Principal amount of new loan(s)		502. Settlement charges to seller *(line 1400)*	
203. Existing loan(s) taken subject to		503. Existing loan(s) taken subject to	
204.		504. Payoff of first mortgage loan	
205.		505. Payoff of second mortgage loan	
206.		506.	
207.		507.	
208.		508.	
209.		509.	
Adjustments for items unpaid by seller:		*Adjustments for items unpaid by seller:*	
210. City/town taxes to		510. City/town taxes to	
211. County taxes to		511. County taxes to	
212. Assessments to		512. Assessments to	
213.		513.	
214.		514.	
215.		515.	
216.		516.	
217.		517.	
218.		518.	
219.		519.	
220. TOTAL PAID BY/FOR BORROWER		520. TOTAL REDUCTION AMOUNT DUE SELLER	
300. CASH AT SETTLEMENT FROM/TO BORROWER		**600. CASH AT SETTLEMENT TO/FROM SELLER**	
301. Gross amount due from borrower *(line 120)*		601. Gross amount due to seller *(line 420)*	
302. Less amounts paid by/for borrower *(line 220)*	( )	602. Less reductions in amt. due to seller *(line 520)*	( )
303. CASH (☐ FROM) (☐ TO) BORROWER		603. CASH (☐ TO) (☐ FROM) SELLER	

(continued)

Figure 11–9 continued

HUD-1 (3-86)

L. SETTLEMENT CHARGES	PAID FROM BORROWER'S FUNDS AT SETTLEMENT	PAID FROM SELLER'S FUNDS AT SETTLEMENT
700. TOTAL SALES/BROKER'S COMMISSION based on price $ @ % = *Division of Commission (line 700) as follows:*		
701. $ to		
702. $ to		
703. Commission paid at Settlement		
704.		
800. ITEMS PAYABLE IN CONNECTION WITH LOAN		
801. Loan Origination Fee %		
802. Loan Discount %		
803. Appraisal Fee to		
804. Credit Report to		
805. Lender's Inspection Fee		
806. Mortgage Insurance Application Fee to		
807. Assumption Fee		
808.		
809.		
810.		
811.		
900. ITEMS REQUIRED BY LENDER TO BE PAID IN ADVANCE		
901. Interest from to @ $ /day		
902. Mortgage Insurance Premium for months to		
903. Hazard Insurance Premium for years to		
904. years to		
905.		
1000. **1000. RESERVES DEPOSITED WITH LENDER**		
1001. Hazard insurance months @ $ per month		
1002. Mortgage insurance months @ $ per month		
1003. City property taxes months @ $ per month		
1004. County property taxes months @ $ per month		
1005. Annual assessments months @ $ per month		
1006. months @ $ per month		
1007. months @ $ per month		
1008. months @ $ per month		
1100. TITLE CHARGES		
1101. Settlement or closing fee to		
1102. Abstract or title search to		
1103. Title examination to		
1104. Title insurance binder to		
1105. Document preparation to		
1106. Notary fees to		
1107. Attorney's fees to		
(includes above items numbers;)		
1108. Title insurance to		
(includes above items numbers;)		
1109. Lender's coverage $		
1110. Owner's coverage $		
1111. Tax Certificate		
1112.		
1113.		
1200. GOVERNMENT RECORDING AND TRANSFER CHARGES		
1201. Recording fees: Deed $; Mortgage $; Releases $		
1202. City/county tax/stamps: Deed $; Mortgage $		
1203. State tax/stamps: Deed $; Mortgage $		
1204.		
1205.		
1300. ADDITIONAL SETTLEMENT CHARGES		
1301. Survey to		
1302. Pest inspection to		
1303.		
1304.		
1305.		
1400. **TOTAL SETTLEMENT CHARGES** *(enter on lines 103, Section J and 502, Section K)*		

I have carefully reviewed the HUD-1 Settlement Statement and to the best of my knowledge and belief, it is a true and accurate statement of all receipts and disbursements made on my account or by me in this transaction. I further certify that I have received a copy of the HUD-1 Settlement Statement.

Borrowers ______________________ Sellers ______________________

To the best of my knowledge, the HUD-1 Settlement Statement which I have prepared is a true and accurate account of this transaction. I have caused or will cause the funds to be disbursed in accordance with this statement.

Settlement Agent ______________________ Date ______________________

WARNING: It is a crime to knowingly make a false statement to the United States on this or any other similar form. Penalties upon conviction can include a fine and imprisonment. For details see: Title 18 U.S. Code Section 1001 and Section 1010.

NEW LOANS

Let's now analyze the difference in the entries when a purchaser is securing a *new loan*. The difference is that the lender will not allow the broker to write checks for certain items to be paid. The lender is concerned about making payoffs of existing loans, recording documents, etc. With an assumption, the broker pays all bills. With a new loan, the broker pays only those bills left to be paid *after* the lender has withheld the money to pay the items the lender is concerned with. The buyer and seller debits and credits will be the same, but the broker reconciliation will show only the money that the broker actually receives and disburses. It is therefore best to enter on the worksheet only the lender figures that affect buyer and seller *before* proceeding to the broker reconciliation and debiting and crediting those items that the lender is not involved in.

New loan		$67,150.00
Pay off old loan	$42,889.88	
Title insurance owner	560.00	
Mortgagee	50.00	
Recording fees: deed	5.00	
New trust deed	15.00	
Release of old loan	15.00	
New insurance policy	552.00	
Reserves: taxes	850.00	
Insurance	46.00	
Loan service fee:	671.50	
Discount 2%	1,343.00	
Total lender payouts	$46,997.38	

Assume that the seller will pay off the old loan and pay for recording the release of the old loan, the owner's title insurance policy, and the discount points. The buyer will pay all other costs.

At this point, the lender has agreed to make a loan of $67,150 (buyer's loan, buyer's credit). The costs then are removed from the loan (buyer debits and seller debits). As a result, there is money *left over*, which is turned over to the broker to pay all other bills necessary. In order to determine the leftover funds (hereafter referred to as net proceeds), subtract the lender payouts, $46,997.38, from the loan of $67,150. This leaves $20,152.62 (net proceeds).

```
  $67,150.00
– 46,997.38
  $20,152.62
```

The net proceeds check is made out to the buyer, who endorses it over to the broker (broker debit). The broker will use this money to continue paying bills that the lender is not involved with. The broker also will settle taxes, water, rent, and so on. See Figure 11–10 for the completed six-column settlement statement.

Note that if you run a total of all debits *including* net proceeds, the total will equal the loan (credit). Therefore debits and credits are equal at this point.

Broker Information to Finalize Closing

1. Close July 1	
2. Sale price	$83,950.00
3. Earnest money	3,000.00
4. Title exam by buyer's attorney	100.00

Figure 11–10 Six-column settlement statement

New Loan Worksheet	SELLER Debit	SELLER Credit	BUYER Debit	BUYER Credit	BROKER Debit	BROKER Credit
1. Selling Price						
2. Deposit, paid to						
3. Trust Deed, payable to				$ 67,150 00		
4. Trust Deed, payable to						
5. Trust Deed, payoff to	$ 42,889 88					
6. Interest on Loan Assumed						
7. Title Ins. Premium	560 00		50 00			
8. Abstracting: Before Sale						
9. After Sale						
10. Title Exam by						
11. Recording: Warranty Deed			5 00			
12. Trust Deed			15 00			
13. Release	15 00					
14. Other						
15. Documentary Fee						
16. Certificate of Taxes Due						
17. Taxes for Preceding Year(s)						
18. Taxes for Current Year						
19. Tax Reserve			850 00			
20. Special Taxes						
21. Personal Property Taxes						
22. Hazard Ins. Prem. Assumed						
23. Premium for New Insurance			552 00			
24. Hazard Ins. Reserve			46 00			
25. FHA Mortgage Ins. Assumed						
26. FHA Mortgage Ins. Reserve						
27. Loan Service Fee (Buyer)			671 50			
28. Loan Discount Fee (Seller)	1,343 00					
29. Interest on New Loan						
30. Survey and/or Credit Report						
31. Appraisal Fee						
32. Water and/or Sewer						
33. Rents						
34. Security Deposits						
35. Loan Transfer Fee						
36. Loan Payment Due						
37. Broker's Fee						
Net Proceeds of Loan					$ 20,152 62	
Sub-Totals						
Balance due to/from Seller						
Balance due to/from Buyer						
TOTALS						

The printed portions of this form aproved by the Colorado Real Estate Commission (SS-61-7-71)

Figure 11–11 Completed six-column settlement statement

New Loan Example	SELLER Debit	SELLER Credit	BUYER Debit	BUYER Credit	BROKER Total $ in to Broker Debit	BROKER Total $ out Credit
1. Selling Price		$ 83,950 00	$ 83,950 00			
2. Deposit, paid to				$ 3,000 00	$ 3,000 00	
3. Trust Deed, payable to				67,150 00		
4. Trust Deed, payable to						
5. Trust Deed, payoff to	$ 42,889 88					
6. Interest on Loan Assumed						
7. Title Ins. Premium	560 00		50 00			
8. Abstracting: Before Sale						
9. After Sale						
10. Title Exam by			100 00			100 00
11. Recording: Warranty Deed			5 00			
12. Trust Deed			15 00			
13. Release	15 00					
14. Other						
15. Documentary Fee						
16. Certificate of Taxes Due						
17. Taxes for Preceding Year(s)						
18. Taxes for Current Year 859.92 ÷ 360 =	431 85			431 85		
19. Tax Reserve 2.385889 x 181 days			850 00			
20. Special Taxes						
21. Personal Property Taxes						
22. Hazard Ins. Prem. Assumed						
23. Premium for New Insurance			552 00			
24. Hazard Ins. Reserve			46 00			
25. FHA Mortgage Ins. Assumed						
26. FHA Mortgage Ins. Reserve						
27. Loan Service Fee (Buyer)			671 50			
28. Loan Discount Fee (~~Seller~~)	1,343 00					
29. Interest on New Loan						
30. Survey and/or Credit Report						
31. Appraisal Fee						
32. Water and/or Sewer $38.00 ÷ 60 = .633333 x 29		18 37	18 37			
33. Rents						
34. Security Deposits						
35. Loan Transfer Fee						
36. Loan Payment Due						
37. Broker's Fee	4,197 50					4,197 50
Net Proceeds					20,152 62	
Sub-Totals	49,437 23	83,968 37	86,257 87	70,581 85	23,152 62	4,297 50
Balance due to/~~from~~ Seller	34,531 14					34,531 14
Balance due ~~to~~/from Buyer				15,676 02	15,676 02	
TOTALS	83,968 37	83,968 37	86,257 87	86,257 87	38,828 64	38,828 64

The printed portions of this form aproved by the Colorado Real Estate Commission (SS-61-7-71)

5. Estimated taxes for current year	858.92
6. Water bill for June and July paid by seller	38.00
7. Commission 5%	4,197.50

As you can see, the broker has debited and credited the parties for the sale price, has settled taxes and water between the parties, has paid the buyer's attorney, paid himself or herself the commission, and drawn a check to the seller for $34,531.14. The broker has received a check from the buyer in the amount of $15,676.02, thus bringing in $38,828.64 and paying out $38,828.64. See Figure 11–11 for the six-column settlement statement.

Practice Problem 3

Lender Information		
New Loan		$76,950.00
Payoff of seller's loan	$49,600.00	
Interest 11% 3–7 thru 3–30	564.30	
Title ins. owner's policy (seller to pay)	525.00	
Title insurance mortgagee policy (buyer to pay)	60.00	
Recording deed	5.00	
Trust deed/mortgage	20.00	
Release seller's loan	15.00	
Documentary fee (buyer)	9.62	
Tax Certificace (buyer)	20.00	
Tax reserves (2 months)	165.00	
Insurance reserves (2 months)	54.00	
New insurance policy	320.00	
Loan service fee	769.50	
Survey (buyer)	100.00	
TOTAL		52,227.42
NET PROCEEDS		$24,722.58

Broker information to finalize closing

1. Close March 7 current year	
2. Sale price	$ 96,200.00
3. Earnest money	$ 5,000.00
4. Taxes paid by seller for current year	$ 985.00
5. Water bill due March 1 for March	$ 18.27
6. Rent (seller has collected rent for March)	$ 900.00
7. Buyer's attorney to examine title	$ 150.00
8. Seller's attorney to review closing	$ 200.00
9. Real estate commission 7%	

Figure 11–12 Six-column settlement statement for practice problem 3

	SELLER		BUYER		BROKER	
	Debit	Credit	Debit	Credit	Debit	Credit
1. Selling Price						
2. Deposit, paid to						
3. Trust Deed, payable to						
4. Trust Deed, payable to						
5. Trust Deed, payoff to						
6. Interest on Loan Assumed						
7. Title Ins. Premium						
8. Abstracting: Before Sale						
9. After Sale						
10. Title Exam by						
11. Recording: Warranty Deed						
12. Trust Deed						
13. Release						
14. Other						
15. Documentary Fee						
16. Certificate of Taxes Due						
17. Taxes for Preceding Year(s)						
18. Taxes for Current Year						
19. Tax Reserve						
20. Special Taxes						
21. Personal Property Taxes						
22. Hazard Ins. Prem. Assumed						
23. Premium for New Insurance						
24. Hazard Ins. Reserve						
25. FHA Mortgage Ins. Assumed						
26. FHA Mortgage Ins. Reserve						
27. Loan Service Fee (Buyer)						
28. Loan Discount Fee (Seller)						
29. Interest on New Loan						
30. Survey and/or Credit Report						
31. Appraisal Fee						
32. Water and/or Sewer						
33. Rents						
34. Security Deposits						
35. Loan Transfer Fee						
36. Loan Payment Due						
37. Broker's Fee						
Sub-Totals						
Balance due to/from Seller						
Balance due to/from Buyer						
TOTALS						

The printed portions of this form aproved by the Colorado Real Estate Commission (88-41-7-71)

Figure 11–13 HUD-1 settlement statement for practice problem 3

HUD-1 (3-86) OMB NO. 2502-0265

A. U.S. DEPARTMENT OF HOUSING AND URBAN DEVELOPMENT SETTLEMENT STATEMENT	B. TYPE OF LOAN 1. ☐FHA 2. ☐FMHA 3. ☐CONV. UNINS. 4. ☐VA 5. ☐CONV. INS.
	6. FILE NUMBER: 7. LOAN NUMBER:
	8. MORTGAGE INSURANCE CASE NUMBER:

C. NOTE: This form is furnished to give you a statement of actual settlement costs. Amounts paid to and by the settlement agent are shown. Items marked *"(p.o.c.)"* were paid outside the closing; they are shown here for informational purposes and are not included in totals.

D. NAME OF BORROWER:	E. NAME OF SELLER:	F. NAME OF LENDER:
G. PROPERTY LOCATION:	H. SETTLEMENT AGENT: I. SETTLEMENT DATE:	PLACE OF SETTLEMENT

J. SUMMARY OF BORROWER'S TRANSACTION		K. SUMMARY OF SELLER'S TRANSACTION	
100. GROSS AMOUNT DUE FROM BORROWER:		**400. GROSS AMOUNT DUE TO SELLER:**	
101. Contract sales price		401. Contract sales price	
102. Personal property		402. Personal property	
103. Settlement charges to borrower *(line 1400)*		403.	
104.		404.	
105.		405.	
Adjustments for items paid by seller in advance		*Adjustments for items paid by seller in advance*	
106. City/town taxes to		406. City/town taxes to	
107. County taxes to		407. County taxes to	
108. Assessments to		408. Assessments to	
109.		409.	
110.		410.	
111.		411.	
112.		412.	
120. GROSS AMOUNT DUE FROM BORROWER		**420. GROSS AMOUNT DUE TO SELLER**	
200. AMOUNTS PAID BY OR IN BEHALF OF BORROWER:		**500. REDUCTIONS IN AMOUNT DUE TO SELLER:**	
201. Deposit or earnest money		501. Excess deposit (see instructions)	
202. Principal amount of new loan(s)		502. Settlement charges to seller *(line 1400)*	
203. Existing loan(s) taken subject to		503. Existing loan(s) taken subject to	
204.		504. Payoff of first mortgage loan	
205.		505. Payoff of second mortgage loan	
206.		506.	
207.		507.	
208.		508.	
209.		509.	
Adjustments for items unpaid by seller:		*Adjustments for items unpaid by seller:*	
210. City/town taxes to		510. City/town taxes to	
211. County taxes to		511. County taxes to	
212. Assessments to		512. Assessments to	
213.		513.	
214.		514.	
215.		515.	
216.		516.	
217.		517.	
218.		518.	
219.		519.	
220. TOTAL PAID BY/FOR BORROWER		**520. TOTAL REDUCTION AMOUNT DUE SELLER**	
300. CASH AT SETTLEMENT FROM/TO BORROWER		**600. CASH AT SETTLEMENT TO/FROM SELLER**	
301. Gross amount due from borrower *(line 120)*		601. Gross amount due to seller *(line 420)*	
302. Less amounts paid by/for borrower *(line 220)*	( )	602. Less reductions in amt. due to seller *(line 520)*	( )
303. CASH (☐ FROM) (☐ TO) BORROWER		**603. CASH (☐ TO) (☐ FROM) SELLER**	

(continued)

Figure 11–13 continued

HUD-1 (3-86)

L. SETTLEMENT CHARGES		
700. TOTAL SALES/BROKER'S COMMISSION based on price $ @ % = *Division of Commission (line 700) as follows:*	PAID FROM BORROWER'S FUNDS AT SETTLEMENT	PAID FROM SELLER'S FUNDS AT SETTLEMENT
701. $ to		
702. $ to		
703. Commission paid at Settlement		
704.		
800. ITEMS PAYABLE IN CONNECTION WITH LOAN		
801. Loan Origination Fee %		
802. Loan Discount %		
803. Appraisal Fee to		
804. Credit Report to		
805. Lender's Inspection Fee		
806. Mortgage Insurance Application Fee to		
807. Assumption Fee		
808.		
809.		
810.		
811.		
900. ITEMS REQUIRED BY LENDER TO BE PAID IN ADVANCE		
901. Interest from to @ $ /day		
902. Mortgage Insurance Premium for months to		
903. Hazard Insurance Premium for years to		
904. years to		
905.		
1000. RESERVES DEPOSITED WITH LENDER		
1001. Hazard insurance months @ $ per month		
1002. Mortgage insurance months @ $ per month		
1003. City property taxes months @ $ per month		
1004. County property taxes months @ $ per month		
1005. Annual assessments months @ $ per month		
1006. months @ $ per month		
1007. months @ $ per month		
1008. months @ $ per month		
1100. TITLE CHARGES		
1101. Settlement or closing fee to		
1102. Abstract or title search to		
1103. Title examination to		
1104. Title insurance binder to		
1105. Document preparation to		
1106. Notary fees to		
1107. Attorney's fees to		
(includes above items numbers;)		
1108. Title insurance to		
(includes above items numbers;)		
1109. Lender's coverage $		
1110. Owner's coverage $		
1111. Tax Certificate		
1112.		
1113.		
1200. GOVERNMENT RECORDING AND TRANSFER CHARGES		
1201. Recording fees: Deed $; Mortgage $; Releases $		
1202. City/county tax/stamps: Deed $; Mortgage $		
1203. State tax/stamps: Deed $; Mortgage $		
1204.		
1205.		
1300. ADDITIONAL SETTLEMENT CHARGES		
1301. Survey to		
1302. Pest inspection to		
1303.		
1304.		
1305.		
1400. TOTAL SETTLEMENT CHARGES *(enter on lines 103, Section J and 502, Section K)*		

I have carefully reviewed the HUD-1 Settlement Statement and to the best of my knowledge and belief, it is a true and accurate statement of all receipts and disbursements made on my account or by me in this transaction. I further certify that I have received a copy of the HUD-1 Settlement Statement.

Borrowers Sellers

To the best of my knowledge, the HUD-1 Settlement Statement which I have prepared is a true and accurate account of this transaction. I have caused or will cause the funds to be disbursed in accordance with this statement.

Settlement Agent Date

WARNING: It is a crime to knowingly make a false statement to the United States on this or any other similar form. Penalties upon conviction can include a fine and imprisonment. For details see: Title 18 U.S. Code Section 1001 and Section 1010.

Practice Problem 4

Lender information:		
New loan		$102,600.00
Interest on new loan at 9% 6–15 thru 6–30		
$25.65 per day (16 days)	$ 410.40	
Private mortgage insurance (1%) (buyer)	1,026.00	
Title insurance owners and mortgagee (buyer to pay)	675.00	
Payoff existing loan	70,280.00	
Recording deed	10.00	
Trust deed/mortgage	20.00	
Seller's release of existing loan	20.00	
Tax certificate (buyer to pay)	15.00	
Tax reserves (2 months)	213.33	
Insurance reserve (2 months)	86.66	
New insurance policy	520.00	
Loan service fee	1,026.00	
TOTAL LOAN PAYOUTS		74,302.39
NET PROCEEDS		$28,297.61

Broker information to finalize closing

1. Closing June 15 current year	
2. Sale price	$114,000.00
3. Earnest money	$10,000.00
4. Estimated taxes for current year	$1,280.00
5. Water and sewer bill for June and July due and unpaid	$36.00
6. Rent for June prepaid	$950.00
7. Security deposit	$400.00
8. Buyer's attorney to examine title	$250.00
9. Seller's attorney	$250.00
10. Broker commission 5%	

Figure 11–14 Six-column settlement statement for practice problem 4

	SELLER		BUYER		BROKER	
	Debit	Credit	Debit	Credit	Debit	Credit
1. Selling Price						
2. Deposit, paid to						
3. Trust Deed, payable to						
4. Trust Deed, payable to						
5. Trust Deed, payoff to						
6. Interest on Loan Assumed						
7. Title Ins. Premium						
8. Abstracting: Before Sale						
9. After Sale						
10. Title Exam by						
11. Recording: Warranty Deed						
12. Trust Deed						
13. Release						
14. Other						
15. Documentary Fee						
16. Certificate of Taxes Due						
17. Taxes for Preceding Year(s)						
18. Taxes for Current Year						
19. Tax Reserve						
20. Special Taxes						
21. Personal Property Taxes						
22. Hazard Ins. Prem. Assumed						
23. Premium for New Insurance						
24. Hazard Ins. Reserve						
25. FHA Mortgage Ins. Assumed						
26. FHA Mortgage Ins. Reserve						
27. Loan Service Fee (Buyer)						
28. Loan Discount Fee (Seller)						
29. Interest on New Loan						
30. Survey and/or Credit Report						
31. Appraisal Fee						
32. Water and/or Sewer						
33. Rents						
34. Security Deposits						
35. Loan Transfer Fee						
36. Loan Payment Due						
37. Broker's Fee						
Sub-Totals						
Balance due to/from Seller						
Balance due to/from Buyer						
TOTALS						

The printed portions of this form aproved by the Colorado Real Estate Commission (88-41-7-71)

Figure 11–15 HUD-1 settlement statement for practice problem 4

HUD-1 (3-86) OMB NO. 2502-0265

A.

U.S. DEPARTMENT OF HOUSING AND URBAN DEVELOPMENT

SETTLEMENT STATEMENT

B. TYPE OF LOAN

1. ☐FHA 2. ☐FMHA 3. ☐CONV. UNINS.
4. ☐VA 5. ☐CONV. INS.

6. FILE NUMBER:

7. LOAN NUMBER:

8. MORTGAGE INSURANCE CASE NUMBER:

C. NOTE: This form is furnished to give you a statement of actual settlement costs. Amounts paid to and by the settlement agent are shown. Items marked *"(p.o.c.)"* were paid outside the closing; they are shown here for informational purposes and are not included in totals.

D. NAME OF BORROWER:	E. NAME OF SELLER:	F. NAME OF LENDER:
G. PROPERTY LOCATION:	H. SETTLEMENT AGENT:	PLACE OF SETTLEMENT
	I. SETTLEMENT DATE:	

J. SUMMARY OF BORROWER'S TRANSACTION		K. SUMMARY OF SELLER'S TRANSACTION	
100. GROSS AMOUNT DUE FROM BORROWER:		**400. GROSS AMOUNT DUE TO SELLER:**	
101. Contract sales price		401. Contract sales price	
102. Personal property		402. Personal property	
103. Settlement charges to borrower *(line 1400)*		403.	
104.		404.	
105.		405.	
Adjustments for items paid by seller in advance		*Adjustments for items paid by seller in advance*	
106. City/town taxes to		406. City/town taxes to	
107. County taxes to		407. County taxes to	
108. Assessments to		408. Assessments to	
109.		409.	
110.		410.	
111.		411.	
112.		412.	
120. GROSS AMOUNT DUE FROM BORROWER		**420. GROSS AMOUNT DUE TO SELLER**	
200. AMOUNTS PAID BY OR IN BEHALF OF BORROWER:		**500. REDUCTIONS IN AMOUNT DUE TO SELLER:**	
201. Deposit or earnest money		501. Excess deposit (see instructions)	
202. Principal amount of new loan(s)		502. Settlement charges to seller *(line 1400)*	
203. Existing loan(s) taken subject to		503. Existing loan(s) taken subject to	
204.		504. Payoff of first mortgage loan	
205.		505. Payoff of second mortgage loan	
206.		506.	
207.		507.	
208.		508.	
209.		509.	
Adjustments for items unpaid by seller:		*Adjustments for items unpaid by seller:*	
210. City/town taxes to		510. City/town taxes to	
211. County taxes to		511. County taxes to	
212. Assessments to		512. Assessments to	
213.		513.	
214.		514.	
215.		515.	
216.		516.	
217.		517.	
218.		518.	
219.		519.	
220. TOTAL PAID BY/FOR BORROWER		**520. TOTAL REDUCTION AMOUNT DUE SELLER**	
300. CASH AT SETTLEMENT FROM/TO BORROWER		**600. CASH AT SETTLEMENT TO/FROM SELLER**	
301. Gross amount due from borrower *(line 120)*		601. Gross amount due to seller *(line 420)*	
302. Less amounts paid by/for borrower *(line 220)*	( )	602. Less reductions in amt. due to seller *(line 520)*	( )
303. CASH (☐ FROM) (☐ TO) BORROWER		**603. CASH (☐ TO) (☐ FROM) SELLER**	

(continued)

Figure 11–15 continued

HUD-1 (3-86)

L. SETTLEMENT CHARGES	PAID FROM BORROWER'S FUNDS AT SETTLEMENT	PAID FROM SELLER'S FUNDS AT SETTLEMENT
700. TOTAL SALES/BROKER'S COMMISSION based on price $ @ % = *Division of Commission (line 700) as follows:*		
701. $ to		
702. $ to		
703. Commission paid at Settlement		
704.		
800. ITEMS PAYABLE IN CONNECTION WITH LOAN		
801. Loan Origination Fee %		
802. Loan Discount %		
803. Appraisal Fee to		
804. Credit Report to		
805. Lender's Inspection Fee		
806. Mortgage Insurance Application Fee to		
807. Assumption Fee		
808.		
809.		
810.		
811.		
900. ITEMS REQUIRED BY LENDER TO BE PAID IN ADVANCE		
901. Interest from to @ $ /day		
902. Mortgage Insurance Premium for months to		
903. Hazard Insurance Premium for years to		
904. years to		
905.		
1000. 1000. RESERVES DEPOSITED WITH LENDER		
1001. Hazard insurance months @ $ per month		
1002. Mortgage insurance months @ $ per month		
1003. City property taxes months @ $ per month		
1004. County property taxes months @ $ per month		
1005. Annual assessments months @ $ per month		
1006. months @ $ per month		
1007. months @ $ per month		
1008. months @ $ per month		
1100. TITLE CHARGES		
1101. Settlement or closing fee to		
1102. Abstract or title search to		
1103. Title examination to		
1104. Title insurance binder to		
1105. Document preparation to		
1106. Notary fees to		
1107. Attorney's fees to		
(includes above items numbers;)		
1108. Title insurance to		
(includes above items numbers;)		
1109. Lender's coverage $		
1110. Owner's coverage $		
1111. Tax Certificate		
1112.		
1113.		
1200. GOVERNMENT RECORDING AND TRANSFER CHARGES		
1201. Recording fees: Deed $; Mortgage $; Releases $		
1202. City/county tax/stamps: Deed $; Mortgage $		
1203. State tax/stamps: Deed $; Mortgage $		
1204.		
1205.		
1300. ADDITIONAL SETTLEMENT CHARGES		
1301. Survey to		
1302. Pest inspection to		
1303.		
1304.		
1305.		
1400. TOTAL SETTLEMENT CHARGES *(enter on lines 103, Section J and 502, Section K)*		

I have carefully reviewed the HUD-1 Settlement Statement and to the best of my knowledge and belief, it is a true and accurate statement of all receipts and disbursements made on my account or by me in this transaction. I further certify that I have received a copy of the HUD-1 Settlement Statement.

Borrowers

Sellers

To the best of my knowledge, the HUD-1 Settlement Statement which I have prepared is a true and accurate account of this transaction. I have caused or will cause the funds to be disbursed in accordance with this statement.

Settlement Agent

Date

WARNING: It is a crime to knowingly make a false statement to the United States on this or any other similar form. Penalties upon conviction can include a fine and imprisonment. For details see: Title 18 U.S. Code Section 1001 and Section 1010.

Individual Statements

After the broker prepares the six-column worksheet, he or she will then transfer the figures to the individual Statement of Settlement for buyer and seller (see Figure 11–16).

GOOD FAITH ESTIMATES AND APRs

The Real Estate Settlement Procedures Act places certain requirements on lenders regarding closing of new loan transactions.

The lender must provide to a borrower a good faith estimate of charges likely to be incurred in connection with the settlement. The lender or the lender's agent must also prepare a Uniform Settlement Sheet as prescribed by the Department of Housing and Urban Development (HUD), and the lender may make no charge for the preparation of the document.

A lender must also, under the Truth in Lending Act, disclose to the purchaser the annual percentage rate (APR). The APR is the true yield to the lender, which includes interest plus other financing charges related to borrowing of the funds. The APR is therefore the relationship of the total finance charge to the total amount to be financed and must be computed to the nearest ⅛th of 1% or ¼th of 1% for irregular payment transactions. To compute the APR, tables must be used.

Figure 11–16

The printed portion of this form approved by the Colorado Real Estate Commission (SS-60-7-71)

STATEMENT OF SETTLEMENT
SELLER'S ☐ PURCHASER'S ☐

PROPERTY ADDRESS__________

SELLER__________ PURCHASER__________

SETTLEMENT DATE__________ DATE OF PRORATION__________

LEGAL DESCRIPTION:

	Debit	Credit
1. Selling Price		
2. Deposit, paid to		
3. Trust Deed, payable to		
4. Trust Deed, payable to		
5. Trust Deed, payoff to		
6. Interest on Loan Assumed		
7. Title Ins. Premium		
8. Abstracting: Before Sale		
9. After Sale		
10. Title Exam. by		
11. Recording: Warranty Deed		
12. Trust Deed		
13. Release		
14. Other		
15. Documentary Fee		
16. Certificate of Taxes Due		
17. Taxes for Preceding Year(s)		
18. Taxes for Current Year		
19. Tax Reserve		
20. Special Taxes		
21. Personal Property Taxes		
22. Hazard Ins. Prem. Assumed—Policy No. Co.		
$ Yr. Term Expires		
Premium $ Days Unused at ¢ per day		
23. Premium for New Insurance		
24. Hazard Ins. Reserve		
25. FHA Mortgage Ins. Assumed		
26. FHA Mortgage Ins. Reserve		
27. Loan Service Fee (Buyer)		
28. Loan Discount Fee (Seller)		
29. Interest on New Loan		
30. Survey and/or Credit Report		
31. Appraisal Fee		
32. Water and/or Sewer		
33. Rents		
34. Security Deposits		
35. Loan Transfer Fee		
36. Loan Payment Due		
37. Broker's Fee		
Sub-Totals		
Balance due to/from Seller		
Balance due to/from Buyer		
TOTALS		

The above figures do not include sales or use taxes on personal property

APPROVED and ACCEPTED

Purchaser/Seller__________ Broker__________

Purchaser/Seller__________ By__________

CHAPTER TEST

Complete the following assumption closing. Use the blank statements (Figures 11–17 and 11–18) provided on the following pages. Use a 30-day month and charge the seller the date of closing.

Carl Smith is purchasing a 10-unit apartment building from Joseph Crowley. The closing is to be November 18 of the current year. The sale price is $280,000. Smith will assume the existing loan of $210,000 with interest at 10% payable in arrears. This is the balance after the November 1 payment, which is unpaid in the amount of $2,430, including principal, interest, taxes, and insurance. Taxes are $2,400 per year, payable in arrears with last year's paid, and insurance is $900 per year, paid through next March 10. The buyer will assume the seller's insurance. The earnest deposit is $20,000. The tax reserve account is $1,900 and the insurance reserve account is $600. The loan transfer fee is $1,000, which the buyer has agreed to pay. The water bill is $78, paid in advance monthly. The buyer and seller have agreed to split the cost of title insurance, which costs $980. The recording charge to record the deed is $10. Tax stamps, which the seller is to pay, are $28. The buyer has obtained a survey costing $600 and provided the seller with a credit report costing $60. Rents are all collected in advance on the first of the month. Four units rent for $600 per month and six units rent for $480 per month. Each tenant has given the seller a security deposit of $250. The broker commission is 5%.

Figure 11–17 Six-column settlement statement for Chapter Test

	SELLER		BUYER		BROKER	
	Debit	Credit	Debit	Credit	Debit	Credit
1. Selling Price						
2. Deposit, paid to						
3. Trust Deed, payable to						
4. Trust Deed, payable to						
5. Trust Deed, payoff to						
6. Interest on Loan Assumed						
7. Title Ins. Premium						
8. Abstracting: Before Sale						
9. After Sale						
10. Title Exam by						
11. Recording: Warranty Deed						
12. Trust Deed						
13. Release						
14. Other						
15. Documentary Fee						
16. Certificate of Taxes Due						
17. Taxes for Preceding Year(s)						
18. Taxes for Current Year						
19. Tax Reserve						
20. Special Taxes						
21. Personal Property Taxes						
22. Hazard Ins. Prem. Assumed						
23. Premium for New Insurance						
24. Hazard Ins. Reserve						
25. FHA Mortgage Ins. Assumed						
26. FHA Mortgage Ins. Reserve						
27. Loan Service Fee (Buyer)						
28. Loan Discount Fee (Seller)						
29. Interest on New Loan						
30. Survey and/or Credit Report						
31. Appraisal Fee						
32. Water and/or Sewer						
33. Rents						
34. Security Deposits						
35. Loan Transfer Fee						
36. Loan Payment Due						
37. Broker's Fee						
Sub-Totals						
Balance due to/from Seller						
Balance due to/from Buyer						
TOTALS						

The printed portions of this form aproved by the Colorado Real Estate Commission (SS-41-7-71)

Figure 11–18 HUD-1 settlement statement for Chapter Test

HUD-1 (3-86) OMB NO. 2502-0265

A.	B. TYPE OF LOAN	
U.S. DEPARTMENT OF HOUSING AND URBAN DEVELOPMENT	1. ☐FHA 2. ☐FMHA 3. ☐CONV. UNINS. 4. ☐VA 5. ☐CONV. INS.	
SETTLEMENT STATEMENT	6. FILE NUMBER:	7. LOAN NUMBER:
	8. MORTGAGE INSURANCE CASE NUMBER:	

C. NOTE: This form is furnished to give you a statement of actual settlement costs. Amounts paid to and by the settlement agent are shown. Items marked *"(p.o.c.)"* were paid outside the closing; they are shown here for informational purposes and are not included in totals.

D. NAME OF BORROWER:	E. NAME OF SELLER:	F. NAME OF LENDER:
G. PROPERTY LOCATION:	H. SETTLEMENT AGENT:	PLACE OF SETTLEMENT
	I. SETTLEMENT DATE:	

J. SUMMARY OF BORROWER'S TRANSACTION		K. SUMMARY OF SELLER'S TRANSACTION	
100. GROSS AMOUNT DUE FROM BORROWER:		**400. GROSS AMOUNT DUE TO SELLER:**	
101. Contract sales price		401. Contract sales price	
102. Personal property		402. Personal property	
103. Settlement charges to borrower *(line 1400)*		403.	
104.		404.	
105.		405.	
Adjustments for items paid by seller in advance		*Adjustments for items paid by seller in advance*	
106. City/town taxes to		406. City/town taxes to	
107. County taxes to		407. County taxes to	
108. Assessments to		408. Assessments to	
109.		409.	
110.		410.	
111.		411.	
112.		412.	
120. GROSS AMOUNT DUE FROM BORROWER		**420. GROSS AMOUNT DUE TO SELLER**	
200. AMOUNTS PAID BY OR IN BEHALF OF BORROWER:		**500. REDUCTIONS IN AMOUNT DUE TO SELLER:**	
201. Deposit or earnest money		501. Excess deposit (see instructions)	
202. Principal amount of new loan(s)		502. Settlement charges to seller *(line 1400)*	
203. Existing loan(s) taken subject to		503. Existing loan(s) taken subject to	
204.		504. Payoff of first mortgage loan	
205.		505. Payoff of second mortgage loan	
206.		506.	
207.		507.	
208.		508.	
209.		509.	
Adjustments for items unpaid by seller:		*Adjustments for items unpaid by seller:*	
210. City/town taxes to		510. City/town taxes to	
211. County taxes to		511. County taxes to	
212. Assessments to		512. Assessments to	
213.		513.	
214.		514.	
215.		515.	
216.		516.	
217.		517.	
218.		518.	
219.		519.	
220. TOTAL PAID BY/FOR BORROWER		**520. TOTAL REDUCTION AMOUNT DUE SELLER**	
300. CASH AT SETTLEMENT FROM/TO BORROWER		**600. CASH AT SETTLEMENT TO/FROM SELLER**	
301. Gross amount due from borrower *(line 120)*		601. Gross amount due to seller *(line 420)*	
302. Less amounts paid by/for borrower *(line 220)*	( )	602. Less reductions in amt. due to seller *(line 520)*	( )
303. CASH (☐ FROM) (☐ TO) BORROWER		**603. CASH (☐ TO) (☐ FROM) SELLER**	

(continued)

Figure 11–18 continued

HUD-1 (3-86)

L. SETTLEMENT CHARGES	PAID FROM BORROWER'S FUNDS AT SETTLEMENT	PAID FROM SELLER'S FUNDS AT SETTLEMENT
700. TOTAL SALES/BROKER'S COMMISSION based on price $ @ % = *Division of Commission (line 700) as follows:*		
701. $ to		
702. $ to		
703. Commission paid at Settlement		
704.		
800. ITEMS PAYABLE IN CONNECTION WITH LOAN		
801. Loan Origination Fee %		
802. Loan Discount %		
803. Appraisal Fee to		
804. Credit Report to		
805. Lender's Inspection Fee		
806. Mortgage Insurance Application Fee to		
807. Assumption Fee		
808.		
809.		
810.		
811.		
900. ITEMS REQUIRED BY LENDER TO BE PAID IN ADVANCE		
901. Interest from to @ $ /day		
902. Mortgage Insurance Premium for months to		
903. Hazard Insurance Premium for years to		
904. years to		
905.		
1000. **1000. RESERVES DEPOSITED WITH LENDER**		
1001. Hazard insurance months @ $ per month		
1002. Mortgage insurance months @ $ per month		
1003. City property taxes months @ $ per month		
1004. County property taxes months @ $ per month		
1005. Annual assessments months @ $ per month		
1006. months @ $ per month		
1007. months @ $ per month		
1008. months @ $ per month		
1100. TITLE CHARGES		
1101. Settlement or closing fee to		
1102. Abstract or title search to		
1103. Title examination to		
1104. Title insurance binder to		
1105. Document preparation to		
1106. Notary fees to		
1107. Attorney's fees to		
(includes above items numbers;)		
1108. Title insurance to		
(includes above items numbers;)		
1109. Lender's coverage $		
1110. Owner's coverage $		
1111. Tax Certificate		
1112.		
1113.		
1200. GOVERNMENT RECORDING AND TRANSFER CHARGES		
1201. Recording fees: Deed $; Mortgage $; Releases $		
1202. City/county tax/stamps: Deed $; Mortgage $		
1203. State tax/stamps: Deed $; Mortgage $		
1204.		
1205.		
1300. ADDITIONAL SETTLEMENT CHARGES		
1301. Survey to		
1302. Pest inspection to		
1303.		
1304.		
1305.		
1400. **TOTAL SETTLEMENT CHARGES** *(enter on lines 103, Section J and 502, Section K)*		

I have carefully reviewed the HUD-1 Settlement Statement and to the best of my knowledge and belief, it is a true and accurate statement of all receipts and disbursements made on my account or by me in this transaction. I further certify that I have received a copy of the HUD-1 Settlement Statement.

Borrowers

Sellers

To the best of my knowledge, the HUD-1 Settlement Statement which I have prepared is a true and accurate account of this transaction. I have caused or will cause the funds to be disbursed in accordance with this statement.

Settlement Agent

Date

WARNING: It is a crime to knowingly make a false statement to the United States on this or any other similar form. Penalties upon conviction can include a fine and imprisonment. For details see: Title 18 U.S. Code Section 1001 and Section 1010.

12

SIMPLE INVESTMENT MATH

Goals

1. Understand basic real estate investment math, including cash flows, time value of money, and rate of return.
2. Perform basic calculations with these concepts, including using calculators and compound interest tables.
3. Consider tax depreciation as it will affect investment decisions.

Regardless of what is used as a vehicle to increase one's wealth, the old adage "the higher the risk the greater the return" holds true. This is the basis for evaluating all real estate investments. A price is paid (in lower returns) for security and certainty, as in purchasing a certificate of deposit. A dividend is gained (in higher returns) for risk over time, as in land speculation. Evaluating the final cash outcome of such investments along with the cash flows received over the investment period helps one determine the *present value* of such an investment, or *how much one should invest right now.* This principle of evaluating various cash flows, cash outcomes, and present values is known as the *time value of money.* Along with related income tax benefits, it forms the basis for analyzing and comparing investment decisions. This chapter will introduce you to some of the more common calculations needed to make such decisions.

CASH FLOW

Ideally, an investment property will yield a positive *cash flow.* The cash flow represents the net proceeds after all expenses are met and may be measured before or after taxes are considered. If an investor has a property that generates an annual income of $44,000 and expenses total $35,000, a net return (cash flow) of $9,000 has been earned.

Income from office building		$44,000
Expenses	17,000	
Debt service (mortgage payment)	18,000	
Cash flow		$ 9,000

If the tax deductible expenses involved in a property are greater than the income, there will be, for tax purposes, a *negative cash flow.*

Exercises

1. An office building took in $1,200 per month in rent and had annual expenses of $3,100. Monthly debt service on this building is $325. What is the annual cash flow? Is it positive or negative?

2. Tabor Medical Center rents for $25,000 annually. The building is older, and monthly expenses have averaged $1,800 per month. The monthly debt service is $500. What is the annual cash flow? Is it positive or negative?

RATE OF RETURN

The value of an asset is determined by the stream of income it produces over the expected life of the investment. The return on the individual's cash investment can vary greatly, depending on the ratio of cash invested to the purchase price as well as on the cost of financing.

To evaluate the feasibility of an investment, the investors decide what percentage of return they want on their investment and examine the return on the actual investment. If they know they can receive a certain percentage return on CDs or Treasury bonds, they will expect more from a real estate investment because of the risks involved.

In the income approach technique for evaluating property investments, the property's net annual income is divided by the desired rate of return. If an investor requires a 12 percent annual return and the property has a $15,000 net annual income, he should pay no more than $125,000.

$$\frac{\$15{,}000 \text{ net annual income}}{12\% \text{ investor's desired rate of return}} = \$125{,}000 \text{ value of property if investor is willing to accept a } 12\% \text{ rate of return}$$

The rate of investor's desired rate of return relates net operating income to the investment.

In using this *capitalization method* of evaluating an income-producing property, the future income is converted to a present value. When the risk is greater, the capitalization rate must be higher to offset the risk or make it worthwhile. The value of the income stream is lessened as the capitalization rate increases. A property will depreciate and lessen in value as its economic life is depleted, and this must be taken into consideration when analyzing the possibility of recapturing the investment. If the remaining life of the property is 25 years, and it is depreciated on a straight-line basis, the property will depreciate at 4 percent per year (100% divided by 25 years equals 4% per year). As the property depreciates, the income may likewise decline. Since the investor desired a 12 percent return on her investment, the 4 percent annual investment must be added to supply the full return on the investment. This 4 percent is called a recapture rate, as it recaptures for the investor what otherwise would have been lost through depreciation. With the 4 percent recapture rate added to the 12 percent desired rate of return, the investor would now be looking for a 16 percent return, and the value of the property in the previous example is now reduced to $93,750.

$$\frac{\$15{,}000 \text{ income}}{16\% \text{ rate of return}} = \$93{,}750 \text{ property value to investor}$$

(See page 231 for more on depreciation.)

Exercises

1. Sam is determining whether to invest in Land View Office Park. His purchase price will be $200,000. His net annual income from the property will be $20,000. He desires an 11% annual return on his money. Should he invest?

2. Swooshball Enterprises plans to invest some of its employee pension funds in real estate. In order to meet its current investment goals they must earn 12% on real estate investments. Currently they are considering purchasing Willamette Warehouse for $85,000. Its annual income would be $13,000. Should they invest?

TIME VALUE OF MONEY

The payment of a return on investment attracts capital to real estate just as to any other type of investment. Investors forego present benefits or the immediate use of capital in favor of accepting future benefits. These payments are a return on the investment called "yield." The interest rate, or yield, represents the "time value of money."

To evaluate and compare real estate investments, one evaluates two types of cash flows (or payments): (1) the rental income and (2) the proceeds of a future sale or the estimated or projected future sale. Problems involving the valuation estimate consider the future value of money at interest "compounding," or the present value of money to be received in the future, called "discounting." The amount to be received or deposited can be a single, lump sum payment or a series of payments discounted or compounded at a given rate of interest and time period.

Compound Interest/Discounting

Compounding or *compound interest* takes place when interest is added to a principal amount in addition to the interest already earned, reflecting compound growth or interest on interest. Compound interest tables are used for compounding or discounting various types of cash flows. *Discounting* is a process of calculating compound interest and deducting it from a sum of money to be received in the future.

Compound interest/discount tables and/or financial calculators are used extensively in the analysis of investment real estate. Several examples of these tables, which you will need to calculate answers to sample problems in this chapter, are found at the end of the chapter on pages 237–242. The tables generally consist of six columns, often referred to as the six functions of a dollar:

Column 1 calculates the growth of a single sum at a given rate over time.

Column 2 calculates the growth of a series of payments at a given rate over time.

Column 3 is known as a sinking fund factor and is used to calculate the amount of equal payments needed to achieve a specified future value or sum.

Column 4 is used to calculate the present value of a lump sum to be received in the future at a given rate.

Column 5 is used to calculate the present value of a series of payments to be received over time at a given rate.

Column 6 is the installment to amortize one table, also known as the amortization or mortgage constant table, used to calculate the principal and interest payments for a

Figure 12–1

Examples of basic routines for calculating factors for the six functions of a dollar with the HP-12C calculator, using an interest rate of 10 percent and a compounding factor of 5 years.

ANNUAL COMPOUNDING:

Keystrokes								Display
To get factor for Column #1:								
(f)	(CLX)	5 (n)	10 (i)	1 (CHS)	(PV)	(FV)	=	1.610051
To get factor for Column #2:								
(f)	(CLX)	5 (n)	10 (i)	1 (CHS)	(PMT)	(FV)	=	6.10510
To get factor for Column #3:								
(f)	(CLX)	5 (n)	10 (i)	1 (CHS)	(FV)	(PMT)	=	0.16380
To get factor for Column #4:								
(f)	(CLX)	5 (n)	10 (i)	1 (CHS)	(FV)	(PV)	=	0.62092
To get factor for Column #5:								
(f)	(CLX)	5 (n)	10 (i)	1 (CHS)	(PMT)	(PV)	=	3.79079
To get factor for Column #6:								
(f)	(CLX)	5 (n)	10 (i)	1 (CHS)	(PV)	(PMT)	=	0.26380

MONTHLY COMPOUNDING:

To get factor for Column #1:								
(f)	(CLX)	5 (gn)	10 (gi)	1 (CHS)	(PV)	(FV)	=	1.64531
To get factor for Column #2:								
(f)	(CLX)	5 (gn)	10 (gi)	1 (CHS)	(PMT)	(FV)	=	77.43707
To get factor for Column #3:								
(f)	(CLX)	5 (gn)	10 (gi)	1 (CHS)	(FV)	(PMT)	=	0.012913
To get factor for Column #4:								
(f)	(CLX)	5 (gn)	10 (gi)	1 (CHS)	(FV)	(PV)	=	0.60779
To get factor for Column #5:								
(f)	(CLX)	5 (gn)	10 (gi)	1 (CHS)	(PMT)	(PV)	=	47.06537
To get factor for Column #6:								
(f)	(CLX)	5 (gn)	10 (gi)	1 (CHS)	(PV)	(PMT)	=	0.02125
		Annual constant		12x			=	0.25496

mortgage. For example: to calculate the monthly mortgage payment for a $50,000 loan at 9% for 30 years, the factor from the 9% monthly table, column 6 is .008046. $50,000 x .008046 = $402.30 = the monthly mortgage payment.

With the HP-12C, the keystrokes are:
$50,000 (PV)
30 (gn)
9 (gi)
PMT = $402.31 (slight difference due to rounding)

Columns 1, 2 and 3 are referred to as future value factors, while columns 4 and 5 are present value factors.

Present Value

Present value can be defined as the amount you are willing to pay today to receive a greater sum in the future, depending on your required rate of return (or interest rate).

The present value of the following cash flows is $1,000, demonstrating that money to be received in the future does not have the same value as money in hand today. For example, if you were to receive a cash payment of $2,012.20 at the end of 12 years and you discounted that payment at a compound rate of 6%, the present value of the future receivable would be $1,000.

Years	**6%**	**8%**	**10%**	**12%**
2.00	$1,123.66	$1,166.40	$1,210.00	$1,254.00
3.00	1,191.02	1,259.71	1,331.00	1,404.93
4.00	1,262.48	1,360.49	1,464.10	1,573.52
5.00	1,338.23	1,469.33	1,610.57	1,762.34
6.00	1,418.52	1,586.87	1,771.56	1,973.82
7.00	1,503.63	1,713.82	1,948.72	2,210.68
8.00	1,593.85	1,805.93	2,143.59	
9.00	1,689.48	1,999.00		
10.0	1,790.85	2,158.93		
11.0	1,898.30			
12.0	2,012.20			

Exercise

1. Jane deposits $1,000 at 8% interest in a compound interest bearing account. What will be the balance of her account at the end of three years?

Figure 12–2

Compound interest is interest earned on interest as it accumulates.

Jones borrows $3,000 with interest at 10% compounded. She plans to pay nothing for three years and at the end of that time to pay the loan off in full. What will her total payment be?

Step 1: $3,000 x .10 = $300 year one.
At the end of year one, Jones owes $3,300.
$3,000 + $300 = $3,300 principal and accumulated interest now due.

Step 2: At the end of year two, she owes $3,300 x .10 = $330.
$3,300 + $330 = $3,630 principal and accumulated interest now due.

Step 3: At the end of year three, she owes $3,630 x .10 = $363.
$3,630 + $363 = $3,993

Answer: $3,993 required payback including accumulated interest.

DISCOUNTED CASH FLOW ANALYSIS

Income-producing property delivers cash flows over future time periods. By discounting the cash flows to be received in the future, the investor determines how much can be paid for the property today to yield a desired rate of return.

To calculate the present value of these future cash flows, the analyst can use compound interest tables or a financial calculator.

Example 1

Calculate the present value of the following cash flows to be received over 3 years, with a desired rate of return of 12%.

Refer to the compound interest table on page 242 (12% annual compounding, column 4).

End of Year	Cash flow	Present value x factor =	Present value
1.	$8,500	.892857	$7,589.28
2.	$9,700	.797194	$7,732.78
3.	$11,000	.711780	$7,829.58
Present value		=	$23,151.64

HP–12C

f clear fin.

1 n	=1.00	2 n	=2.00	3 n	=3.00
12 i	=12.00	12 i	=12.00	12 i	=12.00
8500 fv	= $8,500.00	9700 fv	= $9,700.00	11000 fv	= $11,000.00
PV	= $7,589.29	PV	= $7,732.78	PV	= $7,829.58

The HP-12C calculates to 10 digits. Therefore, the answers may vary slightly due to rounding.

Example 2

What is the present value of a property producing the following cash flows and a sale of $280,000 at the end of the fifth year, utilizing 9% rate of return.

Refer to the compound interest tables on page 238 (9% annual compounding, Column 4).

End of year	Cash flow	Present value × factor	=	Present value
1.	$33,500	.917431		$ 30,734
2.	$26,000	.841680		$ 21,884
3.	$44,000	.772183		$ 33,976
4.	$50,000	.708425		$ 35,421
5.	$57,000	.649931		$ 37,046
				$159,061

Sale at end of year 5

$280,000 × .649931	=	$181,981
Present value	=	$341,042

HP–12C			Property value
f clear fin			
1 n	=	1.00	
9 i	=	9.00	
33500 fv	=	$33,500.00	
PV	=	$30,734.00	$ 30,734
2 n	=	2.00	
9 i	=	9.00	
26000fv	=	$26,000.00	
PV	=	$21,884.00	$ 21,884
3 n	=	3.00	
9 i	=	9.00	
44000 fv	=	$44,000.00	
PV	=	$33,976.00	$ 33,976
4 n	=	4.00	
9 i	=	9.00	
50000 fv	=	$50,000.00	
PV	=	$35,421.00	$ 35,421
5 n	=	5.00	
9 i	=	9.00	
57000 fv	=	$57,000.00	
PV	=	$37,046.00	$ 37,046
Sale $280,000 end of year 5.			
5 n	=	5.00	
9 i	=	9.00	
280000 fv	=	$280,000.00	
PV	=	$181,981.00	$181,981
		Present value	$341,042

Discounting a note: Find the present value of a future lump sum (using the HP–12C).

If your required return is 19%, what should you pay for a $15,000 (present value) new note at 14 1/2% for five years with payments of $275.00 per month?

Keystroke		Display
15,000	(PV)	15,000.00
14.5	(g) (i)	1.21
5	(g) (N)	60.00
275	(CHS) (PMT)	275.00
FV		-6,808.61
19	(g) (i)	1.58
PV		13,254.00

Figure 12–3

Net Present Value (NPV) of a Series of Payments

The net present value (NPV) is used to evaluate uneven cash flows when you wish to achieve a specific rate of return. The financial keys involved are: i, CFo, CFj, Nj, and NPV.

Example:

A project requires an initial investment of $50,000. The forecast after-tax cash flows are:

1st year	=	4,000
2nd year	=	6,000
3rd year	=	8,000
4th year	=	10,000
5th year	=	62,000

The required rate of return is 12%.
Is this project *GO* or *NO GO?*

Keystroke	Display
FIN	
(f) (x⇄y) (Clears financial registers)	
50000 (CHS) (g) (PV)	
(CFo)	-50,000.00
4000 (g) (PMT)	
(CFj)	4,000.00
6000 (g) (PMT)	
(CFj)	6,000.00
8000 (g) (PMT)	
(CFj)	8,000.00
10000 (g) (PMT)	
(CFj)	10,000.00
62000 (g) (PMT)	62,000.00
12 (i)	12.00
(NPV)	
(f) (PV)	5,584.48

Since the answer is positive the project is *GO.*

THE RULE OF 72

Future Value

The Rule of 72 is used to estimate the amount to which an initial deposit into a savings account or investment will grow. It demonstrates the power of compound interest and the "time value of money."

The deposit will double in the number of years obtained by dividing 72 by the rate of annual interest received from the investment.

72 divided by 6% = 12 years (until the deposit doubles)
72 divided by 8% = 9 years (until the deposit doubles)
72 divided by 10% = 7.2 years (until the deposit doubles)
72 divided by 12% = 6 years (until the deposit doubles)

This formula will also provide the rate of interest needed to double the deposit in a predetermined time frame.

72 divided by 12 years = 6% (needed to double the deposit)
72 divided by 9 years = 8% (needed to double the deposit)
72 divided by 7.2 years = 10% (needed to double the deposit)
72 divided by 6 years = 12% (needed to double the deposit)

Figure 12–4
Growth of $1.00 at 5% interest compounded annually.

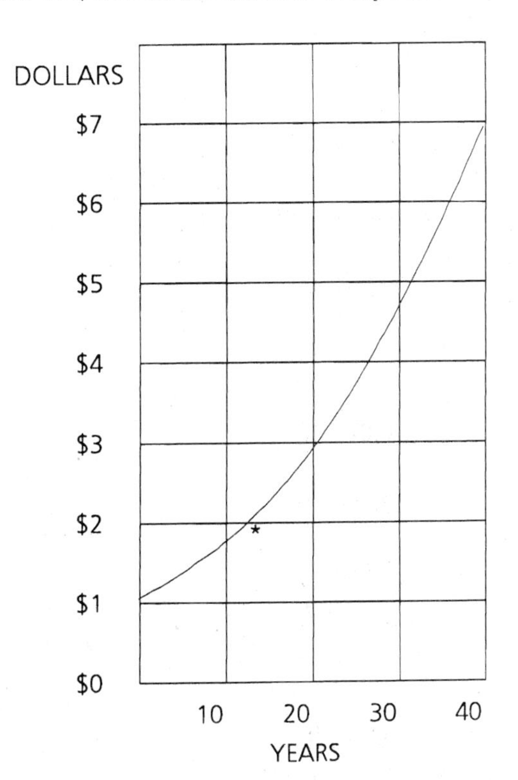

The magic of compound interest is dramatically demonstrated by "The Rule of 72." Money at compound interest will double at the point obtained by dividing 72 by the interest rate:

72 ÷ 5% = 14.4 years

• ▼ • •

Exercises

(Due to the complexity of the problems, solutions are provided using the HP–12C and compound interest tables.)

1. How much money would be accumulated in a 9% savings account with a monthly deposit of $200.00 for 10 years, compounded monthly?

Tables: Column 2, 9%, monthly table, 10 years, factor = 193.514276
Accumulated amount: $200.00 x 193.514276 = $38,702.86
HP 12C: 10gn, 9gi, $200 chs, pmt, *fv* = $38,702.86

2. A piece of residential land has been purchased for $400,000.00. Sales have been appreciating at the rate of 12% compounded annually. Find the value in six years.

Tables: Column 1, 12% annual table, 6 years, factor = 1.973823
Future value: $400,000 x 1.973823 = $789,529.20
HP 12C: 6n, 12i, $400,000 pv, *fv* = $789,529.07

3. An apartment building owner plans to re-roof the building in five years at an estimated cost of $15,000. What is the amount of the annual deposit needed to accumulate the $15,000 in five years with a savings account rate of 10%?

Tables: Column 3, 10%, annual table, 5 years, factor = .163979
Annual payment: $15,000 x .163797 = $2,456.96
HP 12C: 5n, 10i, $15,000 chs fv, *pmt* = $2,456.96

4. A piece of commercial land cannot be utilized until the end of a 10-year mineral lease. If unencumbered by the lease, the land is worth $60,000. What is the present value of the property, assuming no change in value and a yield rate of 12%?

Tables: Column 4, 12%, annual table, 10 years, factor = .32197
Present value: .32197 x $60,000 = $19,318
HP 12C: $60,000 fv, 10n, 12i, *pv* = $19,318.39

5. Calculate the present value of a triple-net lease (NNN) paying $72,000 annually for 12 years using a yield rate of 10%.

Tables: Column 5, 10% annual table, 12 years, factor = 6.813692
Present value: $72,000 x 6.813692 = $490,586.00
HP 12C: $72,000 pmt, 12n, 10i, *pv* = $490,585.81

6. Calculate the monthly payment for a $150,000 loan at 12% for 20 years.

Tables: Column 6, 12%, monthly factor = .011010
$150,000 x .011010 = $1,651.50 monthly payment
HP 12C: $150,000 chs pv, 20 gn, 12 gi, *pmt* = $1,651.63

DEPRECIATION

Depreciation, as we will discuss it here, is an accounting concept used in federal tax law. It makes available to an investor in real estate a deduction from income derived from a property. For accounting and tax purposes, depreciation is based on estimates of a property's future decrease in value. Even as the investor depreciates his property, it continues to increase in value due to rising construction costs and land values. The realization of this depreciation allowance is further enhanced if the investor has used little of his resources to purchase the property. (For example, if a $60,000 property was acquired with $12,000 in cash and the balance from a loan, the investor is still able to depreciate on the *full* value of the structure.) After the value of its *useful life* (economic life) is over, the *salvage value* remains.

The past 10 years have brought dramatic changes in the depreciation methods allowed by the Internal Revenue Service. Prior to 1981, an investor chose one of four methods to depreciate any property or asset eligible for the depreciation allowance. In 1981 Congress passed the Tax Recovery Act, referred to as the Accelerated Cost Recovery System (ACRS). This act replaced the concept of "depreciating" the property with "recovering the cost," enabling the investor to use short-term write-off periods for tax purposes. Losses resulting from depreciation cannot be used to shelter other "earned" income.

Further changes were introduced as a result of the Tax Reform Act (TRA) of 1986. This act stated that residential rental property placed in service after January 1, 1987 must be depreciated on a straight-line basis over 27-1/2 years, and that nonresidential real estate must be depreciated on a straight-line basis over 31-1/2 years. TRA 1993 stated that non-residential property placed in service on or after May 13, 1993 must be depreciated over 39 years. Straight-line depreciation is depreciation of the asset figured in equal installments over a predetermined period of time.

Depreciation can be taken only on the improvements on land and not on the land itself, since land does not diminish in value—literally, it does not wear out. Tax assessors separate the land and improvements when they appraise the property for tax purposes. Assuming that the market value and the cost of the property were the same as the assessed value, Figure 12–5 is an example of the annual depreciation cost of a single-family residential rental.

Figure 12–5
Example of tax depreciation calculation.

This is depreciation on real estate investments used for tax calculations, known as book depreciation or cost recovery.

Steps to calculate depreciation

1. Allocate or separate the depreciable and non-depreciable portions of the asset.
2. Select the recovery period, 27.5 or 31.5 years.
3. Divide the depreciable asset by the recovery period.

$$\frac{\text{Building Value} \quad \$88{,}000}{\text{Recovery Period} \quad 27.5} = \$3{,}200 \text{ annual depreciation}$$

Address	7007 Mulberry Drive
Legal	Lot 3, Block 7, Fall Rapids Subdivision
Land value	$ 32,000
Improvements	$ 88,000
Assessed value	$120,000

Since the example that we have used here is a residential property rental, the amount that can be depreciated must be done over 27.5 years.

Improvements $88,000 ÷ 27.5 (years) = $3,200 = annual amount available for depreciation

Many investments require analysis of the final capital gain, or gain in cash, when the property is sold in order to assess final tax liability. On residential investment properties, capital gain equals the net sale price minus the adjusted basis. The net sale price is the final sale price minus the commission, discount points paid by the seller, and legal fees. The adjusted basis is the original purchase price (also known as the original or initial basis) with improvement costs added and allowable depreciation subtracted.

Figure 12–6 is an example of an investment, which, when sold, generated a federal tax liability on the capital gain.

Figure 12–6
Example of more complex tax depreciation calculation.

Sale price		$110,000
Less: commission	$5,000	
legal fees	$1,000	
discount points	$3,000	
		9,000
Net sales		$101,000
Initial basis	$75,000	
Improvements	4,000	
Allowable depreciation	−5,000	
Adjusted basis		$ 74,000
Capital gain		$ 27,000

CAPITAL GAIN x INVESTOR'S TAX RATE = TAX LIABILITY
(e.g., 27,000 x .27 = $7,290 due)

Figure 12–7
Capital gain, net sale price, adjusted basis.

Capital Gain = *Net Sale Price* – *Adjusted Basis*

Net Sale Price = Sale Price – Commission – Seller Paid Discount Points – Legal Fees

Adjusted Basis = Initial Basis + Improvements – Allowed Depreciation

• ▼ • •

Exercises

1. Susan and John purchased a residential rental in a growing suburb of Dallas. They paid $175,000 for the property, $135,000 of which was determined to be the value of the improvements (house). How much can they depreciate each year?

2. Les and Grace recently sold their long-time residential rental for $125,000. Their commission totaled $7,500 and their legal fees were $800. They paid $2,000 in discount points toward the buyer's new loan. They originally bought this house for $80,000 (initial basis). They made $5,000 worth of improvements, and were allowed $8,700 in depreciation. What is their adjusted basis? What is their capital gain? If their federal tax rate is 27%, what is their federal tax liability?

CHAPTER TEST

1. You purchased a 10-acre parcel of land 15 years ago as a long-term investment. Your original purchase price was $20,000. What sale price today would provide a 12% rate of return?

2. You plan to establish a college fund for your child, who will be ready for college in six years. The amount needed will be $25,000. At an annual return of 10%, how much should you deposit each year?

3. As part of a purchase of an investment property, you agree to pay the seller $10,000 in five years. At a 10% rate, how much should you set aside each month?

4. An income property will produce a $5,000 negative cash flow the first year due to fix-up costs and the following positive cash flows for years two through five: second year, $5,000; third year, $8,000; fourth year, $12,000; and fifth year, $15,000. Calculate the present value of this income stream using a 10% discount rate.

5. You are planning to purchase a new home. The mortgage amount will be $125,000 and the lender will amortize the loan over 25 years at 10%. What is the monthly principal and interest payment?

6. The compound interest tables reflect payments received at the end of each period. Rent typically is received in advance; therefore, the tables must be modified to reflect payments in advance. This is done by multiplying the factor times 1 + the effective rate of interest. For example, the annual 10% factor for 10 years would be 1.10 times the factor for the last period.

   A warehouse lease calls for annual payments of $10,000, payable in advance each year for 10 years. At a 10% discount rate, what is the present value of this income stream?

7. You anticipate receiving a lump sum payment of $50,000 in five years as an estate settlement. If you had this money in hand today, you could invest it and receive a 9% return. Based on this information, what is the present value of this deferred cash flow?

8. A tenant agrees to pay an additional $150.00 per month in rent, payable in advance, in exchange for additional interior improvements. The lease term is 10 years. How much can you afford to spend on these improvements, assuming an annual 10% discount rate? *(Remember:* The present value of one per period factor must be multiplied by 1.00 + i or 1.008333 to convert to payments paid in advance. The modified factor is then 75.671163 x 1.008333 = 76.301731.)

9. You are comparing two $5,000 income streams from alternative investments, both with 10-year terms. One is payable at the end of each year with a 10% yield, and the other is payable in advance with a 12% yield. Which income stream has the highest present value, and what is the difference in dollars?

10. Five years ago you purchased a parcel of vacant land for $10,000. During the five years the carrying costs and property taxes totaled $500.00 per year. You have now decided to sell the property and you wish to receive a 12% return. Calculate your asking price using column 1 and column 2.

11. Sunny Breezes Shopping Strip takes in a monthly rent of $2,300. Its monthly expenses total $800 and there is an annual debt service of $12,000. What is the annual cash flow? Is it positive or negative?

12. Somers and Steel, a law firm, wants to invest in a shopping strip. They desire to earn 10% annually on their investment and have $100,000 with which to purchase a building. How much must their annual income be to meet their goals?

13. Eduardo purchased a nice home in a growing section of Portland as a rental home. He paid $175,000 for the property, $150,000 of which was allocated as the value of the improvements (house). How much will he be able to write off as a depreciated asset after five years, when he plans to sell?

14. Sara Stone wants to purchase a duplex. She found one she likes, and the purchase price is $60,000. The current rents total $650 per month. If she purchases the building, what will be her rate of return?

9% Monthly Compounding Interest

Years	Future worth of 1 1	Future worth of 1 per period 2	Sinking fund factor 3	Present worth of 1 4	Present worth of 1 per period 5	Installment to amortize 1 6
1	1.093806	12.507586	.079951	.914238	11.434912	.087451
2	1.196413	26.188470	.038184	.835831	21.889146	.045684
3	1.308645	41.152716	.024299	.764148	31.446805	.031799
4	1.431405	57.520711	.017385	.698614	40.184781	.024885
5	1.565681	75.424136	.013258	.638699	48.173373	.020758
6	1.712552	95.007027	.010525	.583923	55.476848	.018025
7	1.873201	116.426928	.008589	.533845	62.153964	.016089
8	2.048921	139.856163	.007150	.488061	68.258438	.014650
9	2.241124	165.483222	.006042	.446204	73.839381	.013542
10	2.451357	193.514276	.005167	.407937	78.941692	.012667
11	2.681311	224.174837	.004460	.372951	83.606419	.011960
12	2.932836	257.711569	.003880	.340966	87.871091	.011380
13	3.207957	294.394278	.003396	.311724	91.770017	.010896
14	3.508885	334.518079	.002989	.284990	95.334563	.010489
15	3.838043	378.405768	.002642	.260549	98.593409	.010142
16	4.198078	426.410426	.002345	.238204	101.572769	.009845
17	4.591886	478.918251	.002088	.217775	104.296613	.009588
18	5.022637	536.351673	.001864	.199098	106.786855	.009364
19	5.493795	599.172746	.001668	.182023	109.063530	.009168
20	6.009151	667.886868	.001497	.166412	111.144953	.008997
21	6.572851	743.046850	.001345	.152140	113.047869	.008845
22	7.189430	825.257356	.001211	.139093	114.787589	.008711
23	7.863848	915.179775	.001092	.127164	116.378106	.008592
24	8.601531	1013.537537	.000986	.116258	117.832217	.008486
25	9.408414	1121.121935	.000891	.106287	119.161622	.008391
26	10.290988	1238.798492	.000807	.097172	120.377014	.008307
27	11.256354	1367.513922	.000731	.088838	121.488171	.008231
28	12.312278	1508.303747	.000662	.081219	122.504035	.008162
29	13.467254	1662.300628	.000601	.074254	123.432775	.008101
30	14.730576	1830.743479	.000546	.067886	124.281865	.008046
31	16.112405	2014.987432	.000496	.062063	125.058136	.007996
32	17.623860	2216.514738	.000451	.056741	125.767833	.007951
33	19.277100	2436.946695	.000410	.051875	126.416663	.007910
34	21.085425	2678.056691	.000373	.047426	127.009849	.007873
35	23.063383	2941.784467	.000339	.043358	127.552164	.007839
36	25.226887	3230.251727	.000309	.039640	128.047967	.007809
37	27.593344	3545.779207	.000282	.036240	128.501249	.007782
38	30.181790	3890.905340	.000257	.033132	128.915658	.007757
39	33.013050	4268.406685	.000234	.030291	129.294525	.007734
40	36.109901	4681.320260	.000213	.027693	129.640901	.007713
41	39.497259	5132.967977	.000194	.025318	129.957571	.007694
42	43.202375	5626.983364	.000177	.023146	130.247083	.007677
43	47.255056	6167.340803	.000162	.021161	130.511766	.007662
44	51.687906	6758.387497	.000147	.019346	130.753748	.007647
45	56.536588	7404.878447	.000135	.017687	130.974978	.007635
46	61.840110	8112.014707	.000123	.016170	131.177236	.007623
47	67.641139	8885.485227	.000112	.014783	131.362146	.007612
48	73.986344	9731.512616	.000102	.013516	131.531199	.007602
49	80.926774	10656.903210	.000093	.012356	131.685753	.007593
50	88.518263	11669.101820	.000085	.011297	131.827052	.007585

9% Annual Compounding Interest

Years	Future worth of 1 1	Future worth of 1 per period 2	Sinking fund factor 3	Present worth of 1 4	Present worth of 1 per period 5	Installment to amortize 1 6
1	1.090000	1.000000	1.000000	.917431	.917431	1.090000
2	1.188100	2.090000	.478469	.841680	1.759111	.568469
3	1.295029	3.278100	.305055	.772183	2.531295	.395055
4	1.411582	4.573129	.218669	.708425	3.239720	.308669
5	1.538624	5.984711	.167092	.649931	3.889651	.257092
6	1.667100	7.523335	.132920	.596267	4.485919	.222920
7	1.828039	9.200435	.108691	.547034	5.032953	.198691
8	1.992563	11.028474	.090674	.501866	5.534819	.180674
9	2.171893	13.021036	.076799	.460428	5.995247	.166799
10	2.367364	15.192930	.065820	.422411	6.417658	.155820
11	2.580426	17.560293	.056947	.387533	6.805191	.146947
12	2.812665	20.140720	.049651	.355535	7.160725	.139651
13	3.065805	22.953385	.043567	.326179	7.486904	.133567
14	3.341727	26.019189	.038433	.299246	7.786150	.128433
15	3.642482	29.360916	.034059	.274538	8.060688	.124059
16	3.970306	33.003399	.030300	.251870	8.312558	.120300
17	4.327633	36.973705	.027046	.231073	8.543631	.117046
18	4.717120	41.301338	.024212	.211994	8.755625	.114212
19	5.141661	46.018458	.021730	.194490	8.950115	.111730
20	5.604411	51.160120	.019546	.178431	9.128546	.109546
21	6.108808	56.764530	.017617	.163698	9.292244	.107617
22	6.658600	62.873338	.015905	.150182	9.442425	.105905
23	7.257874	69.531939	.014382	.137781	9.580207	.104382
24	7.911083	76.789813	.013023	.126405	9.706612	.103023
25	8.623081	84.700896	.011806	.115968	9.822580	.101806
26	9.399158	93.323977	.010715	.106393	9.928972	.100715
27	10.245082	102.723135	.009735	.097608	10.026580	.099735
28	11.167140	112.968217	.008852	.089548	10.116128	.098852
29	12.172182	124.135356	.008056	.082155	10.198283	.098056
30	13.267678	136.307539	.007336	.075371	10.273654	.097336
31	14.461770	149.575217	.006686	.069148	10.342802	.096686
32	15.763329	164.036987	.006096	.063438	10.406240	.096096
33	17.182028	179.800315	.005562	.058200	10.464441	.095562
34	18.728411	196.982344	.005077	.053395	10.517835	.095077
35	20.413968	215.710755	.004636	.048986	10.566821	.094636
36	22.251225	236.124723	.004235	.044941	10.611763	.094235
37	24.253835	258.375948	.003870	.041231	10.652993	.093870
38	26.436680	282.629783	.003538	.037826	10.690820	.093538
39	28.815982	309.066463	.003236	.034703	10.725523	.093236
40	31.409420	337.882445	.002960	.031838	10.757360	.092960
41	34.236268	369.291865	.002708	.029209	10.786569	.092708
42	37.317532	403.528133	.002478	.026797	10.813366	.092478
43	40.676110	440.845665	.002268	.024584	10.837951	.092268
44	44.336960	481.521775	.002077	.022555	10.860505	.092077
45	48.327286	525.858735	.001902	.020692	10.881197	.091902
46	52.676742	574.186021	.001742	.018984	10.900181	.091742
47	57.417649	626.862762	.001595	.017416	10.917597	.091595
48	62.585237	684.280411	.001461	.015978	10.933575	.091461
49	68.217908	746.865648	.001339	.014659	10.948234	.091339
50	74.357520	815.083556	.001227	.013449	10.961683	.091227
51	81.049697	889.441077	.001124	.012338	10.974021	.091124
52	88.344170	970.490773	.001030	.011319	10.985340	.091030
53	96.295145	1058.834943	.000944	.010385	10.995725	.090944
54	104.961708	1155.130088	.000866	.009527	11.005252	.090866
55	114.408262	1260.091796	.000794	.008741	11.013993	.090794
56	124.705005	1374.500057	.000728	.008019	11.022012	.090728
57	135.928456	1499.205063	.000667	.007357	11.029369	.090667
58	148.162017	1635.133518	.000612	.006749	11.036118	.090612
59	161.496598	1783.295535	.000561	.006192	11.042310	.090561
60	176.031292	1944.792133	.000514	.005681	11.047991	.090514

10% Monthly Compounding Interest

Years	Future worth of 1 1	Future worth of 1 per period 2	Sinking fund factor 3	Present worth of 1 4	Present worth of 1 per period 5	Installment to amortize 1 6
1	1.104713	12.565568	.079582	.905212	11.374508	.087915
2	1.220390	26.446915	.037811	.819409	21.670854	.046144
3	1.348181	41.781821	.023933	.741739	30.991235	.032267
4	1.489354	58.722491	.017029	.671432	39.428160	.025362
5	1.645308	77.437072	.012913	.607788	47.065369	.021247
6	1.817594	98.111313	.010192	.550177	53.978665	.018525
7	2.007920	120.950418	.008267	.498027	60.236667	.016601
8	2.218175	146.181075	.006840	.450820	65.901488	.015174
9	2.450447	174.053712	.005745	.408088	71.029355	.014078
10	2.707041	204.844978	.004881	.369406	75.671163	.013215
11	2.990504	238.860492	.004186	.334391	79.872985	.012519
12	3.303648	276.437875	.003617	.302695	83.676528	.011950
13	3.649584	317.950100	.003145	.274003	87.119542	.011478
14	4.031743	363.809198	.002748	.248031	90.236200	.011082
15	4.453919	414.470344	.002412	.224521	93.057438	.010746
16	4.920303	470.436373	.002125	.203239	95.611258	.010459
17	5.435523	532.262776	.001878	.183974	97.923008	.010212
18	6.004693	600.563212	.001665	.166536	100.015632	.009998
19	6.633463	676.015596	.001479	.150750	101.909902	.009812
20	7.328073	759.368830	.001316	.136461	103.624619	.009650
21	8.095418	851.450237	.001174	.123526	105.176801	.009507
22	8.943114	953.173772	.001049	.111817	106.581857	.009382
23	9.879575	1065.549089	.000938	.101218	107.853729	.009271
24	10.914096	1189.691570	.000840	.091624	109.005045	.009173
25	12.056944	1326.833392	.000753	.082939	110.047230	.009087
26	13.319464	1478.335753	.000676	.075078	110.990629	.009009
27	14.714186	1645.702391	.000607	.067961	111.844605	.008940
28	16.254954	1830.594505	.000546	.061519	112.617636	.008879
29	17.957060	2034.847238	.000491	.055688	113.317391	.008824
30	19.837399	2260.487900	.000442	.050409	113.950820	.008775
31	21.914633	2509.756088	.000398	.045631	114.524207	.008731
32	24.209382	2785.125915	.000359	.041306	115.043244	.008692
33	26.744421	3089.330559	.000323	.037390	115.513083	.008657
34	29.544911	3425.389403	.000291	.033846	115.938387	.008625
35	32.638649	3796.638004	.000263	.030638	116.323378	.008596
36	36.056343	4206.761180	.000237	.027734	116.671875	.008571
37	39.831913	4659.829611	.000214	.025105	116.987341	.008547
38	44.002835	5160.340233	.000193	.022725	117.272903	.008527
39	48.610506	5713.260852	.000175	.020571	117.531398	.008508
40	53.700662	6324.079483	.000158	.018621	117.765390	.008491
41	59.323823	6998.858807	.000142	.016856	117.977204	.008476
42	65.535802	7744.296352	.000129	.015258	118.168940	.008462
43	72.398257	8567.790939	.000116	.013812	118.342502	.008450
44	79.979301	9477.516170	.000105	.012503	118.499611	.008438
45	88.354179	10482.501530	.000095	.011318	118.641830	.008428
46	97.606016	11592.721980	.000086	.010245	118.770568	.008419
47	107.826641	12819.197020	.000078	.009274	118.887103	.008411
48	119.117499	14174.100030	.000070	.008395	118.992592	.008403
49	131.590658	15670.879080	.000063	.007599	119.088082	.008397
50	145.369919	17324.390450	.000057	.006879	119.174520	.008391

10% Annual Compounding Interest

Years	Future worth of 1 1	Future worth of 1 per period 2	Sinking fund factor 3	Present worth of 1 4	Present worth of 1 per period 5	Installment to amortize 1 6
1	1.100000	1.000000	1.000000	.909091	.909091	1.100000
2	1.210000	2.100000	.476190	.826446	1.735537	.576190
3	1.331000	3.310000	.302115	.751315	2.486852	.402115
4	1.464100	4.641000	.215471	.683013	3.169865	.315471
5	1.610510	6.105100	.163797	.620921	3.790787	.263797
6	1.771561	7.715610	.129607	.564474	4.355261	.229607
7	1.948717	9.487171	.105405	.513158	4.868419	.205405
8	2.143589	11.435888	.087444	.466507	5.334926	.187444
9	2.357948	13.579477	.073641	.424098	5.759024	.173641
10	2.593742	15.937425	.062745	.385543	6.144567	.162745
11	2.853117	18.531167	.053963	.350494	6.495061	.153963
12	3.138428	21.384284	.046763	.318631	6.813692	.146763
13	3.452271	24.522712	.040779	.289664	7.103356	.140779
14	3.797498	27.974983	.035746	.263331	7.366687	.135746
15	4.177248	31.772482	.031474	.239392	7.606080	.131474
16	4.594973	35.949730	.027817	.217629	7.823709	.127817
17	5.054470	40.544703	.024664	.197845	8.021553	.124664
18	5.559917	45.599173	.021930	.179859	8.201412	.121930
19	6.115909	51.159090	.019547	.163508	8.364920	.119547
20	6.727500	57.274999	.017460	.148644	8.513564	.117460
21	7.400250	64.002499	.015624	.135131	8.648694	.115624
22	8.140275	71.402749	.014005	.122846	8.771540	.114005
23	8.954302	79.543024	.012572	.111678	8.883218	.112572
24	9.849733	88.497327	.011300	.101526	8.984744	.111300
25	10.834706	98.347059	.010168	.092296	9.077040	.110168
26	11.918177	109.181765	.009159	.083905	9.160945	.109159
27	13.109994	121.099942	.008258	.076278	9.237223	.108258
28	14.420994	134.209936	.007451	.069343	9.306567	.107451
29	15.863093	148.630930	.006728	.063039	9.369606	.106728
30	17.449402	164.494023	.006079	.057309	9.426914	.106079
31	19.194342	181.943425	.005496	.052099	9.479013	.105496
32	21.113777	201.137767	.004972	.047362	9.526376	.104972
33	23.225154	222.251544	.004499	.043057	9.569432	.104499
34	25.547670	245.476699	.004074	.039143	9.608575	.104074
35	28.102437	271.024368	.003690	.035584	9.644159	.103690
36	30.912681	299.126805	.003343	.032349	9.676508	.103343
37	34.003949	330.039486	.003030	.029408	9.705917	.103030
38	37.404343	364.043434	.002747	.026735	9.732651	.102747
39	41.144778	401.447778	.002491	.024304	9.756956	.102491
40	45.259256	442.592556	.002259	.022095	9.779051	.102259
41	49.785181	487.851811	.002050	.020086	9.799137	.102050
42	54.763699	537.636992	.001860	.018260	9.817397	.101860
43	60.240069	592.400692	.001688	.016600	9.833998	.101688
44	66.264076	652.640761	.001532	.015091	9.849089	.101532
45	72.890484	718.904837	.001391	.013719	9.862808	.101391
46	80.179532	791.795321	.001263	.012472	9.875280	.101263
47	88.197485	871.974853	.001147	.011338	9.886618	.101147
48	97.017234	960.172338	.001041	.010307	9.896926	.101041
49	106.718957	1057.189572	.000946	.009370	9.906296	.100946
50	117.390853	1163.908529	.000859	.008519	9.914814	.100859
51	129.129938	1281.299382	.000780	.007744	9.922559	.100780
52	142.042932	1410.429320	.000709	.007040	9.929599	.100709
53	156.247225	1552.472252	.000644	.006400	9.935999	.100644
54	171.871948	1708.719477	.000585	.005818	9.941817	.100585
55	189.059142	1880.591425	.000532	.005289	9.947106	.100532
56	207.965057	2069.650567	.000483	.004809	9.951915	.100483
57	228.761562	2277.615624	.000439	.004371	9.956286	.100439
58	251.637719	2506.377186	.000399	.003974	9.960260	.100399
59	276.801490	2758.014905	.000363	.003613	9.963873	.100363
60	304.481640	3034.816395	.000330	.003284	9.967157	.100330

12% Monthly Compounding Interest

Years	Future worth of 1 1	Future worth of 1 per period 2	Sinking fund factor 3	Present worth of 1 4	Present worth of 1 per period 5	Installment to amortize 1 6
1	1.126825	12.682503	.078848	.887449	11.255077	.088848
2	1.269734	26.973464	.037073	.787566	21.243387	.047073
3	1.430768	43.076878	.023214	.698924	30.107505	.033214
4	1.612226	61.222607	.016333	.620260	37.973959	.026333
5	1.816696	81.669669	.012244	.550449	44.955038	.022244
6	2.047099	104.709931	.009550	.488496	51.150391	.019550
7	2.306722	130.672274	.007652	.433515	56.648452	.017652
8	2.599272	159.927292	.006252	.384722	61.527703	.016252
9	2.928925	192.892579	.005184	.341422	65.857789	.015184
10	3.300386	230.038689	.004347	.302994	69.700522	.014347
11	3.718958	271.895856	.003677	.268892	73.110751	.013677
12	4.190615	319.061559	.003134	.238628	76.137157	.013134
13	4.722090	372.209054	.002686	.211770	78.822938	.012686
14	5.320969	432.096981	.002314	.187935	81.206433	.012314
15	5.995801	499.580197	.002001	.166783	83.321664	.012001
16	6.756219	575.621973	.001737	.148011	85.198823	.011787
17	7.613077	661.307750	.001512	.131352	86.864707	.011512
18	8.578606	757.860629	.001319	.116569	88.343095	.011319
19	9.666588	866.658829	.001153	.103449	89.655088	.011153
20	10.892553	989.255364	.001010	.091805	90.819416	.011010
21	12.274002	1127.400209	.000886	.081473	91.852697	.010886
22	13.830652	1283.065277	.000779	.072303	92.769683	.010779
23	15.584725	1458.472573	.000685	.064165	93.583461	.010685
24	17.561259	1656.125904	.000603	.056943	94.305647	.010603
25	19.788466	1878.846624	.000532	.050534	94.946551	.010532
26	22.298139	2129.813907	.000469	.044846	95.515320	.010469
27	25.126101	2412.610122	.000414	.039799	96.020074	.010414
28	28.312719	2731.271978	.000366	.035319	96.468018	.010366
29	31.903481	3090.348132	.000323	.031344	96.865546	.010323
30	35.949641	3494.964129	.000286	.027816	97.218330	.010286
31	40.508955	3950.895562	.000253	.024685	97.531409	.010253
32	45.646505	4464.650512	.000223	.021907	97.809251	.010223
33	51.435624	5043.562455	.000198	.019441	98.055821	.010198
34	57.958949	5695.894917	.000175	.017253	98.274641	.010175
35	65.309594	6430.959463	.000155	.015311	98.468831	.010155
36	73.592485	7259.248592	.000137	.013588	98.641165	.010137
37	82.925855	8192.585514	.000122	.012058	98.794103	.010122
38	93.442929	9244.292929	.000108	.010701	98.929827	.010108
39	105.293831	10429.383160	.000095	.009497	99.050277	.010095
40	118.647724	11764.772490	.000084	.008428	99.157169	.010084
41	133.695226	13269.522620	.000075	.007479	99.252029	.010075
42	150.651127	14965.112740	.000066	.006637	99.336214	.010066
43	169.757461	16875.746110	.000059	.005890	99.410924	.010059
44	191.286956	19028.695620	.000052	.005227	99.477225	.010052
45	215.546930	21454.693010	.000046	.004639	99.536064	.010046
46	242.883675	24188.367600	.000041	.004117	99.588280	.010041
47	273.687405	27268.740570	.000036	.003653	99.634619	.010036
48	308.397819	30739.781910	.000032	.003242	99.675743	.010032
49	347.510381	34651.038170	.000028	.002877	99.712238	.010028
50	391.583396	39058.339630	.000025	.002553	99.744626	.010025

12% Annual Compounding Interest

Years	Future worth of 1 1	Future worth of 1 per period 2	Sinking fund factor 3	Present worth of 1 4	Present worth of 1 per period 5	Installment to amortize 1 6
1	1.120000	1.000000	1.000000	.892857	.892857	1.120000
2	1.254400	2.120000	.471698	.797194	1.690051	.591698
3	1.404928	3.374400	.296349	.711780	2.401831	.416349
4	1.573519	4.779328	.209234	.635518	3.037349	.329234
5	1.762342	6.352847	.157410	.567427	3.604776	.277410
6	1.973823	8.115189	.123226	.506631	4.111407	.243226
7	2.210681	10.089012	.099118	.452349	4.563757	.219118
8	2.475963	12.299693	.081303	.403883	4.967640	.201303
9	2.773079	14.775656	.067679	.360610	5.328250	.187679
10	3.105848	17.548735	.056984	.321973	5.650223	.176984
11	3.478550	20.654583	.048415	.287476	5.937699	.168415
12	3.895976	24.133133	.041437	.256675	6.194374	.161437
13	4.363493	28.029109	.035677	.229174	6.423548	.155677
14	4.887112	32.392602	.030871	.204620	6.628168	.150871
15	5.473566	37.279715	.026824	.182696	6.810864	.146824
16	6.130394	42.753280	.023390	.163122	6.973986	.143390
17	6.866041	48.883674	.020457	.145644	7.119630	.140457
18	7.689966	55.749715	.017937	.130040	7.249670	.137937
19	8.612762	63.439681	.015763	.116107	7.365777	.135763
20	9.646293	72.052442	.013879	.103667	7.469444	.133879
21	10.803848	81.698736	.012240	.092560	7.562003	.132240
22	12.100310	92.502584	.010811	.082643	7.644646	.130811
23	13.552347	104.602894	.009560	.073788	7.718434	.129560
24	15.178629	118.155241	.008463	.065882	7.784316	.128463
25	17.000064	133.333870	.007500	.058823	7.843139	.127500
26	19.040072	150.333934	.006652	.052521	7.895660	.126652
27	21.324881	169.374007	.005904	.046894	7.942554	.125904
28	23.883866	190.698887	.005244	.041869	7.984423	.125244
29	26.749930	214.582754	.004660	.037383	8.021806	.124660
30	29.959922	241.332684	.004144	.033378	8.055184	.124144
31	33.555113	271.292606	.003686	.029802	8.084986	.123686
32	37.581726	304.847719	.003280	.026609	8.111594	.123280
33	42.091533	342.429445	.002920	.023758	8.135352	.122920
34	47.142517	384.520979	.002601	.021212	8.156564	.122601
35	52.799620	431.663496	.002317	.018940	8.175504	.122317
36	59.135574	484.463116	.002064	.016910	8.192414	.122064
37	66.231843	543.598690	.001840	.015098	8.207513	.121840
38	74.179664	609.830532	.001640	.013481	8.220993	.121640
39	83.081224	684.010196	.001462	.012036	8.233030	.121462
40	93.050970	767.091420	.001304	.010747	8.243777	.121304
41	104.217087	860.142390	.001163	.009595	8.253372	.121163
42	116.723137	964.359477	.001037	.008567	8.261939	.121037
43	130.729914	1081.082614	.000925	.007649	8.269589	.120925
44	146.417503	1211.812527	.000825	.006830	8.276418	.120825
45	163.987604	1358.230031	.000736	.006098	8.282516	.120736
46	183.666116	1522.217634	.000657	.005445	8.287961	.120657
47	205.706050	1705.883750	.000586	.004861	8.292822	.120586
48	230.390776	1911.589800	.000523	.004340	8.297163	.120523
49	258.037669	2141.980576	.000467	.003875	8.301038	.120467
50	289.002189	2400.018245	.000417	.003460	8.304498	.120417

APPENDIX

USING THE CALCULATOR

Most math problems can be solved more easily, more quickly, and often more accurately with the use of a calculator. Today, most states allow the use of a calculator for their real estate examinations. Although calculators reduce the tedium of solving arithmetic problems, their use must be accompanied by an understanding of math and sound arithmetic skills.

This Appendix will discuss the use of standard, or chain logic, calculators, which can be purchased for as little as $10. It will also describe the use of a group of Hewlett-Packard calculators widely used in the real estate industry: HP-12C, HP-10B, HP-17BII, and HP-19BII. We will provide sample problems using all types of calculators.

ARITHMETIC OPERATIONS FOR A STANDARD CALCULATOR

(ON/C)	On and clear key. Used to turn on and clear the calculator. Press this key before beginning a new problem to make certain that the calculator is cleared.
(OFF)	Off key. Press to turn calculator off.
(+)	Add key. Adds the next entered number to the displayed number.
(–)	Subtract key. Subtracts the next entered number from the displayed number.
(×)	Multiply key. Multiplies the displayed number by the next entered number.
(÷)	Divide key. Divides the displayed number by the next entered number.
(=)	Equal key. Used to complete the calculation. Following (=) with a number entry clears previous result.
(.)	Decimal point key.
(0) – (9)	Digit keys. Numbers used in computation.

To add whole numbers, simply press the keys in the logical order of operation. The columns are aligned properly, and numbers are carried correctly and manipulated more quickly than can be done by hand.

Add 285 + 21 + 3,416

Keys to press	*Display*
(ON/C)	0
285 (+)	285
21 (+)	306
3416 (=)	3722

285 + 21 + 3,416 = 3,722

Subtract 30,235 – 17,775

Keys to press	*Display*
(ON/C)	0
30,235 (–)	30,235
17,775 (=)	12,460

30,235 – 17,775 = 12,460

Multiply 38 x 23

Keys to press	*Display*
(ON/C)	0
38 (×)	38
23 (=)	874

38 x 23 = 874

Divide 10,488 ÷ 23

Keys to press	*Display*
(ON/C)	0
10,488 (÷)	10488
23 (=)	456

10,488 ÷ 23 = 456

If you have a problem that includes both addition and subtraction, it does not matter which you do first.

Solve 8 + 6 – 3

Adding first	*Subtracting first*
8 + 6 =	8 – 3 =
14 – 3 = 11	5 + 6 = 11

If you have a problem that includes multiplication and division, it does not matter which you do first. You may prefer to perform multiplication and division in the order they occur.

Solve 8 x 8 ÷ 4

Multiply first	*Divide first*
8 × 8 =	8 ÷ 4 =
64 ÷ 4 = 16	2 × 8 = 16

If a problem combines addition or subtraction with multiplication or division, always multiply or divide *first*.

Solve 8 x 6 − 4

8 × 6 = 48
48 − 4 = 44

or

Solve: 7 + 12 ÷ 6

12 ÷ 6 = 2
2 + 7 = 9

Simplify $\frac{22 + (16 \div 8) + 8}{16}$

Keys to press	*Display*
(ON/C)	0
16	16
(÷)	16
8	8
(=)	2
(+)	2
22	22
(+)	24
8	8
(=)	32
(÷D)	32
16	16
(=)	2

$\frac{22 + 16 \div 8 + 8}{16} = 2$

ARITHMETIC OPERATIONS FOR THE HP-12C

(ON)	On key. Used to turn calculator on.
(CLX)	Clear key. Used to clear the calculator.
ENTER	Enter key. Enters data into calculator.
(+)	Add key. Adds the last entered number to the preceding number.
(−)	Subtract key. Subtracts the last entered number from the preceding number.
(×)	Multiply key. Multiplies the last entered number times the preceding number.
(÷)	Divide key. Divides the last entered number by the preceding number.
(.)	Decimal point key. To extend the number of digits to the right of the decimal point, press the yellow f key, then the number of digits you wish to see, e.g., f 2 = 0.00. f 4 = 0.0000. f 6 = 0.000000, etc.
(0) − (9)	Digit keys. Numbers used in computation.

To work with whole numbers, enter the first number, press enter, press the next number, and select the function.

Add: 285 + 21 + 3,416

Keys to press	*Display*
(ON/CLX)	0
285	285
ENTER	285

21	21
(+)	306
3416	3416
(+)	3722

285 + 21 + 3,416 = 3,722

Subtract 30,235 – 17,775

Keys to press	*Display*
(ON/CLX)	0
30235	30235
ENTER	30235
17775	17775
(–)	12460

30,235 – 17,775 = 12,460

Multiply 38 x 23

Keys to press	*Display*
(ON/CLX)	0
38	38
ENTER	38
23	23
(×)	874

38 × 23 = 874

Divide 10,488 ÷ 23

Keys to press	*Display*
(ON/CLX)	0
10488	10488
ENTER	10488
23	23
(÷)	456

10,488 ÷ 23 = 456

The rules concerning the order of calculations are the same for the HP-12C as for the standard calculator. If you have a problem that includes both addition and subtraction, it does not matter which you do first. If a problem combines addition or subtraction with multiplication or division, always multiply or divide first.

Simplify $\frac{22 + (16 \div 8) + 8}{16}$

Keys to press	*Display*
(ON/CLX)	0
16	16
ENTER	16
8	8
(÷)	2
22	22
(+)	24

8	8
(+)	32
16	16
(÷)	2

$$\frac{22 + (16 \div 8) + 8}{16} = 2$$

PRACTICE CALCULATIONS

As pointed out in Chapter 3, the key to adding and subtracting is to line up the decimal points of all the numbers. The calculator automatically does this. Following are several examples of problems. For those that have the symbol [hp]* use the HP-12C. Use a standard calculator for the other problems.

[hp] Add 3.68 + 2.164 + .4 + 5

Keys to press	*Display*
(ON/CLX)	0.000
3.68	3.68
ENTER	3.680
2.164	2.164
(+)	5.844
.4	0.4
(+)	6.244
5	5
(+)	11.244

Add 3.68 + 2.164 + .4 + 5

Keys to press	*Display*
(ON/C)	0
3.68	3.68
(+)	3.68
2.164	2.164
(+)	5.844
.4	0.400
(+)	6.244
5	5
(=)	11.244

[hp] Subtract 6.930 – .585

Keys to press	*Display*
(ON/CLX)	0.000
6.930	6.930
ENTER	6.930
.585	0.585
(–)	6.345

*Used by permission of Hewlett-Packard

Subtract 6.930 – .585

Keys to press	*Display*
(ON/C)	0
6.930	6.930
(–)	6.93
.585	0.585
(=)	6.345

6.930 – .585 = 6.345

Multiply 7.74 x .625

Keys to press	*Display*
(ON/CLX)	0.000
7.74	7.74
ENTER	7.740
.625	0.625
(×)	4.838 f4 4.8375

Multiply 7.74 x .625

Keys to press	*Display*
(ON/C)	0
7.74	7.74
(×)	7.74
.625	0.625
(=)	4.8375

Note: The calculator determines how many places are needed.

Divide .8 ÷ .296

Keys to press	*Display*
(ON/CLX)	0.00
f 7	0.0000000
.8	0.8
ENTER	0.8000000
.296	0.296
(÷)	2.7027027

Divide .8 ÷ .296

Keys to press	*Display*
(ON/C)	0
.8	0.8
(÷)	0.8
.296	0.296
(=)	2.7027027

Note: Many standard calculators do not extend the digits and simply round off to two places.

[HP] Simplify $\frac{72{,}000 \times .07 \times 40 \div .05}{.5}$

Keys to press	*Display*
(ON/CLX)	0
72000	72000
ENTER	72000
.07	0.07
(×)	5040
40	40
(×)	201600
.05	0.05
(÷)	4032000
.5	0.5
(÷)	8064000

Note: The calculator determines where the decimal point goes.

Simplify: $\frac{72{,}000 \times .07 \times 40 \div .05}{.5}$

Keys to press	*Display*
(ON/C)	0
72000	72000
(×)	72000
.07	0.07
(×)	5040.
40	40
(–)	201600
.05	0.05
(÷)	4032000
.5	0.5
(=)	8064000

Note: The calculator determines where the decimal point goes.

[HP] Compute 286 x 64 – 1,286 ÷ 28 + 3,028

Keys to press	*Display*
(ON/CLX)	0.00
f9	0.0000000000
286	286
ENTER	286.000000000
64	64
(×)	18304.00000
1286	1286
(–)	17018.00000
28	28
(÷)	607.7857143
3028	3028
(+)	3635.785714

Compute 286 x 64 – 1,286 ÷ 28 + 3,028

Keys to press	*Display*
(ON/C)	0
286	286
(×)	286
64	64
(–)	18304
1286	1286
(÷)	17018
28	28
(+)	607.78571
3028	3028
(=)	3635.7857

The calculator will convert fractions to decimals.

Example

$\frac{6}{8} = .75$

Keys to press HP-12C	*Display*
(ON/CLX)	0
f4	0.0000
6	6
ENTER	6.0000
8	8
(÷)	0.7500

Keys to press Standard	*Display*
(ON/C)	0
6	6
(÷)	6
8	8
(=)	0.75

PERCENTAGES WITH THE HP-12C

With the HP-12C, you do not need to convert a percentage to a decimal equivalent. Thus, 7% does not need to be changed to .07.

Example

You have sold a house for $88,000. Your real estate commission is 8%. How much will you earn on this sale?

Keys to press	*Display*
(ON/CLX)	0.00
88000	88000.00
ENTER	88000.00
8	8
%	7040.00

The commission is $7,040.00

The above discussion will help in any state examination. Be sure you are thoroughly familiar with your calculator long before the day of your examination. You are free to use the calculator in all computations in this math book.

FINANCIAL CALCULATIONS USING THE HP-12C

Now let's do financial calculations using the following keys on the HP-12C:

(n) = number of periods
(i) = interest rate
(PMT) = payment
(PV) = present value
(FV) = future value

Calculate a monthly payment on a $50,000 loan at 12% interest per annum and amortized over a 25-year period.

Keys to press	*Display*
(ON/CLX)	0.00
Blue key g	0.00
End (see #8 key)	0.00
50000 (amount of loan)	50000
PV (present value)	50000.00
12 (interest rate)	12
Blue key g	12
i (blue key 12 ÷)	1.00
25	25
Blue key g	25
n (blue key 12x)	300.00
PMT (payment)	–526.61

Note: A minus sign is displayed, meaning cash is to be paid out.

The HP-12C will do many other financial functions that would not be possible on most regular calculators.

Assume the previous problem has a five-year balloon date. Clear previous financial registers by pressing yellow key f then Clear (CLX) then FIN.

Keys to press	*Display*
(ON/CLX)	0.00
5 (representing 5 years)	5
Blue key g	5
n (blue key 12x) (60 months)	60.00
12 (interest rate)	12
Blue key g	12
i (blue key 12 ÷)	1.00
50000 (loan amount)	50000
PV (present value)	50000
526.61 (monthly payment)	526.61
CHS (change sign-represents a negative payment)	–526.61
PMT (payment)	–526.61
Blue key g	–526.61
END (see #8 key)	–526.61
FV (future value)	–47826.77

Note: When you hit FV the word "running" flashes on the screen. This indicates the calculator is computing the balloon payoff.

ARITHMETIC CALCULATIONS FOR THE HP-10B

ON (C) — On key. Turns the calculator on.

CLEAR (C) — Clear key. Clears data from the calculator.

OFF — Off key. Press yellow key then (C) or OFF to turn calculator off.

Yellow key — Activates the yellow-labeled functions.

Problems are entered as read followed by the equals = sign; 12 × 12 = 144.

To set a decimal point, press the yellow key and DISP, then enter the number of digits desired.

HP-10B Business calculator*

* Provided for use by Hewlett-Packard

Add 285 + 21 + 3,416

Keys to press	*Display*
ON (C)	0.00
285+	285.00
21+	306.00
3416=	3722.00

Subtract 30,235 – 17,775

Keys to press	*Display*
ON (C)	0.00
30,235–	30235.00
17,775=	12460.00

Multiply 38 x 23

Keys to press	*Display*
ON (C)	0.00
38×	38.00
23=	874.00

Divide 10,488 ÷ 23

Keys to press	*Display*
ON (C)	0.00
10,488÷	10488.00
23=	456

As with other calculators, if a problem combines addition or subtraction with multiplication or division, always multiply or divide first.

Simplify $\frac{22+(16 \div 8)+8}{16}$

Keys to press	*Display*
ON (C)	0.00
16÷	16.00
8=	2.00
+22=	24.00
+8=	32.00
÷16=	2.00

The HP-10B automatically lines up the decimal places and places the decimal point at the proper location.

Add 3.68 + 2.164 + .4 + 5

Keys to press	*Display*
ON (C)	0.00
3.68+	3.68
2.164=	5.84

+.4=	6.24
+5=	11.24

Subtract 6.930 – .585

Keys to press	*Display*
ON (C)	0.00
6.930–	6.930
.585=	6.345

Multiply 7.74 x .625

Keys to press	*Display*
ON (C)	0.00
7.74×	7.740
.625=	4.838

Divide .8 ÷ .296

Keys to press	*Display*
ON (C)	0.00
.8÷	0.800
.296=	2.703

Simplify $\frac{72{,}000 \times .07 \times 40 \div .05}{.5}$

Keys to press	*Display*
ON (C)	0.00
72,000×	72000.00
.07=	5040.00
×40=	2016000.00
÷.05=	4032000.00
÷.5=	8064000.00

Simplify 286 x 64 – 1286 ÷ 28 + 3028

Keys to press	*Display*
ON (C)	0.00
286×	286.000
64=	18304.000
–1286=	17018.000
÷28=	607.786
+3028=	3635.786

To convert fractions to decimals:

$\frac{6}{8} = .75$

Keys to press	*Display*
ON (C)	0.00
6÷	6.00
8=	0.75

PERCENTAGES WITH THE HP-10B

You have sold a house for $88,000 and your commission is 8%. How much will you earn on this sale?

Keys to press	*Display*
ON (C)	0.00
88,000×	88000.00
.08=	7040.00

Alternative method with % key

Keys to press	*Display*
ON (C)	0.00
88,000×	88000.00
8%=	7040.00

FINANCIAL CALCULATION WITH THE HP-10B

Calculate the monthly payment for a $50,000 loan at 12% per annum and amortized over a 25-year period, then calculate the balloon payment at the end of the fifth year.

Keys to press	*Display*
ON (C)	0.00
12-N	12.00
25-yellow key-PYR	300.00
0-FV	0.00
$50,000-PV	50000.00
12-1Y/R	12.00
PMT	526.61
Yellow-RND-PMT	
60 N	60.00
FV	47826.61

ARITHMETIC OPERATIONS FOR THE HP-19BII AND HP-17BII

The HP-19BII is the most recent addition to the Hewlett-Packard line of handheld calculators. In addition to step-by-step solution books, an infrared printer is available for this unit. The menu and keystrokes shown below are also applicable to the HP-17BII.

For simple arithmetic calculations, the main menu is used and is accessed by pressing the ON key.

Main Menu [FIN] [BUS] [SUM] [TIME] [SOLVE] [TEXT]

Display contrast can be adjusted by holding down the ON key and pressing PLUS + or MINUS −.

To clear the calculator line, press the gold key and CLEAR.

The left arrow key removes one character at a time from the calculator line; use it to correct data entry errors.

To return to the main menu from subsequent menus, press EXIT.

(+) add key
(−) subtract key
(×) multiply key
(÷) divide key

To set decimal places, press DISP, press FIX, type in the number of decimal places desired, (0 to 11), and press INPUT.

The following problems are the same as those previously given for the standard and HP-12C calculators.

To work with whole numbers in simple four-function calculations, press ON and enter the problem.

HP-17BII Business calculator*

HP-19BII Business calculator*

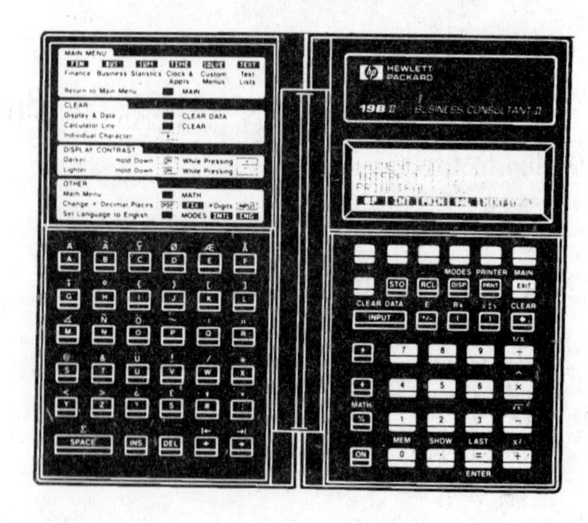

* Provided for use by Hewlett-Packard

Add 285 + 21 + 3,416

Keys to press	*Display*
(ON)	main menu
Gold key + Clear/CLR	0.00
285+	285.00+
21+	306.00+
3416+ or =	3722.00

Subtract 30,235 – 17,775

Keys to press	*Display*
(ON)	main menu
Gold key + Clear/CLR	0.00
30235–	30,235.00–
R17775– or =	12,460.00

Multiply 38 x 23

Keys to press	*Display*
(ON)	main menu
Gold key + Clear/CLR	0.00
38×	38.00×
23× or =	874.00

Divide 10,488 ÷ 23

Keys to press	*Display*
(ON)	main menu
Gold key + Clear/CLR	0.00
10,488–	10,488–
23÷ or =	456.00

If a problem combines addition or subtraction with multiplication or division, always multiply or divide first.

Solve $\frac{22 + (16 \div 8) + 8}{16}$

Keys to press	*Display*
(ON)	main menu
Gold key + Clear/CLR	0.00
16 ÷ 8 =	2.00
+22=	24.00
+8=	32.00
÷16=	2.00

The HP-19BII and HP-17BII automatically place the decimal point at the proper location. For example:

Add 3.68 + 2.164 + .4 + 5

Keys to press	*Display*
(ON)	main menu
Gold key + Clear/CLR	0.00
3.68+	3.68+
2.164+	5.844+
.4+	6.244+
5+ or =	11.244

Subtract 6.930 – .585

Keys to press	*Display*
(ON)	main menu
Gold key + Clear/CLR	0.0
6.930–	6.930–
.585– or =	6.345

Multiply 7.74 × .625

Keys to press	*Display*
(ON)	main menu
Gold key + Clear/CLR	0.00
7.74×	7.740×
.625× or =	4.838

Divide .8 ÷ .296

Keys to press	*Display*
(ON)	main menu
Gold key + Clear/CLR	0.00
.8÷	0.800
.296– or =	2.703

Solve $\frac{72{,}000 \times .07 \times 40 \div .05}{.5}$

Keys to press	*Display*
(ON)	main menu
Gold key + Clear/CLR	0.00
72000×	72,000.00×
.07×	5,040.00×
40	201,600.00
÷.05=	4,032,000.00
÷.5=	8,064,000.00

Solve 286 × 64 − 1286 ÷ 28 + 3,028

Keys to press	*Display*
(ON)	main menu
Gold key + Clear/CLR	0.00
286×	286.000000000×
64=	18,304.000000
−1286=	17,018.000000
÷28=	607.785714286
+3028=	3,635.78571429

The calculator will convert fractions to decimals.

$\frac{6}{8} = .75$

Keys to press	*Display*
(ON)	main menu
Gold key + Clear/CLR	0.00
6÷	6.000
8=	0.7500

PERCENTAGES WITH THE HP-19BII AND HP-17BII

You have sold a house for $88,000 and your commission is 8%. How much will you earn on this sale?

Keys to press	*Display*
(ON)	main menu
Gold key + Clear/CLR	0.000
88,000×	88000.00×
.08=	7040.00

Alternative method

Keys to press	*Display*
(ON)	main menu
Gold key + Clear/CLR	0.00
88,000×	88000.000×
8%	88000.00 × .08
=	7040.00

FINANCIAL CALCULATIONS USING THE HP-19BII AND HP-17BII

For mortgage calculations it is necessary to select the TVM or time value of money menu as follows:

Keys to press	*Display*
(ON)	0.00
Gold key + Clear/CLR	main menu
FIN	select a menu
TVM	12 pmts/yr end mode 0.00

Shows the following menu line:

N I%yr PV PMT FV OTHER

Problem

Calculate the monthly payment for $50,000 loan at 12% interest per annum and amortized over a 25-year period, then calculate the balloon payment at the end of the fifth year.

Keys to press	*Display*
25 gold N	N = 300.00
12 I%yr	I% yr = 12.00
50,000 PV	PV = 50,000.00
PMT	I% yr = 12.00 PV = 50,000.00 PMT = 526.61

To find the balloon payment

5 gold N	PV = 50,000 PMT = 526.61 N= 60.00
FV	FV = 47,826.60

The previous information provides a basic introduction to standard calculators and to a variety of Hewlett-Packard calculators. For more advanced calculations with the HP-19BII, the student should study the handbook available with the unit and the step-by-step solution books, which are available from Hewlett-Packard for both the HP-12C and the HP-19BII. Classes are also available for advanced study of the financial calculators.

Glossary

accrued depreciation All the depreciation that has accrued up to the date of the appraisal. May consist of physical deterioration, functional obsolescence, and external obsolescence.

acre A measure of land that equals 160 square rods, or 4,840 square yards, or 43,560 square feet; a tract about 208.71 feet square.

actual age The chronological age of an improvement.

addend A number that is added to another number.

addition The operation of combining two or more numbers to form a larger number.

add–on interest Interest computed and added on before payments begin.

ad valorem A tax levied by local governments as a percentage of value. (The Latin phrase means "according to value.")

altitude Height of a geometric figure; the perpendicular distance from the base to its highest point.

amortization The reduction of principal by making periodic payments. Payments cover the interest due, with the balance applied to the principal.

angle The space between two lines meeting at a point.

annual Once a year.

apportionment To allocate and distribute an expense.

area Surface contained in a prescribed boundary and measured in square units.

arrears Payment is made at the end of a stated term.

assessed value A percentage of real value used to determine property taxes.

azimuth system A method of describing land using a circle; 360°.

base One of the ratios in a proportion used to solve percent problems is a comparison of two numbers called percentage and base. If 12 is being compared to 33, then 33 is the base.

base line Imaginary line running east and west that intersects a principal meridian.

bearing system A method of describing land using a circle of four quadrants containing 90° each.

biannual Two times a year.

bimonthly Every two months.

capitalization A process for converting an income stream into a lump sum capital value.

capitalization rate A rate expressing the relationship between income and value.

check A square area, 24 miles x 24 miles, formed by the intersection of guide meridians and correction lines; a quadrangle.

circle The set of points on a plane equally distant from a given point (center).

circumference The perimeter of a circle.

closing The settlement between a buyer and a seller; *see* real estate settlement.

closing costs That amount of money required by buyer or seller to close a real estate transaction.

commission A sum of money received for selling something as an agent.

common denominator The bottom number when several fractions are changed to equivalent fractions with the same denominator.

compound interest Interest earned or paid upon interest.

conventional loan A loan that is not insured or guaranteed by the government.

correction line A surveying line used to adjust for the curvature of the earth; these lines are 24 miles apart and run east and west.

cube A solid made up of six squares, each meeting the others at right angles (90°).

debit A decrease in the seller's check; i.e., sale price at the closing. An increase to the amount the buyer must bring to closing.

denominator The number in a fraction written below the line, illustrating into how many equal parts the unit is divided.

diameter A straight line that passes through the center of a circle and divides the circle in half.

difference The number found by subtracting one number from another.

discounting A mathematical process of reducing future income to a present value at a selected rate of interest and for a specific period of time. Printed compound interest tables and most financial calculators can accomplish this process.

discount points *See* points.

dividend In division, the number being divided.

division The procedure in determining how many times one number is contained in another.

divisor The number by which a second number is divided.

economic life The period of time over which the improvements remain competitive in the marketplace and contribute to the total value of the property.

economic rent That amount a parcel of real property would rent for based upon today's market.

effective age The age that the improvements appear to be, based on observed condition and compared to other properties.

equity The net value of a property after subtracting all liens and encumbrances; i.e., the owner's interest.

equivalent fractions Fractions that have the same value, such as $\frac{1}{2}$ and $\frac{4}{8}$.

FHA loan A loan insured by the Federal Housing Administration.

governmental survey A method of describing land using townships and sections.

gross income multiplier The ratio or relationship between sales price and monthly or annual gross income.

height The perpendicular distance from the base of a figure to its highest point.

improper fraction A fraction in which the numerator is as large as or larger than the denominator.

interest Money paid for the use of borrowed money.

interest rate The percentage of interest charged to borrow money.

invert Turn upside down. When a fraction is inverted, the numerator is changed to the denominator and denominator to the numerator.

legal description Method of describing land.

loan origination fee A fee charged by a lender to process a loan application.

loan service fee A loan origination fee.

loss The amount by which expenses are greater than total amount received. In real estate, when cost is greater than selling price.

memory aid A device to aid in finding transformation forms of arithmetic formulas.

metes and bounds A description of land always starting from a point of beginning and returning to the point of beginning.

mile 5,280 feet.

mill 1/10 of one cent, expressed .001; used as a tax rate.

mill levy The tax rate.

minuend The number from which a second number is subtracted.

mixed number A number containing a whole number and a fraction.

mnemonic A device or figure used to simplify problem solving, such as "IS/OF," and to aid the memory.

monthly Once each month; 12 times each year.

multiplicand A number multiplied by a second number.

multiplier A number by which a second number is multiplied.

net proceeds That amount that the lender releases after all bills the lender requires to be paid are paid.

numerator The number in a fraction written above the line, illustrating how many fractional parts are taken.

parallel Lines that are always the same distance apart.

parallelogram A four-sided figure with opposite sides parallel and equal.

percentage One of the ratios in a proportion to solve percent problems. In a comparison of two numbers, if 12 is being compared to 33, then 12 is the percentage and 33 is the base.

perimeter The sum of the measure of the sides of the outer boundary of a figure.

physical life The time period that an improvement will remain standing.

pi (π) The ratio of the circumference of a circle to its diameter. π is approximately equal to 3.1416.

points Amount paid to lender to equalize the yield between market rate and loan rate; one point equals 1% of the loan.

principal meridian An imaginary line upon the face of the earth that runs north and south.

principal payment That amount applied to reduce the debt.

product The result of multiplying two or more numbers.

profit Gain after expenses are taken from the total amount received. In real estate, when cost is less than selling price and transaction costs.

proportion Two ratios that are equal, such as $\frac{2}{3} = \frac{4}{6}$.

prorate The division of expenses between buyer and seller as of the date of closing.

quadrilateral A closed figure that has four straight sides and four angles.

quotient The result from dividing one number by a second number.

radius The straight line from the center of a circle to the circumference. The radius is one-half the diameter.

rate A ratio expressing a fraction as a percent: rate = percentage/base.

ratio The result of one number divided by another number.

real estate settlement The closing. Real property is conveyed and money changes hands.

rectangle A four-sided figure with four right angles, with opposite sides parallel and equal.

rectangular survey *See* governmental survey.

remaining economic life The difference between effective age and total economic life.

return of investment Recapture of the investment over a period of time.

return on investment Investor's risk interest rate of return.

right angle Two intersecting lines meeting perpendicular to each other, i.e., forming a 90° angle.

section A one-mile square tract of land.

semiannual Two times a year.

square A four-sided figure with four right angles and all sides equal in length.

subtraction The operation of taking one quantity or number from another.

subtrahend A number to be subtracted from another.

time value of money That amount that a dollar will be worth in the future, or the present value of a dollar to be received at a future date.

township A six-square mile tract of land; contains 36 sections.

trapezoid A four-sided figure having two and only two sides parallel.

triangle A figure with three sides and three angles.

United States governmental survey system *See* governmental survey.

VA loan A loan guaranteed by the Veterans Administration.

volume Space measured within an object in three dimensions, such as the volume within a right circular cylinder. Measured in cubic units.

whole number A number used for counting.

ANSWER KEY

PRETEST

1. $\frac{7}{9}$
2. C
3. $\frac{3}{4}, \frac{5}{7}, \frac{2}{3}$
4. $\frac{23}{3}$
5. a. $23\frac{9}{11}$
   b. $3\frac{17}{30}$
   c. $13\frac{1}{7}$
   d. $1\frac{1}{3}$
6. $\frac{11}{25}$
7. $4\frac{7}{8}$ yards
8. First puppy
9. a. .53
   b. 4.5
10. a. $62\frac{1}{2}\%$
    b. $87\frac{1}{2}\%$
11. a. .92
    b. 1.12
12. a. $\frac{13}{10}$
    b. $\frac{4}{5}$
13. 20.3118
14. 3.36
15. 9.06
16. 87.4
17. 3.69
18. 5.8
19. $\frac{4}{15}$
20. $\frac{1}{3}$
21. $\frac{3}{8}$
22. 1,400
23. 50
24. 108
25. 20
26. 55
27. $150
28. 24
29. .8
30. $33\frac{1}{3}$ feet
31. $96
32. $100
33. 180
34. 5%
35. $25.44
36. $175
37. $173.63
38. 25%
39. $5,250, $1,050
40. $172.22
41. 197 feet
42. $162
43. $2,850
44. $242.25
45. $8,840
46. $482.13
47. $14,050
48. 116 miles
49. $169,500
50. $517.22

CHAPTER EXERCISES AND CHAPTER TESTS

CHAPTER 1 WORKING WITH WHOLE NUMBERS

Place Value

1. a. 5 ones
   b. 5 billions
   c. 5 thousands
   d. 5 ten thousands
   e. thousands
   f. 5 tens
2. 605
3. 42,800
4. 3,238,000
5. Two thousand, four hundred eight
6. Two billion, eighty-nine million, six hundred fifty-four thousand, two hundred thirteen

Rounding off Numbers

1. a. 570
   b. 530
2. a. 2,800
   b. 3,100
3. a. 13,000
   b. 23,000
4. a. 540,000
   b. 670,000
5. a. 5,700,000
   b. 7,900,000
6. a. 37,000,000
   b. 41,000,000

Adding Whole Numbers

1. 10,276
2. 1,360
3. 601,647
4. 255
5. $395,995

Subtracting Whole Numbers

1. $56,683
2. 18,775
3. $39,653.50
4. 2,457 feet
5. $11,350

Multiplying Whole Numbers

1. 31,500
2. $2,414,100
3. $197,352
4. 770 miles
5. 6,875 sheets

Dividing Whole Numbers

1. $400
2. 40 dozen
3. 9
4. $13\frac{1}{2}$ hours
5. $940.30

Chapter Test

1. a. tens
   b. million
   c. hundreds
2. $1,063 — $\frac{\$19,134}{18} = \$1,063$
3. $2,604 — $217 × 12 = $2,604
4. 11,083 ft. — 14,433 ft. − 3,350 ft. = 11,083 ft.
5. $6,255,984 — $ 3,298,046 + $2,957,938 = $ 6,255,984
6. $422 — $8,995 + $75 + $386 + $125 = $9,581; $9,581 − $3,500 = $6,081
7. $43 — $800 − $112 = $688; $\frac{\$688}{16} = \$43$
8. 945′ — If A = L × W we can use a memory aid.

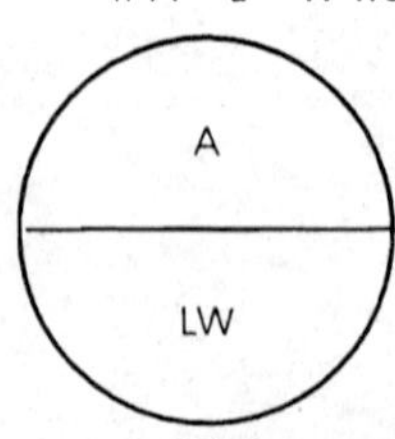

and cover up what we want to find and "do" as the memory aid indicates. So $L = \frac{A}{W}$

Since 9 sq. ft. = 1 sq. yd.

6,300 sq. yds. × 9 = 56,700 sq. ft.

60′

6,300 sq. yds.

56,700 sq. ft.

If $L = \frac{A}{W}$ =

$\frac{56,700}{60} = 945'$

9. $448.75 — P.I. = $372.75
   Monthly tax: $\frac{\$660}{12} = \$55$
   Monthly insurance: $\frac{756}{36} = \$21$
   since 3 yrs. = 3 × 12 = 36 months
   Monthly payment:
   $372.75 + $55 + $21 = $448.75
10. a. 7,500 sq. ft.
    Since 1 acre = 43,560 sq. ft.
    15 × 43,560 sq. ft. = 653,400 sq. ft. total
    a. 75′ × 100′ = 7,500 sq. ft. area of each lot

    b. 72 lots
    b. Subtract for streets, etc.
    653,400 sq. ft. − 112,500 sq. ft. = 540,900 sq. ft. available
    and $\frac{540,900 \text{ sq. ft.}}{7,500 \text{ sq. ft.}} = 72.12$ lots or 72 lots

    In this problem you will note there is information given in the problem that you *do not* need in order to solve the problem.
11. 22 fence posts
    A lot 60′ × 50′ has a total perimeter of 220′.
    $\frac{220}{10} = 22$ fence posts
12. $20,000

Choice 1: 30 acres × $6,000	=$180,000
Choice 2: 60 lots × $4,000	=$240,000
$40,000 costs	− 40,000
Subdividing	$200,000

She will make $20,000 more by subdividing

13. $400

To credit union: $50 × 40	= $2,000
cash	−1,600
savings	$ 400

14. $12,405

$11,250	car
125	power brakes
155	power steering
475	air conditioning
50	undercoating
350	radio and speakers
$12,405	

15. 26 Each car: $.75 + $1.00 for 2 occupants or $1.75 for each car with two occupants

Tolls: $22.75 and $\frac{\$22.75}{\$1.75} = 13$ cars

13 cars × 2 = 26 occupants

16. $75,682

$72,525	house
472	fence
1,575	central air conditioning
835	patio
275	gas barbeque
$75,682	

17. $12,926

$65,756	selling price
−52,830	purchase price
$12,926	profit

18. $68,600

$85,750	purchase price
−17,150	down payment
$68,600	

19. $93,478

$95,875	selling price
− 2,397	commission
$93,478	cost of home

20. $7,925 $317 × 25 = $7,925

21. $199,440 1 year = 12 months

$554 × 12 = $6,648 per year

$6,648 × 30 = $199,440 for 30 years

22. 15.4 $\frac{600}{39}$ = 15.38 or 15.4 miles per gallon

23. $77,050

$4,950	broker's fee
+ 500	closing costs
$5,450	total cost to seller
$82,500	selling price
− 5,450	total cost
$77,050	to seller

24. $180,000

$155,000	
− 25,000	
$130,000	value of double today
$45,000	
+ 5,000	
$50,000	value of land today
$130,000	
+ 50,000	
$180,000	value of property today

25. $391

$92,000	purchase price
$4.25	per $1,000 premium

$\frac{\$92,000}{\$1,000} = 92$

$4.25 × 92 = $391

CHAPTER 2 UNDERSTANDING FRACTIONS

Parts of a Fraction

1. a. $\frac{1}{3}$
   b. $\frac{2}{3}$
2. $\frac{3}{4}$
3. 70
4. a. $\frac{2}{5}$
   b. $\frac{1}{10}$
   c. $\frac{1}{2}$
5. a. $\frac{1}{5}$
   b. $\frac{4}{5}$

Reducing Fractions to Lowest Terms

1. $\frac{1}{4}$
2. $\frac{7}{9}$
3. $\frac{6}{7}$
4. $\frac{1}{6}$
5. $\frac{1}{3}$

Equivalent Fractions

1. 6
2. 12
3. 12
4. 20 inches
5. $\frac{15}{27}$

Comparing Fractions

1. Pitcher
2. Fred
3. Cindy
4. $12\frac{7}{8}\%$
5. $15\frac{5}{8}$

Improper Fractions and Mixed Numbers

1. 43
2. $3\frac{1}{2}$ hours
3. 89
4. $2\frac{7}{8}$
5. $\frac{38}{3}$

Multiplying Fractions

1. $2\frac{7}{9}$ feet
2. 18
3. $\frac{3}{16}$ mile
4. $25\frac{1}{5}$
5. 51,155

Dividing Fractions

1. 6
2. $4\frac{1}{2}$
3. 15
4. 432
5. $\frac{22}{45}$

Fractional Part of a Number

1. 40
2. 72
3. 63
4. 140
5. \$160
6. $\frac{6}{25}$
7. 1,600
8. $\frac{7}{8}$
9. $\frac{1}{4}$
10. 51

Adding and Subtracting Fractions

1. $\frac{7}{12}$
2. $1\frac{7}{8}$
3. $\frac{11}{14}$
4. $1\frac{19}{48}$
5. $1\frac{5}{12}$
6. $\frac{3}{20}$
7. $\frac{1}{10}$
8. $\frac{2}{15}$
9. $\frac{1}{3}$
10. $\frac{1}{8}$

Adding and Subtracting Mixed Numbers

1. $13\frac{5}{12}$
2. 49
3. $14\frac{13}{18}$
4. $7\frac{13}{15}$
5. $34\frac{11}{12}$

Chapter Test

1. 20 — $\frac{20}{20} = 1$

2. $\frac{1}{16}$ — 1 section = 640 acres
   so $\frac{40}{640} = \frac{1}{16}$

3. 480 acres — 1 section = 640 acres
   so $\frac{3}{4} \times 640 = 480.$
   Think of "of" as meaning multiply.

4. $\frac{8}{10}$ — $\frac{8}{10} \times 640 = 512$ acres $512 > 480$
   $\frac{15}{20} \times 640 = 480$ acres
   ">" means "greater than." So $\frac{8}{10}$ of a section has the larger number of acres.

5. 160 acres — Since 1 section = 640 acres, $\frac{1}{4}$ of a section is $\frac{1}{4} \times 640 = 160$ acres.
   Think of "of" as meaning multiply.

6. 160 acres — $\frac{2}{5} \times \frac{5}{8} \times 640 = 160$ acres

7. $1\frac{3}{7}$ — $\frac{5}{6}$ divided by $\frac{7}{12}$ =
   $\frac{5}{6} \times \frac{12}{7} = \frac{10}{7}$ or $1\frac{3}{7}$

8. 40 acres — $\frac{\text{part}}{\text{total}}$ so $\frac{25}{\frac{5}{8}} = 25 \times \frac{8}{5} = 40$ acres

9. 320 acres — We must first find the part that is woodland:
   $$\begin{array}{r} \frac{1}{5} = \frac{8}{40} \\ + \quad \frac{5}{8} = \frac{25}{40} \\ \hline \frac{33}{40} \end{array}$$
   So $\frac{40}{40} - \frac{33}{40} = \frac{7}{40}$ is the part that is woodland.
   Then using $\frac{\text{part}}{\text{total}}$:
   $\frac{56}{\frac{7}{40}} = 56 \times \frac{40}{7} = 320$ acres

10. 14

1 gal. = 4 qts. and 1 qt. = 2 pts.
thus, 1 gal. = 4 × 2 = 8 pts.
or 16 half pints

$\frac{7}{8} = \frac{?}{16}$ $\frac{7}{8} = \frac{14}{16}$ and 14 half-pints

11. Wilson

Wilson: 13 for 28 = $\frac{13}{28}$

Jones: 3 for 7 = $\frac{3}{7} = \frac{12}{28}$

$\frac{13}{28}$ is larger than $\frac{12}{28}$

Therefore, Wilson had the better average.

12. Jim

Fred: $4\frac{9}{10}$ min.

Jim: $4\frac{4}{5} = 4\frac{8}{10}$

Jim won the race.

13. 1 hr. 35 min.

$\frac{3}{4} + \frac{2}{3} + \frac{1}{6}$, LCD = 12

$\frac{9 + 8 + 2}{12} = \frac{19}{12} = 1\frac{7}{12}$ hours

Since 60 min. = 1 hr.

$\frac{7}{12} \times 60 = 35$ min.

so 1 hr. 35 min.

14. $60\frac{1}{8}$

$32\frac{1}{4} = 32\frac{2}{8}$ LCD = 8

$12\frac{3}{8} = 12\frac{3}{8}$

$15\frac{1}{2} = 15\frac{4}{8}$

$59\frac{9}{8}$ $\frac{9}{8} = 1\frac{1}{8}$

$59 + 1\frac{1}{8} = 60\frac{1}{8}$

15. $33\frac{1}{6}$

$13\frac{3}{5} = 13\frac{18}{30}$ LCD = 30

$7\frac{11}{15} = 7\frac{22}{30}$

$11\frac{5}{6} = 11\frac{25}{30}$

$31\frac{65}{30}$

$\frac{65}{30} = 2\frac{5}{30} = 2\frac{1}{6}$

$31 + 2\frac{1}{6} = 33\frac{1}{6}$

16. $\frac{5}{16}$ lb.

$\frac{3}{4} - \frac{7}{16}$ LCD = 16

$\frac{12 - 7}{16} = \frac{5}{16}$

17. $2\frac{3}{16}$

$7\frac{3}{8} = 7\frac{6}{16}$

$- 5\frac{3}{16} = 5\frac{3}{16}$

$2\frac{3}{16}$

18. $7\frac{9}{20}$

$14\frac{1}{5} = 14\frac{4}{20} = 13\frac{24}{20}$

$- 6\frac{3}{4} = 6\frac{15}{20} = 6\frac{15}{20}$

$7\frac{9}{20}$

19. $\frac{7}{64}$

$\frac{\cancel{5}^{1}}{\cancel{16}_{4}} \times \frac{\cancel{4}^{1}}{8} \times \frac{7}{\cancel{10}_{2}} = \frac{7}{64}$

20. **a.** $25\frac{41}{99}$

$8\frac{2}{9} \times 3\frac{1}{11}$

$\frac{74}{9} \times \frac{34}{11} = \frac{74 \times 34}{9 \times 11} = \frac{2{,}516}{99}$

$$\begin{array}{r} 25\ \frac{41}{99} \\ 99\ \overline{)\,2{,}516} \\ \underline{198} \\ 536 \\ \underline{495} \\ 41 \end{array}$$

b. 6,348

$230 \times 27\frac{3}{5}$

$230 \times \frac{138}{5}$

$46 \times 138 = 6{,}348$

21. $\frac{5}{8}$

$\frac{1}{4} \times 800 = 200$ miles first day

$800 - 200 = 600$ miles remaining

$\frac{1}{6} \times 600 = 100$ miles second day

$200 + 100 = 300$ miles covered in two days

$\frac{300}{800} = \frac{3}{8}$ part covered in two days

$\frac{8}{8} - \frac{3}{8} = \frac{5}{8}$ part to be covered

22. $\frac{3}{10}$

$800 × $\frac{1}{2}$ = $400 spent first day

$800 – $400 = $400 remaining after first day

$400 × $\frac{1}{4}$ = $100 spent second day

$400 + $100 = $500 spent after two days

$800 – $500 = $300 remaining after two days

$300 × $\frac{1}{5}$ = $60 spent third day

$400 + $100 + $60 = $560 total spent 3 days

800 – $560 = $240 remaining after 3 days

$\frac{\$240}{\$800} = \frac{3}{10}$ fraction remaining

She had $\frac{3}{10}$ of original sum after three days.

23. C

Change each fraction to an equivalent fraction having a denominator equal to the least common denominator, 64:

$\frac{5}{8} = \frac{40}{64}, \frac{7}{16} = \frac{28}{64}, \frac{23}{64}, \frac{17}{32} = \frac{34}{64}$

$\frac{23}{64}$ is the smallest; therefore, C.

24. $\frac{4}{15}$

$1,200 × $\frac{1}{3}$ = $400 spent for food

$1,200 – $400 = $800 remainder

$800 × $\frac{2}{5}$ = $320 spent for rent

$\frac{\$320}{\$1{,}200} = \frac{4}{15}$ of remaining income for rent

25. $8,700

$49,000 + $38,000 = $87,000 total sale

$87,000 × $\frac{1}{10}$ = $8,700 total commission

CHAPTER 3 MASTERING DECIMALS

Place Value

1. Four hundred twenty-eight and one hundredth
2. Seventy-three and eight hundred one thousandths
3. Eleven and eighty-one thousand two hundred seventy-five hundred thousandths
4. .2116
5. 3.00036

Comparing Decimals and Rounding off Decimals

1. <
2. >
3. 10.43, 11.04, 11.4, 11.44
4. 4.2
5. .01

Changing Fractions to Decimals and Decimals to Fractions

1. 0.875
2. 0.375
3. 0.1875
4. $\frac{5}{8}$
5. $\frac{5}{16}$

Adding, Subtracting, and Multiplying Decimals

1. $13,267.45
2. 77.778
3. $4,116.78
4. 20,259.538
5. 0.0777

Dividing by Decimals

1. 0.8
2. 75
3. 35
4. 16.14
5. 700

Chapter Test

1. 12 acres

$$\begin{array}{r} 2.5 \\ +\ 11.75 \\ \hline 14.25 \end{array} \qquad \begin{array}{r} 26.25 \\ -14.25 \\ \hline 12.00 \text{ acres} \end{array}$$

2. 0.125

$$\frac{12.50}{100} = 0.125$$

3. 0.5875123

$$\begin{array}{r} 1.0000000 \\ -.4124877 \\ \hline 0.5875123 \end{array}$$

4. 0.140, 0.104, 0.014, 0.0014

5. 71.9

71.85
71.9

6. 17 lbs.

$3.45 − .25 = $3.20 1st pound
Since each additional 2 pounds cost 40 cents, then there are $\frac{3.20}{.40}$ or 8 additional 2 pounds or 8 × 2 = 16 pounds.
So total weight is 1 + 16 = 17 pounds.

7. $40,623.50

If profit is .13, always add 1.00 to profit and take 1.13 "of" purchase price. So $35,950 × 1.13 = $40,623.50. Remember "of" means multiply. Or we could solve the problem by finding profit first and then adding to $35,950:

$$\begin{array}{r} \$35,950 \\ \times\ \ .13 \\ \hline \$\ 4,673.50 \text{ Profit} \end{array} \qquad \begin{array}{r} \$35,950 \\ +\ 4,673.50 \\ \hline \$40,623.50 \end{array}$$

(Selling Price)

8. $\frac{13}{40}$

$$0.325 = \frac{325}{1,000} = \frac{13}{40}$$

9. $55.25

For the 8 hours worked from 9 A.M. to 5 P.M. the clerk earned 8 × $4.50, or $36.00.
For the remaining 3.5 hours from 5 P.M. to 8:30 P.M. the clerk earned 3.5 × $5.50, or $19.25.
Total earnings for the day:
$36.00 + $19.25 = $55.25

10. $4,536

$$\frac{\$20,410}{4.5} = \$4,535.56 = \$4,536.00$$

11. a. .005

$.06 \div \frac{.6}{.05}$ use vertical division

Simplify $\frac{.6}{.05} = \frac{.60}{.05} = 12$

$$.06 \div \frac{.6}{.05} = .06 \div 12 = \frac{.060}{12} = .005$$

b. .5

$$.7 \div \frac{7}{5} = .7 \times \frac{5}{7} = .1 \times 5 = .5$$

c. .025

$$8 \div \frac{16}{.05} = 8 \times \frac{.05}{16} = \frac{.05}{2} = .025$$

d. 50

$$4 \div \frac{.4}{5} = 4 \times \frac{5}{.4} = \frac{20}{.4} = \frac{200}{4} = 50$$

12. a. .85

To multiply by 10, move decimal point one place to the right.
10(.073) = .73
To divide by 10, move decimal point one place to the left.

$$\frac{1.32}{10} = .132$$

$$\frac{1}{4} + 10\,(.073) - \frac{1.32}{10}$$

.25 + .73 - .132
.98 − .132 = .848 = .85

b. .20 $\frac{5.72}{10} - \frac{3}{8}$ $\frac{3}{8} = 8\overline{)3.000}$ = .375

$.572 - .375 =$ $.572 - .375 = .197 = .20$

c. .14 $\frac{2}{9} \times .63$

$2 \times .07 = .14$

d. .35 $.83\frac{1}{3} \times 10\ (.0415)$

$.83\frac{1}{3} = \frac{83\frac{1}{3}}{100} = \frac{\frac{250}{3}}{100} = \frac{250}{300} = \frac{5}{6}$

or using table $.83\frac{1}{3} = \frac{5}{6}$

$\frac{5}{6} \times .415$

$\frac{2.075}{6} = .345 = .35$

13. $\frac{5}{.2}$ $\frac{2}{.5} = \frac{20}{5} = 4$

$\frac{.5}{2} = \frac{5}{20} = \frac{1}{4}$

$\frac{5}{.2} = \frac{50}{2} = 25$

$\frac{.5}{.2} = \frac{5}{2} = 2\frac{1}{2}$

14. 21 $.25 = \frac{25}{100} = \frac{1}{4}$ mile

The cost is 20¢ for the first $\frac{1}{4}$ mile. The remaining cost is $2.00 at 10¢ per quarter mile. There are $\frac{2.00}{.10}$, or 20 quarter miles, plus the first quarter mile gives a total of 21.

15. 50 Student ticket receipts
$100 \times \$.75 = \$75$
The balance $150 – $75 = $75 was the amount received from adults. At $1.50 a ticket, the number of adults sold = $\frac{\$75}{\$1.50} = 50$.

CHAPTER 4 PERCENT IN REAL ESTATE

Changing a Percent to a Fraction or Decimal

1. a. $\frac{1}{5}$ b. $\frac{3}{10}$ c. $\frac{13}{10}$ d. $\frac{9}{10}$
2. a. .0621 b. .0071 c. 1.62 d. .36

Changing a Fraction or a Decimal to a Percent

1. a. 39% b. 40% c. 2% d. 87.5%
2. a. 60% b. 40% c. 83.3% d. 41.1%

Finding a Percent of a Given Amount

1. $18,100
2. $72,400
3. $20,000
4. $88
5. 175

Finding What Percent One Number Is of Another Number

1. $33\frac{1}{3}$%
2. 78%
3. 30%
4. 50%
5. 60%

Finding a Number When a Percent of It Is Known

1. 180
2. 64
3. 50
4. $200
5. $200

Applications of Percentage

1. $9,000
2. $522.50
3. 25%
4. $82,500
5. $24,250

Chapter Test

1. .125 $12\frac{1}{2}\% = 12.5\% = .125$
To change a percent to a decimal, remove the % and move the decimal point two places to the left.

or change to decimal .125, then to a fraction, and reduce: $\frac{125}{1{,}000} = \frac{1}{8}$
To change a percent to a fraction, write the percent as a fraction with a denominator 100 and reduce.

2. $\frac{1}{8}$ $\frac{12\frac{1}{2}}{100} = \frac{25}{2} \div 100 = \frac{25}{2} \times \frac{1}{100} = \frac{25}{200} = \frac{1}{8}$

3. 62.5%

$\frac{5}{8} = .625 = 62.5\%$

To change a fraction to a percent, divide the numerator by the denominator and change the decimal to a percent.

4. 25.5%

$.25\frac{1}{2} = .255 = 25.5\%$

To change a decimal to a percent, move the decimal point two places to the right.

5. $16,500

is the down payment, so they have enough.
20% = .20
20% of $82,500 is the down payment. "Of" means to multiply, so .20 × $82,500 = $16,500.
The down payment is $16,500.
To find a percent of a number, write the percent as a decimal or fraction and multiply.

6. 3%

Refer to Figure 4–3.

$\frac{\$2{,}200}{\$72{,}500} = .0303 = .03 = 3\%$

To find the percent one number is of another, write as a fraction comparing the first to the second and then convert the fraction or decimal to a percent.

7. $104,500

20% = .20

$\frac{\$20{,}900}{.20} = \$104{,}500$

To find a number when a percent of a given number is known, divide the known number by the decimal or a fractional equivalent of the percent.

8. $69,167

Refer to Figure 4–4.
Using our memory aid we find that the selling price is:

$SP = \frac{\$4{,}150}{.06} = \$69{,}166.67 =$

$69,167 (rounded off)

9. $82,609

Refer to Figure 4–5.
Selling price = $95,000
1 + % profit = 115% = 1.15
Covering cost in our memory aid we get:

$C = \frac{\$95{,}000}{1.15} = \$82{,}608.70 =$

$82,609 (rounded off)

10. 20%

Refer to Figure 4–5.

so $1 - \%\ \text{loss} = \frac{80{,}000}{100{,}000}$

$1 - \%\ \text{loss} = .8$

and $1 - .8 = \%\ \text{loss}$

$.20 = \%\ \text{loss}$

The percent loss is 20%.
Also, the percent loss is simply a ratio of loss/cost, and loss = $100,000 – $80,000 = $20,000.
cost = $100,000
Then the percent of loss = $\frac{\$20{,}000}{\$100{,}000}$ and the percent of loss is .20 or 20%.

11. 96

Use total = $\frac{\text{part}}{\text{rate}}$

part = 60

rate = $62\frac{1}{2}\% = 62.5\% = .625$

total = $\frac{60}{.625} = 96$

12. $\frac{3}{8}$

$\frac{1}{4} = .25$

$24\frac{1}{2}\% = 24.5\% = .245$

$\frac{3}{8}$ $8\overline{)3.000}$ = .375 hence, $\frac{3}{8} = .375$

The number according to size:

$.24\frac{1}{2}\%,\ .2462,\ \frac{1}{4},\ \frac{3}{8}$

The greatest is $\frac{3}{8}$.

13. $77,900

Use total = $\frac{\text{part}}{\text{rate}}$

part = $15,580
rate = 20%

total = $\frac{\$15{,}580}{.20} = \$77{,}900$

14. 8.5%

Use rate = $\frac{\text{part}}{\text{total}}$

part = $4,930
total = $58,000

rate = $\frac{\$4{,}930}{\$58{,}000} = .085 = 8.5\%$

15. **a.** 7% $\frac{\$3{,}850}{\$55{,}000} = .07 = 7\%$

b. $50,000 $\frac{\$3{,}000}{.06} = \$50{,}000$

c. $5,775 $82,500 × .07 = $5,775

d. $77,687.50 $\frac{\$6{,}215}{.08} = \$77{,}687.50$

16. Total estate $411,111.11

37% husband
18% son
18% son
<u>18%</u> daughter
91%
college receives 9% which is $37,000

use total = $\frac{\text{part}}{\text{rate}}$ or $B = \frac{P}{R}$

total estate = $\frac{\$37{,}000}{.09} = \$411{,}111.11$

Daughter $74,000

Daughter receives 18% of the estate.
Use part = total × rate or P = B × R
part = $411,111.11 × .18 = $74,000 to nearest dollar.

17. $31,495.73

Refer to Figure 4–5.
Selling price = $36,850
1 + % profit = 117% = 1.17

Purchase price = $\frac{\$36{,}850}{1.17} = \$31{,}495.73$

CHAPTER 5 RATIO, PROPORTION, AND SCALE

Ratio and Proportion

1. $17\frac{1}{2}$
2. $1,961.54
3. $1,200
4. $25,000
5. $3,000

Scale Drawing

1. 80 yards, 70 yards
2. $\frac{1}{4}$ inch, $1\frac{7}{8}$ inches
3. 15 inches
4. 495 ft.
5. 188 miles

Chapter Test

1. $333 — This problem can be solved as a ratio-proportion problem.

$\frac{500}{90,000} = \frac{?}{60,000}$ depreciation

$\frac{500}{90,000} \times 60,000$ depreciation

$500 \times \frac{2}{3} = \frac{1,000}{3} = \$333.33 =$ depreciation. Rounding to the nearest dollar, we get $333.00.

2. $947.88 — $\frac{850}{82,500} = \frac{\text{tax}}{92,000}$ cross multiply

$\frac{850}{82,500} \times 92,000 = \text{tax} = \$947.88$

3. 1" — $\frac{\frac{1}{8}}{200} \times \frac{?}{1,600}$ cross multiply

$\frac{\frac{1}{8}}{200} \times 1,600 = ?$

$\frac{1}{1,600} \times 1,600 = ? = 1"$

1" represents 1,600 miles

4. $630 — $\frac{105}{2} = \frac{\text{utilities}}{12}$ cross multiply

$\frac{105}{2} \times 12 = \$105 \times 6 = \$630$ utilities per year

5. $14,375 — $\frac{11,500}{70,000} = \frac{?}{87,500}$ cross multiply

$\frac{11,500}{70,000} \times 87,500 = ?$ (down payment)

$\frac{115}{700} \times 87,500 = \$14,375$ (down payment)

6. $5,913.75 — $\frac{83}{1,000} = \frac{\text{tax}}{71,250}$ cross multiply

$\frac{83}{1,000} \times 71,250 = \text{tax}$

$83 \times 71.250 = \$5,913.75$

7. 440 miles — Jonesville Sunville Hamlet

x———$\frac{3}{4}$"———x———2"———x

Scale $\frac{1}{2}$" = 80 miles

First, find distance (d) from Jonesville to Sunville:

$\frac{80}{\frac{1}{2}} = \frac{d}{\frac{3}{4}}$ cross multiply

$160 \times \frac{3}{4} = \frac{480}{4} = d = 120$ miles

Second, find distance (d) from Sunville to Hamlet:

$\frac{80}{\frac{1}{2}} = \frac{d}{2}$ $160 \times 2 = d = 320$ miles

Finally, distance from Jonesville to Hamlet is 120 miles + 320 miles = 440 miles.

8. 6.8" — The actual line is 15 times the drawing if the scale is 1:15. Changing 8.5′ to inches, 8.5 × 12 = 102". Using a proportion:

$\frac{1}{15} = \frac{\text{inches}}{102}, \frac{1}{15} \times 102 = \text{inches} = 6.8"$

9. 8 — In a proportion, the product of means equals the product of extremes.
The product of extremes (outer terms):
$12 \times 6 = 72$
The product of means (inner terms):
$W \times 9 = 9W$
So $9W = 72$ then $W = \frac{72}{9} = 8$
or if this is easier, 6:W = 9:12
means $\frac{6}{W} = \frac{9}{12}$ or $\frac{W}{6} = \frac{12}{9}$
$W = 6 \times \frac{12}{9}$ $W = 8$

10. 800 sq. ft. — If 4" = 20′ and 6" = 30′ then 1" = 5′ and 1 sq. in. = 25 sq. ft.

$\frac{25}{1} = \frac{?}{32'}$, $\frac{\text{sq. ft.}}{\text{sq. in.}}$

$25 \times 32 = ? = 800$ sq. ft.

11. $200 — Set up proportion

Earns $10 E (earns)
Sales $110 $2,200

$\frac{10}{110} = \frac{E}{2,200}$, cross multiply

$\frac{10}{110} \times 2,200 = E = \$200$

He earns $200

12. 1" — Scale $\frac{3}{8}$ inch = 15 miles

$\frac{\frac{3}{8}}{15} = \frac{\text{inches}}{40}$ cross multiply

$\frac{\frac{3}{8}}{15} \times 40 = \text{inches}$

$\frac{3}{8} \times \frac{1}{15} \times 40 = \text{inches} = 1"$

13. $10,710

Area 1st lot: 60′ × 125′ = 7,500 sq. ft.

Area second lot: 85′ × 105′ = 8,925 sq. ft.

Set up proportion

Cost: $9,000 ? (cost)

Area: 7,500 8,925

$\frac{9,000}{7,500} = \frac{C}{8,925}$, cross multiply

$\frac{90}{75} \times 8,925 = C = 90 \times 119 = \$10,710$

Cost is $10,710.

14. $165 Set up proportion

Cost $54 C

Dozen $4\frac{1}{2}$ $13\frac{3}{4}$

$\frac{54}{4\frac{1}{2}} = \frac{C}{13\frac{3}{4}}$ cross multiply

$\frac{54}{\frac{9}{2}} = \frac{C}{\frac{55}{4}}, \frac{54}{\frac{9}{2}} = 54 \times \frac{2}{9} = 12$

$12 \times \frac{55}{4} = C = 3 \times 55 = \$165$

Cost is $165

15. 10 miles Set up proportion

inches $\frac{3}{4}$ $1\frac{1}{4}$

miles 6 M

$\frac{6}{\frac{3}{4}} = \frac{M}{1\frac{1}{4}}, \frac{6}{\frac{3}{4}} = 6 \times \frac{4}{3} = 8$

$8 \times 1\frac{1}{4} = M$

$8 \times \frac{5}{4} = M = 10$ miles

The north boundary of the farm is 10 miles.

CHAPTER 6 MEASUREMENTS IN REAL ESTATE

Changing a Smaller Measure to a Larger Measure

1. 8.5 ft.
2. 7.25 ft.
3. 55 yds.
4. 5.5 yds.
5. 3.5 miles

Changing a Larger Measure to a Smaller Measure

1. 69 in.
2. 135 ft.
3. 13,200 ft.
4. 31,680 ft.
5. 60 ft.

Finding the Perimeter of Geometric Figures

1. 21 ft.
2. 105 ft.
3. 24 ft.
4. 720 ft.
5. 356.6 ft.
6. 154 yds.
7. 14

Measuring Area

1. 5 sq. mi.
2. 180 sq. ft.
3. $2\frac{2}{9}$ sq. yds.
4. 140 ft.; 84 ft.
5. $1,125
6. 72 sq. yds.
7. 6,969,600 sq. ft.; 160 acres; $320,000
8. 270 sq. ft.
9. 201 sq. yds. (rounded off)
10. 76 sq. ft.

Measuring Volume

1. $150,000
2. 27,000 cu. ft.
3. 1,000 boxes
4. 480 cubes
5. 924 cu. ft.

Chapter Test

1. 252 ft. Changing 2,520 sq. yds. to sq. ft. (We are changing to a smaller unit, so we multiply.)

1 sq. yd. = 9 sq. ft.

2,520 × 9 = 22,680 sq. ft.

Now use our memory aid, Figure 6–8.

Covering L, we get $L = \frac{A}{W}$. We found A = 22,680 sq. ft. and W = 90 ft. of frontage. Then the depth

$L = \frac{22,680}{90} = 252$ ft.

The depth of the lot is 252 ft.

2. $7,600 1 acre = 43,560 sq. ft.

Change 348,480 sq. ft. to acres

$\frac{348,480}{43,560} = 8$ acres

Land sold for $950 per acre.

Selling price is $950 × 8 = $7,600

The selling price is $7,600.

3. $2,500

Using our memory aid for volume of a rectangular solid, V = LWH. (Refer to Figure 6–25.)
So volume excavated,
V = 27 × 50 × 10 = 13,500 cu. ft.
Change 13,500 cu. ft. to cu. yd.
(We are changing to a larger unit, so we divide.)
1 cu. yd. = 27 cu. ft. $\frac{13{,}500}{27} = 500$ cu. yd.
Cost is $5.00 per cu. yd.
Total cost = 500 × 5 = $2,500
The total cost is $2,500.

4. $623

The total perimeter (P) of the lot
P = 160 + 125 + 160 + 125 = 570 ft.
Less gates 4′ + 4′ = 8′
Total linear ft. of fence = 570′ – 8′ = 562′
Cost of fencing = 562 × $1.00 = $562
Cost of two gates = 2 × $30.50 = $61
Total cost = $562 + $61 = $623
The total cost of fence and gates is $623.

5. 50 cu. yds.

Change 30 in. to ft.
(We are changing to a larger unit so we divide.) 1 ft. = 12 in.
30 in. = $\frac{30}{12}$ = 2.5 ft.
Refer to Figure 6–25.
V = 54 × 10 × 2.5 = 1,350 cu. ft.
Change 1,350 cu. ft. to cu. yd.
(We are changing to a larger unit, so we divide.)
1 cu. yd. = 27 cu. ft.
$\frac{1{,}350}{27}$ = 50 cu. yd.
50 cu. yd. of gravel is needed to fill the trench.

6. 11,000 sq. ft.

The shaded lot is a trapezoid, with $s_1 = 80'$, $s_2 = 140'$.
Our memory aid gives the area of a trapezoid. Refer to Figure 6–21.

$$A = \frac{(s_1 + s_2)}{2} \times H$$

$$A = \frac{(80 + 140)}{2} \times 100 = \frac{220}{2} \times 100$$

A = 110 × 100 = 11,000 sq. ft.
The area of the trapezoid is 11,000 sq. ft.

7. 1393.92 ft.

The property forms a right triangle.
We know its area: A = 8 × 43,560
A = 348,480 sq. ft.
We know the side facing East Ave.
Let the side be B = 500
Refer to Figure 6–15.
We need to find H. Covering H in our memory aid we get,

$$H = \frac{A}{\frac{B}{2}} = \frac{348{,}480}{\frac{500}{2}}$$

$$H = \frac{348{,}480}{250} = 1{,}393.92 \text{ ft.}$$

The boundary facing North Street is 1,393.92 ft.

8. 9,000 sq. ft.

The figure is a trapezoid. Using our memory aid, Figure 6–21:

$$A = \frac{(s_1 + s_2)}{2} \times H = \frac{(200 + 160)}{2} \times 50$$

$$A = \frac{360}{2} \times 50 = 180 \times 50$$

= 9,000 sq. ft.

9. 386 cu. ft. Cost: $858

Refer to Figure 6–25.
Let's first find the number of cubic feet of concrete.
Using V = LWH for three sections.
V = 4 × 75 × .5 = 150 cu. ft.
V = 4 × 4 × .5 = 8 cu. ft.
V = 4 × 114 × .5 = 228 cu. ft.
Total cubic feet of concrete:
150 + 8 + 228 = 386 cu. ft.
386 cubic feet of concrete is needed.
Second, the cost is $60 per cubic yard. We must change 386 cu. ft. to cu. yd. 1 cu. yd. = 27 cu. ft.
(We are changing to a larger unit, so we divide.)
$\frac{386}{27}$ = 14.3 cu. yd. (to nearest tenth)
Cost is 14.3 × 60 = $858
The cost is $858.

10. 30,800 cu. ft.

The volume of a cylinder using our memory aid, Figure 6–28:
If diameter D = 28 then radius R = $\frac{28}{2}$ = 14 and $V = \pi R^2 H$,

$$V = \frac{22}{7} \times 14 \times 14 \times 50$$

V = 22 × 2 × 14 × 50 = 30,800 cu. ft.
30,800 cubic feet of corn can be stored.

11. 90 sq. ft.

In a square the measure of each side is the same measure.
A = LW, L = 9.5, W = 9.5 so
A = 9.5 × 9.5 = 90.25
The area is 90 sq. ft.

12. 800 acres

Change miles to ft. (We are changing to a smaller unit, so we multiply.)
1 mile = 5,280 ft.
W = $\frac{1}{2}$ × 5,280 = 2,640 ft.
L = 2.5 × 5,280 = 13,200 ft.
Since A = LW
A = 2,640 × 13,200
A = 34,848,000 sq. ft.
Change square feet to acres.
(We are changing to a larger unit, so we divide.)
1 acre = 43,560 sq. ft.
$\frac{34{,}848{,}000}{43{,}560}$ = 800 acres
The rectangular field contains 800 acres.

13. 7 inches

The perimeter is the sum of each of the four sides:

$1\frac{3}{4} + 1\frac{3}{4} + 1\frac{3}{4} + 1\frac{3}{4}$ or P

$= 4 \times 1\frac{3}{4} = 4 \times \frac{7}{4} = 7"$

The perimeter is 7".

14. 91 cu. in.

$V = L \times W \times H$

Let $4\frac{1}{2} = 4.5$

$V = 4.5 \times 4.5 \times 4.5 = 91.125$ cu. in.

The volume to nearest whole unit is 91 cu. in.

15. $51,300

The figure can be divided into a trapezoid and a rectangle, or two rectangles and a triangle. We will divide it into a trapezoid and a rectangle and then sum the area of each and add them in order to get the total area.

Area of rectangle: A = LW

$A = 30 \times 20 = 600$ sq. ft.

Refer to Figure 6–21.

Area of trapezoid:

$A = \frac{(s_1 + s_2)}{2} \times H$

$A = \frac{(150 + 180)}{2} \times 100 = \frac{330}{2} \times 100$

$A = 165 \times 100 = 16{,}500$ sq. ft.

Total area = 600 + 16,500

Total area = 17,100 sq. ft.

Cost is $3.00 per square foot.

Total cost = 17,100 × 3 = $51,300

The total cost is $51,300.

16. 1,368 sq. ft.

Using $A = L \times W$

$42 \times 6 \times 2 = 504$ sq. ft. (area of the sidewalk on two sides of building).

$60 \times 6 \times 2 = 720$ sq. ft. (area of the sidewalk on two sides of building).

$6 \times 6 \times 4 = 144$ sq. ft. (area of four corners).

Total area: 504 + 720 + 144 = 1,368 sq. ft.

17. $387.50

Changing 18 ft. and 12 ft. 6 in. to yards (divide to change to a larger measure).

1 yd. = 3 ft.

18 ft. $= \frac{18}{3} = 6$ yd.

12 ft. 6 in. $= 12\frac{1}{2}$ ft. $= \frac{25}{2}$ ft.

$= \frac{\frac{25}{2}}{3} = \frac{25}{6} = 4\frac{1}{6}$ yds.

The living room is 6 yds. × $4\frac{1}{6}$ yds.

$A = L \times W$

$A = 6 \times 4\frac{1}{6} = 6 \times \frac{25}{6} = 25$ sq. yds.

If cost is $15.50 per yard, then 25 yards cost $15.50 × 25 = $387.50.

18. 2 gallons

$12 \times 8 \times 2 =$	192	sq. ft. 2 walls
$9\frac{1}{2} \times 8 \times 2 =$	152	sq. ft. 2 walls
$9\frac{1}{2} \times 12 =$	114	sq. ft. ceiling
	458	sq. ft. total
	−72	sq. ft.
	386	sq. ft. total less opening
	× 2	2 coats paint
	772	sq. ft. 2 coats

$\frac{772}{450} = 1.7$ gallons

or 2 gallons needed

19. 19,694 bushels

Refer to Figure 6–28.

$V = \pi R^2 H$

$R = 28 \div 2 = 14$

$H = 40$

$\pi = 3.14$

$V = 3.14 \times 14 \times 14 \times 40$

$= 24{,}617.6$ cu. ft.

$1\frac{1}{4}$ cu. ft. = 1.25 cu. ft.

$\frac{24{,}617.6}{1.25} = 19{,}694.08$ bushels

20. 6 feet

Find H as follows. Refer to Figure 6–21.

$A = \frac{H}{2}(s_1 + s_2)$ $A = 60$, $s_1 = 8$, $s_2 = 12$

$60 = \frac{H}{2}(8 + 12)$

$60 = \frac{H}{2}(20)$

$60 = 10H$

$\frac{1}{10} \times 60 = \frac{1}{10} \times 10H$

$6 = H$

The height is 6 feet.

21. B

A. 41,372 sq. ft.

B. 43,560 sq. ft.

C. 36,153 sq. ft.

9 sq. ft. = 1 sq. yd.

We are changing to a smaller measure so we multiply:

4,017 × 9 = 36,153 sq. ft.

so 4,017 sq. yd. = 36,153 sq. ft.

D. 38,416 sq. ft.

196 × 196 = 38,416 sq. ft.

B has the larger area.

22. 70 lots

50′ × 100′ = 5,000 sq. ft. each lot size

1 acre = 43,560 sq. ft.

so 10 acres gives 10 × 43,560 = 435,600 sq. ft.

Allowing 85,600 sq. ft. for streets

435,600 sq. ft.

−85,600 sq. ft.

350,000 sq. ft. total

Dividing into 5,000 sq. ft. lots gives

$\frac{350{,}000}{5{,}000} = 70$ lots.

CHAPTER 7 LAND DESCRIPTIONS

Bearing and Azimuth

1. see drawing
2. see drawing

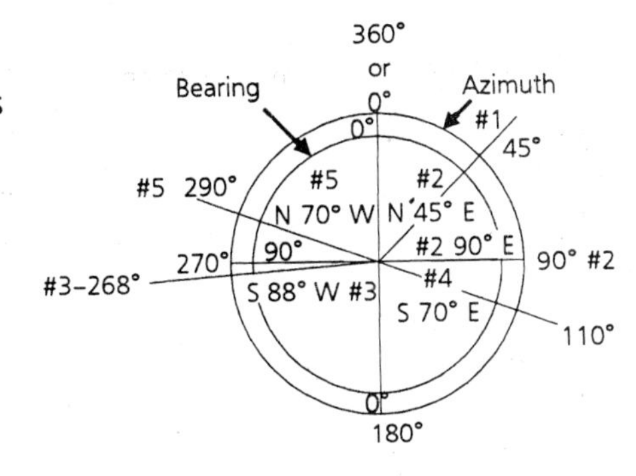

Governmental Survey

1. 576 square miles
2. 36 square miles
3. 6 miles × 4 sides = 24 miles
4. 40 acres $82,000
5. 10 acres
6. 653.40 feet
7. Developed 10 acres
   Sold 30 acres for $90,000
8. 20 acres
9. 40 acres $1960 per acre
10. 50 acres
11. 20 acres $50,000
12.
    1. N½ of the NW¼
    2. SW¼ of the NW¼
    3. N½ of the S½ of the NE¼
    4. NW¼ of the SE¼ of the SE¼
    5. S½ of the SE¼ of the NE¼ of the SW¼
13.
    1. 80
    2. 40
    3. 40
    4. 10
    5. 5

Lot and Block

1. 6,250 square feet — 125′ × 50′ = 6,250
2. 118,000 square feet — 590′ × 200′ = 118,000
3. 2.71 acres — 118,000 ÷ 43,560 = 2.708
4. 36,000 square feet

   6′ × 125′ = 750 sq. ft. each
   × 24
   18,000 sq. ft. for easement

   30′ × 200′ = 6,000 sq. ft. per street
   × 3
   18,000 sq. ft. for street

5. 1,260 square feet

   front/back setback 80′ — 125′ – 80′ = 45′
   side setback 22′ — 50′ – 22′ = 28′
   28′ × 45′ = 1,260 sq. ft.

6. $46,250 — $25,000 + $21,250 = $46,250
7. 67 — 40 – 9 = 31 × 43,560 = $\frac{1,350,360}{20,000}$ = 67.52
8. 22 — $\frac{240,000}{10,890}$ = 22
9. 5.5 acres — $\frac{240,000}{43,560}$ = 5.5 acres
10. 15 — 304,920 ÷ 20,000 = 15.24

Chapter Test

1. 60 acres
2. see diagram

   0°
   N 45° W — N 10° E
   90° — 90°
   S 40° W — S 20° E
   0°

3. $6.00 per square foot and 6.5 acres
4. 1,089 feet
5.
   a. 40 acres
   b. 10 acres
   c. $68,000
6. The SW¼ of the NE¼ and
   the NW¼ of the SE¼ and
   the NE¼ of the SW¼ and
   the SE¼ of the NW¼
7. 36 × 640 = 23,040 × .10 = 2,304 acres
8. 20 acres $10,800
9. 80 acres
10. D

    A. 1 acre = 43,560 sq. ft.
    B. 363′ × 363′ = 43,560 sq. ft.
    C. 180′ × 242′ = 43,560 sq. ft.
    D. 203′ × 203′ = 41,209 sq. ft.

11. 92.5 — 43,560 sq. ft. × 60 acres = 2,613,600 sq. ft.
    – 300,000 streets
    2,313,600

    $\frac{2,313,600}{25,000}$ = 92.5

12. 125 feet — $\frac{25,000}{200}$ = 125
13. $60,000 — 125 × $480 = $60,000
14. 11.5% — $\frac{300,000}{2,613,600}$ = 11.47
15. $600 — $\frac{45,000}{75}$ = $600

CHAPTER 8 MORTGAGE MATH

Mortgage Interest

1. $656
2. $6,598.88
3. 10.75%
4. $101,419.29
5. $1,021.28
6. $633.44 P&I
7. $633.44 × 360 mo. = $228,038.40 total P&I
8. $141,738.40 interest
   $228,038.40 − 86,300.00 = $141,738.40
9. $9.00 × 125 = $1,125.00
10. 20 years
    15 years
    $145,000 interest
    −103,375 interest
    $ 41,625

Amortization

1. $84,000
2. $10,080
3. $840
4. $885.36
5. $885.36 principal
   −840.00 interest
   $ 45.36 principal
6. $45.81 principal payment two
   $84,000.00
   − 45.36
   $83,954.64 balance payment two
   × .12
   $10,074.56 ÷ 12 months = $839.55
   P&I payment $885.36
   −839.55
   $ 45.81
7. $181,608.00
8. $106.10
   $50,000 × .037 = $1,850
   − 1,850
   $48,150 × .14 = $6,741 ÷ 12 = $561.75
   $667.85
   −561.75
   $106.10
9. $280,225.92
   $264,006.72
   + 16,219.20
   $280,225.92
10. $68,748.48
    30 year $264,006.72 P&I
    − 87,200.00 P
    $176,806.72 I
    20 year $195,258.24 P&I
    − 87,200.00 P
    $108,058.24 I
    $176,806.72 interest 30 years
    −108,058.24 interest 20 years
    $ 68,748.48 saved

Add-On Interest

1. $2,108.70
   $1,485 × .14 = 207.90 × 3 years =
   $623.70
   + 1,485.00
   $2,108.70
2. $29,400
3. $490
   $29,400 ÷ 60 months = $490

Discount Points

1. $2,800 discount points $\frac{1}{2}$% less than market is being charged, so $\frac{1}{2}$% converted to 8th = $\frac{4}{8}$% or 4 points will be charged.
   $70,000 × .04 = $2,800 discount points
2. 6 discount points $\frac{3}{4}$% = $\frac{6}{8}$% or 6 points
   $95,000 × .06 = $5,700 discount
3. $3,600
   The difference in market rate 11% and loan rate 10$\frac{1}{4}$% is $\frac{3}{4}$%. = $\frac{6}{8}$%
   $\frac{6}{8}$% = 6 points
   $60,000 × .06 = $3,600 discount amount

Chapter Test

1. $162,034.31
   $162,680.52
   × .09
   interest for 1 year 14,641.25 ÷ 12 =
   $1,220.10 interest for July, paid with the August 1 payment
   $1,542.00 P & I
   −1,220.10 I
   321.90 to be applied to principal
   $162,680.52
   − 321.90
   $162,358.62 × .09 = 14,612.28
   ÷ 12 = $1,217.69
   interest for August
   $1,542.00 P & I
   −1,217.69 I
   $ 324.31 P
   $162,358.62 principal balance after
   − 324.31 August payment
   $162,034.31 principal balance after September payment
2. 8.75%
   $674.48 × 12 months =
   $8,093.76 interest for one year
   $8,093.76 ÷ $92,500.00 = .0875

3. $85,666.67 — $10,280.00 ÷ .12 = $85,666.67

4. $622.38 — Match 11% and 20 years =
$10.33 × 60.25 = $622.38

5. $89,121.20 — $622.38 × 240 months =
$149,371.20 principal and interest
60,250.00 principal
$ 89,121.20 interest

6. 4 points

Market rate	10.5
Required rate	10.0
Under market	.5

or $\frac{1}{2}$ converted to eighths
$= \frac{4}{8} = 4$ points

7. $6,510 — $108,200 × .05 =
$5,410 + $1,100 = $6,510

8. $4,140 — $90,000 × .80 = $72,000 loan
$72,000 × .0575 = $4,140

9. .03 — $105,000 × .90 = $94,500 loan
$2,835 ÷ $94,500 = .03
3 points

10. $93,000 — $682 × 12 = $8,184 per year interest
$ 8,184 ÷ .11 = $74,400 loan
$74,400 ÷ .80 = $93,000
appraised value

11. $1,428 — $119,000 × .80 = $95,200 loan
$ 95,200 × .015 = $1,428

12. $4,800

Sale price	$125,000	
down	– 25,000	
	$100,000	to be paid
	$100,000	
	– 95,200	80% loan
	$ 4,800	short

13. $6,720 — $4,800 × .10 =
$480 × 4 years = $1,920
$4,800 + $1,920 = $6,720

CHAPTER 9 APPRAISAL MATH

Cost Approach

Exercise 1

1. 40 × 19 = 760 sq. ft.
6 × 30 = 180 sq. ft.
Total 940 sq. ft.

2. 25 × 35 × 2 = 1,750 sq. ft.

3.

House	1,750 × $35.00	=	$61,250
Garage 20 × 20 = 400 sq. ft. @ $12.00		=	$ 4,800
Total cost new			$66,050

4. 35 × 25 = 875 × $10.00 = $8,750 + $66,050 =
$74,800

Exercise 2

1. $125,000 ÷ 45 years = $2,778
2. $2,778 × 5 years = $13,890
3. 100 ÷ 45 years = 2.2%
4. 100 ÷ 40 = 2.5% × 7 years = 17.5%
5. $55,000 × 17.5% = $9,625

Exercise 3

1. $75,000 ÷ .75 = $100,000 × .25 = $25,000

2. To three decimal places:
100 ÷ 60 years = 1.667% annual rate of depreciation
5 years × 1.667% = 8.333% accrued depreciation
$75,000 × .08333 = $6,249.75 accrued depreciation
$75,000 – $6,250Rd. = $68,750 + $25,000 = $93,750

To two decimal places:
100 ÷ 60 years = 1.67% annual rate of depreciation
5 years × 1.67% = 8.33% accrued depreciation
$75,000 × .0835 = $6,262.50 accrued depreciation
$75,000 – $6,263Rd. = $68,737 + $25,000 =
$93,737

Market or Sales Comparison Approach

Exercise 1

1. A minus adjustment is applied to the sales price of the comparable.

2. All are true.

3. 1 = plus adjustment
2 = minus adjustment
3 = plus adjustment
4 = no adjustment

Income Approach

Exercise 1 GRM

1. $200.00 × 110 = $22,000 depreciation
2. $850 × 12 × 9 = $91,800
3. $22,800 × 8 = $182,400

Exercise 2 IRV

1. $150,000 × .07 = $10,500 income at .07
   V × R = I
   $10,500 ÷ .09 = $116,667 value at .08
   I ÷ R = V

2. $35 × 12 months = $420 ÷ .12 = $3,500
   I ÷ R = V

3. $15,000 ÷ $200,000 = .075 cap rate
   I ÷ V = R

4. | | |
   |---|---|
   | Scheduled gross income | $45,000 |
   | Vacancy and collection loss 5% | – 2,250 |
   | Effective gross income | $42,750 |
   | Expenses 35% | –14,963 |
   | Net operating income | $27,787 |

   Value = $27,787 ÷ .115 =
   $241,626
   rounded $242,000

5. Cap Rate 12%
   1 ÷ 20 = 5% Return of investment
   7% Return on investment

6. Capitalization rate = 12%
   Return on investment = –8%
   Return of investment 4%
   Remaining economic life = 1 ÷ 4% = 25 years

Economic Rent

1. | | |
   |---|---|
   | 15 units × $250 × 12 months = | $45,000 |
   | 5 units × $300 × 12 months = | 18,000 |
   | Potential gross income | $63,000 |

2. | | |
   |---|---|
   | Vacancy and collection loss @ 5% | – 3,150 |
   | | 59,850 |
   | Laundry income | + 600 |

3. Effective gross income $60,450

4. | | |
   |---|---|
   | Expenses @ 35% × EGI | 21,158 |
   | Net operating income | $39,292 |

5. $39,292 ÷ .09 = $436,578 rounded to $437,000

6. $63,000 × 6.9 = $434,700 rounded to $435,000

7. Value $436,000 × .65 = $283,400 loan
   $2,378.28 × 12 months = $28,539 annual debt service
   $436,000 – $283,400 = $152,600 equity investment

8. | | |
   |---|---|
   | Net operating income | $39,292 |
   | Debt Service | –28,539 |
   | Net cash flow (before taxes) | $10,753 |

9. $10,753 ÷ $152,600 = .070 or 7.0% return on equity

10. $10,753 ÷ $39,292 = .274 or 27.4% profit margin
    $39,292 ÷ $28,539 = 1.377 debt coverage ratio

Chapter Test

1. Cost new – depreciation + site value
2. 10 × 12 × 12 = $1,440
3. $1,200 ÷ .095 = $12,632
4. Vacancy; collection loss
5. $50,000 – $2,500 = $47,500 – $16,625 = $30,875
6. I ÷ V = R $30,875 ÷ $310,000 = 10%
7. $450,000 – $90,000 = $360,000
   1 ÷ 30 = .033 × 10 yrs. = 33.3% total depreciation
   $360,000 × 66.7% = $240,120 + $90,000 =
   $330,120
8. 40 × 28 × 2 = 2,240 s/f × $45.00 = $100,800
   $100,800 × 90% = $90,720 + $25,000 = $115,720
9. $60,000 – $18,000 = $42,000
   $47,000 – $42,000 = $5,000
10. $400,000 × 40% = $160,000 equity investment
    $30,000 ÷ $160,000 = 18.8%
11. 1.20 $30,000 ÷ $25,000 = 1.20
12. 50% $60,000 – $30,000 = $30,000 expense
    $\frac{\$30,000}{\$60,000}$ = .50 or 50%
13. A Always divide *into* income.
14. 10.6 $15,000 – $6,000 = $9,000 $\frac{\$9,000}{\$85,000}$ = 10.6
15. 16% $125,000 × .30 = $37,500 equity investment
    $750 × 12 months = $9,000 debt service
    $15,000 – $9,000 = $6,000 cash flow
    $6,000 ÷ $37,500 = .16 or 16%

CHAPTER 10 REAL ESTATE PRORATIONS

Real Estate Taxes

1. $1,200
2. $550
3. $650
4. At the end of the tax period, at which time purchaser will own the property and will pay the taxes.
5. $309
6. $154.50
7. $413.78, debit buyer and credit seller

Aug.	13 days
Sept. – Dec. = 4 mo. × 30 =	120 days
	133 days seller paid not used

   $\frac{\$1,120}{360}$ = 3.1111 per day × 133 days = $413.78

8. $598.89, debit seller and credit buyer

Jan. – April 4 × 30 = 120 days
May = 20 days
140 days

$\frac{\$1{,}540}{360}$ = 4.277778 per day × 140 days = $598.89

9. $1,025 due now. Debit seller $615. Debit buyer $410. Jan. through June are paid.

Seller owes July, Aug. and Sept. = 90 days
Oct. = 18 days
108 days

Buyer owes Oct. = 12 days
Nov. and Dec. = 60 days
72 days

$\frac{\$2{,}050}{360}$ = $5.694444 per day

$5.69444 × 108 = $615 debit seller

$5.69444 × 72 = $410 debit buyer

10. $416.29, debit seller and credit buyer

Jan - June = 6 months × 30 days or 180 days
July = 21 days
201 days

$\frac{\$745.60}{360}$ = $2.07111 per day × 201 days = $416.29

Insurance

1. 208 days
2. $205.15
3. 66
4. $51.08
5. $231.42
6. $141.56, credit seller and debit buyer

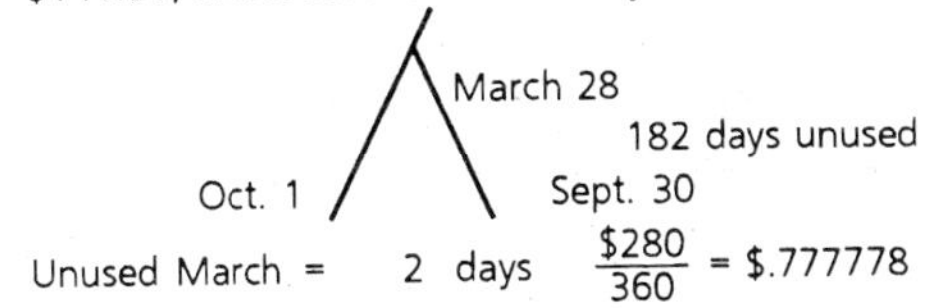

Unused March = 2 days $\frac{\$280}{360}$ = $.777778

6 mo. × 3 = 180 days × 182

182 days unused $ 141.56

7. $281.56, credit seller and debit buyer

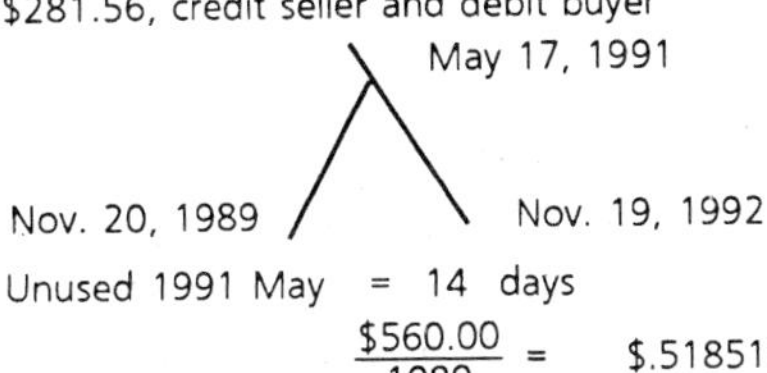

Unused 1991 May = 14 days

$\frac{\$560.00}{1080}$ = $.518519

7 mo. × 30 = 210 days × 543

1992 10 mo. × 30 = 300 days $ 281.56

Nov. = 19 days

543 days

8. $57.61, credit seller and debit buyer

Dec. 17

Feb. 18 Feb. 17

$\frac{\$340.00}{360}$ = $.944444 × 61 days = $57.61

Dec. 14 days
Jan. 30 days
Feb. 17 days
61 days

9. $347.55, credit seller and debit buyer

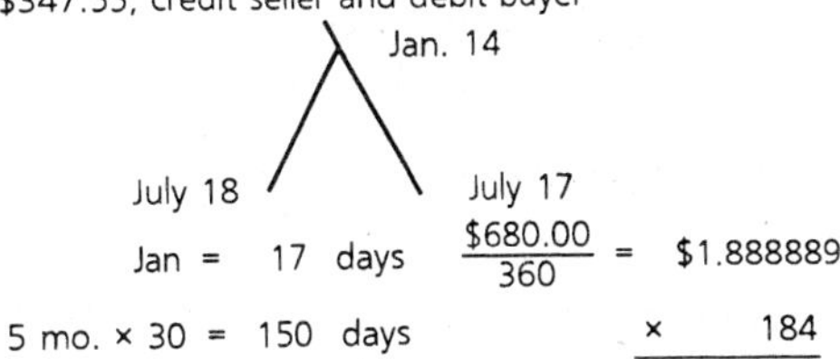

Jan = 17 days $\frac{\$680.00}{360}$ = $1.888889

5 mo. × 30 = 150 days × 184

July = 17 days $ 347.56

184 days

10. $98.00, credit seller and debit buyer

July 27

Oct. 21 Oct. 20

July = 4 days $\frac{\$420.00}{360}$ = $1.166667

2 mo. × 30 = 60 days × 84

Oct = 20 days $ 98.00

84 days

Rental

1. $20.00
2. $24.17
3. $754.17
4. $570.83
5. $57.33, debit seller and credit buyer

   $\frac{\$860.00}{30}$ = $28.666666 per day

   Buyer will own 2 days × $28.666666 = $57.33

6. $1,092.67, debit seller and credit buyer

   $\frac{\$1{,}490}{30}$ = $49.666666 per day

   Buyer will own September 9 through 30 = 22 days

   $49.666666 per day
   × 22 days
   $ 1,092.67

7. $810, debit seller and credit buyer

   $450 × 6 units = $2,700

   $\frac{\$2{,}700}{30}$ days = $90.00 per day

   $90 × 9 days owned by buyer = $810.

8. $516.13, debit seller and credit buyer

$480 × 6 units = $2,880
$560 × 2 units = $1,120
Total rent $4,000

$\frac{\$4{,}000}{31} = \$129.032258$ per day

× 4 days owned by buyer
$ 516.13

9. $328.64, debit seller and credit buyer

$290 ÷ 30 = $9.666 per day per unit
Unit One: July 16 through Aug 4 = 19 days
× $9.666 = $183.65
Unit Two: July 16 through July 30 = 15 days
× $9.666 = $144.99

10. $286.00, debit seller and credit buyer

$\frac{\$780}{30}$ days = $26 rent per day

April 20 through 30 = 11 days × $26 = $286

Water and Sewer

1. 92
2. 42
3. $21.91
4. Credit seller and debit buyer
5. Debit seller 50 days or $21.98, credit buyer same
6. $28.20, debit buyer and credit seller

May 31 $\frac{\$78.62}{92}$ days = $.854565 per day
June 30 $.854564 × 33 days = $28.20
July 31
92 days
June 2 days
July 31 days
33 days remaining unused

7. Debit seller $18.35
Debit buyer $ 6.52
Broker will pay $24.87

$\frac{\$24.87}{61}$ days = $.407705 per day

March 31 days
April 30 days
61 days
Seller owes March 31 days
April 14 days
45 days
× .407705
$ 18.35

Buyer owes April 16 days
× .407705
$ 6.52

8. $12.48, debit buyer and credit seller

$\frac{\$86.40}{90} = \$.96$ per day

January, February and March paid.
13 days remaining in March. $.96 × 13 = $12.48

9. Debit seller $13.09
Debit buyer $110.91
Credit broker $124.00

$\frac{\$124.00}{360} = \$.344444$ per day

Seller owes September 20 through October 27 =
38 days
× .344444
$ 13.09
Buyer owes October 28 through September 19 =
3 days
10 mo. × 30= 300 days
September = 19 days
322 days
× .344444
$ 110.91

10. Debit seller $9.90
Credit buyer $9.90

$\frac{\$19.80}{30} = \$.66$ per day

Seller owes 15 days × .66 = $9.90.

Interest

1. 12 days
2. $280.80
3. $272.17, debit seller and credit buyer

$42,600
× .10
$ $\frac{4{,}260}{12}$ mo. = $355 per month

$\frac{\$355}{30} = \$11.833333$ per day

$11.833333 per day
× 23 days owned by seller
$ 272.17

4. $427.74, debit buyer and credit seller

$\frac{\$780.00}{31} = \$25.161290$ per day

$25.161290 per day
× 17 days paid by seller
$ 427.74

5. $334.76, debit seller and credit buyer

$86,480.00
× .08
$\frac{\$6{,}918.40}{12}$ mo. = $\frac{\$576.533333}{31}$ days =
$18.597849 per day
× 18 days
$ 334.76

6. $261.21, debit seller and credit buyer

$60,280.00
× .12
$ $\frac{7{,}233.60}{12}$ mo. = $\frac{\$602.80}{30}$ days =
$20.093333 per day
× 13 days
$ 261.21

7. $93.00, debit buyer and credit seller
$36,000.00
× .0775
$ 2,790.00 / 12 mo. = $232.50 / 30 days = $7.75 per day
× 12 days
$ 93

8. $187, debit buyer and credit seller
$52,800.00
× .085
$ 4,488.00 / 12 mo. = $374.00 / 30 days = $12.46666
× 15 days
$ 187

9. $77.28, debit buyer and credit seller
$42,800.00
× .065
$ 2,782.00 / 12 mo. = $231.833333 / 30 days =
$7.727778
× 10 days
$77.27777

10. $477.36, debit buyer and credit seller
$98,200.00
× .125
$12,275.00 / 12 mo. = $1,026.91666 / 30 days =
$34.09722
× 14 days
$ 477.36

Chapter Test

1. $218.10
$43,500.00 principal
× .095 interest rate
$ 4,132.50 interest for one year
$4,132.50 ÷ 12 months = $344.38 this month
$ 344.38 ÷ 30 days = $ 11.48 per day
× 19
$218.10 debit seller and credit buyer

2. $1,213.23
$82,600 × .18 = $14,868 assessed value
$14,868 × .0816 = $1,213.23 taxes

3. $180
$325 + $350 = $675 total rent
$675 ÷ 30 days = $22.50 per day
$22.50 × 8 days = $180

4. $54.43
71 days × .766666 = $54.43 remaining

5. $172.45
$86,222.60 × .08 =
$6,897.80 ÷ 12 = $547.82
$547.82 ÷ 30 days =
19.16 × 9 = $172.45

6. $56.35
$12,000 × .0805 =
$966 taxes per year.
$966 ÷ 360 = $2.68333 per day
× 21 days
$ 56.35

7. $15.29
$41.69 ÷ 30 = $1.389666 per day
11 days seller debit = $15.29
11 days buyer credit = $15.29

8. $461.23
$858.92 ÷ 365 = $2.353205
Seller has owned 196 days × $2.353205 = $461.23, debit seller and credit buyer

9. $132.87
$198.76 ÷ 365 = .544548 per day
Seller has paid and buyer will use August 14 through April 14, or 244 days × .544548 = $132.87, debit buyer and credit seller

10. $153.26
$964.50 ÷ 365 days = $2.642465 per day. 58 days remaining in the year × $2.642465 = $153.26, credit seller and debit buyer

11. $32,000
$616 ÷ .0385 = $16,000 × 2 = $32,000

12. $248.01
$846 ÷ 365 = $2.31780
× 107
$ 248.01 credit seller

13. $1312.50
$525 per year
× 2.5
$1312.50

Chapter 11
Six-column settlement statement, solutions to practice problem 1

Close October 20	SELLER Debit	SELLER Credit	BUYER Debit	BUYER Credit	BROKER Debit	BROKER Credit
1. Selling Price		$ 105,000 00	$ 105,000 00			
2. Deposit, paid to				$ 2,000 00	$ 2,000 00	
3. Trust Deed, payable to	$ 84,600 00			84,600 00		
4. Trust Deed, payable to						
5. Trust Deed, payoff to						
6. Interest on Loan Assumed 20 days x $23.50	470 00			470 00		
7. Title Ins. Premium $84,600 x .10 = $8,460	627 00					627 00
8. Abstracting: Before Sale ÷ 12 = 705 ÷ 30 =						
9. After Sale $23.50 day						
10. Title Exam by						
11. Recording: Warranty Deed			5 00			5 00
12. Trust Deed						
13. Release						
14. Other						
15. Documentary Fee or Tax Stamp			10 50			10 50
16. Certificate of Taxes Due			13 00			13 00
17. Taxes for Preceding Year(s)						
18. Taxes for Current Year $1,082 ÷ 360 =	871 61			871 61		
19. Tax Reserve 3.005556 per day x 290 days		880 00	880 00			
20. Special Taxes						
21. Personal Property Taxes						
22. Hazard Ins. Prem. Assumed 380 ÷ 360 =		210.06	210 06			
23. Premium for New Insurance 1.055556/day						
24. Hazard Ins. Reserve x 199 days = 210.06		192 00	192 00			
25. FHA Mortgage Ins. Assumed						
26. FHA Mortgage Ins. Reserve						
27. Loan Service Fee (Buyer)						
28. Loan Discount Fee (Seller)						
29. Interest on New Loan						
30. Survey and/or Credit Report						
31. Appraisal Fee						
32. Water and/or Sewer 32 ÷ 30 = 1.066667	21 33		10 67			32 00
33. Rents per day S 20 days B 10 days						
34. Security Deposits						
35. Loan Transfer Fee						
36. Loan Payment Due Paid $918 paid Sept. Interest						
37. Broker's Fee	6,300 00					6,300 00
Sub-Totals	$ 92,889 94	$ 106,282 06	$ 106.321 23	$ 87,941 61	$ 2,000 00	$ 6,987 50
Balance due to/~~from~~ Seller	13,392 12					13,392 12
Balance due ~~to~~/from Buyer				18,379 62	18,379 62	
TOTALS	106,282 06	106,282 06	106,321 23	106,321 23	20,379 62	20,379 62

Chapter 11
HUD-1 settlement statement, solutions to practice problem 1

HUD-1 (3-86) OMB NO. 2502-0265

A.
U.S. DEPARTMENT OF HOUSING AND URBAN DEVELOPMENT

SETTLEMENT STATEMENT

B. TYPE OF LOAN
1. ☐ FHA 2. ☐ FMHA 3. ☒ CONV. UNINS.
4. ☐ VA 5. ☐ CONV. INS. assumption
6. FILE NUMBER 52649
7. LOAN NUMBER 268-342-0001
8. MORTGAGE INSURANCE CASE NUMBER —

C. NOTE: This form is furnished to give you a statement of actual settlement costs. Amounts paid to and by the settlement agent are shown. Items marked "(p.o.c.)" were paid outside the closing; they are shown here for informational purposes and are not included in totals.

D. NAME OF BORROWER: SOLUTION TO CLOSING PROBLEM NUMBER ONE
E. NAME OF SELLER:
F. NAME OF LENDER:
G. PROPERTY LOCATION:
H. SETTLEMENT AGENT:
PLACE OF SETTLEMENT:
I. SETTLEMENT DATE: OCTOBER 20,

J. SUMMARY OF BORROWER'S TRANSACTION		K. SUMMARY OF SELLER'S TRANSACTION	
100. GROSS AMOUNT DUE FROM BORROWER:		400. GROSS AMOUNT DUE TO SELLER:	
101. Contract sales price	$105,000.00	401. Contract sales price	$105,000.00
102. Personal property		402. Personal property	
103. Settlement charges to borrower (line 1400)	28.50	403.	
104. Water/sewer charges 10 days	10.67	404.	
105.		405.	
Adjustments for items paid by seller in advance		*Adjustments for items paid by seller in advance*	
106. City/town taxes to		406. City/town taxes to	
107. County taxes to		407. County taxes to	
108. Assessments to		408. Assessments to	
109. Reserves held by lender	880.00	409. Reserves held by lender	880.00
110. Hazard insurance reserve	192.00	410. Hazard insurance reserve	192.00
111. Hazard insurance prepaid	210.06	411. Hazard insurance prepaid	210.06
112.		412.	
120. GROSS AMOUNT DUE FROM BORROWER	$106,321.23	420. GROSS AMOUNT DUE TO SELLER	$106,282.06
200. AMOUNTS PAID BY OR IN BEHALF OF BORROWER:		500. REDUCTIONS IN AMOUNT DUE TO SELLER:	
201. Deposit or earnest money	2,000.00	501. Excess deposit (see instructions)	6,927.00
202. Principal amount of new loan(s)		502. Settlement charges to seller (line 1400)	
203. Existing loan(s) ~~taken subject to~~ assumed	84,000.00	503. Existing loan(s) ~~taken subject to~~ assumed	84,600.00
204.		504. Payoff of first mortgage loan	
205.		505. Payoff of second mortgage loan	
206.		506. Water/sewer charges 20 days	21.33
207.		507.	
208.		508.	
209.		509.	
Adjustments for items unpaid by seller		*Adjustments for items unpaid by seller:*	
210. City/town taxes to		510. City/town taxes to	
211. County taxes 1,082 ÷ 360 ~~to~~ 3.00556 day	871.61	511. County taxes 1,082 ÷ 360 = ~~to~~ 3.00556 day	871.61
212. Assessments 290 days Jan. 1 to October 20		512. Assessments 290 days Jan 1 to October 20	
213. Interest on loan assumed 20 days	470.00	513. Interest on loan assumed 20 days	470.00
214.		514.	
215.		515.	
216.		516.	
217.		517.	
218.		518.	
219.		519.	
220. TOTAL PAID BY/FOR BORROWER	$87,941.61	520. TOTAL REDUCTION AMOUNT DUE SELLER	$92,889.94
300. CASH AT SETTLEMENT FROM/TO BORROWER		600. CASH AT SETTLEMENT TO/FROM SELLER	
301. Gross amount due from borrower (line 120)	106,321.23	601. Gross amount due to seller (line 420)	106,282.06
302. Less amounts paid by/for borrower (line 220)	(87,941.61)	602. Less reductions in amt. due to seller (line 520)	(92,889.94)
303. CASH (☒ FROM) (☐ TO) BORROWER	$18,379.62	603. CASH (☒ TO) (☐ FROM) SELLER	$13,392.12

continued

Chapter 11
HUD-1 settlement statement, continued, solutions to practice problem 1

HUD-1 (3-86)

L. SETTLEMENT CHARGES	PAID FROM BORROWER'S FUNDS AT SETTLEMENT	PAID FROM SELLER'S FUNDS AT SETTLEMENT
700. TOTAL SALES/BROKER'S COMMISSION based on price $ 105,000.00 @ % =$6,300 *Division of Commission (line 700) as follows:*		
701. $ 3,150.00 to ABC Realty Co.		
702. $ 3,150.00 to XYZ Realty Co.		
703. Commission paid at Settlement		$ 6,300.00
704		
800. ITEMS PAYABLE IN CONNECTION WITH LOAN N/A		
801. Loan Origination Fee %		
802. Loan Discount %		
803. Appraisal Fee to		
804. Credit Report to		
805. Lender's Inspection Fee		
806. Mortgage Insurance Application Fee to		
807. Assumption Fee		
808.		
809.		
810.		
811.		
900. ITEMS REQUIRED BY LENDER TO BE PAID IN ADVANCE		
901. Interest from to @ $ /day		
902. Mortgage Insurance Premium for months to		
903. Hazard Insurance Premium for years to		
904. years to		
905.		
1000. **1000. RESERVES DEPOSITED WITH LENDER**		
1001. Hazard insurance months @ $ per month		
1002. Mortgage insurance months @ $ per month		
1003. City property taxes months @ $ per month		
1004. County property taxes months @ $ per month		
1005. Annual assessments months @ $ per month		
1006. months @ $ per month		
1007. months @ $ per month		
1008. months @ $ per month		
1100. TITLE CHARGES		
1101. Settlement or closing fee to		
1102. Abstract or title search to		
1103. Title examination to		
1104. Title insurance binder to		
1105. Document preparation to		627.00
1106. Notary fees to		
1107. Attorney's fees to *(includes above items numbers:*)		
1108. Title insurance to *(includes above items numbers:*)		
1109. Lender's coverage $		
1110. Owner's coverage $ 627.00		
1111. Tax Certificate	13.00	
1112.		
1113.		
1200. GOVERNMENT RECORDING AND TRANSFER CHARGES		
1201. Recording fees: Deed $ 5.00 ; Mortgage $; Releases $	5.00	
1202. City/county tax/stamps: Deed $; Mortgage $		
1203. State tax/stamps: Deed $ 10.50 ; Mortgage $	10.50	
1204.		
1205.		
1300. ADDITIONAL SETTLEMENT CHARGES		
1301. Survey to		
1302. Pest inspection to		
1303.		
1304.		
1305.		
1400. TOTAL SETTLEMENT CHARGES *(enter on lines 103, Section J and 502, Section K)*	28.50	6,927.00

I have carefully reviewed the HUD-1 Settlement Statement and to the best of my knowledge and belief, it is a true and accurate statement of all receipts and disbursements made on my account or by me in this transaction. I further certify that I have received a copy of the HUD-1 Settlement Statement.

Borrowers

Sellers

To the best of my knowledge, the HUD-1 Settlement Statement which I have prepared is a true and accurate account of this transaction. I have caused or will cause the funds to be disbursed in accordance with this statement.

Settlement Agent

Date

WARNING: It is a crime to knowingly make a false statement to the United States on this or any other similar form. Penalties upon conviction can include a fine and imprisonment. For details see: Title 18 U.S. Code Section 1001 and Section 1010.

Broker Reconciliation
HUD-1 Practice Problem #1

Funds Received

Earnest deposit	$2,000.00
Buyer funds to close	18,379.62
Total funds received	$20,379.62

Funds to Disburse

Seller funds	$13,392.12
Title insurance	627.00
Record warranty deed	5.00
Tax stamps	10.50
Certificate of taxes	13.00
Water	32.00
Broker fee	
ABC Realty	3,150.00
XYZ Realty	3,150.00
	$20,379.62

Chapter 11
Six-column settlement statement, solutions to practice problem 2

Close May 4	SELLER Debit		SELLER Credit		BUYER Debit		BUYER Credit		BROKER Debit		BROKER Credit	
1. Selling Price			86,800	00	86,800	00						
2. Deposit, paid to Broker							5,000	00	5,000	00		
3. Trust Deed, payable to	72,600	00					72,600	00				
4. Trust Deed, payable to												
5. Trust Deed, payoff to												
6. Interest on Loan Assumed 72600. x .105=			550	55	550	55						
7. Title Ins. Premium 7,623/12 mo.=635.25/30					584	00					584	00
8. Abstracting: Before Sale = 21.1750 x 26												
9. After Sale												
10. Title Exam by												
11. Recording: Warranty Deed					10	00					10	00
12. Trust Deed												
13. Release												
14. Other												
15. Documentary Fee					8	68					8	68
16. Certificate of Taxes Due	15	00									15	00
17. Taxes for Preceding Year(s)												
18. Taxes for Current Year 720/360=2.00 day x			472	00	472	00						
19. Tax Reserve 236 days = $472.00			315	00	315	00						
20. Special Taxes												
21. Personal Property Taxes												
22. Hazard Ins. Prem. Assumed 320/360=			168	89	168	89						
23. Premium for New Insurance .888888x190												
24. Hazard Ins. Reserve			187	00	187	00						
25. FHA Mortgage Ins. Assumed												
26. FHA Mortgage Ins. Reserve												
27. Loan Service Fee (Buyer)												
28. Loan Discount Fee (Seller)												
29. Interest on New Loan												
30. Survey and/or Credit Report												
31. Appraisal Fee												
32. Water and/or Sewer 45.00/60=.75dayx34	25	50					25	50				
33. Rents $1120/30=$37.333333 x 26 days	970	67					970	67				
34. Security Deposits $200 x 2 units	400	00					400	00				
35. Loan Transfer Fee					125	00					125	00
36. Loan Payment Due pays May interest	773	25									773	25
37. Broker's Fee	6,944	00									6,944	00
Sub-Totals	81,728	42	88,493	44	89,221	12	78,996	17	5,000	00	8,459	93
Balance due to/~~from~~ Seller	6,765	02									6,765	02
Balance due to/from Buyer							10,224	95	10,224	95		
TOTALS	88,493	44	88,493	44	89,221	12	89,221	12	15,224	95	15,224	95

Chapter 11
HUD-1 settlement statement, solutions to practice problem 2

HUD-1 (3-86) — OMB NO. 2502-0265

A. U.S. DEPARTMENT OF HOUSING AND URBAN DEVELOPMENT

SETTLEMENT STATEMENT

B. TYPE OF LOAN
1. ☐ FHA 2. ☐ FMHA 3. ☐ CONV. UNINS.
4. ☐ VA 5. ☐ CONV. INS.
6. FILE NUMBER 7. LOAN NUMBER
8. MORTGAGE INSURANCE CASE NUMBER

C. NOTE: This form is furnished to give you a statement of actual settlement costs. Amounts paid to and by the settlement agent are shown. Items marked "(p.o.c.)" were paid outside the closing; they are shown here for informational purposes and are not included in totals.

D. NAME OF BORROWER	E. NAME OF SELLER	F. NAME OF LENDER
SOLUTION TO CLOSING PROBLEM NUMBER TWO		

G. PROPERTY LOCATION	H. SETTLEMENT AGENT	PLACE OF SETTLEMENT
	I. SETTLEMENT DATE: MAY 4,	

J. SUMMARY OF BORROWER'S TRANSACTION		K. SUMMARY OF SELLER'S TRANSACTION	
100. GROSS AMOUNT DUE FROM BORROWER:		**400. GROSS AMOUNT DUE TO SELLER:**	
101. Contract sales price	86,800.00	401. Contract sales price	86,800.00
102. Personal property		402. Personal property	
103. Settlement charges to borrower *(line 1400)*	727.68	403.	
104.		404.	
105.		405.	
Adjustments for items paid by seller in advance		*Adjustments for items paid by seller in advance*	
106. City/town taxes to		406. City/town taxes to	
107. County taxes May 5 to Dec. 30	472.00	407. County taxes May 5 to Dec. 30	472.00
108. ~~Assessments~~ 2.00 day x 236 days		408. ~~Assessments~~ 2.00 day x 236 days	
109. Tax reserves held by lender	315.00	409. Tax Reserves held by lender	315.00
110. Insurance reserves held by lender	187.00	410. Hazard insurance reserve	187.00
111. Hazard insurance prepaid 190 days x.88888	168.89	411. Hazard insurance prepaid 190 days x.88888	168.89
112. Interest May 5-May 30 @ 21.1750 day	550.55	412. Interest May 5-May 30 @ 21.1750 day	550.55
120. GROSS AMOUNT DUE FROM BORROWER	89,221.12	**420. GROSS AMOUNT DUE TO SELLER**	88,493.44
200. AMOUNTS PAID BY OR IN BEHALF OF BORROWER:		**500. REDUCTIONS IN AMOUNT DUE TO SELLER:**	
201. Deposit or earnest money	5,000.00	501. Excess deposit (see instructions)	
202. Principal amount of new loan(s)		502. Settlement charges to seller *(line 1400)*	6,959.00
203. Existing loan(s) taken ~~subject to~~ assume	72,600.00	503. Existing loan(s) taken ~~subject to~~ assume	72,600.00
204.		504. Payoff of first mortgage loan	
205.		505. Payoff of second mortgage loan	
206.		506. Loan payment due May 1	773.25
207.		507.	
208.		508.	
209.		509.	
Adjustments for items unpaid by seller		*Adjustments for items unpaid by seller*	
210. City/town taxes to		510. City/town taxes to	
211. County taxes to		511. County taxes to	
212. Assessments to		512. Assessments to	
213. Water/sewer 45.00/60 = .75 x 34 days	25.50	513. Water/sewer 45.00/60 = .75 x 34 days	25.50
214. Rents 1120/30 = 37.333333 day x 26 days	970.67	514. Rents 1120/30 =37.333333 day x 26 days	970.67
215. Security deposits 200.00 x 2 units	400.00	515. Security deposits 200.00 x 2 units	400.00
216.		516.	
217.		517.	
218.		518.	
219.		519.	
220. TOTAL PAID BY/FOR BORROWER	78,996.17	**520. TOTAL REDUCTION AMOUNT DUE SELLER**	81,728.42
300. CASH AT SETTLEMENT FROM/TO BORROWER		**600. CASH AT SETTLEMENT TO/FROM SELLER**	
301. Gross amount due from borrower *(line 120)*	89,221.12	601. Gross amount due to seller *(line 420)*	88,493.44
302. Less amounts paid by/for borrower *(line 220)*	(78,996.17)	602. Less reductions in amt. due to seller *(line 520)*	(81,728.42)
303. CASH (☒ FROM) (☐ TO) BORROWER	10,224.95	603. CASH (☒ TO) (☐ FROM) SELLER	6,765.02

continued

Chapter 11

HUD-1 settlement statement, continued, solutions to practice problem 2

HUD-1 (3-86)

L. SETTLEMENT CHARGES	PAID FROM BORROWER'S FUNDS AT SETTLEMENT	PAID FROM SELLER'S FUNDS AT SETTLEMENT
700. TOTAL SALES/BROKER'S COMMISSION based on price $ 86,800.00 @ 8 % = 6,944. *Division of Commission (line 700) as follows:*		
701. $ 6,944.00 to Listing & Selling broker		
702. $ to		
703. Commission paid at Settlement		6,944.00
704.		
800. ITEMS PAYABLE IN CONNECTION WITH LOAN		
801. Loan Origination Fee % N/A		
802. Loan Discount % N/A		
803. Appraisal Fee to N/A		
804. Credit Report to		
805. Lender's Inspection Fee		
806. Mortgage Insurance Application Fee to		
807. Assumption Fee	125.00	
808.		
809.		
810.		
811.		
900. ITEMS REQUIRED BY LENDER TO BE PAID IN ADVANCE		
901. Interest from to @$ /day		
902. Mortgage Insurance Premium for months to		
903. Hazard Insurance Premium for years to		
904. years to		
905.		
1000. RESERVES DEPOSITED WITH LENDER		
1001. Hazard insurance months @ $ N/A per month		
1002. Mortgage insurance months @ $ N/A per month		
1003. City property taxes months @ $ N/A per month		
1004. County property taxes months @ $ N/A per month		
1005. Annual assessments months @ $ N/A per month		
1006. months @ $ per month		
1007. months @ $ per month		
1008. months @ $ per month		
1100. TITLE CHARGES		
1101. Settlement or closing fee to		
1102. Abstract or title search to		
1103. Title examination to		
1104. Title insurance binder to	584.00	
1105. Document preparation to		
1106. Notary fees to		
1107. Attorney's fees to		
(includes above items numbers:)		
1108. Title insurance to		
(includes above items numbers:)		
1109. Lender's coverage $		
1110. Owner's coverage $ 584.00		
1111. Tax Certificate		15.00
1112.		
1113.		
1200. GOVERNMENT RECORDING AND TRANSFER CHARGES		
1201. Recording fees: Deed $; Mortgage $; Releases $		
1202. City/county tax/stamps: Deed $ 10.00 ; Mortgage $	10.00	
1203. State tax/stamps: Deed $ 8.68 ; Mortgage $	8.68	
1204.		
1205.		
1300. ADDITIONAL SETTLEMENT CHARGES		
1301. Survey to		
1302. Pest inspection to		
1303.		
1304.		
1305.		
1400. TOTAL SETTLEMENT CHARGES *(enter on lines 103, Section J and 502, Section K)*	727.68	6,959.00

I have carefully reviewed the HUD-1 Settlement Statement and to the best of my knowledge and belief, it is a true and accurate statement of all receipts and disbursements made on my account or by me in this transaction. I further certify that I have received a copy of the HUD-1 Settlement Statement.

Borrowers

Sellers

To the best of my knowledge, the HUD-1 Settlement Statement which I have prepared is a true and accurate account of this transaction. I have caused or will cause the funds to be disbursed in accordance with this statement.

Settlement Agent

Date

WARNING: It is a crime to knowingly make a false statement to the United States on this or any other similar form. Penalties upon conviction can include a fine and imprisonment. For details see: Title 18 U.S. Code Section 1001 and Section 1010

Broker Reconciliation
HUD-1 Practice Problem #2

Funds Received	
Earnest deposit	$5,000.00
Buyer funds to close	10,224.95
Total funds received	$15,224.95

Funds to Disburse	
Seller funds	$6,765.02
Title insurance	584.00
Record warranty deed	10.00
Tax stamps	8.68
Certificate of taxes	15.00
Loan transfer fee	125.00
Loan payment fee	773.25
Broker fee	6,944.00
Total funds to disburse	$15,224.95

Chapter 11
Six-column settlement statement, solutions to practice problem 3

Close March 7	SELLER Debit	SELLER Credit	BUYER Debit	BUYER Credit	BROKER Debit	BROKER Credit
1. Selling Price		$ 96,200 00	$ 96,200 00			
2. Deposit, paid to				$ 5,000 00	$ 5,000 00	
3. Trust Deed, payable to				76,950 00		
4. Trust Deed, payable to						
5. Trust Deed, payoff to	$ 49,600 00					
6. Interest on Loan Assumed						
7. Title Ins. Premium	525 00		60 00			
8. Abstracting: Before Sale						
9. After Sale						
10. Title Exam by			150 00			150 00
11. Recording: Warranty Deed			5 00			
12. Trust Deed			20 00			
13. Release	15 00					
14. Other						
15. Documentary Fee			9 62			
16. Certificate of Taxes Due			20 00			
17. Taxes for Preceding Year(s)						
18. Taxes for Current Year 985 ÷ 360 = 2.736111		801 68	801 68			
19. Tax Reserve x 293 days			165 00			
20. Special Taxes						
21. Personal Property Taxes						
22. Hazard Ins. Prem. Assumed						
23. Premium for New Insurance			320 00			
24. Hazard Ins. Reserve			54 00			
25. FHA Mortgage Ins. Assumed						
26. FHA Mortgage Ins. Reserve						
27. Loan Service Fee (Buyer)			769 50			
28. Loan Discount Fee (Seller)						
29. Interest on New Loan			564 30			
30. Survey and/or Credit Report			100 00			
31. Appraisal Fee						
32. Water and/or Sewer 18.27 ÷ 30 = .6090/day seller 7 day buyer 23 day	4 26		14 01			18 27
33. Rents $30.00 x 23 days	690 00			690 00		
34. Security Deposits						
35. Loan Transfer Fee						
36. Loan Payment Due						
37. Broker's Fee	6,734 00					6,734 00
Seller Attorney	200 00					200 00
Net Proceeds					24,722 58	
Sub-Totals	$ 57,768 26	$ 97,001 68	$ 99,253 11	$ 82,640 00	$ 29,722 58	$ 7,102 27
Balance due to/~~from~~ Seller	39,233 42					39,233 42
Balance due ~~to~~/from Buyer				16,613 11	16,613 11	
TOTALS	$ 97,001 68	$ 97,001 68	$ 99,253 11	$ 99,253 11	$ 46,335 69	$ 46,335 69

Chapter 11
HUD-1 settlement statement, solutions to practice problem 3

HUD-1 (3-86) OMB NO. 2502-0265

A.

U.S. DEPARTMENT OF HOUSING AND URBAN DEVELOPMENT

SETTLEMENT STATEMENT

B. TYPE OF LOAN

1. ☐ FHA 2. ☐ FMHA 3. ☐ CONV. UNINS.
4. ☐ VA 5. ☐ CONV. INS.

6. FILE NUMBER | 7. LOAN NUMBER

8. MORTGAGE INSURANCE CASE NUMBER

C. NOTE: This form is furnished to give you a statement of actual settlement costs. Amounts paid to and by the settlement agent are shown. Items marked "(p.o.c.)" were paid outside the closing; they are shown here for informational purposes and are not included in totals.

D. NAME OF BORROWER	E. NAME OF SELLER	F. NAME OF LENDER
Solution to Closing Problem Number three		

G. PROPERTY LOCATION	H. SETTLEMENT AGENT	PLACE OF SETTLEMENT
	I. SETTLEMENT DATE March 7, 19 __	

J. SUMMARY OF BORROWER'S TRANSACTION		K. SUMMARY OF SELLER'S TRANSACTION	
100. GROSS AMOUNT DUE FROM BORROWER:		**400. GROSS AMOUNT DUE TO SELLER:**	
101. Contract sales price	$ 96,200.00	401. Contract sales price	$ 96,200.00
102. Personal property		402. Personal property	
103. Settlement charges to borrower *(line 1400)*	2,087.42	403.	
104. Buyer Attorney	150.00	404.	
105.		405.	
Adjustments for items paid by seller in advance		*Adjustments for items paid by seller in advance*	
106. City/town taxes to		406. City/town taxes to	
107. County taxes 985.00/360 = 2.736111x293 day	801.68	407. County taxes 985/360=2.736111dx293days	801.68
108. Assessments to		408. Assessments to	
109. Water 18.27/30=.6090 day Buyer 23 days	14.01	409.	
110.		410.	
111.		411.	
112.		412.	
120. GROSS AMOUNT DUE FROM BORROWER	$ 99,253.11	**420. GROSS AMOUNT DUE TO SELLER**	$ 97,001.68
200. AMOUNTS PAID BY OR IN BEHALF OF BORROWER:		**500. REDUCTIONS IN AMOUNT DUE TO SELLER:**	
201. Deposit or earnest money	5,000.00	501. Excess deposit (see instructions)	
202. Principal amount of new loan(s)	76,950.00	502. Settlement charges to seller *(line 1400)*	7,274.00
203. Existing loan(s) taken subject to		503. Existing loan(s) taken subject to	
204.		504. Payoff of first mortgage loan	49,600.00
205.		505. Payoff of second mortgage loan	
206.		506. Seller Attorney	200.00
207.		507.	
208.		508.	
209.		509.	
Adjustments for items unpaid by seller		*Adjustments for items unpaid by seller*	
210. City/town taxes to		510. City/town taxes to	
211. County taxes to		511. County taxes to	
212. Assessments to		512. Assessments to	
213.		513. Water 18.27/30 = .6090 day Seller 7 days	4.26
214. Rent 30.00 x 23 days	690.00	514. Rent 30.00 x 23 days	690.00
215.		515.	
216.		516.	
217.		517.	
218.		518.	
219.		519.	
220. TOTAL PAID BY/FOR BORROWER	$ 82,640.00	**520. TOTAL REDUCTION AMOUNT DUE SELLER**	$ 57,768.26
300. CASH AT SETTLEMENT FROM/TO BORROWER		**600. CASH AT SETTLEMENT TO/FROM SELLER**	
301. Gross amount due from borrower *(line 120)*		601. Gross amount due to seller *(line 420)*	97,001.68
302. Less amounts paid by/for borrower *(line 220)*	( )	602. Less reductions in amt. due to seller *(line 520)*	(57,768.26)
303. CASH (☒ FROM) (☐ TO) BORROWER	$ 16,613.11	603. CASH (☒ TO) (☐ FROM) SELLER	$ 39,233.42

continued

Chapter 11
HUD-1 settlement statement, continued, solutions to practice problem 3

HUD- 3-86)

L. SETTLEMENT CHARGES	PAID FROM BORROWER'S FUNDS AT SETTLEMENT	PAID FROM SELLER'S FUNDS AT SETTLEMENT
700. TOTAL SALES/BROKER'S COMMISSION based on price $ 96,200.00 @ 7 % = 6734. *Division of Commission (line 700) as follows:*		
701. $ to		
702. $ to		
703. Commission paid at Settlement		$ 6734.00
704.		
800. ITEMS PAYABLE IN CONNECTION WITH LOAN		
801. Loan Origination Fee %	769.50	
802. Loan Discount %		
803. Appraisal Fee to		
804. Credit Report to		
805. Lender's Inspection Fee		
806. Mortgage Insurance Application Fee to		
807. Assumption Fee		
808.		
809.		
810.		
811.		
900. ITEMS REQUIRED BY LENDER TO BE PAID IN ADVANCE		
901. Interest from 3-7 thru 3-30 @ $ /day	564.30	
902. Mortgage Insurance Premium for 12 months to	320.00	
903. Hazard Insurance Premium for years to		
904. years to		
905.		
1000. RESERVES DEPOSITED WITH LENDER		
1001. Hazard insurance 2 months @ $ 27.00 per month	54.00	
1002. Mortgage insurance months @ $ per month		
1003. City property taxes months @ $ per month		
1004. County property taxes 2 months @ $ 82.50 per month	165.00	
1005. Annual assessments months @ $ per month		
1006. months @ $ per month		
1007. months @ $ per month		
1008. months @ $ per month		
1100. TITLE CHARGES		
1101. Settlement or closing fee to		
1102. Abstract or title search to		
1103. Title examination to		
1104. Title insurance binder to		
1105. Document preparation to		
1106. Notary fees to		
1107. Attorney's fees to		
(includes above items numbers:)		
1108. Title insurance to	60.00	525.00
(includes above items numbers:)		
1109. Lender's coverage $ 60.00		
1110. Owner's coverage $ 525.00		
1111. Tax Certificate	20.00	
1112.		
1113.		
1200. GOVERNMENT RECORDING AND TRANSFER CHARGES		
1201. Recording fees: Deed $ 5.00 ; Mortgage $ 20.00 ; Releases $ 15.00	25.00	15.00
1202. City/county tax/stamps: Deed $; Mortgage $		
1203. State tax/stamps: Deed $ 9.62 ; Mortgage $	9.62	
1204.		
1205.		
1300. ADDITIONAL SETTLEMENT CHARGES		
1301. Survey to Survey Company	100.00	
1302. Pest inspection to		
1303.		
1304.		
1305.		
1400. TOTAL SETTLEMENT CHARGES *(enter on lines 103, Section J and 502, Section K)*	$ 2087.42	$ 7274.00

I have carefully reviewed the HUD-1 Settlement Statement and to the best of my knowledge and belief, it is a true and accurate statement of all receipts and disbursements made on my account or by me in this transaction. I further certify that I have received a copy of the HUD-1 Settlement Statement.

Borrowers Sellers

To the best of my knowledge, the HUD-1 Settlement Statement which I have prepared is a true and accurate account of this transaction. I have caused or will cause the funds to be disbursed in accordance with this statement.

Settlement Agent Date

WARNING: It is a crime to knowingly make a false statement to the United States on this or any other similar form. Penalties upon conviction can include a fine and imprisonment. For details see: Title 18 U.S. Code Section 1001 and Section 1010.

Broker Reconciliation
HUD-1 Practice Problem #3

Funds Received	
Earnest deposit	$5,000.00
Net proceeds	24,722.58
Buyer funds	16,613.11
Total funds received	$46,335.69

Funds to Disburse	
Seller funds	$39,233.42
Buyer attorney	150.00
Seller attorney	200.00
Water (sewer)	18.27
Broker commission	6,734.00
Total funds to disburse	$46,335.69

Chapter 11
Six-column settlement statement, solutions to practice problem 4

Close June 15	SELLER Debit		SELLER Credit		BUYER Debit		BUYER Credit		BROKER Debit		BROKER Credit	
1. Selling Price			$ 114,000	00	$ 114,000	00						
2. Deposit, paid to							$ 10,000	00	$ 10,000	00		
3. Trust Deed, payable to							102,600	00				
4. Trust Deed, payable to												
5. Trust Deed, payoff to	$ 70,280	00										
6. Interest on Loan Assumed					675	00						
7. Title Ins. Premium												
8. Abstracting: Before Sale												
9. After Sale												
10. Title Exam by Buyers Attorney					250	00					250	00
11. Recording: Warranty Deed					10	00						
12. Trust Deed					20	00						
13. Release	20	00										
14. Other												
15. Documentary Fee												
16. Certificate of Taxes Due					15	00						
17. Taxes for Preceding Year(s)												
18. Taxes for Current Year $1280 ÷ 12 =	586	67					586	67				
19. Tax Reserve 106.666 x 5.5 mos.					213	33						
20. Special Taxes												
21. Personal Property Taxes												
22. Hazard Ins. Prem. Assumed												
23. Premium for New Insurance					520	00						
24. Hazard Ins. Reserve					86	66						
25. FHA Mortgage Ins. Assumed												
26. FHA Mortgage Ins. Reserve					1,026	00						
27. Loan Service Fee (Buyer)					1,026	00						
28. Loan Discount Fee (Seller)												
29. Interest on New Loan					410	40						
30. Survey and/or Credit Report												
31. Appraisal Fee												
32. Water and/or Sewer seller ½ mo. buyer 1½ mo	9	00			27	00					36	00
33. Rents	475	00					475	00				
34. Security Deposits	400	00					400	00				
35. Loan Transfer Fee												
36. Loan Payment Due												
37. Broker's Fee	5,700	00									5,700	00
Sellers Attorney	250	00									250	00
Net Proceeds									28,297	61		
Sub-Totals	$ 77,720	67	$ 114,000	00	$ 118,279	39	$ 114,061	67	$ 38,297	61	$ 6,236	00
Balance due to/~~from~~ Seller	36,279	33									36,279	33
Balance due ~~to~~/from Buyer							4,217	72	4,217	72		
TOTALS	$ 114,000	00	$ 114,000		$ 118,279	39	$ 118,279	39	$ 42,515	33	$ 42,515	33

Chapter 11
HUD-1 settlement statement, solutions to practice problem 4

HUD-1 (3-86) OMB NO. 2502-0265

A. U.S. DEPARTMENT OF HOUSING AND URBAN DEVELOPMENT

SETTLEMENT STATEMENT

B. TYPE OF LOAN
1. ☐ FHA 2. ☐ FMHA 3. ☐ CONV. UNINS.
4. ☐ VA 5. ☒ CONV. INS.
6. FILE NUMBER 7. LOAN NUMBER
8. MORTGAGE INSURANCE CASE NUMBER

C. NOTE: This form is furnished to give you a statement of actual settlement costs. Amounts paid to and by the settlement agent are shown. Items marked "(p.o.c.)" were paid outside the closing; they are shown here for informational purposes and are not included in totals.

D. NAME OF BORROWER: Solution to Closing Problem Number four
E. NAME OF SELLER:
F. NAME OF LENDER:

G. PROPERTY LOCATION:
H. SETTLEMENT AGENT:
PLACE OF SETTLEMENT:
I. SETTLEMENT DATE: June 15, 19__

J. SUMMARY OF BORROWER'S TRANSACTION		K. SUMMARY OF SELLER'S TRANSACTION	
100. GROSS AMOUNT DUE FROM BORROWER:		**400. GROSS AMOUNT DUE TO SELLER:**	
101. Contract sales price	$ 114,000.00	401. Contract sales price	$114,000.00
102. Personal property		402. Personal property	
103. Settlement charges to borrower *(line 1400)*	4,002.39	403	
104. Water 1 1/2 month	27.00	404	
105. Buyer Attorney	250.00	405	
Adjustments for items paid by seller in advance		*Adjustments for items paid by seller in advance*	
106. City/town taxes to		406. City/town taxes to	
107. County taxes to		407. County taxes to	
108. Assessments to		408. Assessments to	
109		409	
110		410	
111		411	
112		412	
120. GROSS AMOUNT DUE FROM BORROWER	$118,279.39	**420. GROSS AMOUNT DUE TO SELLER**	$ 114,000.00
200. AMOUNTS PAID BY OR IN BEHALF OF BORROWER:		**500. REDUCTIONS IN AMOUNT DUE TO SELLER:**	
201. Deposit or earnest money	$ 10,000.00	501. Excess deposit (see instructions)	
202. Principal amount of new loan(s)	102,600.00	502. Settlement charges to seller *(line 1400)*	$ 5,720.00
203. Existing loan(s) taken subject to		503. Existing loan(s) taken subject to	
204.		504. Payoff of first mortgage loan	70,280.00
205		505. Payoff of second mortgage loan	
206.		506. Water 1/2 month	9.00
207		507 Seller Attorney	250.00
208		508	
209		509	
Adjustments for items unpaid by seller		*Adjustments for items unpaid by seller*	
210. City/town taxes to		510. City/town taxes to	
211. County taxes 1280/12 = 106.666 x 5.5 month	586.67	511. County taxes 1280/12 = 106.666 x 5.5 month	586.67
212. Assessments to		512. Assessments to	
213. Rent	475.00	513 Rent	475.00
214. Security Deposit	400.00	514. Security Deposit	400.00
215.		515	
216		516	
217		517	
218		518	
219		519	
220. TOTAL PAID BY/FOR BORROWER	114,061.67	**520. TOTAL REDUCTION AMOUNT DUE SELLER**	77,720.67
300. CASH AT SETTLEMENT FROM/TO BORROWER		**600. CASH AT SETTLEMENT TO/FROM SELLER**	
301. Gross amount due from borrower *(line 120)*	$ 118,279.39	601. Gross amount due to seller *(line 420)*	114,000.00
302. Less amounts paid by/for borrower *(line 220)*	(114,061.67)	602. Less reductions in amt. due to seller *(line 520)*	(77,720.67)
303. CASH (☒ FROM) (☐ TO) BORROWER	$ 4,217.72	**603. CASH (☒ TO) (☐ FROM) SELLER**	$ 36,279.33

continued

Chapter 11

HUD-1 settlement statement, continued, solutions to practice problem 4

HUD-1 (3-86)

L. SETTLEMENT CHARGES	PAID FROM BORROWER'S FUNDS AT SETTLEMENT	PAID FROM SELLER'S FUNDS AT SETTLEMENT
700. TOTAL SALES/BROKER'S COMMISSION based on price $ 114,000 @ 6% = 5700. *Division of Commission (line 700) as follows:*		
701. $ to		
702. $ to		
703. Commission paid at Settlement		$ 5700.00
704.		
800. ITEMS PAYABLE IN CONNECTION WITH LOAN		
801. Loan Origination Fee 1 %	$ 1026.00	
802. Loan Discount %		
803. Appraisal Fee to		
804. Credit Report to		
805. Lender's Inspection Fee		
806. Mortgage Insurance Application Fee to		
807. Assumption Fee		
808.		
809.		
810.		
811.		
900. ITEMS REQUIRED BY LENDER TO BE PAID IN ADVANCE		
901. Interest from 6-15 thru 6-30 @ $ 25.65 /day 16 days	410.40	
902. Mortgage Insurance Premium for 1 year	1026.00	
903. Hazard Insurance Premium for years to	520.00	
904. years to		
905.		
1000. RESERVES DEPOSITED WITH LENDER		
1001. Hazard insurance 2 months @ $ 43.33 per month	86.66	
1002. Mortgage insurance months @ $ per month		
1003. City property taxes months @ $ per month		
1004. County property taxes 2 months @ $ 106.67 per month	213.33	
1005. Annual assessments months @ $ per month		
1006. months @ $ per month		
1007. months @ $ per month		
1008. months @ $ per month		
1100. TITLE CHARGES		
1101. Settlement or closing fee to		
1102. Abstract or title search to		
1103. Title examination to		
1104. Title insurance binder to		
1105. Document preparation to		
1106. Notary fees to		
1107. Attorney's fees to		
(includes above items numbers:)		
1108. Title insurance to	675.00	
(includes above items numbers:)		
1109. Lender's coverage $		
1110. Owner's coverage $ 675.00		
1111. Tax Certificate	15.00	
1112.		
1113.		
1200. GOVERNMENT RECORDING AND TRANSFER CHARGES		
1201. Recording fees: Deed $ 10.00 ; Mortgage $ 20.00 ; Releases $ 20.00	30.00	20.00
1202. City/county tax/stamps: Deed $; Mortgage $		
1203. State tax/stamps: Deed $; Mortgage $		
1204.		
1205.		
1300. ADDITIONAL SETTLEMENT CHARGES		
1301. Survey to		
1302. Pest inspection to		
1303.		
1304.		
1305.		
1400. TOTAL SETTLEMENT CHARGES *(enter on lines 103, Section J and 502, Section K)*	$ 4002.39	$ 5720.00

I have carefully reviewed the HUD-1 Settlement Statement and to the best of my knowledge and belief, it is a true and accurate statement of all receipts and disbursements made on my account or by me in this transaction. I further certify that I have received a copy of the HUD-1 Settlement Statement.

Borrowers ______________________ Sellers ______________________

To the best of my knowledge, the HUD-1 Settlement Statement which I have prepared is a true and accurate account of this transaction. I have caused or will cause the funds to be disbursed in accordance with this statement.

Settlement Agent ______________________ Date ______________________

WARNING: It is a crime to knowingly make a false statement to the United States on this or any other similar form. Penalties upon conviction can include a fine and imprisonment. For details see: Title 18 U.S. Code Section 1001 and Section 1010.

Broker Reconciliation
HUD-1 Practice Problem #4

Funds Received	
Earnest deposit	$10,000.00
Net proceeds	28.297.61
Buyer funds	4,217.72
Total funds received	$42,515.33

Funds to Disburse	
Seller funds	$36,279.33
Buyer attorney	250.00
Seller attorney	250.00
Water (sewer)	36.00
Broker commission	5,700.00
Total funds to disburse	$42,515.33

Chapter 11
Six-column settlement statement, solutions to chapter test

Close November 18	SELLER Debit	SELLER Credit	BUYER Debit	BUYER Credit	BROKER Debit	BROKER Credit
1. Selling Price		$ 280,000 00	$ 280,000 00			
2. Deposit, paid to				$ 20,000 00	$ 20,000 00	
3. Trust Deed, payable to 1st	$ 210,000 00			210,000 00		
4. Trust Deed, payable to						
5. Trust Deed, payoff to						
6. Interest on Loan Assumed $58.3333 day x 18 days November	1,050 00			1,050 00		
7. Title Ins. Premium	490 00		490 00			980 00
8. Abstracting: Before Sale						
9. After Sale						
10. Title Exam by						
11. Recording: Warranty Deed			10 00			10 00
12. Trust Deed						
13. Release						
14. Other						
15. Tax Stamps	28 00					28 00
16. Certificate of Taxes Due						
17. Taxes for Preceding Year(s)						
18. Taxes for Current Year 318 x $6.6666 day	2,120 00			2,120 00		
19. Tax Reserve		1,900 00	1,900 00			
20. Special Taxes						
21. Personal Property Taxes						
22. Hazard Ins. Prem. Assumed 112 days x 2.50 day		280 00	280 00			
23. Premium for New Insurance						
24. Hazard Ins. Reserve		600 00	600 00			
25. FHA Mortgage Ins. Assumed						
26. FHA Mortgage Ins. Reserve						
27. Loan Service Fee (Buyer)						
28. Loan Discount Fee (Seller)						
29. Interest on New Loan						
30. Survey and/or Credit Report $600/$60			660 00			660 00
31. Appraisal Fee						
32. Water and/or Sewer paid November 12 days remaining x 2.60		31 20	31 20			
33. Rents $176 x 12 days	2,112 00			2,112 00		
34. Security Deposits $250 x 10 units	2,500 00			2,500 00		
35. Loan Transfer Fee			1,000 00			1,000 00
36. Loan Payment Due Nov. 1 pays Oct. interest	2,430 00					2,430 00
37. Broker's Fee	14,000 00					14,000 00
Sub-Totals	$ 234,730 00	$ 282,811 20	$ 284,971 20	$ 237,782 00	$ 20,000 00	$ 19,108 00
Balance due to/~~from~~ Seller	48,081 20					48,081 20
Balance due ~~to~~/from Buyer				47,189 20	47,189 20	
TOTALS	$ 282,811 20	$ 282,811 20	$ 284,971 20	$ 284,972 20	67,189 20	67,189 20

Chapter 11
HUD-1 settlement statement, solutions to chapter test

HUD-1 (3-86) OMB NO. 2502-0265

A. U.S. DEPARTMENT OF HOUSING AND URBAN DEVELOPMENT

SETTLEMENT STATEMENT

B. TYPE OF LOAN
1. ☐ FHA 2. ☐ FMHA 3. ☐ CONV. UNINS.
4. ☐ VA 5. ☐ CONV. INS.
6. FILE NUMBER 7. LOAN NUMBER
8. MORTGAGE INSURANCE CASE NUMBER

C. NOTE. This form is furnished to give you a statement of actual settlement costs. Amounts paid to and by the settlement agent are shown. Items marked "(p.o.c.)" were paid outside the closing; they are shown here for informational purposes and are not included in totals

D. NAME OF BORROWER	E. NAME OF SELLER	F. NAME OF LENDER
Chapter Test Solution		

G. PROPERTY LOCATION	H. SETTLEMENT AGENT	PLACE OF SETTLEMENT
	I. SETTLEMENT DATE November 18, current year	

J. SUMMARY OF BORROWER'S TRANSACTION		K. SUMMARY OF SELLER'S TRANSACTION	
100. GROSS AMOUNT DUE FROM BORROWER:		400. GROSS AMOUNT DUE TO SELLER:	
101. Contract sales price	$280,000.00	401. Contract sales price	$280,000.00
102. Personal property		402. Personal property	
103. Settlement charges to borrower *(line 1400)*	2,160.00	403.	
104.		404.	
105.		405.	
Adjustments for items paid by seller in advance		*Adjustments for items paid by seller in advance*	
106. City/town taxes to		406. City/town taxes to	
107. County taxes to		407. County taxes to	
108. Assessments to		408. Assessments to	
109. Hazard insurance 900.00/360=2.50x112	280.00	409. Hazard insurance 900.00/360=2.50x112	280.00
110. Tax reserve	1,900.00	410. Tax reserve	1,900.00
111. Insurance reserve	600.00	411. Insurance reserve	600.00
112. Water $78/30=$2.60x12	31.20	412. Water $78/30=$2.60x12	31.20
120. GROSS AMOUNT DUE FROM BORROWER	$284,971.20	420. GROSS AMOUNT DUE TO SELLER	$282,811.20
200. AMOUNTS PAID BY OR IN BEHALF OF BORROWER:		500. REDUCTIONS IN AMOUNT DUE TO SELLER:	
201. Deposit or earnest money	$ 20,000.00	501. Excess deposit (see instructions)	
202. Principal amount of new loan(s)		502. Settlement charges to seller *(line 1400)*	$ 14,518.00
203. Existing loan(s) taken ~~subject to~~ Assume	210,000.00	503. Existing loan(s) taken ~~subject to~~ Assume	210,000.00
204.		504. Payoff of first mortgage loan	
205.		505. Payoff of second mortgage loan	
206.		506.	
207.		507.	
208.		508.	
209.		509.	
Adjustments for items unpaid by seller		*Adjustments for items unpaid by seller*	
210. City/town taxes to		510. City/town taxes to	
211. County taxes 318 days x ~~to~~ 6.6666	2,120.00	511. County taxes 318 days ~~to~~ 6.6666	2,120.00
212. Assessments to		512. Assessments to	
213.		513. Loan payment due (Oct. int.)	2,430.00
214. Interest 18 days Nov. $58.3333 x 18	1,050.00	514. Interest 18 days Nov. $58.3333 x 18	1,050.00
215. Rent 5280/30 = 176.00 x 12	2,112.00	515. Rent 5280/30 = 176.00 x 12	2,112.00
216. Security deposit 250 x 10	2,500.00	516. Security deposit 250 x 10	2,500.00
217.		517.	
218.		518.	
219.		519.	
220. TOTAL PAID BY/FOR BORROWER	$237,782.00	520. TOTAL REDUCTION AMOUNT DUE SELLER	$234,730.00
300. CASH AT SETTLEMENT FROM/TO BORROWER		600. CASH AT SETTLEMENT TO/FROM SELLER	
301. Gross amount due from borrower *(line 120)*	284,971.20	601. Gross amount due to seller *(line 420)*	282,811.20
302. Less amounts paid by/for borrower *(line 220)*	(237,782.00)	602. Less reductions in amt. due to seller *(line 520)*	(234,730.00)
303. CASH (☒ FROM) (☐ TO) BORROWER	$ 47,189.20	603. CASH (☐ TO) (☐ FROM) SELLER	$ 48,081.20

continued

Chapter 11
HUD-1 settlement statement, continued, solutions to chapter test

JD-1 (3-86)

L. SETTLEMENT CHARGES	PAID FROM BORROWER'S FUNDS AT SETTLEMENT	PAID FROM SELLER'S FUNDS AT SETTLEMENT
700. TOTAL SALES/BROKER'S COMMISSION based on price $ 280,000.00 @ 5 % = 14,000 *Division of Commission (line 700) as follows:*		
701. $ to		
702. $ to		
703. Commission paid at Settlement		$ 14,000.00
704.		
800. ITEMS PAYABLE IN CONNECTION WITH LOAN		
801. Loan Origination Fee %		
802. Loan Discount %		
803. Appraisal Fee to		
804. Credit Report to		
805. Lender's Inspection Fee		
806. Mortgage Insurance Application Fee to		
807. Assumption Fee	1,000.00	
808.		
809.		
810.		
811.		
900. ITEMS REQUIRED BY LENDER TO BE PAID IN ADVANCE		
901. Interest from to @ $ /day		
902. Mortgage Insurance Premium for months to		
903. Hazard Insurance Premium for years to		
904. years to		
905.		
1000. RESERVES DEPOSITED WITH LENDER		
1001. Hazard insurance months @ $ per month		
1002. Mortgage insurance months @ $ per month		
1003. City property taxes months @ $ per month		
1004. County property taxes months @ $ per month		
1005. Annual assessments months @ $ per month		
1006. months @ $ per month		
1007. months @ $ per month		
1008. months @ $ per month		
1100. TITLE CHARGES		
1101. Settlement or closing fee to		
1102. Abstract or title search to		
1103. Title examination to		
1104. Title insurance binder to		
1105. Document preparation to		
1106. Notary fees to		
1107. Attorney's fees to *(includes above items numbers:)*		
1108. Title insurance to *(includes above items numbers:)*	490.00	490.00
1109. Lender's coverage $		
1110. Owner's coverage $ 980.00		
1111. Tax Certificate		
1112.		
1113.		
1200. GOVERNMENT RECORDING AND TRANSFER CHARGES		
1201. Recording fees: Deed $ 10.00 ; Mortgage $; Releases $	10.00	
1202. City/county tax/stamps: Deed $; Mortgage $		
1203. State tax/stamps: Deed $ 28.00 ; Mortgage $		28.00
1204.		
1205.		
1300. ADDITIONAL SETTLEMENT CHARGES		
1301. Survey to Survey Company	600.00	
1302. Pest inspection to		
1303. Credit report	60.00	
1304.		
1305.		
1400. TOTAL SETTLEMENT CHARGES *(enter on lines 103, Section J and 502, Section K)*	$ 2,160.00	$ 14,518.00

I have carefully reviewed the HUD-1 Settlement Statement and to the best of my knowledge and belief, it is a true and accurate statement of all receipts and disbursements made on my account or by me in this transaction. I further certify that I have received a copy of the HUD-1 Settlement Statement.

Borrowers ______________________ Sellers ______________________

To the best of my knowledge, the HUD-1 Settlement Statement which I have prepared is a true and accurate account of this transaction. I have caused or will cause the funds to be disbursed in accordance with this statement.

Settlement Agent ______________________ Date ____________

WARNING: It is a crime to knowingly make a false statement to the United States on this or any other similar form. Penalties upon conviction can include a fine and imprisonment. For details see: Title 18 U.S. Code Section 1001 and Section 1010.

Broker Reconciliation
HUD-1 Chapter Test

Funds Received

Earnest deposit	$20,000.00
Buyer funds	47,189.20
Total funds received	$67,189.20

Funds to Disburse

Seller funds	$48,081.20
Title insurance	980.00
Recording deed	10.00
Tax stamps	28.00
Survey credit report	660.00
Loan transfer fee	1,000.00
Nov. 1 payment	2,430.00
Broker fee	14,000.00
	$67,189.20

CHAPTER 12 SIMPLE INVESTMENT MATH

Cash Flow

1. Annual income (rent) ($1,200 per month x 12 months) = $14,400
   Annual expenses = $(3,100)
   Annual debt service ($325 x 12 months) = $(3,900)
   Positive annual cash flow = $7,400

2. Annual income (rent) = $ 25,000
   Annual expenses ($1,800 x 12 months) = $(21,600)
   Annual debt service ($500 x 12 months) = $ (6,000)
   Negative annual cash flow = $ (2,600)

Rate of Return

1. $\frac{\$20{,}000 \text{ annual income}}{11\% \ (.11)} = \$181{,}818$
   This property is worth only $181,818 to Sam if he wants to earn 11% on his money. Therefore, he should not invest $200,000.

2. $\frac{\$13{,}000 \text{ annual income}}{\$85{,}000 \text{ investment}} = 15\% \text{ return}$
   They will earn 15% on their money, well over the 12% necessary to invest. So, yes, they should invest.

Compound Interest

1. Year 1 - $1,080.00 Year 2 = $1,166.40 Year 3 = $1,259.71

Depreciation

1. $\frac{\$135{,}000 \text{ purchase price}}{27.5 \text{ years}} = \$4{,}909.09 \text{ per year}$

2. Sale Price: $125,000
   Less: Commission $7,500
   Legal fees $800
   Discount points $2,000
   $10,300
   Realized selling price $114,700

   Initial basis $80,000
   Improvements + $5,000
   Allowable depreciation – $8,700
   Adjusted basis $76,300
   Capital gain $38,400
   (Capital gain x tax rate = federal tax liability)
   For example, $38,400 x .27 = $10,368 federal tax liability

Chapter Test

1. $20,000 x 5.473566 (col. 1) = $109,471
   HP-12C f clear fin, 15n, 12i, $20,000 chs, pv, fv = $109,471

2. $25,000 x .129607 (col. 3) = $3,240.18
   HP-12C f clear fin, 6n, 10i, $25,000 fv, pmt = $3,240.18

3. $10,000 x .012913 (col. 3 monthly) = $129.13
   HP-12C f clear fin, 5gn, 10gi, $10,000 fv, pmt = $129.13

4.

Year	*Income*	*PV factor*	*Present Value*
1	$ (5,000)	.909091	= $(4,545.45)
2	$ 5,000	.826446	=$ 4,132.23
3	$ 3,000	.751315	=$ 2,253.95
4	$12,000	.683013	=$ 8,196.16
5	$ 8,000	.620921	=$ 4,967.36

   Present value of the income stream $15,004.25
   HP-12C f clear fin, 10i, $5,000 chs, g CFj, $5,000 g CFj, $3,000 g CFj, $12,000 g CFj, $8,000 g CFj, f NPV = $15,004.25 present value of the income stream with a negative cash flow the first year.

5. $125,000 x .009087 (col 6 monthly) = $1,135.88
   HP-12C f clear fin, 25gn, 10gi, $125,000 pv, pmt = $1,135.88.

6. $10,000 x 6.759024 (col 5 annual) = $67,590.24
   HP-12C f clear fin, g beg, 10n, 10i, $10,000 chs, pmt, pv = $67,590.24.

7. $50,000 x .649931 (col 4 annual) = $32,497
   HP-12C f clear fin, 5n, 9i, $50,000 fv, pv = $32,497.

8. $150.00 x 76.301731 (col 5 monthly modified) - $11,445 HP-12C f clear fin, g beg, 10gn, 10gi, $150 pmt, pv = $11,445.

9. Ordinary annuity paid in arrears
   $5,000 x 6.144567 (col 5 annual) = $30,723
   HP-12C f clear fin, 10n, 10i, $5,000 chs, pmt, pv = $30,723.
   Annuity due paid in advance
   $5,000 x 6.328250 (col 5 annual modified) = $31,641
   HP 12C f clear fin, g beg, 10n, 12i, $5,000 chs, pmt, pv = $31,641.
   Dollar difference, $31,641 – $30,723 = $918.00

10. $10,000 x 1.762342 (col 1 annual) = $17,623
    $500 x 6.352847 (col 2 annual) = $ 3,176
    Asking price $20,800 rounded
    HP-12C f clear fin, 5n, 12i, $10,000 chs, pv, $500 chs, pmt, fv = $20,800 = asking price

11. Annual income (rent) ($2,300 x 12 months) $ 27,600
    –Annual expenses ($800 x 12 months) $ (9,600)
    –Annual debt service $(12,000)
    Positive annual cash flow $ 6,000

12. $\frac{\$100{,}000 \text{ investment}}{10\% \ (.10) \text{ rate of return}} = \$10{,}000 \text{ per year}$

13. $\frac{\$150{,}000}{27.5 \text{ years}} = \$5{,}455/\text{year}$
    $5,455 per year x 5 years = $27,275 allowed depreciation

14. $\frac{\$650 \times 12 = \$7{,}800 \text{ annual income}}{\$60{,}000 \text{ purchase price}} = 13\% \text{ rate of return}$

INDEX